T0244398

OUR NATION AT RISK

OUR NATION AT RISK

ELECTION INTEGRITY AS A NATIONAL SECURITY ISSUE

EDITED BY
JULIAN E. ZELIZER AND
KAREN J. GREENBERG

NEW YORK UNIVERSITY PRESS
New York, New York

NEW YORK UNIVERSITY PRESS
New York
www.nyupress.org

Library of Congress Cataloging-in-Publication Data
Names: Greenberg, Karen J., editor. | Zelizer, Julian E., editor.
Title: Our nation at risk : election integrity as a national security issue / edited by Karen J. Greenberg and Julian E. Zelizer.
Description: New York, New York : New York University Press, 2024. | Includes bibliographical references and index. | Summary: "This book, will bring together some of the nation's top political scientists, historians, and legal scholars to examine different areas where the stability and integrity of the electoral process has become a threat to national security"—Provided by publisher.
Identifiers: LCCN 2024002636 (print) | LCCN 2024002637 (ebook) | ISBN 9781479830916 (hardback) | ISBN 9781479830923 (ebook) | ISBN 9781479830930 (ebook other)
Subjects: LCSH: Election security—United States. | Elections—United States—Management. | Foreign interference in elections—United States. | National security—United States. | Voting—United States. | Voter suppression—United States.
Classification: LCC JK1976 .087 2024 (print) | LCC JK1976 (ebook) | DDC 324.973—dc23/eng/20240326
LC record available at https://lccn.loc.gov/2024002636
LC ebook record available at https://lccn.loc.gov/2024002637

This book is printed on acid-free paper, and its binding materials are chosen for strength and durability. We strive to use environmentally responsible suppliers and materials to the greatest extent possible in publishing our books.

Manufactured in the United States of America

10 9 8 7 6 5 4 3 2 1

Also available as an ebook

To all the poll workers who work tirelessly

to make sure that our democracy works

CONTENTS

Introduction 1
Karen J. Greenberg and Julian E. Zelizer

PART I: THE HISTORICAL SOURCES OF INSECURE ELECTIONS

1 On a Wing and a Prayer: The Perilous Path of Our Contested Presidential Elections 11
Karen J. Greenberg

2 "An Instrument of Justice and Fulfillment": The Lost Promise of the Voting Rights Act 32
Julian E. Zelizer

3 The History of Foreign Election Interference and an Alternative Future 55
Jeremi Suri

4 Election Deception: Disinformation, Election Security, and the History of Voter Suppression 73
Nicole Hemmer

5 After the Civil Rights Revolution 90
Thomas B. Edsall

PART II: OVERSEEING SECURE ELECTIONS

6 Presidential Power and Federal Elections 107
Trevor W. Morrison

7 Election Security, Election Integrity, and the Role of Congress 127
Matthew N. Green

8 The Supreme Court 145
Michael Waldman

9 Political Reforms to Combat Extremism 163
Richard H. Pildes

PART III: ADMINISTERING SECURE ELECTIONS

10 Election Administration and the Right to Vote 191
Nathaniel Persily

11 The Deep Roots of the "Big Lie" 216
Julilly Kohler-Hausmann

12 HBCUs and Election Integrity 238
Kareem Crayton

13 States as Bulwarks against, or Potential Facilitators of, Election Subversion 253
Richard L. Hasen

14 Voting Machines: Friend or Foe? 271
Charles Stewart III

15 The Transition Period: The Disruption of the Election of a President Due to the Death of Presidential Candidates after Election Day 294
John C. Fortier

16 The Potential Impact and Limitations of the Electoral Count Reform Act of 2022 309
Russ Feingold and Lindsay Langholz

Epilogue 331
Karen J. Greenberg and Julian E. Zelizer

Acknowledgments 335

About the Contributors 337

Index 347

INTRODUCTION

KAREN J. GREENBERG AND JULIAN E. ZELIZER

Our election system is not secure. The attack on the US Capitol on January 6, 2021, was a wake-up call. The 2020 election and its aftermath showed the nation that our electoral system was fraught with peril, posing an existential risk to our democracy. Not only did powerful forces in American politics, including the president of the United States, display a willingness to challenge and subvert the basic operations of the democratic process, and not only did the nation discover that there were many ways that this could be achieved, but the country learned in an unforgettable manner that the protections in place for our elections are searingly vulnerable. "To cast a vote in the United States of America is an act of both hope and faith. When you drop that ballot in the ballot box, you do so with the confidence that every person named on that ballot will hold up their end of the bargain," warned the congressional committee that investigated the events of January 6. "The person who wins must swear an oath and live up to it. The people who come up short must accept the ultimate results and abide by the will of the voters and the rule of law. This faith in our institutions and laws is what upholds our democracy. If that faith is broken—if those who seek power accept only the results of elections that they win—then American democracy, only a few centuries old, comes tumbling down."[1]

The danger posed by election denialism was not simply that it could take hold over one of the nation's major political parties but that there were accessible ways to achieve the goal of declaring an election's outcome illegitimate. The constitutional system on which we rely to determine who will be our president has multiple points of vulnerability that can be manipulated, exploited, and weaponized, despite long-standing efforts to implement safeguards. Layered on top of the process is a communications environment where misinformation and disinformation—from at home and abroad—easily permeate the ecosystem on which we depend to understand the outcomes of democratic contests. While it is true that the election of 2020 ended with the rightful person in office, largely as a result of individuals who refused to interfere with lawfully cast and counted votes, the potential for an illegitimate outcome remains. Had Vice President Mike Pence made a different decision on January 6, yielding to the pressure of the president and his counsel to delay counting the votes, or if one state official in Michigan or Wisconsin had moved forward in sending an alternative slate of delegates, it is not difficult to imagine how Donald Trump might still be sitting in the Oval Office.

This is not the first time that our democracy has been under threat. The worst moment took place during the nineteenth century, when the political system proved incapable of resolving the immense divisions that emerged over the institution of slavery and disintegrated into a devastating civil war that almost destroyed the republic. The promise of Reconstruction was undone by organized Southern white violence and a deal struck after the contested presidential election in 1876 that was part of the dismantling of the ambitious federal programs that had been put into place by Northern Republicans. During the early twentieth century, the Deep South put into place Jim Crow laws that fundamentally undercut efforts to broaden political rights and create a truly democratic system that offered representation to all citizens regardless of their race. It took a grassroots movement and a sympathetic president to enact the Voting Rights Act (VRA) of 1965 that finally brought the muscle of the federal government to bear in service of protecting every American's right to vote. When a Republican Senate and president agreed to reauthorize and extend the reach of the legislation in 1982, it appeared that the VRA had entrenched a new era in which the right to vote would retain newfound strength within American political culture.

But the election of 2000, in which the Electoral College winner lost the popular vote, and in which a close election led to the Supreme Court deciding the election, ushered in a whole new set of problems hindering trust in the democratic process and put into motion a number of initiatives that aimed to improve election administration. In 2013, the Supreme Court knocked down Section 5 of the VRA and helped open the door to state efforts that put into place new kinds of restrictions—not explicitly racial but often falling hardest on Black and Latino communities—that became the center of political battles over democratic rights. "Beyond question," Justice Ruth Bader Ginsburg wrote in her dissent, "the V.R.A. is no ordinary legislation. It is extraordinary because Congress embarked on a mission long delayed and of extraordinary importance: to realize the purpose and promise of the Fifteenth Amendment. . . . For a half century a concerted effort has been made to end racial discrimination in voting. Thanks to the Voting Rights Act, progress once the subject of a dream has been achieved and continues to be made. The court errs egregiously by overriding Congress's decision."[2] Despite the fact that the nation has been able to overcome moments of vulnerability in our history, the survival of the system in the past is not evidence that a fragile democracy will always endure. January 6 was so perilous, taking place in an era where autocratic forces in other countries have been eroding democratic politics, that it has forced the nation into a reckoning with the threats that the security of our electoral system faces.

In the 2020s, we have clearly entered into a new moment of political instability. While other Western democracies are also confronting unprecedented challenges to fair and just elections, the full array of dangers here at home is uniquely threatening.

The nation can't afford to continue in this way. Presidential and congressional elections determine the future. With each election comes the promise and the peril of change. Domestic policy, foreign affairs, economic viability, and safety in our streets are but a few of the realities of life that the country's leadership stands to affect.

The definition of national security must take into account the challenges that are posed to our free and fair elections, the bulwark that we depend on to prevent authoritarian forces from gaining a strong hold in the United States. Whereas many of the national security risks we have focused on stem from external sources—such as authoritarian governments in Europe or nonstate terrorist networks—it has become increasingly clear that some of the most serious challenges stem from within. Indeed, the two threats are interconnected. Not only do foreign adversaries seek to capitalize on the nation's political instability, but the vulnerabilities themselves offer avenues for overseas actors to influence our process.

This is the subject of our book. *Our Nation at Risk* brings together some of our leading political scientists, historians, law professors, and journalists to address the biggest vulnerabilities that our election system faces and to provide numerous recommendations to fix it. The following chapters take seriously Benjamin Franklin's famous admonition to Elizabeth Willing Powel, who asked, "Well, Doctor what have we got, a republic or a monarchy?" to which he responded, "A Republic, if you can keep it." Whereas just a decade ago most Americans would have agreed that we can automatically keep it, today we know that maintaining democracy requires substantive institutional reforms that can provide stability and predictability to the mechanisms through which we make our decisions. While the lessons of the past helped lay the groundwork for recent abuses, they also shine a light on remedies available for more robust, secure, and trusted elections. This volume tries to offer pathways toward making sure we can keep our republic.

There are three pillars to the democratic system that are especially important to the security of our politics, none of which has been as stable as we assume. The first, inscribed into the Constitution, is the Electoral College. Under the constitutional system, each state is allotted a certain number of electors, based on the number of members the state has in Congress, who vote for a candidate to be president. Although it is not stipulated in the Constitution, most electors have voted for the candidate whom a majority of the electorate in their state selected. In 1887, Congress passed the Electoral Count Act, which laid out more specific procedures for how electoral votes should be counted. While the system has generally provided for a smooth and peaceful transition of power, there have been a number of messy and contested election outcomes, as the following chapters document, where the underlying problems with the process were exposed. The 2020 election also showed how the process could be purposely exploited by bad-faith actors should the will exist to do so. The 2022 Electoral Count Reform Act endeavored to address some of the fissures that had been exploited, though as our authors point out, much more remains to be addressed.

The second pillar has been the right to vote. At the heart of the ideal democratic system is the ability of each person to exercise their right to citizenship by voting for who their leader should be. The Constitution did not articulate a right to vote. Only white male citizens, twenty-one years and over, were eligible to do so. In subsequent decades, Congress gradually took it upon themselves to protect the franchise. The resistance toward extending the franchise was fierce. From the beginning, white men intently fought against granting this key element of citizenship to other Americans. The Fifteenth Amendment was a landmark moment when the nation vowed that individuals would not be denied the vote based on race. The promise was fleeting as restrictionist measures were put into place after Reconstruction. Women did not gain the right to vote until 1920 with the ratification of the Nineteenth Amendment, while Americans between the ages of eighteen and twenty-one, though eligible to serve in the military, were only able to go to the ballot box after 1971 as a result of the Twenty-Sixth Amendment. The VRA of 1965 prohibited racial discrimination against voting and established mechanisms empowering the federal government to take action when there was evidence of wrongdoing within the states. When the Supreme Court knocked down a major provision in the VRA in 2013, conservative states rushed to impose limitations on voting based on unfounded allegations of mass fraud. And, as we write, the VRA remains under attack.

Finally, the third pillar revolves around a multiplicity of other institutions within the democratic system that have been extremely important to the security and stability of the process. The news media, for instance, has functioned as the main platform through which citizens receive information about public issues, their elected officials, and the election itself. The proliferation of social media has only enhanced the possibilities for distortion. When these platforms have been filled with disinformation or even foreign propaganda, the democracy has become unstable. The capacity of state and local government to administer elections has likewise been pivotal to ensuring that citizens can express their will at the ballot box. The campaign finance system, which has structured the nexus between money and politics, has created processes that enable a flow of private dollars to influence elections, and in turn decision-making by elected officials. There have been times when Congress and the states were able to pass measures that limited some of this money and offered alternative methods for financing campaigns, including public funds. But there have been many other turning points, such as the Supreme Court's *Citizen United* decision in 2010, that undercut regulations that had been put into place.

The chapters in this volume are intended to bring to public attention this complex array of issues that have come to bear on American elections, particularly for the presidency. Long-standing concerns such as election tampering, racial discrimination at the polls, and "corrupt bargains" still persist. Meanwhile, new realities have come into play in the twenty-first century. Technology, disinformation, and foreign influences pose novel and evolving challenges to the electoral process. The essays included here reflect on the major challenges confronting our electoral process and the consequences for the security of our democracy. The authors examine the historical and structural reforms pertaining to executive powers, voting rights, and the presidential transition that have led us to this moment. They examine the effect of foreign influences and corporate entities on campaigns; the impact of voting restrictions, gerrymandering, racial discrimination, and political polarization; and the role played by state legislatures as well as the courts in guiding election processes and outcomes. With the dangers to our democracy—in which election security is a crucial element—our experts offer recommendations for reform and best practices going forward. Our hope is that these chapters will enlighten readers not just about the threats to national security that our elections pose but about meaningful ways to strengthen the structural and legal underpinnings as well as the public's understanding of our presidential elections.

The authors explore these problems from different angles, ranging from the foreign policy and election interference interconnection to the basic technology used to tabulate voting and to the use and abuse of laws, authorities, and policies surrounding elections. A holistic approach to reforming and strengthening the way we decide on our elected officials will be essential to breaking through some of the structural problems that were exposed in recent years.

The book is organized into three sections. The first section examines the sources that caused, and continue to cause, insecurity in our election system (Greenberg, Zelizer, Suri, Hemmer, and Edsall). Examining forces that date back to the design of the Constitution itself, several contributors explore the ways in which the Electoral College, voting rights, overseas interference, disinformation and misinformation, polarization, and racial discrimination have led to instability and a declining trust in our elections. The next section turns to the different forces—presidents, Congress, the Supreme Court, and the states—that have considerable capacity to stabilize weaknesses in our democracy yet, for different reasons, have been limited in effect (Morrison, Green, Waldman, and Pildes). Finally, the last section centers on the important realm of administration, the nuts and bolts of the election system, from those who tabulate the votes to the moment when Congress certifies the Electoral College results, when the selection process has the greatest capacity to be undermined (Persily, Kohler-Hausmann, Crayton, Hasen, Stewart, Fortier, and Feingold and Langholz).

Our authors underscore the long-standing reliance on trust that a just and transparent system, and a legitimized (or widely accepted) outcome, will eventually prevail. Although our authors are not in agreement on all issues and express differences on key questions, collectively they believe there are ways in which our democratic system can be strengthened given the strains it has encountered in recent decades. The election of 2000 breached that trust. The election of 2020 poked more and deeper holes in the comforting assumption that all would eventually be well. While fraught elections in the past ultimately found their way to peaceful resolution, future elections, we now know, may stumble and even fail to reach a trusted outcome. Our authors reason that hoping for well-intentioned, law-abiding actors as a bulwark against corrupt elections is not enough. All of the authors agree that passively waiting is not an option. Election security and our national security go hand in hand. All the weapons in the world and all of the best defense systems won't protect us if the core of the democracy is broken. With this book, we offer a path to achieving a better republic—sooner rather than later.

NOTES

1 *The January 6th Report: The Report of the Select Committee to Investigate the January 6 Attack on the United States Capitol* (New York: Cleadon, 2022), xi–xii.
2 Adam Liptak, "Supreme Court Invalidates Key Part of the Voting Rights Act," *New York Times*, June 25, 2013.

PART I

THE HISTORICAL SOURCES OF INSECURE ELECTIONS

1

ON A WING AND A PRAYER

THE PERILOUS PATH OF OUR CONTESTED PRESIDENTIAL ELECTIONS

KAREN J. GREENBERG

"Democracy is sometimes messy," reflected Joe Biden, counseling patience in the aftermath of the 2020 election while he and the country awaited official results.[1] Messy outcomes in US presidential elections, foundational to our democracy, have certainly proved him right. Over the course of the country's two and a quarter centuries, tallies have been left in disarray, outcomes mired in doubt, and losing candidates certain that they had been victorious. Repeatedly, lawmakers have endeavored to fix the vulnerabilities exposed by fraught elections—often with too little effect. Nonetheless, contested elections—from those that were formally disputed to those that were sent to the dustbin of history amid whispers of inaccuracies, manipulation, and deceit—have long been a piece of the story of American presidential elections. As the twenty-first century dawned, the nation's long legacy of electoral vulnerabilities caught up with itself. The 2000 election rang as a wake-up call to the vulnerabilities that still existed after fifty-four presidential elections.

"Welcome to Guatemala." These were the words with which Ron Klain, Vice President Al Gore's chief of staff and general counsel for Gore's recount committee, greeted Gore lawyer David Boies five days after the 2020 election.[2] Boies had made an unscheduled last-minute trip to Florida, summoned to help devise a legal strategy for addressing the yet-to-be-decided election results in the state. Gore's lawyers were deep in the weeds of their legal and legislative options, convinced that the vote count was tainted and the election set to be inaccurately called for George W. Bush. For Klain, the chaos of the moment and the options for remedy resembled, as he later recalled, the conditions found in an unstable "Third World banana republic," not American democracy. Legal experts, pundits, and others echoed Klain's sentiment, labeling the election outcome a "coup" and more precisely "a constitutional coup."[3]

Twenty years later, the country experienced a full-scale alarm. The 2020 election took the issue of election security and election legitimacy to new heights with the attempt of the incumbent president, Donald Trump, to overturn the election results through a series of illegal overreaches involving Congress, the courts, and the White House itself. Once again, cries of "banana republic" filled the air, this time abroad as well as at home.[4]

A trip down history lane might have led observers to temper, however slightly, their sense of the foreignness of the moment. They might instead have cast a look over the frightening prior instances where accusations of stolen, corrupt, mismanaged, or manipulated election results had followed on the heels of US presidential elections. If the 2000 election was a wake-up call and the 2020 election a full-scale alarm, other elections had also stumbled to the finish line—most famously in 1800, 1824, and 1876—where the outcomes teetered on the brink of irresolution and illegitimacy. When questions arose, the final resolution was often the result of an individual candidate choosing to concede. Over time, in fact, the five candidates who won the popular vote but lost the electoral vote eventually chose to concede the election, though at times with continuing allegations of unfairness.

EARLY FLAWS AND FIXES

Concerns about the knotty challenges inherent in creating a fair and trusted system for electing a president arose in the founding days of the republic. Attendees at the Constitutional Convention of 1787 recognized the ambitiousness—and potential pitfalls—of the task they had set for themselves in devising the electoral system for choosing a president. It was, after all, a complex and unprecedented task. As Rufus King, a delegate from Massachusetts, explained, the numerous potential dangers inherent in deciding how to choose a country's chief executive had led other nations "to prefer hereditary to elective Executives."[5] As James Madison reminded his colleagues, "The elective mode of obtaining rulers is the characteristic policy of republican government."[6]

For King, the Constitution's prescription for peaceful and productive elections—which he summed up as "apportioning, limiting, and confining the Electors within their respective States, and by the guarded manner of giving and transmitting the ballots of the Electors to the Seat of Government"—included an unspoken assumption. The delegates, he acknowledged, "did indulge the hope" that the guardrails and specifications imposed in the Constitution on the electoral process would prevail over the dangers such "that intrigue, combination, and corruption, would be effectually shut out, and a free and pure election of the President of the United States made perpetual."[7] King's reliance on "hope" among the tools designed to dispel "intrigue" and "corruption" provides a telling lens for understanding the history of American presidential election.

From the very establishment of the republic, the founders knew that the Constitution's prescription for presidential elections included potential vulnerabilities. Drafted in the final rushed days of the Constitutional Convention, the Constitution's requirements for elections succumbed to what Madison later referred to as "the hurrying influence" as well as the "fatigue and impatience" of the moment.[8] In so doing, it left many potential fault lines exposed, among them vague directions. When it came to vote counting, for example, it prescribed only that "the President of the Senate shall . . . open all the Certificates, and the Votes shall then be counted." The use of the passive voice left it unclear who exactly should do the counting. Nor did the founding document consider a variety of problems that vote counts could encounter.

Consequently, the infant republic tripped over the uncertainty and flaws within the electoral process in its first years. In fact, the very first attempt to transfer political power underlined the dangers inherent in this lack of clarity, and the role that wishful thinking played in considerations of a peaceful outcome.

Hopeful thinking, combined with the absence of specific guidance when it came to unanticipated election complications, was visible as early as 1796 when George Washington decided against a third term. In the electoral tabulations of the election, the insufficiencies of the electoral system as laid out in Article II of the Constitution were immediately apparent. As the Constitution originally specified, electors were to cast two votes, the winner to be president, the second-place finisher to assume the vice presidency. Federalist candidate and Washington's vice president John Adams won the election, only to have the Democratic-Republican Thomas Jefferson win the vice presidency. In other words, as Madison surmised, "the Ultimate choice is extremely uncertain."[9]

The founders hadn't accounted for the rise of the party system and the possibility of an election that yielded a president from one party and a vice president from another—at best an uncomfortable alliance. Though exposing a flaw in the Constitution's structural understanding of elections, the outcome itself, with Adams winning by three electoral votes, did not rise to the level of a dispute, and therefore did not lead to successful efforts to produce a system beyond that provided for in the Constitution. In place of efforts at reform, trust that the system would work going forward prevailed.

With the very next election, however, the two-vote system, unaddressed in the interim, led to more concerning troubles. In 1800, Adams sought a second term. Disunion within the Federalist Party helped lead not only to Adams garnering third place when the vote was tallied but also to a tie between Jefferson and his running mate, Aaron Burr. The dispute, as the Constitution provided, was sent to the House of Representatives. After thirty-six ballots, Jefferson was declared the third president of the United States. It was a messy resolution at best, recalling the kind of "intrigue" that King had worried over.

This time, crossing fingers that things would work out gave way to the more responsible consensus that the provisions in the Constitution warranted additional guidance. In 1804, Congress passed the Twelfth Amendment. It amended the two-vote system and specified that each member of the Electoral College would cast one vote for president and one for vice president.

But even with reform, fault lines remained. Notably, the Twelfth Amendment did not clarify what the Constitution itself had failed to clearly provide—namely, sufficient guidance on how to resolve disputes about the vote count. As Supreme Court justice Elena Kagan would later lament, the Constitution provided merely "bare bones" in terms of guidance for the future.[10]

Accordingly, electoral troubles lay in wait as the 1824 election revealed unaddressed inadequacies in the system. While the Twelfth Amendment had addressed several lapses in the casting and counting of votes, more dimensions of the electoral process remained in need of reform. In his bid for the presidency, John Quincy Adams lost the popular vote, but his opponent, Andrew Jackson, who led in both the popular vote and the electoral vote, had failed to win a majority, sending the decision to the House of Representatives as the Constitution required. Adams won by one vote, after a number of votes were switched, with Henry Clay's intervention, from Jackson to Adams. In place of widespread acceptance of the result, allegations lingered of a "corrupt bargain" in which Clay was accused of lining up votes for Adams in exchange for his appointment as secretary of state.

The 1824 election could have led lawmakers to design new measures and clear and transparent processes for resolving disputes. But in fact it would be many decades before they rose to the occasion.

As the century progressed, lawmakers did, however, attempt to address the acknowledged lapses in the law, often to little effect. In 1865, Congress adopted the Twenty-Second Joint Rule as a means of setting out procedures for resolving electoral disputes. The joint rule specified that any member of the House or Senate could, during the counting of the electoral votes by president of the Senate, object to the counting of an individual state's electoral vote. For the vote to then be counted, the consent of both House and Senate was required. Any nay vote in either chamber would render the vote ineligible. In other words, as one scholar has noted, the joint rule "not only claimed the power to count but defined that power as permitting it to reject an invalid state canvass."[11] It thus opened up a Pandora's box of ways for Congress to disallow votes from states.

The 1872 election contest between incumbent Republican Ulysses S. Grant and Democrat Horace Greeley underscored the dangers of applying the joint rule. That year, the first time the rule was invoked, Louisiana submitted two slates of electors to Congress, both certified by the governor. Congress empowered itself to investigate further and subsequently rejected both slates. Louisiana was thereby deprived of casting a vote for president. And Congress was left with the takeaway that the road to resolving contested elections remained uncertain.

In 1875, in further efforts at reform, Congress briefly considered a proposed constitutional amendment that would allow states to elect all but two electors from congressional districts rather than honor statewide slates pledged to one winner. It failed, however, to gain momentum. Meanwhile, a chastened Senate rescinded the joint rule in 1876, just before the election that would expose with greater clarity than ever before the fragile constraints and guidelines in place for contested presidential elections.

THE ELECTION OF 1876

As the 1876 contest between Democrat Samuel Tilden and Republican Rutherford B. Hayes loomed, the country was left with little more than the vague and insufficient guidance that Article II and the Twelfth Amendment had provided. In the shadow of the Civil War, the election threatened to divide the nation to the point of violence. And as in earlier disputes, the blame for the disarray would fall directly on the lapses in the law.

By election night, disputes raged in three states—Louisiana, Florida, and South Carolina—as both parties claimed victory. Tilden had won the national popular vote but did not have an Electoral College majority. In all three states, the returning boards claimed that intimidation and threats of violence, along with fraud, had led to invalidated vote counts. Republicans faced the possibility of losing the election due to widespread disenfranchisement of freedmen, in violation of the Fifteenth Amendment. Once again, a dual slate of electors seemed possible. And once again, neither the Constitution nor the Twelfth Amendment offered sufficiently helpful direction.

Debates followed as to which votes to count, which to discard, and how to address the alleged improprieties involved in vote counting. Three separate slates of electors were sent to Congress from Florida and Louisiana, while South Carolina submitted two. To make matters worse, in a fourth state—Oregon, where the signatures of both the secretary and the governor were required on the certificate—a dispute took place over the validity of one of the electors. Noting that it was unconstitutional for a federal official—in this case, a postmaster—to serve as an elector, the Democratic governor disqualified the elector, replaced him with a Democrat, and certified a slate of two votes for Hayes and one for Tilden. The secretary of state, however, certified a slate of all Hayes electors,[12] leading to yet another set of conflicting electoral certificates.

When each of these four states submitted multiple slates of electors to Congress, there was still no playbook in place for specifying who should decide which one to count. As the slogan "Tilden or Blood" illustrated, time was of the essence. Notably, President Grant secured the Capitol with troops and readied for the possibility of deploying troops elsewhere if needed.

Fearing violence and finding no applicable law or precedent to guide them, Congress opted for a new reform: the Electoral Commissions Act. Passed on January 29, 1877, nearly three months after the election, the act established a commission tasked with deciding the election. The bipartisan commission would consist of fifteen individuals—five members from the Senate, five from the House, and five from the Supreme Court—who would jointly resolve the disputed votes and decide the winner.

It was not the first time such a commission had been proposed. The original draft of the Twelfth Amendment had envisioned the creation of a committee that would be appointed to resolve a deadlocked dispute. Both the House and the Senate passed versions of what was known as the "Grand Committee Bill," a provision whereby a panel consisting of members of Congress and the chief justice of the Supreme Court would together resolve such disputes. The two bodies could not, however, agree on the details of the bill. As a result, it failed to become law.[13] In the early 1870s, lawmakers similarly had put forth proposals for resolving future election disputes via tribunals, but to no avail. Now, in efforts to resolve the outcome of the 1876 election, the idea of a committee to decide an election had taken hold.

The understanding among lawmakers was that seven Democrats, seven Republicans, and a true independent chosen from the Supreme Court—Justice David Davis—would constitute membership on the commission. When Davis refused to serve, having been named by the state legislator to be a senator (in the days before senators were elected by the people), the commission went from being nonpartisan in its makeup to being divided between the two parties, with the once agreed-on neutral justice replaced by a Republican. The die was thereby cast. Once the agreed-on independent member of the commission withdrew, the 1876 commission was destined to fall short of constituting a neutral arbitration. The result, predictably, in Davis's absence, came down along party lines—one vote more for Hayes than Tilden.

Contentious and uncertain to the end, the Tilden-Hayes election controversy further demonstrated the dangers of continuing to ignore the fault lines in the electoral process. The events resulted in an election whose results have been doubted ever since, leaving the legacy of a "stolen election," a "monster fraud," forever in its wake.

Nonetheless, the election of 1876 led to the addition of several new tools for resolving disputed elections. On a procedural level, it brought justices of the Supreme Court into the mix, albeit not acting in the role of justices but, as Chief Justice William Rehnquist later explained, nodding approval, in an "extrajudicial" role.[14] As such, it was an incremental step toward engaging the Supreme Court in the matter of elections. Second, on a structural level, the election heightened the sense that a plan for resolving disputes in presidential elections was imperative. The popular vote tallies in the two following elections—1880 and 1884—were, like those in the Tilden-Hayes election, uncomfortably close, further exacerbating concerns about the vagueness of the law when it came to counting votes and resolving electoral confusions.

A decade later, in 1887, Congress finally passed the Electoral Count Act (ECA), intending to avoid the pitfalls that many had predicted would occur without new legislation. As contemporary observer John Burgess commented, "It is almost marvelous that any people should have preserved political unity for a century under such a loose and decentralized system of election of its chief magistrate. It is certainly indubitable evidence of great popular self-control."[15] Rushed into place in anticipation of the 1888 election, the ECA laid out specific procedures for resolving disputed elections. It placed much of the vote counting in the hands of the states, giving "the executive" of the state authority to decide a tiebreaker and to choose what slate to send to Congress, and carved out a small set of disputes that would fall to Congress for resolution, including the prospect of two slates of electors being submitted to Congress. The ECA thus narrowed the areas of dispute in which Congress could engage. As the House Select Committee on the bill report maintained, Congress could "only count legal votes, and in doing so must determine from the best evidence to be had, what are legal votes." In case of disagreement over legal votes, though, Congress would decide. With a scolding note, the House Select Committee report added, "It will be the State's own fault if the matter is left in doubt."[16]

Yet despite adding new procedures for resolving disputes, it still left many unanswered questions about procedures, exact interpretations, and ultimate authorities for a resolution, including the precise meaning of the "executive" of the state. Nonetheless, the election of 1888 did not end up testing the efficacy of the ECA. Grover Cleveland won the popular vote but lost the electoral vote. He chose not to challenge the outcome, preferring to wait for the 1892 rematch, in which he "clobbered Harrison."[17]

Meanwhile, as the country continued forward with at best convoluted directions for the role of Congress vis-à-vis the states, the Supreme Court backed away from future iterations of its own involvement in presidential outcomes. In 1900, in *Taylor v. Beckham*, a case involving a gubernatorial election dispute in Kentucky, the Supreme Court opined that it did not have jurisdiction on the grounds that there was no Fourteenth Amendment concern as alleged and therefore no federal issue to be adjudicated. It thus dismissed the case and in so doing set a clear and powerful precedent on the Court's distance from such matters.[18]

As the twentieth century approached, a process to ensure against two candidates vying for the presidency on the day of the inauguration remained absent and the possibilities for manipulating election results remained insufficiently addressed, as did the prospects for a protracted contingent election as had occurred in 1800. On a wing and a prayer, then, the country went forward ill-equipped to face future disputes. Indeed, the matter of contested elections continued to rely essentially on the hope that either one candidate would eventually concede defeat or a deft ad hoc solution would emerge to resolve any disputes.

TWENTIETH-CENTURY REFORMS

Compared with the turbulent 1876 election, twentieth-century presidential elections, though hardly dispute-free, did not give rise to the virulent levels of upheaval that had marked the 1876 election. Nevertheless, the issues at hand did not disappear, especially when it came to vote casting.

Over the course of the century, voter discrimination persisted, especially in the South, as poll taxes, illiteracy tests, and redistricting led to voter suppression.

In the 1960s, attempting to counter racial discrimination at the polls, Congress and the courts took up the matter of discriminatory voting disparities. In three Supreme Court cases, the Warren Court, relying on the Fourteenth Amendment, set new rules for extending voting rights to an increasing array of citizens. In 1962, in *Baker v. Carr*, the Court moved away from the long-standing norm of being hands-off when it came to the "political questions" doctrine as it had held in *Taylor v. Beckham*, ruling that the Court could decide—in this case on the issue of legislative apportionment—to adjudicate challenges to states' drawing of district lines.[19] The decision, in addition to bringing the Court into the matter of contested elections after a century of remaining firmly outside matters of vote counting in the states, opened the door to engaging in contested election disputes, especially when there was an alleged constitutional violation involved. In 1962, in *Reynolds v. Sims*, and in 1964 in *Wesberry v. Sanders*, the Court ruled that legislative districts needed to be drawn according to similarly populous areas, extending the one-person, one-vote rule in *Reynolds* to state legislative districts and in *Wesberry* to congressional districts in accordance with the Fourteenth Amendment, thus leading to redistricting around the country.[20] Ultimately, the 1965 Voting Rights Act, outlawing discriminatory voting practices, gave additional power to the courts for addressing voter disenfranchisement.

Moreover, while the second half of the twentieth century followed, on the one hand, a path toward democratically minded efforts at inclusion in legislation and the involvement of the courts,[21] on the other hand it began to set the stage for undermining trust in the electoral process—notably in the Indiana congressional election of 1984. Although there had been many contested House elections in the nineteenth century, their frequency vastly diminished as a result of the institutionalization of the lower chamber as well as disenfranchisement. Their infrequency heightened the political tension in 1984. Though the battle was not over a presidential election, its extreme partisanship and fraught recount set the stage for the election of 2000. In what became known as the Bloody Eighth, Democrats contested the validity of the candidate who was originally declared the victor, Republican Rick

McIntyre. Six months later, following an intensive recount process that resulted from differential treatments of unnotarized and unwitnessed absentee ballots, the Democrats won out and the incumbent, Frank McCloskey, was declared the winner by a mere four-vote lead.[22] As one election official summed it up, "It took a process that should be ministerial and turned it adversarial."[23]

Thus, as the twenty-first century dawned, it was inevitable that, should disputes arise, both legal and constitutional challenges would involve the country's newfound—and untested—tools for addressing those disputes.

BUSH V. GORE

However perilous the 1876 election had been, it was the 2000 election that let Americans know that their system was, if not broken, breakable. The problems had caught up with the times, exposing the lingering reliance on a strategy of hope and trust that things would inevitably right themselves in times of election dispute and upheaval—as they always had. "Our political system blew up on Tuesday," *Washington Post* columnist E. J. Dionne Jr. warned, lacking hope in a noncontroversial resolution. "No matter who takes office as president next January, the legitimacy of his election will be in doubt."[24]

Political polarization had greatly intensified during the 1990s. As a result of the sorting of votes and changes to the rules of Congress, the relevance and presence of centrists in either party vastly diminished. Each party was more disciplined and less willing to enter into bargains with the other. More broadly, partisan tensions between Democratic and Republican voters worsened over the decade. For many citizens, the decision by the House to impeach President Bill Clinton in 1998 was a culmination of this development, a fierce partisan bludgeon wielded against the president without justifiable cause. When the 2000 election took place, the sentiment in the public culture was extraordinarily tense.

On election night, November 7, 2000, returns showed Democratic candidate Al Gore leading the popular vote over his Republican opponent, George W. Bush. The electoral count remained uncertain. Shortly after two o'clock on the morning of November 8, the news channels called the race for Bush. Gore, defying advice from his team, called Bush to congratulate him. But overnight counts showed Bush with four fewer electoral votes than Gore, and by dawn, the full tally remained uncertain. While three states—Oregon, New Mexico, and Florida—faced inconclusive counts, it was Florida's twenty-five electoral votes that could prove decisive for the overall results.

In Florida, the uncertainty was caused by apparent irregularities including undercounting due to sloppy paper punching on ballots, confusion in the list of names on the ballots, and overcounting due to votes cast for two presidential candidates. Gore, accordingly, withdrew his concession.

For six weeks, the country waited, shrouded in confusion, with no confirmed winner as Gore sought hand recounts in four counties as well as an extension of the deadline for submission of vote counts to the secretary of state. The Bush teamed attempted to block both attempts. On December 8, the Florida Supreme Court ordered a recount. The next day, Bush appealed to the Supreme Court.

Setting aside the long precedent of staying out of presidential disputes, the Court, led by Chief Justice William Rehnquist, ordered a stay to the recount and agreed to hear the appeal. On December 11 the Court heard oral arguments. On December 12, in compliance with the "safe harbor" date set by the ECA, the Court, exercising what it referred to as its "unsought responsibility," returned its decision. In a per curiam decision, with John Paul Stevens and Ruth Bader Ginsburg dissenting, the Court acknowledged the legal framework that the latter twentieth century had put into place. The Court relied not only on Article II and the Twelfth Amendment for its reasoning but also on the path set by more recent Supreme Court rulings that underscored the Fourteenth Amendment's Equal Protection Clause and its one-person, one-vote mandate. The Court now reasoned that "having once granted the right to vote on equal terms, Florida may not, by later arbitrary and disparate treatment, value one person's vote over that of another." Because there was no consistently followed standard for "accepting or rejecting contested ballots," the "minimum requirement for non-arbitrary treatment of voters" had not been satisfied.[25]

Other options were available. The Court could have taken into consideration lapses that characterized the history of electoral disputes—particularly the increasingly recognized need for specificity rather than generalized statements about procedures for resolving disputes. As legal scholar Richard Pildes explains, "The Court could have gone so far as to specify the processes and rules required for a constitutional recount."[26] "The choice," he adds, "need not have been an all-or-nothing one between constitutional law and democratic politics." But the Court, weighing legal clarity against the prospect of delaying the outcome even further, chose to conclude the story on its own. "Upon due consideration of the difficulties identified to this point, it is obvious that the recount cannot be conducted in compliance with the requirements of equal protection and due process without substantial additional work."[27] The next day, Gore conceded.

While the Supreme Court had defied tradition, reversing its historical reluctance to be involved in presidential election disputes, it nonetheless shied away from setting a precedent for the role of the Court in future elections. "Our consideration," the Court concluded, "is limited to the present circumstances." Further, the Court acknowledged the concerning absence of sufficient protocols needed for true reform, just as so many candidates, Congresses, and observers had done for centuries. In its opinion, the Court registered its hope for change, considering it "likely" that "legislative bodies nationwide will examine ways to improve the mechanisms and machinery for voting."[28]

The Court's wish for reform proved prescient. In 2002, Congress passed the Help America Vote Act (HAVA). What the US Election Assistance Commission—established under the statute for the purpose of promoting an exchange of ideas over standards and practices in voting across the country—called "sweeping reforms"[29] were thereby lawfully implemented, including the replacement of punch-card and lever voting machines so as to remove the potential for mistakes such as those discovered in 2000, as well as the institution of policies for the counting of provisional votes, in-precinct early voting, and voting for individuals with disabilities.

But in terms of the true vulnerabilities exposed by the election of 2000—and by the longer historical arc of disputed presidential elections—HAVA, like its predecessors, fell short. Although the Court had set out important guidelines for vote casting and counting, the kind of "specific mechanisms" that the Court had wishfully referenced remained lacking.

Once again, blind hope that nips and tucks would be enough had prevailed over acknowledgment of the need for major reform. Notably, as the 2020 election approached, the Supreme Court weighed in once more, addressing the issue of "faithless electors" and reaffirming the power of the states to appoint their electors and the obligation of the electors to cast their votes as pledged. The opinion written by Justice Kagan goes to great lengths to clarify the long-standing vagueness of Article II and the Twelfth Amendment. But like HAVA, it proved to be too little too late.[30]

THE 2020 ELECTION

The dangers of unaddressed fault lines in the electoral process therefore remained all too securely in place as an increasingly divided country faced the 2020 election contest between norms-breaking Republican candidate Donald Trump and his Democratic opponent, former vice president Joe Biden.

Even before Election Day, pundits noted the dangers inherent in the now-perpetual reluctance to tackle the grimy issues attendant on elections. As Election Day approached, there was no dearth of warnings about the dangers that lay ahead. Law professors weighed in with predictions of foul play and how to counter and prevent it.[31] Law enforcement took note as well. So dire were the predictions that, six weeks before the election, the FBI issued a warning about election crimes, offering up a long list of potential crimes, among them the accusations that had fueled the 2000 election controversy—ballot fraud, poorly formatted ballots, abuse of office by election officials, and voter suppression.[32]

Unsurprisingly, the Trump-Biden contest replayed many of the frictions passed along from contested election to contested election.

In the run-up to the election, it became clear that the Trump team had studied the vulnerabilities exposed in past presidential elections. Even before Election Day, Trump and his advisers, fearing defeat, set out to discredit the results of the election, appealing to the Supreme Court, which, due to Trump's appointments, was now decidedly Republican. The Court, however, refused to get involved.

Under the tutelage of lawyer John Eastman, Trump and his allies continued to reach back over the full set of lessons garnered from disputed elections, looking for ammunition with which to overturn the results of a Biden victory. Eastman had done his homework. In late September, he produced a two-page memo outlining "a January 6 scenario," referring to the upcoming date for congressional certification of the electoral votes. Subsequently expanded to a six-pager that included a section titled "War-Gaming the Alternatives," Eastman set out nine scenarios, four of which would result in a Biden victory, five of which would result in a second term for Trump.[33]

Eastman's memos were, in essence, a mere litany of the very fault lines that had been pushed forward without adequate reforms in the country's prior contested elections. He argued that both the Constitution and the Twelfth Amendment lay silent as to the specifics for who decides which votes to count—for example, in the case of two slates of electors presented to Congress by a state. In addition, he declared the ECA "likely unconstitutional,"[34] reasoning that it violated the Twelfth Amendment, which called not for the two chambers to decide disputes separately but for a joint session to hear the certification.

According to Eastman, the Twelfth Amendment deferred to the state executive, not to Congress, for determining the result of a dispute, "regardless of the evidence that exists regarding the election, and regardless of whether there was ever fair review of what happened in the election, by judges and/or state legislatures."[35] He further argued that the charge to the president of the Senate to count the "regularly given votes" was too vague to implement. Counseling that "we are no longer playing by Queensbury rules," Eastman claimed that Vice President Pence, as president of the Senate, had the authority to reduce the number of votes counted in both the House and the Senate.[36]

In the lead-up to Election Day, worries surfaced about other lessons from the past that were reportedly informing the Trump team. In late September, journalist Barton Gellman reported in *The Atlantic* on an incipient plan by the Trump campaign team that relied in part on the Supreme Court ruling in *Bush v. Gore*, in which state legislatures "can take back the power to appoint electors." In battleground states with Republican-dominated legislatures, Trump allies could, the reasoning went, set aside the popular vote and "exercise their power to choose a slate of electors directly." The confusions over who had the last say—the legislature, the courts, the governor, or Congress—could lead, in Gellman's thinking, to a "constitutional crisis." Given this dire scenario, Gellman ultimately concluded that, given all the undecided, and confusing, fault lines of the law, Trump "may win or lose, but he will never concede."[37]

And although returns showed Biden had won the electoral vote on election night, it took days for states with close contests to determine the winner. On November 7, Biden was named president. For the first time in history, his opponent refused to concede.

Determined to use all tools to subvert the election results, the Trump campaign pursued a judicial as well as a political course. His team filed two suits in Pennsylvania. Both relied on the *Bush v. Gore* Supreme Court decision. In one suit, filed on Election Day, lawyers argued that practices at some of the Pennsylvania polling places violated the Equal Protection Clause of the Constitution. And in a second suit Trump's lawyers argued, following the controversial Rehnquist concurrence in *Bush v. Gore*, that, based on Article II, state legislatures have the "plenary" power over all decisions involving an election. The Pennsylvania Supreme Court did not, therefore, have the right to extend the deadline for mail-in ballots as it had done.[38]

This time, the Supreme Court refused to play a role in resolving the disputes. The country could no longer afford to run from the need for substantial reform. One remedy came in the form of legislation, long overdue. Congress got to work on a revised ECA, passing the Electoral Count Reform Act in December 2022. In contrast to prior election reform efforts, the ECRA tackled some of the more challenging questions surrounding election disputes, providing needed clarity on several issues. It encapsulated and codified lessons learned from the past that had escaped legislative attention for centuries. It clarified the vice president's role as purely "ministerial." It raised the threshold for the number of senators and representatives required to object to electoral votes. It narrowed exceptions to the requirement that electors be appointed on Election Day. And it eliminated the ECA's provision that had given legislatures the power to appoint electors in the instance of a "failed election."[39] It also amended the Presidential Transition Act in order to provide safeguards for the period of dispute.

In addition to clarifying the mechanism for resolution that the Supreme Court had underscored in *Bush v. Gore*, the ECRA included the federal courts and the Supreme Court in its prescriptions for resolving disputes. In "any action brought by an aggrieved candidate for President or Vice President" with regard to the certification of the vote, the federal courts, in the form of a three-judge panel, would henceforth play a part in deciding the dispute and were tasked "to expedite to the greatest possible extent" their decision. Further, "any appeal from the judgment of the panel" could be heard by the Supreme Court, also "on an expedited basis."[40] The Supreme Court's long-standing reluctance to get involved on a statutory matter was now over.

Heralded as "nothing short of a miracle in the annals of democracy reform" by leading legal experts Bob Bauer and Jack Goldsmith, commended by the ACLU for its attempt "to ensure access to and protect the right to vote," and praised by the likes of senior fellow at the American Enterprise Institute Kevin Kosar as an act "for which we should all be thankful," the ECRA has received praise from across the political spectrum.[41]

While some have expressed concern over unaddressed issues that remain at the state level, the ECRA is nonetheless a much-warranted step forward.

The potential for a future role for the Supreme Court in presidential election outcomes received yet another push forward in 2023 when the Court issued its ruling in *Moore v. Harper* and weighed in anew on the powers of the federal courts. Although the case concerned congressional elections, not presidential elections, its legal reasoning has resonance for presidential elections. In a six-to-three decision, written by Chief Justice John Roberts, the Court rejected a maximalist view of the independent state legislature theory, ruling that the federal Elections Clause of the Constitution does not empower state legislatures to independently set rules, free from judicial review by state courts. Tearing away at the full power of the independent state legislature review standard that had been unleashed in *Bush v. Gore*, the decision—in this way echoing *Bush v. Gore*—gave courts a say in state election practices as well as the authority to strike down rules and procedures that violated a state's constitution.[42] The decision noted also that there were limits on state courts in terms of their review of laws pertaining to federal elections. It thus gave the federal courts a potential role in assessing a state court's ruling that went beyond the "ordinary bounds of judicial review."[43] The very vagueness of that standard arguably created more opportunities for federal court involvement. In so doing, the decision created new avenues for the federal courts, and thus the Supreme Court, to play a role in future electoral disputes.[44]

Hailed by many as "a solid victory for a system of free and fair elections,"[45] the *Moore* decision left a great deal unsaid, leading to uncertainty in the applicability of the ruling. The Court did not specify the limits on state courts or the standards for federal review in the matter of elections. Yet one thing was clear, if buried by the headlines focused on the ruling's new restrictions on the independent state legislature theory. The *Moore* decision had in fact opened up a path for federal courts to have a say over state election laws, and thus for the Supreme Court "to meddle" in future presidential elections.[46]

As we approach the 2024 presidential election, the dangers to democracy of a contested election are now indisputably clear, but the ECRA remains untested. The fallout of *Moore v. Harper* is unclear. Granted, there are more guardrails in place than before, and some remedy is certainly better than none. Nonetheless, Rufus King's "hope"—that "a free and pure election of the President of the United States" could be made "perpetual"—may still outpace the reforms necessary for American election security. In other words, let's keep our fingers crossed.

NOTES

1 Bloomberg Television, "Biden Says Democracy 'Sometimes Messy' as Count Drags On," YouTube video, 1:39, November 5, 2020, www.youtube.com/watch?v =UHfoUzaYj30.
2 Ena Alvarado et al., "The Bush-Gore Recount Is an Omen for 2020," *The Atlantic*, August 17, 2020, www.theatlantic.com.
3 Bruce Ackerman, "Anatomy of a Constitutional Coup," *London Review of Books*, February 8, 2001, www.lrb.co.uk.
4 See, for example, "'Who's the Banana Republic Now?': Nations Long Targeted by US Chide Trump's Claims of Fraud," *Times of India*, November 7, 2020, https:// timesofindia.indiatimes.com.
5 "Rufus King in the Senate of the United States," in *The Records of the Federal Convention of 1787*, ed. Max Farrand (New Haven, CT: Yale University Press, 1911), 3:461, https://tile.loc.gov/storage-services/service/ll/llscd/llfr003/llfr003.pdf.
6 "The Federalist Papers: No. 57," Avalon Project, https://avalon.law.yale.edu.
7 King in the Senate, 461.

8 James Madison to George Hay, August 23, 1823, in *The Writings of James Madison*, ed. Gaillard Hunt (New York: G. P. Putnam's Sons, 1900–1910), https://tile.loc.gov.
9 James Madison to James Madison Sr., November 27, 1796, Founders Online, https://founders.archives.gov.
10 Chiafalo et al. v. Washington, No. 19-465, slip op. (U.S. July 6, 2020), www.supremecourt.gov.
11 L. Kinvin Roth, "Election Contests and the Electoral Vote," *Dickinson Law Review* 65, no. 4 (1960–61): 330, https://ideas.dickinsonlaw.psu.edu.
12 Nathan Colvin and Edward B. Foley, "The Twelfth Amendment: A Constitutional Ticking Time Bomb," *University of Miami Law Review* 64, no. 2 (2010): 475, https://repository.law.miami.edu.
13 Matthew A. Seligman, "John Eastman Is Right: His Election Memo Was 'Crazy,'" *Slate*, October 22, 2021, https://slate.com.
14 William H. Rehnquist, *Centennial Crisis: The Disputed Election of 1876* (New York: Vintage Books, 2004), 145–50.
15 John Burgess, "The Law of the Electoral Count," *Political Science Quarterly* 3, no. 4 (December 1888): 634–35, www.jstor.org.
16 H.R. REP. No. 1638, 49th Cong., 2d Sess., 18 CONG. REC. 30 (1886); see also L. Kinvin Wroth, "Election Contests and the Electoral Vote," *Dickinson Law Review* 65 (1961): 335, https://ideas.dickinsonlaw.psu.edu.
17 Edward B. Foley, *Ballot Battles: The History of Disputed Elections in the United States* (New York: Oxford University Press, 2016), 355; Stephen A. Siegel, "The Conscientious Congressman's Guide to the Electoral Count Act of 1887," *Florida Law Review* 56 (2004): 160, www.floridalawreview.com/article/80375.
18 Taylor and Marshall v. Beckham, 178 U.S. 548 (1900).
19 Baker v. Carr, 369 U.S. 186 (1962).
20 Reynolds v. Sims, 377 U.S. 533 (1964); Wesberry v. Sanders, 376 U.S. 1 (1964).
21 Caroline Sulllivan, "Ten Voting Rights Cases That Shaped History," Democracy Docket, March 22, 2022, www.democracydocket.com.
22 Michael Kruse, "The 'Stolen' Election That Poisoned American Politics. It Happened in 1984," *Politico*, January 6, 2023, www.politico.com.
23 Kruse.
24 E. J. Dionne Jr., "Scrap This System," in *Bush v. Gore: The Court Cases and the Commentary*, ed. E. J. Dionne Jr. and William Kristol (Washington, DC: Brookings Institution Press, 2001), 165.
25 Bush v. Gore, 531 U.S. 98 (December 12, 2000), https://supreme.justia.com/cases/federal/us/531/98/.
26 Richard H. Pildes, "Constitutionalizing Democratic Politics," in *A Badly Flawed Election: Debating "Bush v. Gore," the Supreme Court and American Democracy*, ed. Ronald Dworkin (New York: New Press, 2002), 181.
27 Bush v. Gore, 531 U.S. 98.
28 Bush v. Gore, 531 U.S. 98.

29 "Help America Vote Act," US Election Assistance Commission, June 7, 2023, www.eac.gov.

30 Chiafalo v. Washington, 140 S. Ct. 2316 (2020).

31 Ad Hoc Committee for 2020 Election Fairness and Legitimacy, *Fair Elections during a Crisis: Urgent Recommendations in Law, Media, Politics and Tech to Advance the Legitimacy of, and the Public's Confidence in, the November 2020 U.S. Elections* (Irvine, CA: UCI Law, April 2020); Michelle Onibokun and Chuck Rosenberg, "The Justice Department's Policy against Election Interference Is Open to Abuse," Lawfare, September 11, 2020, www.lawfaremedia.org.

32 "FBI Warns Voters about Election Crimes ahead of the November 2020 Election," press release, FBI, September 24, 2020, www.fbi.gov.

33 Bob Woodward and Robert Costa, *Peril* (New York: Simon and Schuster, 2021), 226.

34 He reiterated the unconstitutionality argument more specifically in "Discussing the John Eastman Memo with John Eastman," *Another Way*, podcast, hosted by Lawrence Lessig, September 27, 2021, https://podcasts.apple.com.

35 John Eastman, "January 6 Scenario," January 2, 2021, https://www.cnn.com/2021/09/21/politics/read-eastman-memo/index.html.

36 John Eastman, "January 6 Scenario," January 3, 2021, https://https://www.cnn.com/2021/09/21/politics/read-eastman-full-memo-pence-overturn-election/index.html.

37 Barton Gellman, "The Election That Could Break America," *The Atlantic*, November 20, 2020, first published September 23, 2020, www.theatlantic.com.

38 Steven Mulroy, "Trump's Pennsylvania Lawsuits Invoke Bush v. Gore—but the Supreme Court Probably Won't Decide the 2020 Election," *The Conversation*, November 5, 2020, https://theconversation.com.

39 Jason D'Andrea, Sonia Monejano, and Matthew Vaughn, "Presidential Election Disruptions: Balancing the Rule of Law and Emergency Response," Voting Rights and Democracy Project, Fordham Law, May 8, 2023, https://fordhamdemocracyproject.com.

40 Electoral Count Reform and Presidential Transition Improvement Act of 2022, S.4573, *Ballotpedia*, https://ballotpedia.org/Electoral_Count_Reform_and_Presidential_Transition_Improvement_Act_of_2022#Text_of_the_bill.

41 Bob Bauer and Jack Goldsmith, "The Lessons of the Electoral Count Reform Act: Next Steps in Reform," Lawfare, January 31, 2023, www.lawfaremedia.org; Kristen Lee, "Why the ACLU Supports the Electoral Count Reform Act," ACLU News and Commentary, December 2, 2022, www.aclu.org; Kevin Kosar, "The Electoral Count Act Is Fixed; Presidential Transition Remains in Jeopardy," *The Hill*, January 10, 2023, https://thehill.com.

42 Amy Howe, "Supreme Court Rules against North Carolina Republicans over Election Law Theory," *SCOTUSBlog*, June 27, 2023, www.scotusblog.com.

43 Michael Sozan, "Supreme Court's Decision in Moore v. Harper Is a Win for Democracy, but Some Questions Remain Unanswered," Center for American Progress, July 24, 2023, www.americanprogress.org.

44 "Leading Case: *Moore v. Harper*," *Harvard Law Review* 137, no. 1 (November 2023): 290, https://harvardlawreview.org; Sozan, "Supreme Court's Decision."

45 Sozan, "Supreme Court's Decision."

46 Rick Hasen, "There's a Time Bomb in Progressives' Big Supreme Court Voting Case Win," *Slate*, June 27, 2023, https://slate.com.

2

"AN INSTRUMENT OF JUSTICE AND FULFILLMENT"

THE LOST PROMISE OF THE VOTING RIGHTS ACT

JULIAN E. ZELIZER

Democracy has never come easily in the United States. From the beginning, the founding fathers refused to extend the franchise to most Americans. Black, female, young, Native American, and other people were excluded from the democratic process at the moment of the nation's founding. The challenge of expanding the franchise grew out of an illiberalism that remained integral to the American political tradition and in tension with other ideological pulses.[1] The right to vote, as the historian Alexander Keyssar has argued in his epic account of the subject, would remain contested and would only be secured through difficult grassroots struggle. It also took war to create windows of opportunity to obtain legislation or executive actions to democratize a nation that was not committed domestically to the ideals they professed overseas.[2]

A strong federal government has always been essential to securing the most elemental part of American democracy, especially with regard to racial justice: voting. The Constitution did not make that protection effortless to achieve. The law granted primary authority over the election system to state and local governments. Article I, Section 4, declared that states retained the power to determine the "times, places and manner" of holding congressional elections. The Constitution also outlines the Electoral College system that would be used to elect the president. Voting became an essential component to the Reconstruction program undertaken after the Civil War. "I am for negro suffrage in every rebel state," argued Pennsylvania House Republican Thaddeus Stevens in 1867. "If it be just, it should not be denied; if it be necessary, it should be adopted; if it be a punishment to traitors, they deserve it."[3] As a result of the effort by Radical Republicans like Stevens to achieve racial justice in the aftermath of slavery, a crucial turning point took place in 1870. The GOP, which controlled the House and Senate, as well as the White House, passed the Fifteenth Amendment in 1869, ratified by the states one year later, prohibiting racial discrimination against men who wanted to vote based on their race. According to the text, "The right of citizens of the United States to vote shall not be denied or abridged by the United States or by any State on account of race, color, or previous condition of servitude." Equally relevant, Section 2 stated that "the Congress shall have the power to enforce this article by appropriate legislation." The amendment was at the heart of what historian Eric Foner calls the nation's second founding—Reconstruction—by empowering a population literally just freed from white bondage.[4] President Ulysses S. Grant praised the amendment as the "most important event that has occurred since the nation came to life." The Speaker of the House, Ohio Republican James Garfield, proclaimed that the amendment "confers upon the African race the care of its own destiny. It places their fortunes in their own hands."[5]

Despite the historic victory, the same antidemocratic forces that had been embedded in American political culture have endured. Over the decades that followed, opponents of universal suffrage would reemerge and continually struggle to dismantle the advances toward racial justice that were made in the era.

RETRENCHING RECONSTRUCTION, 1877–1965

The Fifteenth Amendment was far from perfect. Its basic design left ample opportunities for opponents to subvert the changes it was meant to achieve. Most important was the fact that the amendment was structured around preventing racial discrimination rather than guaranteeing universal suffrage. Women were excluded from the extension of citizenship. Other groups, such as Catholics, likewise faced electoral discrimination. Southern states imposed Jim Crow laws that undermined the promise of Reconstruction. Under the control of Southern Democrats, elected officials in every state of the Deep South responded to the threat that the Black vote posed to their power by passing numerous discriminatory laws in the late nineteenth and early twentieth centuries that entrenched racial inequality at the ballot box.

Mississippi was arguably the worst of the lot. The state constitution that was adopted in 1890 imposed the most draconian measures in the region. The new laws required that people who wanted to register to vote needed to pass an extraordinarily difficult in-person test that made it easier for the examiner to fail them. According to the law, in the exam—which was administered by the registrars, none of whom were supportive of racial justice—they had to transcribe and analyze specific sections of the Constitution that were randomly assigned. If a person made even the slightest technical error, then that was enough for them to fail. And the registrars maintained total discretion over evaluating the results, without having to justify their decision. Furthermore, local newspapers would publish the names of people who attempted to register, which for a Black Mississippian meant that everyone in their community—employers, police, white neighbors—would know what they had attempted to do. In addition, poll taxes imposed an economic burden on most Black voters, who could barely afford to eat. Racial disenfranchisement was also enforced through outright intimidation. Paramilitary groups such as the Ku Klux Klan relied on violence, employers imposed economic reprisals, and police intimidated any nonwhite American who dared to enter into a courthouse, as they were armed with rifles and ferocious dogs. Although Mississippi earned a reputation as the most brutal state in the region, all of its neighbors implemented variations of these same strategies. The only difference was scale and scope, as well as the amount of violence that was tolerated by state authorities. As a result, levels of registration for Black Americans in all of these states remained extraordinarily low throughout the twentieth century. In Mississippi, merely 6.7 percent of the Black population would be able to vote before 1965. The numbers were slightly better in Alabama, but only about 19 percent.[6]

Even as the United States entered into a modern era defined by industrialization, urbanization, and technological progress—and even after the nation granted women the right to vote following the ratification of the Nineteenth Amendment in 1920—Black Americans thus had to continue fighting to be treated as full citizens. Modernity in America did not translate into racial equality.

Electoral discrimination was not just a southern practice. Under the umbrella of progressivism, as the historian Steven Hahn argues, there were systematic efforts in northern cities by reformers to restrict the ability of working-class, largely first-generation immigrants to vote, in order to undercut the power of party machines. New voter registration systems that were put into place to diminish fraud likewise were intended to make voting more difficult.[7]

The right to vote remained paramount to those who fought for racial justice. "So long as I do not firmly and irrevocably possess the right to vote," stated Martin Luther King Jr., "I do not possess myself."[8] Black Americans who migrated to the North ramped up the pressure within the Democratic Party. As they became part of the New Deal coalition that President Franklin Roosevelt created in the 1930s and 1940s, they exercised their ability to vote to maintain some influence on legislators and local officials in cities like New York and Chicago. Although the Electoral College tended to benefit the small, rural states that were least liberal on racial issues, the system also caused Black voters in pivotal northern swing states to matter to candidates who wanted to win national office. This was evident as Republicans and Democrats began to more aggressively court this vote in the 1950s and Black leaders such as New York congressman Adam Clayton Powell Jr. could effectively threaten parties that refused to take their issues seriously.[9] The civil rights organizations that took form between the 1940s and early 1960s, including the Congress of Racial Equality, the Southern Christian Leadership Conference, and the Student Nonviolent Coordinating Committee, as well as older groups such as the NAACP, all prioritized voting rights. They understood that all other gains would remain precarious unless Black Americans could vote. The vote would empower Black citizens by allowing them to remove and replace the elected officials—from legislators to sheriffs—who upheld white supremacy. Service in World War II also led many Black veterans who returned from the battlefront in Europe and Asia to take a more proactive stand in their states, insisting that the United States live up to the ideals they had fought for overseas and for which many of their fellow soldiers had died. Many also came home burning mad from the virulent racism they had encountered when they had stepped off military bases that were in southern towns.[10]

The movement created sufficient pressure on Congress that Republican president Dwight Eisenhower and Senate Majority Leader Lyndon Johnson—a Texan closely connected to the southern barons of Capitol Hill—expended political capital to push through Congress the first major piece of civil rights legislation since Reconstruction, the Civil Rights Act of 1957. The legislation reaffirmed the voting rights provided by the Fifteenth Amendment and established the Civil Rights Division within the Department of Justice, whose prosecutors could obtain court injunctions to stop people from abridging voting rights, as well as the Civil Rights Commission in the executive branch, which was charged with investigating discrimination. Despite the victory, liberals were frustrated. They complained that the legislation had been so watered down as to be meaningless.[11] That frustration, combined with some evidence that grassroots pressure could work, nonetheless inspired the movement to keep mobilizing in pursuit of bolder voting rights legislation. Until 1964, the Civil Rights Division under John Doar, a Republican whom the historian Taylor Branch called the "Gary Cooper" of the civil rights movement,[12] emerged as the main point of contact between Washington and grassroots activists.

JOHNSON'S LEGISLATIVE SOLUTION, 1965

As civil rights organizations intensified their drive for a bill that would truly commit the federal government to making the Fifteenth Amendment real, with enforcement mechanisms, the movement tried to capitalize on the election of a northern Democrat, Massachusetts senator John Kennedy, to the presidency in 1960. Johnson had argued that if he could convince southerners to allow one bill to go through, as occurred three years earlier, then it would be much easier to move forward with more. The dam, in his mind, would be broken.[13]

Yet activists continued to encounter stiff resistance from Democrats, not only from southerners but also from a White House that remained terrified of angering this wing of the party. The perennial concern about the potential of a white backlash remained more powerful than the imperative to move forward with legislation that they knew was necessary and right.[14] Kennedy feared that if he sent any civil rights legislation to Congress, the Dixiecrats who chaired over half of the major committees would tie up the rest of his agenda, including a health care program for the elderly (called Medicare) that was his priority.[15] Given that he was deeply unpopular in the South, the president doubted that he could re-create his success against Vice President Richard Nixon, even with Johnson by his side, in a reelection campaign that followed any major battle over civil rights. Southerners were the backbone of the Democratic Party, and he had nightmares thinking about what would happen should these voters defect in a contest against someone such as the right-wing Arizona senator Barry Goldwater.

But over time, the movement made such positions untenable for him or his successor. In June 1963, following clashes in Birmingham, Alabama, where police under Sheriff Bull Connor violently attacked peaceful civil rights protesters, including children, with batons, guns, and water hoses, Kennedy finally sent legislation to Capitol Hill that would end legal racial discrimination in public accommodations. "We are confronted primarily with a moral issue," Kennedy told the nation in a televised address on June 11, 1963. "It is as old as the scriptures and is as clear as the American Constitution."[16] On August 28, 1963, hundreds of thousands of civil rights supporters descended on the nation's capital to participate in the March on Washington, which aimed to generate stronger support for the legislation. The peaceful protest was such a smashing success that the possibility of passage suddenly seemed inevitable to more Americans. Kennedy's political fears had not disappeared. In fact, they intensified. "I may lose the next election because of this," he acknowledged.[17] But the president didn't live to find out the effects. Kennedy was assassinated on November 22, 1963, and he never saw what happened to the proposal, which was still being considered by the House Judiciary Committee. By the time that Johnson took over the presidency following Kennedy's death, he concluded that there was no turning back. He used all of his political muscle to push the bill forward regardless of the risks. The Civil Rights Act of 1964, which King called the "second emancipation," ended segregation in public accommodations (restaurants, parks, courthouses, hotels, and more), established the Equal Employment Opportunity Commission to ensure equality in the workplace, and restated the guarantee that there would be equal voting rights throughout the nation. Kennedy, as well as Johnson, had left stronger voting rights provisions outside this bill for fear that their inclusion would be too bold and undermine the support that was needed to close down the southern filibuster.

Civil rights leaders considered the legislation to be the first part of a broader agenda, not the final step. Though elated with the legislative victory, the movement kept demanding more, with the most important goal being the voting rights measures that had been left off the previous legislation. Black Americans demonstrated their potential political power in the 1964 election when they achieved a higher turnout than in previous elections that reached 72 percent outside the South. A large majority of the vote went to the victorious President Johnson against Senator Goldwater. Goldwater's vote against the Civil Rights Act had proved to be a major liability despite all the fears that Johnson had expressed about a backlash.

Facing mounting pressure to complete the civil rights revolution, Johnson still hemmed and hawed about dealing with voting rights. He supported federal protection for Black voters but wanted to wait until the end of the year, at a minimum, so that he could focus attention on Medicare, federal education assistance, and other matters. But movement leaders and activists refused to wait any longer. They were emboldened by the victory a few months earlier and inspired by King's call to act according to the fierce urgency of now. In February, the Mississippi Freedom Democratic Party documented and publicized evidence of voting discrimination in their state as part of a challenge (unsuccessful) to unseat the elected Democratic legislators whose power rested on their disenfranchisement. A few months earlier, they had already gained national attention for the issue when they had attempted to unseat the Mississippi delegates at the Democratic Convention in Atlantic City; though the effort failed, the entire nation heard from and was deeply moved by the riveting testimony of a former sharecropper, Fannie Lou Hamer, about just how far southern whites went to brutalize Black Americans trying to register. In March 1965, civil rights leaders traveled to Selma, Alabama, in order to attract national attention for marches that were taking place to build support for a bill. On March 7, hundreds of protesters tried to walk peacefully from Selma to Montgomery, the state capital. The notorious county sheriff, James Clark, stopped them in their tracks. Standing alongside his troops, Clark wore his military-style helmet and dark sunglasses, with a button on his jacket that said "Never," and greeted the activists when they reached the Edmund Pettus Bridge as his officers violently attacked the peaceful protesters. The chairman of the Student Nonviolent Coordinating Committee, John Lewis, had his skull cracked open by police batons. Television cameras captured the horrific images of what was happening. Americans who had been watching ABC's Sunday-night movie, *Judgment at Nuremberg*, couldn't believe the brutality when the network cut away from the film to show images from the clash in Selma. "I don't see how President Johnson can send troops to Vietnam—I don't see how he can send troops to the Congo—I don't see how he can send troops to Africa," Lewis angrily argued, "and can't send troops to Selma, Alabama."[18]

The scenes of state-sanctioned racial violence were so shocking that Democrats in Congress—who had huge liberal majorities after the 1964 election and faced a Republican Party terrified of looking like reactionary extremists after Goldwater's landslide defeat in 1964—called for an immediate response. President Johnson decided to send a voting rights bill to Capitol Hill right away. On March 15, eight days after "Bloody Sunday" unfolded, Johnson delivered a stirring address to the nation in which he prioritized a bill in no uncertain terms. "Our fathers believed that if this noble view of the rights of man was to flourish, it must be rooted in democracy. The most basic right of all was the right to choose your own leaders. The history of this country, in large measure, is the history of expansion of that right to all of our people. Many of the issues of civil rights are very complex and most difficult," Johnson said, "but about this there can and should be no argument: every American citizen must have an equal right to vote."[19] In a stirring moment, the president repeated the words, "We shall overcome," the chorus of the most popular civil rights song of the time. "There was an instant of silence, the gradually apprehended realization that the president has proclaimed, adopted as his own rallying cry, the anthem of black protest, the hymn of a hundred embattled black marchers," speechwriter Richard Goodwin recalled in his memoirs.[20] Martin Luther King Jr. shed tears upon hearing the address.

Unlike with the 1964 legislation, the resistance in Congress was minimal this time around. The GOP was in no shape to join southern Democrats in obstructing the bill. "Republicans having nothing to gain," one quipped, "from being for a civil rights bill, but they have everything to lose by being against one."[21] Senate Minority Leader Everett Dirksen made it clear that his caucus would not support another prolonged filibuster. "The right to vote is still an issue in this free country," Dirksen said on television. "There has to be a real remedy. There has to be something durable and worthwhile. This cannot go on forever, this denial of the right to vote by ruses and devises and tests and whatever the mind can contrive to either make it very difficult or to make it impossible to vote."[22] The conservative coalition of southern Democrats and Republicans who had mounted the longest filibuster in history one year earlier barely tried this time.[23] The Senate ended a twenty-four-day filibuster on June 10 by a 71 to 29 vote and passed the measure 73 to 27.

On August 6, 1965, President Johnson signed the Voting Rights Act (VRA) into law. The historic legislation prohibited states from using literacy tests and required states and local governments that had a history of denying the vote to obtain preclearance if they were going to implement any changes in their voting laws. The VRA established a specific formula that the government could use to determine which jurisdictions would fall under the preclearance requirements (Section 5). The legislation complemented the Supreme Court's one-man, one-vote decisions (*Baker v. Carr* [1962] and *Reynolds v. Sims* [1964])—which outlawed legislative districts that had given conservative, rural voters disproportionate power compared with the residents of heavily populated, and more liberal, cities—as well as ratification of the Twenty-Fourth Amendment in 1964, which banned poll taxes. At the signing ceremony, Johnson praised the bill as "one of the most monumental laws in the entire history of American freedom."[24] Many keen observers, sensitive to the long tradition of presidential exaggeration, agreed that with this bold statement, LBJ was spot on. A new era of American democracy, or so it seemed, had dawned.

Although opponents challenged the legislation, the Supreme Court repeatedly defended its constitutionality in several cases. Before the dust had even settled, South Carolina attorney general Daniel McLeod attempted to undermine the bill by challenging the law in the Supreme Court, claiming that the VRA didn't square with states' rights. The law, he argued, would also treat voting systems differently in different parts of the country. In *South Carolina v. Katzenbach* (1966), the Supreme

Court under Chief Justice Earl Warren upheld the VRA by eight to one. The Fifteenth Amendment, according to the majority, "authorizes the National Legislature to effectuate by 'appropriate' measures the constitutional prohibition against racial discrimination in voting."[25] In the 1969 case *Allen v. State Board of Elections*, the Court affirmed by a seven-to-two majority that the preclearance rules covered every kind of change in the voting laws and that in states where such changes had not been approved, individuals could not be deprived of the ability to vote.[26] According to Warren in the majority opinion, voting rights were "aimed at the subtle, as well as the obvious, state regulations which have the effect of denying citizens their right to vote because of their race." Protected by the Court, the VRA was the law of the land.

AMERICAN POLITICAL CULTURE IN THE AGE OF THE VRA, 1966–1982

For several decades thereafter, the voting rights legislation worked. Racial disenfranchisement diminished, and democracy grew stronger. Our election system was more secure. Almost 250,000 Black Americans registered by the end of 1965. Nine out of thirteen states had over 50 percent of their Black population registered to vote one year after Congress passed the bill.[27] A record number of Black Alabamians lined up for over four hours to exercise their right to vote in the 1966 Democratic primaries.[28] Throughout the country, moreover, there was a significant increase in the number of Black elected officials winning national, state, and local office unlike in any period since Reconstruction.[29] In 1971, there were enough representatives in the House to form the Congressional Black Caucus.

Two decades after Congress passed the VRA, the legislation seemed to have gained strong bipartisan support. Despite growing Republican opposition to the measure, in 1982 Kansas Republican Robert Dole headed a bipartisan coalition to reauthorize the VRA, a huge victory for the civil rights community that mobilized to obtain this decision. He overcame the opposition of North Carolina Republican Jesse Helms, a staunch conservative and loyal ally of President Reagan, who used every parliamentary trick at his disposal in an attempt to stop the bill from moving forward. Helms wanted "to reach an understanding that the 40 counties in North Carolina will no longer be treated as second class citizens . . .

they should no longer be required to clear with Big Brother in Washington every change."[30] Dole wanted to protect the protect the image of the GOP with marginalized constituencies. The reauthorization not only preserved the law but also expanded protections under Section 5 and strengthened Section 2 to cover a broader range of factors producing racial inequities by shifting focus from intent to impact. The legislation also determined that Section 2 would cover the entire nation. Dole's primary reasons were practical, just as they had been when President Richard Nixon decided to back away from opposing the preclearance provisions after facing stiff opposition from Democrats. One of his aides explained that the senator was attempting to "save the Republican party," as Black Americans felt increasingly alienated from what was happening as the Party of Lincoln transformed into the rightward Party of Reagan.[31] The notion of dismantling the legislation seemed to be off the table. "This victory," proclaimed Massachusetts Democratic senator Ted Kennedy, "is a heartening sign that Congress will not endlessly turn its back on the needy in our society and the minority who are not white."[32]

Not surprisingly, these years also witnessed a proliferation of rights-based movements that built on the achievements of the civil rights movement and demanded that the government protect the ability of every citizen to live a full and equal life, including in the realm of immigration.[33]

The VRA propelled major advances in democratic politics. In 1971, the states had also ratified the Twenty-Sixth Amendment, which lowered the voting age to eighteen years old, thus vastly broadening the potential youth vote. Voter registration steadily rose, early and absentee voting became much more common, restrictions on felons' voting were lowered (with bipartisan support), and overt racial discrimination vastly diminished.

RETRENCHMENT, 1983–2020

Yet just as the post-Reconstruction period proved the inherently precarious state of legislative gains for voting rights, the twenty-first century likewise revealed that this moment of democratic expansion would not be as durable as many had hoped for. While Senator Dole had been able to push back against members of his party who didn't want to reauthorize the legislation, he turned out to be on the losing side of the debate. A growing number of Republicans had been fighting against expanded suffrage as operatives began to see the virtues of dampening the vote in Black and Latino communities that tended to support Democrats. "I don't want everybody to vote," the conservative activist Paul Weyrich frankly acknowledged in 1980. "As a matter of fact our leverage in the elections quite candidly goes up as the voting populace goes down."[34]

Indeed, at the same time that Congress had voted to continue with the legislation, prominent political and legal voices within the Reagan administration were starting to develop legal challenges to the VRA. Under Attorney Generals William French Smith and Edwin Meese, the Department of Justice emerged as a hothouse for a new generation of right-wing lawyers who were enthralled by the conservative movement and Reagan's presidency. These lawyers were connected to an organization called the Federalist Society, formed in 1982, that aimed to nurture networks of conservative lawyers and judges to elevate them into the federal courts. Meese, according to Harvard professor Lawrence Tribe, was "successful in making it look like he and his disciples were carrying out the intentions of the great founders, where the liberals were making it up as they went along."[35]

One figure from this cohort was a Harvard Law School graduate named John Roberts. He arrived in Washington at twenty-five years of age. He first served as a clerk for Supreme Court justice William Rehnquist, a long-time opponent of voting rights. Throughout the early 1960s, Rehnquist had helped lead a Republican program in Phoenix that set out to challenge the qualifications of nonwhite voters. Roberts's next job was at the Department of Justice, where in the fall of 1981 he joined other up-and-coming conservatives such as Kenneth Starr, Roger Clegg, and Bruce Fein in taking on all elements of the Great Society, including voting rights. Roberts agreed with a growing number of Republicans who believed that Senator Dole was wrong to support reauthorization of the VRA. Indeed, Roberts's first job had been to write a brief to challenge the reauthorization. As the bill moved forward, he lamented that the legislation was "constitutionally suspect, but also contrary to the most fundamental tenants [*sic*] of the legislative process on which the laws of the country are based."[36]

Roberts and his colleagues continued to draft legal analysis that could be used to challenge the legislation when the next opportunity occurred. He agreed with the conservative Heritage Foundation, which had argued that legislation that centered on outcomes rather than intent—whether voting systems had discriminatory effects rather than whether officials intended to discriminate—was unconstitutional.[37] "There is no reason to change the permanent nationwide provisions of the Voting Rights Act," he complained, "from an intent test to a results test." Writing drafts of opinion articles for his superiors, Roberts warned colleagues that "the frequent writings in this area by our adversaries have gone unanswered for too long."[38] The arguments about intent fit into a broader critique that had developed against civil rights policy since 1969.[39]

In his writing, Roberts argued that the VRA imposed racial quotas that were antithetical to individual liberties. He veered so much to the right on this issue in the 1980s that even colleagues in the Civil Rights Division concluded he had gone too far. "John seemed like he always had it in for the Voting Rights Act," Gerald Herbert recalled. "I remember him being a zealot when it came to having fundamental suspicions about the Voting Rights Act's utility."[40] But Herbert miscalculated where the arc of the political universe seemed to be bending. The influence of conservatives such as Roberts grew during the presidency of George H. W. Bush, who, after taking over the Oval Office in 1989, worked hard to bring more of these voices into his administration. Bush appointed several major adherents to the philosophy of originalism, a legal theory stipulating that justices had to stick to the original intention of the founders, by appointing Clarence Thomas to the Supreme Court in 1991, as well as Samuel Alito to the Third US Circuit Court of Appeals and Roberts to the US Court of Appeals for the DC Circuit (though the Democratic Senate never took a confirmation vote).

The legal strategy merged with renewed Republican determination to depress the vote. There was a strong perception in the GOP that higher rates of voting tended to benefit Democrats, who were stronger in larger, urban, and cosmopolitan areas. As the source of Republican electoral strength shifted toward southern states and rural areas in the North, they became even more eager to stand as roadblocks toward higher levels of voting. In 1993, Republican Ed Rollins admitted that he and Republican Christine Whitman had distributed money to Democratic poll workers and Black ministers in exchange for their remaining at home on election day and also refraining from participating in get-out-the-vote operations for the Democratic campaign. "We went into the black churches and basically said to ministers who had endorsed Florio [incumbent Democratic governor James Florio]: 'Do you have a special project? We see you have already endorsed Florio. That's fine. But don't get up in the Sunday pulpit . . . and say it's your moral obligation to vote on Tuesday, to vote for Jim Florio.'"[41] Republican officials and campaign strategists often referenced massive voting fraud—despite lacking evidence to prove this was a problem—that dated back to the Jim Crow era as a tool for advancing this agenda.[42]

Whatever the motivation behind the push to restrict the vote, a sharp asymmetry took form between Democrats, who emerged as the party that stood behind stronger voting rights legislation, and Republicans as opponents. Voting rights were folded into the polarized fault lines of American politics as the two major parties came to embrace very different approaches to the right to vote. With Democrats since Jimmy Carter pushing for Election Day holidays and rules to facilitate early and absentee voting, Republicans coalesced around legislative packages that imposed stronger restrictions.

Just as 1965 was a turning point in the struggle over racial justice and voting, the 2000 presidential election marked the start of the next big phase in this fraught history. The election pitted Democratic vice president Al Gore against Texas governor George W. Bush. The contest came down to the state of Florida, where the fact that fewer than six hundred votes separated the candidates resulted in a lengthy and bitter recount that lasted into December.

The battle over the ballots exposed a number of underlying problems with the election system. Black and Latino voters in Miami, the US Commission on Civil Rights reported, "confronted inexperienced poll workers, antiquated machinery, inaccessible polling locations, and other barriers to being able to exercise their right to vote. The Commission's findings make one thing clear: widespread voter disenfranchisement not the dead-heat contest was the extraordinary feature in the Florida election."[43] Public attention to confusion over the butterfly ballot and other irregularities, which culminated with the Court's *Bush v. Gore* decision in December 2000, took the media focus away from racial discrimination and directed it toward the weaknesses in election administration that would dominate much of the postelection conversation about reform. Many celebrated after the election of Barack Obama in 2008, when the victory of the first Black American president symbolized the positive impact that expanded suffrage could have on the character of the nation's democracy.

The drive to roll back the VRA accelerated after the 2010 midterms. Following Operation Red-Map, through which the national Republican Party invested heavily in local races, red states imposed tougher controls on voting that fell hardest on Black and lower-income Americans as well as immigrants. The project grew out of Karl Rove's *Wall Street Journal* column calling on the party to focus on state races, with the aim to control redistricting in 2011 after the census: "He who controls redistricting can control Congress." Several states passed measures requiring proof of citizenship as well as prohibitions on voting registration efforts.[44]

Since the 1970s, there had been several Supreme Court decisions that weakened Section 5 of the VRA, including *Shaw v. Reno* (1993) and *Georgia v. Ashcroft* (2003). This was seen as the most vulnerable element of the legislation. But the Supreme Court had rejected efforts to challenge the constitutionality of the provision, including in a 2009 decision.[45]

This campaign against the constitutionality of the voting rights law was finally legitimized by the Supreme Court in 2013 when it issued a landmark ruling with *Shelby v. Holder*, which eliminated the heart of the VRA—the preclearance formula and the requirement that the federal government would have the authority and responsibility to review and approve changes in voting laws in states where there was historical evidence of discrimination. John Roberts, who was confirmed as Chief Justice of the Supreme Court in 2005, drafted the majority opinion and argued that because voting discrimination had diminished, there was no longer a need for those parts of the law. According to Roberts, there "was no longer such a disparity" as "old data and eradicated practices" had revealed in previous years.[46] Many, including his colleague Ruth Bader Ginsburg, would see this as twisted logic. "Hubris," she wrote, "is a fit word for today's demolition of the VRA." According to Ginsburg in her dissent, "Throwing out preclearance when it has worked and is continuing to work to stop discriminatory changes is like throwing away your umbrella in a rainstorm because you are not getting wet."

As civil rights activists feared, the decision unleashed efforts in red states to impose voting restrictions. Texas, for instance, immediately enacted legislation that required voters to show photo identification. Six hundred thousand eligible voters in the state did not have that documentation. Even worse, huge swaths of the state's Black and Latino populations lived in areas where there was no Department of Public Safety office that was easily accessible. After reviewing the situation, US district judge Nelva Gonzales Ramos determined in her 147-page opinion that the legislation imposed an "unconstitutional burden on the right to vote, has an impermissible discriminatory effect against Hispanics and African Americans, and was imposed with an unconstitutional discriminatory purpose."[47] About one year later, the Supreme Court undermined that decision by saying that the Texas restrictions were legitimate. The Texas legislature revised the law by adding measures through which a person without photo identification could sign a legal document stating why they didn't have that documentation. Critics argued that the new provision would be intimidating to many voters who were suspicious of authorities and what would happen with the information they provided. Texas was just the start. Within a year, fourteen other states—from Alabama to Wisconsin—had put new restrictions on the books. Voters who went to the polls in the 2014 midterm elections found a complex web of regulations and procedural barriers toward casting their ballot. In addition to requiring photo identification, many states put into effect limits or prohibitions on early voting and same-day registration. The push was on.

Although some social scientists have disputed the overall impact of these measures—and some have pointed to misperceptions about who was hurt most politically by their implementation—there is substantial evidence that these largely red-state initiatives aimed to suppress Black and Latino votes while stoking fears of massive voting fraud, especially in large urban areas. Republican strategists have continued to believe that lower levels of voter turnout benefit them. And even when proposed measures did not pass, the legislative debates surrounding them worsened distrust in the electoral system. Unsubstantiated claims about millions of voters cheating the system and casting false votes filled the chambers of state legislative bodies and the stories by reporters who covered them. Moreover, new technology created so many platforms to disseminate information without filters, as Nicole Hemmer shows in her chapter, that the allegations surrounding these proposals became difficult to contain or correct.

The proliferation of restrictive voting laws also took place within the context of a Republican Party that was shifting far to the right on social and cultural issues, fueled by a profound illiberalism that has strong roots in American politics.[48] The same GOP that was championing voting restrictions had a growing number of elected officials in the 2010s operating in the same space as—or in alliance with—hardline nativists, white supremacist organizations, Christian nationalists, and "Birthers" who challenged the legitimacy of the first Black American president. This was the same party disproportionately responsible for defiantly pushing voting measures that civil rights organizations warned were having a detrimental impact on the political rights achieved for Black Americans in 1965.

The voting restrictions worked in tandem with other mechanisms that limited or harmed the franchise. Increasingly sophisticated mechanisms of redistricting based on computer technology, for instance, were used in red states to diminish the power of voters in liberal, cosmopolitan areas. All of these initiatives hurt the movement to increase rates of voting and levels of participation.

The campaign for voting restrictions culminated with the presidency of Donald Trump. Throughout his 2016 campaign and one term as president, Trump elevated the theme of voting fraud to the top of his agenda. Even when he defeated Hillary Clinton in 2016 through a narrow victory in the Electoral College, Trump constantly spoke about massive levels of voting fraud as the reason he lost the popular vote, and he supported the kinds of restrictions that were put into place. Although a commission set up by the Trump administration, cochaired by Vice President Mike Pence and Kansas secretary of state Kris Kobach, could not find any credible evidence of widespread voting fraud, the president did not pull back with his rhetoric. In 2018, he claimed that "millions and millions of people" voted illegally. "In many places, like California, the same person votes many times," he claimed as the midterms approached. "You've probably heard about that. They always like to say that's a conspiracy theory. Not a conspiracy theory, folks."[49]

The strategy picked up steam in the 2020 election. Many states put into effect measures that eased early voting and mail-in voting as a result of the COVID-19 pandemic. The goal was to offer accessible and safe mechanisms for all eligible Americans to vote without having to go to a polling place and risk infection. Most of the measures had been expanding in states like California as well as conservative states like Tennessee for many years as an effort to increase voting rates. As Americans were scared to wait in long lines and enter into crowded polling centers, with public health officials agreeing on the risks, state governments offered a response. Trump feared that the higher rates of voting would hurt his chances to win. He claimed that Democrats were attempting to steal the election from him, though he once again failed to provide any evidence. In March, saying the silent part out loud, as he tended to do, Trump commented on a stimulus bill that contained provisions to ease voting by saying on *Fox & Friends*, "The things they had in there were crazy. They had things—levels of voting that if you ever agreed to it, you'd never have a Republican elected in this country again."[50]

On election night, as the votes were being counted, Trump held a press conference where he alleged that the election was being stolen and that votes were being manufactured to support Joe Biden. "This is a fraud on the American public. This is an embarrassment to our country," he said. "We were getting ready to win this election. Frankly, we did win this election. We did win this election. . . . This is a major fraud in our nation."[51] Although some dismissed the moment as just Trump being Trump, the press conference was a small part of a concerted effort to overturn the presidential election, with voting fraud as the central pillar—an effort that would only end on January 6 with violence in the Capitol. Even though his own advisers were privately telling him the claims were false, with some resigning in response to his continuing to spread these lies, the arguments gained a strong hold. Conservative media outlets such as Fox News promoted Trump's claims even as they themselves privately knew they were not true. On November 12, Fox host Dana Perino emailed someone at work to say that allegations of a big conspiracy by a company that was involved in the production of voting machines, Dominion, was "total bs."[52]

Trump's argument stuck. In 2021, Pew Research found that the share of Republicans who supported measures to make voting less cumbersome, such as early and absentee voting, was falling fast. According to its data, only 27 percent of Democrats backed taking people off voter registration lists if they had failed to confirm their registration (or vote), compared with 68 percent of Republicans.[53]

Election denialism would become a central theme of the 2022 midterms as Republicans ramped up their efforts to support candidates who had been part of the effort to overturn the 2020 election or were intent on winning positions in usually low-level positions, such as secretary of state, that would determine elections. In 2022, the Republican embrace of these ideas produced good outcomes for their Democratic opponents, as most candidates who championed election denialism lost. Moreover, Congress followed up with the Electoral Count Reform Act that tightened holes in the system created back in 1877.

The most important firewall to all of these efforts was what remained of the VRA, as well as the strong cultural commitment to the franchise that Johnson's legislation had inscribed into the body politic. Even as red-state Republicans moved to make voting harder, the legacy of 1965 lived on. At the federal level, conservatives were resigned to working through the legal process rather than pursuing legislation. The courts threw out the administration's efforts to overturn or discount votes.

There has even been some change of heart, or at least a realization of limitations, from Chief Justice Roberts. In *Allen v. Milligan* (2023), the Court ruled that based on Section 2 of the VRA, the State of Alabama would have to draw a new Black majority district and affirmed the constitutionality of this section of the law. Siding with Justices Ketanji Brown Jackson, Elena Kagan, Brett Kavanaugh, and Sonia Sotomayor, the ruling was significant in that it protected the elements of the law designed to strengthen minority representation. "The ruling in Milligan," writes Richard Hasen, "disrupts the narrative that the court is relentlessly revolutionary in its conservative jurisprudence."[54]

The fact that the "system worked," however, is not evidence that the system is secure. Indeed, had several key figures, including Vice President Pence, decided to support the president's attempt to overturn the election, the outcome might have been different. Red states, moreover, have continued to move forward with the effort to create new restrictions on the franchise.

The right to vote remains under threat. There was the second highest number of restrictive laws passed in 2023 than in any other year over the past decade.[55] The *Milligan* decision did not expand minority rights—it just preserved what exists. "A win is a win," Hasen adds, "even though it's a little sad to have to say so, these days, a Supreme Court decision preserving the status quo on voting rights is worthy of celebration."[56] Moreover, in November 2023, one year before the election, the US Court of Appeals for the Eighth Circuit ruled that only the federal government could bring legal challenges under Section 2 and *not* private citizens or civil rights organizations, which, if upheld by the Supreme Court, would strike another major blow to Johnson's legislation.

Legislation to protect voting rights entitled the John Lewis Voting Rights Advancement Act never made it through the Senate as a result of a Republican filibuster. Brookings Institution scholar Elaine Kamarck estimates that restrictive laws could have an impact in several key swing states in 2024, including Arizona, Florida, and Georgia.[57] Numerous red states in 2023 continued the push to restrict voting, including an effort by national Republicans to adjust the rules to influence a specific election in Montana as well as another push, which failed, to raise the barriers toward passing ballot initiatives in Ohio.[58] When Trump, running for presidential election in 2024 while facing not only two major indictments stemming from his effort to overturn the 2020 election but also two additional indictments, won the Iowa Caucus in January, polls showed that almost two-thirds of Republicans in the state did not believe President Biden's election had been legitimate.[59] The results of the 2022 midterms did not weaken the grip that this trope, which was usually connected to false allegations of voting fraud, held on elected officials and voters.

If Americans don't have the right to vote, and if that right is not protected by the federal government, we don't have a fully functioning democracy. Some reformers have called for an amendment that would place an affirmative right to vote in the Constitution, once and for all eliminating the kinds of recurring threats citizenship has faced.[60] The integrity of the entire system rests on that fundamental right. We had a major breakthrough in 1965 when Congress passed the VRA. But in recent decades we have moved into reverse, inflicting immense damage on the process by dismantling the policies put in place by that legislation. The security of our elections will depend on whether we can restore the promise.

NOTES

1 Steven Hahn, *Illiberal America: A History* (New York: Norton, 2024). I started to explore these themes in "So Far Away from 1965," *Perspectives on History*, August 24, 2020, https://www.historians.org.

2 Alexander Keyssar, *The Right to Vote: The Contested History of Democracy in the United States* (New York: Basic Books, 2000).

3 Thaddeus Stevens, "Speech on Reconstruction," January 3, 1867, https://teachingamericanhistory.org.

4 Eric Foner, *The Second Founding: How the Civil War and Reconstruction Remade the Constitution* (New York: Norton, 2019).

5 Andrew Glass, "U.S. Adopts 15th Amendment, March 30 1870," *Politico*, March 30, 2016, https://www.politico.com.

6 German Lopez, "How the Voting Rights Act Transformed Black Voting Rights in the South, in One Chart," August 6, 2015; Hearings before Subcommittee No. 5, Judiciary Committee, House of Representatives, 89th Cong., 1st Sess. on H.R. 6400, Serial No. 2 (US Government Printing Office, 1965), 135, 142, 160, 176, 185, 193, 196, 201, and 257.

7 Hahn, *Illiberal America*, 190.

8 Martin Luther King Jr., "Give Us the Ballot, We Will Transform the South," May 1957, https://archive.pov.org.

9 Paul Frymer, *Race and Party Competition in America* (Princeton, NJ: Princeton University Press, 1999).

10 Matthew F. Delmont, *Half American: The Epic Story of African Americans Fighting World War II at Home and Abroad* (New York: Viking, 2022).

11 Robert A. Caro, *Master of the Senate: The Years of Lyndon Johnson* (New York: Knopf, 2002); Julian E. Zelizer, *On Capitol Hill: The Struggle to Reform Congress and Its Consequences, 1948–2000* (New York: Cambridge University Press, 2004).

12 Cited in Nicholas Lemann, "John Doar's Civil Rights Struggle," *New Yorker*, November 12, 2014.

13 Caro, *Master of the Senate*, 893–94.

14 Larry B. Glickman, "White Backlash," in *Myth America: Historians Take on the Biggest Legends and Lies about Our Past*, edited by Kevin M. Kruse and Julian E. Zelizer (New York: Basic Books, 2023), 211–23.

15 Robert Dallek, *An Unfinished Life: John F. Kennedy, 1917–1963* (Boston: Little Brown, 2003), 330–33; 641–45.

16 John F. Kennedy, "Radio and Television Report to the American People on Civil Rights," June 11, 1963, The American Presidency Project, https://www.presidency.ucsb.edu.

17 Dallek, *An Unfinished Life*, 642.

18 Roy Reed, "Alabama Police Use Gas and Clubs to Rout Negros," *New York Times*, March 8, 1965.

19 Lyndon Johnson, "Speech before Congress on Voting Rights," March 15, 1965, https://millercenter.org.

20 Julian E. Zelizer, *The Fierce Urgency of Now: Lyndon Johnson, Congress, and the Battle for the Great Society* (New York: Penguin, 2015), 214.

21 Zelizer, 203–4.

22 Zelizer, 206–7.

23 Zelizer, 125–27.
24 Caroll Kilpatrick, "Vote Rights Bill Signed in Ceremony at Capitol," *Washington Post*, 7 August 7, 1965.
25 South Carolina v. Katzenbach, March 7, 1966.
26 Allen v. State Board of Elections, March 3, 1969, https://www.oyez.org.
27 "Voting Rights Act (1965)," National Archives, https://www.archives.gov.
28 "First Time Voters," Newsreel, 1966, National Archives, http://recordsofrights.org.
29 Thomas J. Sugrue, *Sweet Land of Liberty: The Forgotten Struggle for Civil Rights in the North* (New York: Random House, 2008); David Goldfield, *Black White and Southern: Race Relations and Southern Culture, 1940–Present* (Baton Rouge: Louisiana State Press, 1990), 176.
30 Mary Thornton, "Helms Threatens to Stall Voting Rights Bill," *Washington Post*, June 10, 1982.
31 Robert Pear, "Compromise Likely on Voting Rights," *New York Times*, May 1, 1982.
32 "Voting Rights Act Renewed in the Senate by a Margin of 85–8," *New York Times*, June 19, 1982.
33 Peniel E. Joseph, *The Third Reconstruction: America's Struggle for Racial Justice in the Twenty-First Century* (New York: Basic Books, 2022); Sarah Coleman, *The Walls Within: The Politics of Immigration in Modern America* (Princeton, NJ: Princeton University Press, 2021).
34 Cited in Allen J. Lichtman, *The Embattled Vote in America: From the Founding to the Present* (Cambridge, MA: Harvard University Press, 2018).
35 Julian E. Zelizer, "How Conservatives Won the Battle over the Courts," *The Atlantic*, July 7, 2018.
36 Ian Millhiser, "Chief Jusice Roberts's Lifelong Crusade against Voting Rights, Explained," Vox, September 18, 2020, www.vox.com.
37 Walter Berns, The Heritage Foundation, "The Voting Rights Act," *The Issue Bulletin*, February 23, 1982.
38 Ari Berman, "Inside John Roberts' Decades-Long Crusade against the Voting Rights Act," *Politico*, August 10, 2015.
39 Hugh Davis Graham, *The Civil Rights Era: Origins and Development of National Policy* (New York: Oxford University Press, 1990).
40 Carol Anderson, *One Person, No Vote: How Voter Suppression Is Destroying Our Democracy* (New York: Bloomsbury, 2018), 39.
41 "The Boasting of Ed Rollins," *Washington Post*, November 11, 1993.
42 Ari Berman, *Give Us the Ballot: The Modern Struggle for Voting Rights in America* (New York: Farrar, Straus and Giroux, 2015); Michael Waldman, *The Fight to Vote* (New York: Simon and Schuster, 2016); Carol Anderson, "Voter Fraud," in Kruse and Zelizer, *Myth America*; Anderson, *One Person, No Vote*.
43 "Voting Irregularities in Florida during the 2000 Election," US Commission on Civil Rights, accessed January 19, 2024, www.usccr.gov.
44 Wendy Weiser and Nhu-Y Ngo, "Voting Rights in 2011: A Legislative Round-Up," Brennan Center for Justice, July 15, 2011, www.brennancenter.org; Dave Dayen,

*Ratf**ked: The True Story behind the Secret Plan to Steal America's Democracy* (New York: Liveright, 2016); Karl Rove, "The GOP Targets State Legislatures," *Wall Street Journal*, March 2010, 4.

45 Nick Corasinti, "How the Voting Rights Act, Newly Challenged, Has Long Been under Attack," *New York Times*, November 21, 2023.

46 Shelby County v. Holder, 2013.

47 Ross Ramsey, "Judge Rules Texas Voter ID Law Unconstitutional," *Texas Tribune*, October 9, 2014, https://www.texastribune.org.

48 Hahn, *Illiberal America*, 314–47.

49 Jane C. Timm, "Trump Again Claims Massive Vote Fraud: A Massive Search for Evidence Finds None," NBC News, April 5, 2018, www.nbcnews.com.

50 Aaron Blake, "Trump Just Comes Out and Says It: The GOP Is Hurt When It's Easiest to Vote," *Washington Post*, March 30, 2020.

51 "Donald Trump 2020 Election Night Transcript," November 2020, National Archives, https://trumpwhitehouse.archives.gov.

52 David Folkenflik, "Judge Rules Fox Hosts' Claims about Dominion Were False, Says Trial Can Proceed," NPR, March 31, 2023, www.npr.org.

53 "Republicans and Democrats Move Further Apart in Views of Voting Access," Pew Research Center, April 22, 2021, www.pewresearch.org.

54 Richard Hasen, "John Roberts Throws a Curveball," *New York Times*, June 8, 2023.

55 "Voting Laws Roundup: October 2023," Brennan Center, October 19, 2023, www.brennancenter.org.

56 Hasen, "John Roberts."

57 Ellen Kamarck, "Voter Suppression or Voter Expansion? What's Happening and Does It Matter?," Brookings, October 26, 2021, www.brookings.edu.

58 Nick Corasaniti and Alexandra Berzon, "Under the Radar, Right Wing Push to Tighten Voting Law Persists," *New York Times*, May 8, 2023.

59 Sarah Fortinksy, "Almost Two-Thirds of Iowa Caucus Goers Say Biden 2020 Win Was Not Legitimate," *The Hill*, January 16, 2024.

60 On the long history of the effort to provide an affirmative right to vote in the Constitution, see Richard Hasen, *A Real Right to Vote: How a Constitutional Amendment Can Safeguard American Democracy* (Princeton, NJ: Princeton University Press, 2024).

3

THE HISTORY OF FOREIGN ELECTION INTERFERENCE AND AN ALTERNATIVE FUTURE

JEREMI SURI

Although sanguine about many parts of early American democracy, Alexis de Tocqueville was not impressed with American elections. He called the every-four-year choice of president a recurring "national crisis."[1] With the expansion of white male suffrage in Jacksonian America, elections became a mass phenomenon for the first time. They divided a large number of voting citizens against one another, they encouraged corrupt vote-getting, they rewarded demagoguery, and they distracted leaders from the real work of governing. Tocqueville minced no words in his criticism of mass campaigns: "The president, for his part, is consumed by the need to defend his record. He no longer governs in the interest of the state but rather in the interest of his reelection. He prostrates himself before the majority, and often, rather than resist its passions as his duty requires, he courts favor by catering to its whims. As the election draws near, intrigues intensify, and agitation increases and spreads. The citizens divide into several camps, each behind its candidate. A fever grips the entire nation."[2]

Tocqueville believed that similar conditions in Europe would lead to civil war, as divided citizens fought one another to hold power, or conquest, as aggressive neighbors attacked a distracted country. The United States escaped the latter danger, Tocqueville believed, because its foreign enemies were far away; it was very difficult for them to exploit the internal weaknesses of the United States during election season.

Foreign governments did not care deeply about the outcome of American elections in Tocqueville's time: "The policy of the Americans toward the rest of the world is simple. One might almost say that no one needs them, nor do they need anyone. Their independence is never threatened."[3] These conditions would change, but slowly.

Civil war in the United States, however, remained a worry, especially as Tocqueville witnessed the deepening divisions over the expansion of slavery. For the century and a half after the full publication of Tocqueville's *Democracy in America* in 1840, what he called the internal "agitation" surrounding US elections preoccupied the attention of American democracy activists and their opponents. Textbooks give a contrary impression, but for much of the nation's history, American elections were riven with violence, corruption, and outright cheating. As late as 1964, African Americans in the American South faced violent mobs for trying to vote. The Student Nonviolent Coordinating Committee, for instance, documented countless acts of violence against Black Americans attempting to register in 1963 and 1964, as well as white civil rights workers seeking to help. Prominent American national politicians, most notably Lyndon Johnson, gained election from stuffed ballot boxes and votes from the graveyard.[4]

Until the last third of the twentieth century, domestic agitation prevented fair and secure elections in the United States. As early as 1870, during Ulysses Grant's presidency, the federal government developed law enforcement institutions, particularly the national Justice Department, to protect voters and limit violence and cheating. These efforts were only partially successful. The passage of the Voting Rights Act in 1965 finally gave the federal government extensive enforcement powers for election security against domestic lawbreaking. Even those powers were constrained, most especially by the Supreme Court's ruling in *Shelby County v. Holder* in 2013.

Federal efforts to combat foreign interference were much more shallow. That is largely because there were, as Tocqueville anticipated, few threats to American elections from abroad. Interference at the ballot box was entirely internal. The Justice Department (founded in 1870), the Federal Bureau of Investigation (first created in 1908), and the Federal Election Commission (legislated in 1974) each targeted almost exclusively domestic sources of violence and fraud. They hired few personnel, if any, with expertise on foreign governments and their potential interest in American elections. Even as they investigated radicals, communists, and other internal threats—often obsessively—these agencies paid little attention to foreign threats to US elections. Limiting federal scrutiny of the conduct of elections, especially before the 1960s, enabled meddling by local bullies, especially white supremacists. That was not an accident.

US election security had a very small role in national security before the late twentieth century. That is one way in which American history was exceptional compared with other democracies, which contended with frequent foreign meddling in their elections. Ironically, the United States was, after World War II, the most aggressive and pervasive foreign election meddler. The Cold War national security state enabled Washington's reach into the elections of other societies, but the country's own elections remained largely insulated, until the twenty-first century. Safe and complacent at home, the United States pioneered election interference abroad, with a belated blowback.

US FOREIGN ELECTION INTERFERENCE

Compared with other expanding nations at the end of the nineteenth century, the United States was slow to develop foreign intelligence capabilities. (The country was also slow to develop a professional foreign service.) Washington had a long history of intervening in other societies through military force, but diplomatic intrigue and spying were depicted as unsavory and undemocratic. One of the most respected early twentieth-century figures in American foreign policy, Henry Stimson, famously quipped that "gentlemen do not read each other's mail." When he was secretary of state, under President Herbert Hoover, Stimson shut down nascent espionage efforts based in the State Department.[5]

A decade later, when Stimson moved to the War Department, the United States created its first serious foreign intelligence capabilities. These were a response to the pressures of World War II and the overwhelming evidence that America's enemies were spying on the country and using the intelligence they acquired to their military advantage. President Franklin Roosevelt believed that the United States needed new capabilities to defend itself and to support forward military operations in Europe and Asia.

The Office of Strategic Services (OSS), formed by presidential order in June 1942, allowed the United States to infiltrate foreign societies. The OSS recruited highly educated men (often from Yale) and eccentric women (including Julia Child) to collect information on America's enemies, slip behind their boundaries, spread propaganda, organize resistance, and even plan assassinations. By the end of the war, the OSS employed more than twenty thousand people on four continents, and they reported to the president alone, not Congress.[6]

This was a very powerful tool, especially for postwar presidents concerned about the spying and aggression of the Soviet Union around the world. The evidence of Moscow's infiltration of the Manhattan Project, and the public uproar over those allegations, made it clear that the United States needed more foreign intelligence capabilities, not fewer. Accordingly, President Harry Truman used the National Security Act of 1947—the most far-reaching reform of the American national security apparatus—to create the Central Intelligence Agency (CIA) as a statutory and congressionally authorized successor to the OSS.

The CIA became a cornerstone of the new national security state quickly constructed by Truman and Congress for continuous Cold War conflict. For the first time in its history, the United States occupied large parts of Europe and Asia, and it was committed to building liberal capitalist states in those regions, as it also prevented the spread of communist alternatives, sponsored by the Soviet Union. Creating military, economic, and espionage capabilities for defending American interests abroad was an overriding priority for Cold War presidents and congressional leaders. Their actions limited public oversight and transparency, both at home and abroad. Henry Stimson's admonition against reading others' mail was turned on its head: serious statesmen now needed to penetrate the secrets of dangerous enemies as they also protected their own.

The key point for this chapter is that the CIA began its operations by interfering in foreign societies and tampering with their elections. The Agency, as it came to be called, was charged to prevent communists from getting elected in Western Europe, Japan, South Korea, and soon other parts of the world. The first major CIA operation surrounded the Italian elections of 1948, where communists were running strong. Coordinating with George Kennan, director of policy planning in the

State Department, the Agency sent bags of money to major Italian cities. These bags were distributed to Catholic priests with clear instructions to tell their parishioners to vote against the communists. With help from the State Department and Italian Americans, including a young Frank Sinatra, the CIA circulated rumors that the communists were criminals, traitors, and rapists. Truman's newly formed National Security Council affirmed these covert actions, agreeing that the United States had to assist anticommunist parties "by all feasible means." Foreign election interference had the full support of the White House.[7]

The Soviet Union also intervened in Italy, to support communist candidates, but Moscow did not have the resources to match the CIA's efforts. In April 1948 the Christian Democratic pro-American conservative party, led by Alcide De Gasperi, won an outright majority in the new Italian parliament—a very rare occurrence. Although the Left parties in Italy would remain influential for the next five decades, the United States had struck a fatal blow against the communists, who had been popular before the 1948 election. Within the US government, and across allied governments, the CIA's meddling in Italy was seen as a major success, and a model for other countries.[8]

France also had a very popular communist party that challenged American dominance in Western Europe and favored Soviet alternatives. The CIA and the State Department transferred many of their tactics from Italy to France. Through the US embassy, Washington provided funds to both the Gaullist conservative party and the socialist anticommunist party. The CIA worked closely with noncommunist union leaders and various conservative newspapers to spread favorable messages about the United States and the Western alliance while denigrating communist politicians.

France had a series of coalition governments that largely excluded communists, and the United States helped to tilt the elections against its perceived enemies. Washington funded the anticommunist press, and even shared Hollywood talent to advocate for America's friends. The United States tied military and political aid to internal French party negotiations that isolated the communists. And the CIA worked to spread dissension within communist ranks, often through fake news and character assassination. The United States observed few boundaries in its obsession with shaping politics in Paris.[9]

Apparent success in postwar Italy and France turned an American experiment in foreign election interference—almost unthinkable before World War II—into a standard foreign policy tool. *Political warfare* was the term of art at the time: "the employment of all the means at a nation's command, short of war," to exert influence abroad. American policy-makers came to assume that they could manipulate how other societies vote and choose leaders. They also carried a self-righteousness about the American "duty" to ensure that new democracies made the correct choices, which were our choices.[10]

Washington quickly spread this logic of foreign election interference far beyond Europe. It became a core element of American Cold War strategy. Containing the spread of communism across the globe justified aggressive efforts to keep communists out of government. When communists and other Soviet sympathizers gained power, the United States worked to unseat them, often violently. Despite their advocacy of free elections, American leaders did not respect the freedom of other societies to elect their own leaders.[11]

The United States, and especially the CIA, pioneered innovative and intrusive tactics for foreign election interference. These included the distribution of money to candidates, collaboration with local strongmen, the spread of propaganda through newspapers and radio, and targeted violence. What made the United States innovative was the covert deployment of these capabilities so far from the United States with density and deniability. By the 1950s the United States had election interference capabilities on all continents, and it had local allies who would do the dirty work for American patrons.[12]

President Dwight Eisenhower, who was both anticommunist and hesitant to deploy the US military abroad, relied heavily on these capabilities. His "New Look" strategy built nuclear weapons to deter war while expanding covert capabilities to influence foreign societies short of war. He began in Iran in 1953 and Guatemala in 1954. In both countries, on two different continents, the CIA equipped, trained, and encouraged unpopular anticommunist groups to overthrow popular governments that were sympathetic to communists. After the American-sponsored coups, the United States worked with the replacement governments to prevent elections anytime soon. Eisenhower was quite satisfied with these "victories" for the United States over what he perceived as communist threats. The contradiction between America's public promotion of democracy and covert support for coups did not trouble him very much.[13]

Eisenhower's successors followed a similar playbook, sponsoring coups in Brazil (1964), Indonesia (1965), and Chile (1973), among other countries. In South Korea and South Vietnam, the United States propped up dictators and resisted popular calls for open elections. Throughout Central America, the United States funded right-wing parties that promised to resist communist influences and protect American interests. It was difficult, and often deadly, to run for office south of the American border as a critic of the northern colossus.[14]

Washington's postwar habits of election interference reached a culminating point in the elections of Hamid Karzai as president of US-occupied Afghanistan. Karzai returned to his native country with US assistance in October 2001. A tribal congress (*loya jirga*) elected him as interim president in 2002, and he was elected president in nationwide voting in 2004 and again in 2009. At every step in his presidential career, Karzai was financed and promoted by the United States. He had American military bodyguards and he received daily cash allowances from Washington. Political consultants paid for by the US government guided his campaigns.

The United States also prevented any serious electoral opposition. Karzai's elections were designed as sure things. Alternative candidates were condemned through the American-sponsored press in Afghanistan, they were denied financing for their campaigns, and they and their supporters were frequently threatened by American personnel. Most often, political critics were encouraged by the United States to join Karzai's regime, often with well-paid positions. The United States engineered Karzai's twelve-year presidency in Afghanistan, and it undermined any possible faith in a fair and open electoral process thereafter.[15]

Most striking in retrospect is not only how American policy in Afghanistan followed established precedent for foreign electoral interference from Washington but also how oblivious Americans were to the behavior they were modeling for the world to see. Anyone observing the government in Kabul recognized that the United States was distorting democratic procedures, violating sovereignty, and picking the winners it wanted. This was more than hypocrisy. For Russia, China, and many European counterparts, the United States was acting in reckless and unilateral ways that threatened more than just Afghanistan.

The end of the Cold War increased the willingness of Washington to shape the outcomes of foreign elections. Leaders in the White House and Congress felt emboldened and nearly infallible; they believed history was on their side. Many Americans, including President George W. Bush, appeared to believe they had a right to choose leaders for citizens far away. Russia and China worried about this dynamic in their immediate regions, filled with new governments dependent on American trade and finance. Europeans perceived threats to their efforts to promote social democracy and other alternatives to American dominance.

By the second decade of the twenty-first century, flagrant US electoral interference in Afghanistan had become a global issue. Russian president Vladimir Putin had numerous international supporters when he condemned the United States for trying to "build democracy in other countries according to foreign templates." Although she did not repeat the sharpness of the Russian leader's condemnations, German chancellor Angela Merkel, who stood up to Putin on some issues, shared his concerns about American foreign meddling, including Washington's surveillance of her phone calls.[16]

US DOUBLE STANDARDS

Americans did not really understand these criticisms of their meddling in foreign elections. For national security officials and members of Congress, the United States was simply protecting democracy as we understood it. Chosen figures, like Hamid Karzai, were the partners we needed in other countries. American intervention in foreign elections appeared justified because it ensured the outcomes we knew these governments needed. On this point, President Barack Obama echoed his predecessor in claiming American intervention was essential to build democracy in Afghanistan, where he increased US forces and funding during the first years of his presidency. Republicans and Democrats felt a "duty" to help direct new democracies.[17]

Neither party believed that foreign countries could or should do the same in the United States. Washington has never accepted the legitimacy of foreign standards or tests for American democracy. This is one of the reasons the United States does not recognize the domestic jurisdiction of international human rights tribunals, although we encourage their work abroad. Foreign intervention in American elections and other politics has always been beyond the pale—unthinkable for most citizens.

Distance enabled this double standard. So did the decentralized nature of American elections, which made any systemic effort to shift national outcomes very difficult. During the Cold War, the United States added a strong deterrent as well, especially for the Soviet Union and other communist adversaries. The United States' draconian reaction to evidence of communist espionage, especially during the decade after World War II, made it clear that the US government was prepared to use force against any adversary who crossed into the domestic space.

International competition was fair game, but a norm quickly emerged in the Cold War that foreign enemies of the United States would not tamper with American internal democratic institutions. In return, the United States generally refrained from interfering in internal Soviet and Chinese leadership selection. Even as they intervened in smaller states, the biggest powers agreed that attacks on their domestic succession would be too destabilizing. (Imagine what would have happened if American leaders had seriously suspected the Soviet Union was involved in the assassination of President John F. Kennedy.)

By the end of the Cold War and the dawn of the twenty-first century, the United States had a long history of insecure elections that were, however, free of foreign interference. When experts spoke of protecting fair elections in the United States, they meant protections from other Americans. *National security* became a ubiquitous phrase in American politics, with many domestic implications, but not for election security. The phrase largely excluded concerns about foreign countries influencing US elections, and it simultaneously justified Washington's intervention in elections abroad.

This double standard was integral to American conceptions of national security in the early twenty-first century. Despite the end of the Cold War, the United States continued to use its military, diplomatic, and covert capabilities to exert control over foreign societies. At the same time, it expected zero intervention or violence from abroad at home.

If anything, the United States expanded its reach across the oceans as it also sought to build a higher wall of separation against people and influences it did not like.

The terrorist attacks of September 11, 2001, only deepened this dynamic, as the United States waged a global war on terror, including foreign election interference, while Washington sought to ensure complete safety within its borders. National security became a vision of two worlds: a foreign Hobbesian arena of conflict and subversion, separated from an American safe space of freedom, openness, and nonintervention. This dichotomy seemed so axiomatic to most Americans—even policy experts—that it was taken for granted.

BLOWBACK

Foreign leaders not only resented the American double standard on elections; they found it personally threatening. For dictators like Vladimir Putin and Xi Jinping, American foreign election interference challenged their influence in vital regions, and there were few ways to deter this behavior by Washington. Despite rhetoric about sovereignty and independence, the United States seemed more determined than ever to shape foreign governments, especially in places that Russia and China long sought to dominate: Ukraine, Georgia, Taiwan, and Myanmar. American presidents faced few risks in their foreign election interference because they did not believe any other country could or would do the same in the United States. American presidents could swing a big bat freely, with few worries of anyone swinging back at them. Or so they thought . . .

Before he became president of Russia, Putin spent a long career in the Soviet KGB, the CIA's counterpart. He understood American covert capabilities very well, and he was aware of Soviet efforts to infiltrate other societies and thwart US meddling. Confronting what he perceived as pervasive American expansion after 2001, Putin began early in his presidency to consider ways of breaching American security at home. He continued to maintain a large nuclear arsenal capable of reaching the United States, but he also looked to deploy more flexible and, for the KGB, traditional tools: propaganda and covert influence peddling.[18]

Although the Russian economy and military could not compete with the innovative and plentiful capabilities of the United States, Putin benefited from lucrative hard currency revenues acquired from the sale of oil and other commodities mined in Russia. Despite population decline, his country benefited from a talented engineering and computer science labor pool, as well as a strong tradition of training in mathematics and the sciences. Russia had the cash and the talent to use new technologies to infiltrate American society. This was an obvious asymmetrical strategy for unsteadying the United States without direct military conflict. Americans were slow to recognize this threat because it challenged long-held assumptions of safety at home.

Putin's efforts began with propaganda promoting Russia's ability to control potential Muslim and other perceived terrorist communities in Chechnya, Dagestan, Georgia, and central Asia. Russia hired public relations firms in New York to depict the country as a white and Christian actor that Americans should trust in a world filled with terrorists and other restive non-Christian peoples. In addition to planting news articles, the Russian government also hired lobbyists in the United States, including Paul Manafort, who made appeals on behalf of Moscow to members of Congress and parts of the executive branch.[19]

During the years of Obama's presidency, Russian influence operations focused on the Republican Party. Putin had a particular hatred for Democratic secretary of state Hillary Clinton, following her criticisms of his heavy-handed efforts to control Ukrainian politics. Republicans also hated Clinton, especially because she was the likely front-runner to succeed Obama. The Russian government targeted Clinton with vicious lies and threats, and it enlisted Republicans to help spread them, knowingly and unknowingly. Russian cash fueled an avalanche of anti-Clinton attacks. The group of advisers who eventually worked for Donald Trump's presidential campaign—Manafort, Roger Stone, and Michael Flynn, among others—were given compromising material on Clinton by Russia, and assistance spreading it.[20]

Putin created an army of computer hackers and internet trolls to disrupt Clinton's campaign and American democracy in general. He gave this group an innocuous name, the Internet Research Agency (IRA), and he funded it initially through his paramilitary surrogate (and later critic) Yevgeny Prigozhin. The report that resulted from the investigation led by former FBI director Robert Mueller after the 2016 election (the Mueller Report) detailed the reach of the IRA in the United States. Through

Facebook, 126 million people unknowingly read Russian propaganda disguised as news revelations about Clinton and others. Through Twitter, 1.4 million people received trolling messages from Russia that appeared to be something else.[21]

The Mueller Report showed that these communications aimed at "influencing the U.S. presidential election."[22] On March 18, 2016, for example, the Russian agency ran an advertisement on Facebook disguised as the post of an American user, including a photo of Clinton and the message, "If one day God lets this liar enter the White House as a president—that day would be a real national tragedy." A month later, the Russian agency bought an advertisement on Instagram, also while posing as an American user, calling for photos and other actions on behalf of "#KIDS4TRUMP." Follow-up advertisements included the phrases "Stop All Invaders" and "Secure Borders." As their posts were shared and retweeted, the IRA was triggering a wave against Clinton and one for Trump.[23]

Russian activities went beyond election propaganda. Through its disguised social media sites, the IRA organized pro-Trump rallies in New York, Pennsylvania, Florida, and other locations.[24] The Main Intelligence Directorate of the Russian General Staff devoted its resources to hacking the email accounts of Clinton campaign personnel, including campaign chair John Podesta. The Mueller Report concluded that the directorate "stole hundreds of thousands of documents." Russia selectively released the hacked materials to the public, often in conjunction with the Trump campaign.[25]

Most troubling, Russian agents pierced the security of state and local elections offices. Russian hackers broke into public voter databases, injected malicious code, and extracted data about registered voters. These intrusions occurred in Illinois and Florida, among other states. Russian agents also attacked the email accounts of elections officials and those who worked for election machine companies. There is no evidence that Moscow's hackers counterfeited any votes, but they appear to have been working toward major disruptions in voting systems.[26]

Russian interference in the 2016 presidential election was uniquely aggressive and technologically sophisticated. It also benefited from a candidate willing to collaborate. The efforts of China and perhaps other countries to influence American elections were real, but much more limited at the time. Putin acted with a chilling determination to disrupt

American democracy. The people and institutions of the United States were unprepared.

Americans were not, however, blameless. Although the aggression and lawlessness exhibited by Putin were his responsibility and worthy of criminal prosecution for all parties involved, they were also echoes of American actions during the last half century. Russia tried to turn the electoral process in another country to its advantage by manipulating voters and infiltrating voting processes. The United States had indeed done the same, repeatedly, for more than a half century. This was the distortion of a foreign democracy by a powerful and distant actor. It was what American leaders, as early as 1948, called legitimate "political warfare."

I want to be clear: this observation does not justify or apologize for Putin's crimes or Trump's collaboration. What it does offer is a necessary historical explanation for how we came to the current moment. Russia improved on and redirected a tactic for international power projection, pioneered by the United States, against its creator. Americans failed to nurture a credible and widespread taboo against foreign election interference. Even though they made that claim, especially about their own elections, their repeated behavior belied its reality. Americans did not disavow the tool that they demanded others reject.

Putin's ideas about election interference in the United States, his understanding of the tactics, and his self-righteousness came from studying, in his KGB days, what Washington had done for years before. Putin found support for his electoral aggression, in Russia and abroad, from those who were familiar with that part of American history. For all his uniquely horrible dictatorial qualities (and there are many!), one must conclude that the Russian leader learned how to tamper with foreign elections, at least in part, from the United States. Presidents from Truman to Obama offered an unintended model. And Putin was encouraged by the apparent successes Americans had in this dirty antidemocratic endeavor. How could American leaders flagrantly deploy this weapon so often, and still expect to remain immune from its effects?[27]

NONINTERFERENCE IN FOREIGN ELECTIONS

Like the citizens of any democracy, Americans have a right to free and secure elections. The United States must defend its elections from the kinds of propaganda, influence peddling, and manipulation practiced by Russia in 2016. There is every reason to believe that Russia and other countries will try to do the same again, if given the opportunity. It seems obvious, as many experts have argued, that the United States must develop a robust cyber-defense capability, effective protections against social media propaganda, and even some forward measures to punish and deter potential aggressors.[28]

Equally important, however, will be American efforts to establish a firm international norm against foreign election interference. The historical record shows that when the United States and its allies have pushed, through international law and other forms of persuasion, to declare a tool of conflict out of bounds, the frequency of its occurrence has dropped. The two primary examples are chemical and nuclear weapons, both transformed into "unthinkable" instruments of war after years of public activism and US government pressure. The nonuse of these weapons, especially by the United States, has made their use by others far less common.[29]

Norms constraining behaviors are indeed common in all areas of domestic and international politics, and they emerge when a tool of power is deemed so damaging and self-defeating by its most prominent practitioners that they turn its efficacy into a reason for prohibition. Potential users nurture a consciousness that the instrument is inherently antisocial and inhumane. This was the case for chemical and nuclear weapons. A similar dynamic explains the near-universal rejection of particular interpersonal forms of behavior, including cannibalism and incest.[30]

The moral heinousness of an action (a perceived "crime"), when strongly renounced by powerful actors, acquires a normative prohibition—a public threshold of widespread revulsion that few will consider crossing. Torture and the flagrant bombing of innocent civilians are in this category. International agreements give these normative prohibitions a clarity and a permanence that encourage enforcement and penalize transgression. The Geneva Conventions on the treatment of prisoners of war and the Nuclear Non-proliferation Treaty are effective instances of international law constraining damaging political behavior.[31]

Manipulating a foreign country's democratic elections can and should become another strongly enforced normative taboo. The actions of the United States after World War II, as described earlier, normalized this form of intervention; the United States should now take the lead to re-criminalize it, morally and institutionally. This obviously requires that the United States renounce its own long-standing foreign election interference practices. Washington should also join allies and international institutions, including the United Nations, in making foreign election interference a recognized and penalized violation of international law. Building an international community of agreement that renounces this behavior will create strong presumptions against it and raise the costs—moral and material—for continuing perpetrators.

The definition of election interference is somewhat nebulous. Expressions of favoritism for a candidate and advocacy of particular policies in a foreign country cannot be completely disallowed. Nor is it reasonable to expect even-handedness from external actors who have a lot at stake in another country's elections. What can be prohibited, and what the United States perpetrated abroad and recently suffered from at home, are actions to manipulate voters through deception, disinformation, bribery, intimidation, and thievery. In most countries these are domestic crimes. They should be identified, condemned, and resisted as international elections crimes as well.

The United States must take the lead in renouncing its own past actions; otherwise no credible norm can stand. American leaders must admit that their own country has violated stated principles in the past. That historical reckoning can become a source of policy leverage today if the United States pledges not to interfere in foreign elections again. Showing restraint in American behavior justifies international cooperation to restrain others in the same way. Disavowing the electoral interference weapon gives other countries that wish to shield themselves (especially Russia and China) reason to disavow the weapon too. Just as repeated foreign intervention exposed the United States to blowback, concerted foreign restraint can help secure America's democratic practices.

The process will be slow, but essential. And it must start now, as the technologies for electoral manipulation proliferate. The history of the last century has shown that aggressive new capabilities—from nuclear weapons to computer hacks—require international normative cooperation, supported by the United States.

Alexis de Tocqueville would probably embrace this argument. Although he was a critic of presidential elections, he revered the ability of Americans to devise mechanisms for cooperation and mutual benefit, despite their differences. Elections work better, he would recognize, when the strongest actors defend common rules. At its core, *Democracy in America* reminds readers that democracy is a set of practices nourished by behaviors that promote self-governance, at home and abroad. That is why Tocqueville was so keen to examine American society as a case study in what true democracy could mean for the wider world. Securing American elections requires securing elections outside the United States.[32]

NOTES

1. Alexis de Tocqueville, *Democracy in America*, trans. Arthur Goldhammer (New York: Library of America, 2004), 152.
2. Tocqueville, 152.
3. Tocqueville, 147.
4. See, among many others, Alexander Keyssar, *The Right to Vote: The Contested History of Democracy in the United States* (New York: Basic Books, 2000). On Lyndon Johnson's successful effort to steal the 1948 Democratic primary for the US Senate in Texas, see Robert Caro, *Means of Ascent: The Years of Lyndon Johnson* (New York: Random House, 1990).
5. See William Safire, "Each Other's Mail," *New York Times*, May 9, 1974, 43.
6. See Bradley F. Smith, *The Shadow Warriors: OSS and the Origins of the CIA* (New York: Basic Books, 1983).
7. Alessandro Brogi, *Confronting America: The Cold War between the United States and the Communists in France and Italy* (Chapel Hill: University of North Carolina Press, 2011), 107.
8. See James E. Miller, "Taking Off the Gloves: The United States and Italian Elections of 1948," *Diplomatic History* 7 (January 1983): 35–56; Mario Del Pero, "The United States and 'Psychological Warfare' in Italy, 1948–1955," *Journal of American History* 87 (March 2001): 1304–34; and Brogi, *Confronting America*, 108.
9. Edward Rice-Maximin, "The United States and the French Left, 1945–1949: The View from the State Department," *Journal of Contemporary History* 19 (October 1984): 729–47; Brogi, *Confronting America*, 110–21, 136–46.
10. Brogi, *Confronting America*, 108.
11. This is a central point in Paul Thomas Chamberlin, *The Cold War's Killing Fields: Rethinking the Long Peace* (New York: Harper, 2018).
12. See Tim Weiner, *Legacy of Ashes: The History of the CIA* (New York: Doubleday, 2007).
13. See Robert R. Bowie and Richard H. Immerman, *Waging Peace: How Eisenhower Shaped an Enduring Cold War Strategy* (New York: Oxford University Press, 1998).

14 See Stephen G. Rabe, *The Killing Zone: The United States Wages Cold War in Latin America*, 2nd ed. (New York: Oxford University Press, 2015).

15 For one of many accounts of this dynamic in Afghanistan, see Rajiv Chandrasekaran, *Little America: The War within the War for Afghanistan* (New York: Alfred Knopf, 2012).

16 Andrew Roth, "Vladimir Putin Warns West to Stop Meddling in Afghanistan," *The Guardian*, August 20, 2021; Michael Birnbaum and Ellen Nakashima, "German Leader Calls Obama about Alleged Cellphone Tapping," *Washington Post*, October 24, 2013.

17 Jeremi Suri, *Liberty's Surest Guardian: American Nation-Building from the Founders to Obama* (New York: Free Press, 2011), 210–65.

18 For an excellent examination of Putin's career in the KGB and its influence on his presidency, see Fiona Hill and Clifford Gaddy, *Mr. Putin: Operative in the Kremlin*, expanded ed. (Washington, DC: Brookings Institution Press, 2015).

19 See Franklin Foer, "Paul Manafort, American Hustler," *The Atlantic*, March 2018.

20 The first volume of the *Report on the Investigation into Russian Interference in the 2016 Presidential Election*, March 2019 (the Mueller Report), details the communications between the Russian government and Trump campaign officials about Hillary Clinton. See Robert S. Mueller III, *Report on the Investigation into Russian Interference in the 2016 Presidential Election*, vol. 1 (Washington, DC: Department of Justice, 2019), www.justice.gov.

21 Mueller, 15.

22 Mueller, 24.

23 Mueller, 25.

24 Mueller, 31.

25 Mueller, 36.

26 Mueller, 50–51.

27 This is the central argument of Alfred W. McCoy's trenchant criticism of the entire covert apparatus developed by the United States in the twentieth century. See Alfred W. McCoy, *A Question of Torture: CIA Interrogation, from the Cold War to the War on Terror* (New York: Henry Holt, 2006). See also Chalmers Johnson, *Blowback: The Costs and Consequences of American Empire* (New York: Henry Holt, 2000).

28 See the conversation with Christopher Krebs, former director of the Department of Homeland Security's Cybersecurity and Infrastructure Security Agency: Robert Strauss Center, "A Conversation with Christopher Krebs," YouTube video, 1:13:44, March 21, 2022, www.youtube.com/watch?v=5IvKghCf8FM.

29 See, among many others, Nina Tannenwald, *The Nuclear Taboo: The United States and the Non-use of Nuclear Weapons since 1945* (New York: Cambridge University Press, 2008); and Richard M. Price, *The Chemical Weapons Taboo* (Ithaca, NY: Cornell University Press, 2007).

30 The classic work on the structural impediments to self-destructive behaviors in human communities is Claude Lévi-Strauss, *Structural Anthropology*, trans. Claire Jacobson and Brooke Grundfest Schoepf (New York: Basic Books, 1963).

31 There is a very large literature on this topic. See, among many others, Hedley Bull, *The Anarchical Society: A Study of Order in World Politics* (London: Macmillan, 1977); and Peter Katzenstein, ed., *The Culture of National Security: Norms and Identity in World Politics* (New York: Columbia University Press, 1996).

32 See Olivier Zunz's compelling biography of Tocqueville, *The Man Who Understood Democracy: The Life of Alexis de Tocqueville* (Princeton, NJ: Princeton University Press, 2022).

4

ELECTION DECEPTION

DISINFORMATION, ELECTION SECURITY, AND THE HISTORY OF VOTER SUPPRESSION

NICOLE HEMMER

In 1949, Russian speakers coined a new term: *dezinformatsiya.* Within a few years, the word would be imported into the United States and Anglicized as *disinformation.* Born in the Cold War, disinformation involved a deliberate campaign by authoritarian governments (and their corporate and media allies) to mislead and deceive, in the hope of influencing public opinion, political decision-making, and electoral outcomes. In the United States, the word largely remained relegated to discussions of propaganda and foreign policy. Until 2016.[1]

During the 2016 election, Russian efforts to influence the outcome of the US presidential election, along with the discovery of "fake news" factories in places like Macedonia, moved disinformation to the center of US electoral analysis. Concern over election security came to include protecting not only voting machines and voting rolls but the information environment more broadly. Soon, new scholarly fields and governing bodies were born. In 2019, Harvard Kennedy School launched the *Misinformation Review*, which, a few years later, outlined the tenets of a new field, critical disinformation studies. A year earlier, the Cybersecurity and Infrastructure Security Agency, a section of the Department of Homeland Security, expanded its mission to include election security. As part of its efforts, it developed a guide for election officials on mis-, dis-, and malinformation, highlighting the information environment as a potential weakness in the US election security infrastructure.[2]

That application of the disinformation framework to understand US electoral politics resonated with a subset of voters trying to make sense of the results of the 2016 presidential election. It brought together the specter of foreign interference, internal subversion, and critical analysis of social media, a communications technology that had long lost its techno-utopian sheen. The focus on election security as a response to disinformation likewise resonated: a narrative emerged that Russia had "hacked" the election not by manipulating voting machines but by corrupting the information environment; to secure elections meant securing the nation's information infrastructure. As a bonus, it allowed analysts to reorient the idea of "election security" away from Republican talking points about voter fraud and toward more reality-based concerns about deliberate political deception.

But while both the disinformation and election security frameworks are powerful sense-making devices for the specific case of the 2016 election, they sever the connection between contemporary deception campaigns and the longer history of deception as a form of voter suppression. This essay will reconnect those histories, exploring the growing role of deception in voter suppression and how a broader understanding of election security can promote not only more trust in election results but higher participation in electoral politics.

THE LIMITS OF THE DISINFORMATION AND ELECTION SECURITY FRAMEWORKS

In the years since 2016, disinformation has become the go-to framework for thinking about election manipulation. At conferences and convenings over the intervening years, historians have applied that framework retrospectively, conceptualizing the information environment in the United States through the lens of politically motivated and heavily coordinated disinformation campaigns.

When it comes to the histories of election and voter suppression, the disinformation framework is especially tempting. Concerns about the quality of information have particular implications for a democratic society. The theory of US democracy has, from the beginning, been rooted in the concept of an informed citizenry. The protections of speech and the press, support for nationwide mail service with special rates for newspapers, investment in public education and libraries, and even racist and nativist policies like literacy tests and understanding clauses for voting were rationalized by the need for the electorate to have access to good information. If citizens were to have the power to choose their leaders, the thinking went, they should have the tools necessary to make informed evaluations of those leaders.[3]

If that was the ideal, however, it was not the reality. Elite white male citizens often had access to quality education and could purchase periodicals, even in the days of the early republic. But even before the electorate and the press expanded, newspapers in the United States—the primary medium through which political information spread within and between communities—took on distinctly partisan identities. The content of those papers matched the agenda of their party backers. By the end of the nineteenth century, the electorate had widened to include unpropertied men, some immigrants, and an ever-decreasing number of Black men who accessed the ballot in the face of growing legal restrictions and extralegal violence. Despite a rising literacy rate and a nation awash in newsprint, the information environment did not necessarily improve. Tabloid journalism joined the partisan press to offer readers a sensationalized and slanted depiction of the world. The nation was flooded with political misinformation, campaign rumormongering, and biased reports—sensationalized stories about the explosion of the USS *Maine* in Havana's harbor, insinuations about Grover Cleveland's secret child—but there was little expectation that the information could, or even should, look otherwise.[4]

To think of that misinformation as a form of voter suppression does not get us very far, not only because the standard of objectivity was not yet the norm in journalism but also because there were so many more effective ways of suppressing votes. Elections in the nineteenth century were often corrupt affairs, especially in the years before the secret ballot. Nor was there any concept of universal or even widespread democracy; ballot access was formally limited by sex and race, even after the Fifteenth Amendment, as well as by literacy and wealth in states with tests and poll taxes. It was also limited by organized violence and terrorism campaigns. In light of those tools, disinformation efforts had a minimal role to play. Manipulation of the information environment as a meaningful voter suppression tactic would have to wait until there was both an expectation of trustworthy information and new constraints on formal suppression.

The election security framework likewise has limitations. Thinking of election security as a form of national security invites people to think of greater surveillance and tighter restrictions, of a piece with Republican strategies around the notion of voter fraud. Certainly there are concerns, heightened by the 2016 and 2020 campaigns, that foreign actors will continue to target US elections, both to sow chaos and to ensure the instillation of their preferred candidate. But precisely because of the resonances with Republican voter fraud messaging, as well as the anxieties a security framework creates for those people most likely to be the subjects of scrutiny, we should be wary of emphasizing election security in this way.

What I suggest is that we think of election security in the same way we think of social security or economic security: not a system that seeks to surveil and restrict but one that seeks to maximize the opportunities for people to exercise the rights of citizenship. That includes preventing attacks on the voting system, from both within and without, as well as making electoral processes from registration to voting free and accessible, making accurate information easy to find, and fostering a culture that views participation in competitive and fair elections as essential to sustaining a democratic society.

For that vision of election security, we need to address one of the main limits of the disinformation and election security frameworks: they encourage people to see threats as foreign rather than domestic. But the most significant challenges to free and fair elections in the United States have not, and do not, come from abroad; they have come from domestic actors. As I will explore in the remainder of this essay, it is that history that we need to center as we think about how best to address the contemporary challenges facing US elections.

ELECTION DAY DECEPTIONS

The sun had not yet risen on Election Day in 2006 when nearly three hundred Black Philadelphians boarded six Trailways buses headed for Baltimore, Maryland. The passengers, mostly poor, had been promised three meals and one hundred dollars each, courtesy of the campaigns to reelect Maryland's Republican governor, Robert L. Ehrlich Jr., and to send his lieutenant governor, Michael S. Steele, to the Senate. As the buses rumbled to a halt, campaign workers handed the passengers hot coffee, fresh donuts, and thousands of glossy flyers that read, "Democratic Sample Ballot." The flyers showed checks next to Ehrlich's and Steele's names—with no indication they were Republicans—followed by a list of local Democratic candidates. The goal: to leaflet Black neighborhoods in Baltimore and Prince George's County in the hope that some people would be tricked into voting for the Republican candidates.

By the time the state Democratic Party got the issue in front of a judge, arguing that the fraudulent flyers had to be pulled from circulation, polls were preparing to close. "I'm not going to do it," Judge Ron Silkworth reportedly told the parties' attorneys on a conference call. "It's too late."[5]

The deception did not win the election for Ehrlich or Steele. In a strong Democratic year, in a strong Democratic state, both Republicans lost by wide margins. But the flyers were part of a disturbing trend in the 2000s, when robocalls, posters, and social media sites transmitting deceptive information about elections—about voter registration, polling hours, candidates, and voting eligibility—became more visible.[6]

Ten days after the 2006 election, a first-term senator put forward a bill to address deceptive campaign practices. When Barack Obama announced the proposed legislation, the Deceptive Practices and Voter Intimidation Prevention Act, he pointed to the Ehrlich-Steele flyers, in addition to scores of robocalls, noting they were paid for by Republican campaigns and targeted poor and minority voters. His proposed legislation would have prohibited deceiving voters about the logistics of the election, qualifications for voting, the party affiliation of candidates, or the sponsor of campaign advertisements.[7]

The bill died in committee, only to be revived again and again in the years that followed. Concerns over these efforts, which used deception to change or suppress votes, deepened in the years leading up to the 2021 insurrection at the US Capitol. Yet no new legislation was enacted. Democratic senators Ben Cardin and Amy Klobuchar promoted the bill as part of the broader For the People Act, which passed the House in 2019 and 2021, but both times it was killed by a Republican filibuster in the Senate. Rather than new legislation to protect the vote, the 2010s instead saw voter protections stripped away by Republican states and a conservative Supreme Court.[8]

This type of deception—misleading voters to prevent them from casting a ballot or to cause them to miscast their votes—became increasingly popular thanks to the enactment of new protections for voting rights, which limited methods of voter suppression. New technologies made it possible to conduct robocalls and spread misinformation through social media, but as the case of the Philadelphians in Baltimore suggests, shoe-leather deception campaigns were at least as prevalent, and likely more effective. That's because in the United States, elections are carried out at the district and precinct level, creating a bewildering patchwork of election laws and procedures. Voters who have to navigate those procedures can be easily misled about registration requirements, deadlines, voting procedures, and even when elections are held.

Evidence of this sort of deception abounds. In 2006, robocalls targeted at districts in Virginia with significant Black populations told voters that their polling place had been changed. Four years later, in Maryland, a Republican campaign robocalled one hundred thousand Democratic households on Election Day to say that the Democratic candidates had won enough votes and no more were needed (a case that ended in a prosecution for conspiracy to commit election fraud). Students at Bates University in Maine in 2016 received flyers warning, falsely, that students could only vote if they paid hundreds of dollars to change their driver's licenses and car registrations to Lewiston, Maine—a false claim repeated by Republican governor Paul LePage.[9]

Yet such deceptions extend beyond simply misleading voters, as troubling as that may be. They can also be wielded as a form of intimidation. Consider the case of New Jersey's state and local elections in 1981. On Election Day, a group of men wearing armbands that read, "National Ballot Security Task Force," appeared in Black and Latino neighborhoods, demanding registration cards from nonwhite voters and saying, falsely, that they couldn't vote without those cards. The "task force," which included several armed men and off-duty police officers, also tacked up signs warning that police would be at the polls, looking for people casting fraudulent ballots.

None of this was true. The men swarming New Jersey neighborhoods were part of an effort by the Republican Party to deceive and intimidate

Black and Latino voters. When initial returns showed Thomas Kean, the Republican candidate, winning by a narrow two thousand votes in the state's gubernatorial race, party leaders shared that they planned to unleash similar "task forces" in other states to help tip elections to Republicans. Richard Richards, then chair of the Republican National Committee, defended the decision to the *New York Times*: "Anyone opposed to ballot security obviously must be supportive of election fraud. We would have been cheated out of that race if we hadn't been alert."[10]

In the New Jersey case, Democrats pushed back, arguing that the task force hadn't simply been spreading misinformation but was engaged in voter intimidation. Because they targeted Black and Latino neighborhoods, the party's actions violated the 1965 Voting Rights Act. The Republican Party entered into a consent decree a year later that prevented them from engaging in further acts of intimidation.[11]

Even without the implicit threats of violence or racist targeting, deception that dissuades voters from registering to vote or participating in elections violates the more capacious notion of election security outlined earlier. Lying to voters so they will not cast a ballot they wish to cast can skew the result of an election, divorcing election outcomes from popular will and making Americans less confident in the outcome of elections. Conceivably, these types of violations of election security could be addressed by bills like those backed by Obama, Klobuchar, and Cardin (though the consequences of voter suppression and dilution make it unlikely such a bill will pass in the foreseeable future). There is, however, a broad field of voter deception that has damaged national election security and is much harder to address through legislation.

THE VOTER-FRAUD FRAUD

The modern obsession with rampant voter fraud—an obsession that, despite a persistent search for evidence, has been found to have no basis—came to the fore after the 2010 midterm elections loaded Congress and statehouses with Republicans who were well to the right of the previous generation (which was itself well to the right of the generation of Republicans that preceded it). Assuming power after significant losses in 2006 and 2008, Republicans took aim at the machinery of elections, purging voter rolls, enacting strict voter ID laws, closing polling sites, and limiting election hours. They justified this crackdown on voting with a story: voter fraud was rampant in the United States, undermining the legitimacy of elections and weakening US democracy. Only strict surveillance and heightened barriers—intensified election security—would protect the nation's elections.[12]

The problem with that story, though, was that it was not true. Cases of in-person voting fraud were vanishingly rare, which served as evidence that elections were surprisingly secure, given their decentralized nature and the billions of ballots cast over the course of even just one decade. Broader concerns about election security, worries about tampering with voting machines or more systemic types of fraud, also did not pan out. As warnings of the dangers of voter fraud mounted, so too did the evidence that no such fraud existed.

If the 2010s marked a turning point in state-level legislation around voter fraud, they did not mark the start of the fearmongering around voter fraud. To chart that history, it's important to distinguish among a few phases of voter fraud history. As mentioned earlier, election corruption has a long history in the United States, with efforts to safeguard the vote enacted over several decades in the twentieth century. The most notable reform, of course, was the 1965 Voting Rights Act. But early laws instituting secret ballots and civil service reform, as well as later laws that helped codify a set of rules around electioneering and ballot security, meant that by the 1980s and 1990s, mass voter fraud was largely a thing of the past.

But while voter fraud had become rare, its utility for throwing into question the validity of election outcomes remained as strong as ever. Notably, the modern voter fraud deception—the voter-fraud fraud—emerged in the 1990s at the same moment, and in the same place, that a useful hysteria over undocumented immigration had begun to boil over. In California in 1994, activists had transformed the issue of undocumented immigrants from a low-level concern for some voters into a top state (and national) priority. Proposition 187, which appeared on the ballot in that year's midterm elections, moved both Republicans and Democrats sharply right on the issue of immigration. Rhetoric around undocumented immigrants reached a fever pitch that year, as politicians insisted that those immigrants were the source of most of the state's problems: overcrowded schools, high unemployment, rising housing costs, and even pollution.[13]

Michael Huffington, running for US Senate against incumbent Democrat Dianne Feinstein, saw another way to scapegoat undocumented immigrants: accuse them of a coordinated campaign of mass voter fraud. Despite losing the race to Feinstein by more than 150,000 votes, he refused to concede, arguing the race had been tainted by widespread noncitizen voting. In an appearance on *Larry King Live* a few weeks after the election, Huffington vowed that his supporters would go door-to-door in California to quiz voters—certain voters, anyway—about their citizenship status. Supporters of Proposition 187 put together a Voter Fraud Task Force to aid Huffington's efforts.[14]

Huffington's team failed to unearth evidence that undocumented immigrants had voted en masse to deny him a seat in the Senate. But his efforts to call into question the legitimacy of the election's outcome, coming at the very moment that nativist sentiment had spiked in California, showed how, from the start, the new, unsupported narrative of voter fraud was intertwined with racism and nativism. Some voters were naturally legitimate and their votes were sacrosanct; others were inherently suspect and deserved closer scrutiny.

The voter-fraud fraud began to cohere in the mid-1990s. Over the next fifteen years, the targets would broaden: voters in urban areas, college students, Black churches organizing Souls to the Polls. But the underlying story was the same. People who had no right to vote were corrupting elections and stealing Republican victories. That story, repeated again and again in right-wing media outlets and by Republican politicians, created what could be thought of as an electoral disinformation campaign: the persistent and deliberate repetition of false information in an effort to affect the outcome of an election. But it also has to be understood as part of a much longer project aimed at disenfranchising voters, especially nonwhite voters, in order to secure Republican power.

WHY DISINFORMATION HAS A PARTISAN BIAS

The voter-fraud fraud flourished on the right in large part because of the unique media ecosystem that conservatives had developed. That ecosystem was impervious to outside intervention. No matter how many studies showed that voter fraud was not happening, no matter how many fact-checks and debunking articles circulated online, the voter fraud narrative persisted, becoming an article of faith on the right. It did so in part because it was politically useful, but also because a generation of conservatives had been taught to treat nonconservative sources of information with suspicion, to base trustworthiness on ideology rather than accuracy.

Before digging into the construction of that media ecosystem, it is important to sketch out the information environment in which it emerged, one much different from the age of the partisan press in the nineteenth century. By the 1920s, the idea of journalistic objectivity had emerged, not only as a value statement from journalists—that they were committed to producing accurate, verifiable reporting from a dispassionate, nonpartisan perspective—but also as a set of professional practices that determined everything from sources and fact-checking to the voice and layout of a piece of journalism. Objectivity was always more a goal than a reality, and it was mostly blind to the biases that structured it (in the United States, a faith in capitalism, technocracy, and certain racial and gender hierarchies). But it set expectations for Americans encountering the news and shaped ideas about what informed citizens should know, as well as how they should get their information.[15]

By the mid-twentieth century, the notion of objectivity had embedded itself at the heart of US news media. But it had also gained a competitor. On the right, activists questioned the idea of objectivity. Rather than seeing it as a noble goal, they saw it as a dangerous fiction, a way that liberal elites had gained control not only over media but over truth itself. If journalists could sell the public liberal ideas shrouded in the guise of neutrality and factuality, then they could brainwash a generation of Americans into their ideology.

Nowhere was this objectivity sleight of hand clearer than during election season. The new conservative print publications *Human Events* (founded in 1944) and *National Review* (founded in 1955) obsessed over presidential elections they believed had been rigged. The 1940 election, they argued, had been manipulated so that both parties put forward a pro-intervention candidate, leaving those Americans who opposed US entry into the expanding world war without an option on the ballot. Similarly, the opening issues of *National Review* seethed over the 1952 Republican presidential primary, which the editors argued had been stolen from the more conservative candidate, Senator Robert Taft, and handed to Dwight Eisenhower. In both cases, though, their response was not political organizing but political publishing. They believed, as other conservative media activists of the time did, that control over communications would determine control over election outcomes.[16]

What the Right built in the years that followed—the magazines, the newsletters, the radio shows, the publishing houses—did not immediately unwind the widespread belief in the United States that news media were objective and trustworthy. But the ecosystem they were creating taught a generation of conservatives to distrust sources of information that were not avowedly conservative. In doing so, they created a separate conservative epistemology: the accuracy of a source was decided primarily not by the quality of evidence it used but by the political ideology of its creator.[17]

In such an environment, election deception thrived. The 1964 election, which saw conservative favorite Barry Goldwater win the Republican presidential nomination, was awash with conspiracies. The most notable came from a Texan conservative, J. Evetts Haley, who took aim at Goldwater's opponent, fellow Texan (and sitting president) Lyndon B. Johnson. Millions of copies of Haley's self-published paperback, *A Texan Looks at Lyndon*, circulated among conservatives in the summer of 1964. The contents were pure, uncut conspiracy, a lascivious account of Johnson's corruption that attributed more than a dozen murders to him and his wife during his pursuit of the White House (a storyline that would be repeated thirty years later when Bill Clinton was in the Oval Office).[18]

Conservative media outlets were already beginning to construct an information world for the Right separate and apart from the existing media ecosystem. They accomplished that during the Cold War with shoestring budgets and often less-than-gripping content. With the rise of talk radio and cable news in the 1990s, the power and influence of conservative media expanded exponentially. By the start of the new millennium, the US information landscape had dramatically changed, with the Right living in a world apart, one where information was evaluated largely in terms of its ideological content and its partisan utility.

This transformation of the media environment was not solely a conservative problem, however. From the Nixon administration on, the Right had spread its attacks on objectivity far beyond the confines of the conservative movement. Aided by a journalism profession that had regularly fallen short of its professed commitment to relay information with no regard to party or power, the Right successfully seeded the idea of liberal media bias as the primary way of critiquing objectivity, helping to chip away not only at the authority that journalists had once wielded but also at the very idea that media could, or should, strive to be a reliable and accurate source of information.[19]

Americans as a whole had lost considerable trust in journalism by the 2000s. But on the right, there was still considerable faith in media—so long as it was *their* media. Divorced from outside measures of factuality and accuracy, the conservative media ecosystem became particularly vulnerable to both domestic and foreign efforts to manipulate the information conservatives received. Politicians seeking to sway conservatives on issues like immigration appealed to conservative media outlets to seed their talking points and mute criticism of their policies. Campaigns could infuse right-wing media with anti-Democratic conspiracies, whether Swift Boat Vets for Truth or accusations about Barack Obama's birthplace or false stories about Hillary Clinton's health. Consumers of those media found such stories useful and repeated them time and again, both in person and on social media.

New media technologies and the desire for partisan advantage also made Democrats vulnerable to misinformation at times. In 2004, in the midst of a heated election, CBS News anchor Dan Rather appeared on the television news magazine *60 Minutes II* with documents that purported to show that George W. Bush had used his political connections to get out of his obligations as a member of the National Guard—a key campaign issue given Republican attacks on Democratic candidate John Kerry's service in Vietnam.

The documents, it turned out, were forgeries. But unlike, say, the conspiracies around Obama's birthplace, the forged-document episode became a scandal. CBS News and Rather had to retract their report and apologize. The network convened a panel to investigate how the newsroom had been deceived, and several high-level executives were fired. The misinformation did not become an article of faith; it launched no careers. How the mainstream news ecosystem dealt with deceptive information looked decidedly different from its conservative counterpart's approach.[20]

These dynamics help explain why election deception is particularly prominent on the right. So long as it advances conservative goals, such deception violates no core principle of the conservative information sphere. It raises no protest from information consumers. Deceivers pay no price when a gauntlet of external investigations and fact-checkers expose the fraud, since sources outside the conservative information sphere are easily rejected as false.

The advent of social media supercharged election deception because of the way platforms presented and distributed information. Platforms like Facebook and Twitter allowed users to share links, but all links looked the same: the same font, the same layout. A link from a fringe blog looked the same as a link from the *New York Times*. Democratizing, yes, but also a significant diminution of context clues. And posts and links could spread rapidly through networks, often on the strength of their emotional content (and negative emotions, studies showed, drove far more engagement that positive ones). The platforms also shaped and reinforced networks of influence and affinity: posts spread among friends, family, and ideological allies, contributing to both a fracturing of common sources of information and a solidifying of ideological allegiances.[21]

The information environment nurtured by social media platforms and their users was thus fractured, fast-paced, and emotional, with little in the way of oversight and fact-checking before 2016. Heightened concerns about "fake news" led to greater moderation: tweaked algorithms that would amplify trusted sources over those with a history of publishing misleading content; notes and warning flags to alert users to misleading or false information; and burgeoning oversight teams that had to assess and evaluate the masses of data flowing through the platforms every second of every day.[22]

Yet for all these efforts to slow the spread of deceptive information, platforms struggled with misinformation. Take the story of the discovery of a laptop filled with potentially damaging information about Democratic presidential nominee Joe Biden in the closing days of the 2020 election. The laptop, purportedly belonging to Biden's son Hunter, had been delivered to the *New York Post* by allies of the sitting Republican president, Donald Trump, and journalists at the paper began mining it for stories.

Platforms had been prepared for something like this: a salacious story of unprovable provenance appearing right before the election to pollute the election information environment right as voters were headed to the polls. When a story about Joe Biden, sourced to Hunter Biden's laptop, appeared in the *New York Post* on October 14, 2020, Facebook and Twitter throttled the story, making links difficult to find and share on their platforms. Twitter eventually banned links to the story under its ban on sharing hacked materials.[23]

While the measures may have momentarily slowed the spread of the *New York Post* story—though on Facebook it received fifty-four million views in the first week of its publication—they also brought significant attention to both the laptop story and the platforms as criticism, primarily but not exclusively from the right, mounted. On the right, it quickly became an article of faith that the story had been censored not because platforms suspected it was deceptive but because they sought to help Joe Biden win the election. In the months that followed, the election policies of social media platforms became the subject of congressional hearings, Federal Election Commission complaints, and countless segments on conservative outlets. Under the weight of those recriminations, social media companies slowly began to remove themselves from the role of arbiters, abandoning responsibility for the quality of the information environment their platforms produced. YouTube has dropped its election integrity initiative; Meta, the parent company of Facebook, has downsized its moderation team. Twitter, after being bought by Elon Musk in 2022, has stripped away nearly all its integrity tools and now regularly boosts accounts that spread misinformation.[24]

Those hoping that government might fill the regulatory void that these companies have left will be disappointed. The free speech clause of the First Amendment has more power to protect the circulation of misinformation than to curb its reach or stop its production. Outside of narrowly defined acts of fraud, the type that Obama and Klobuchar attempted to counter through legislation, current First Amendment jurisprudence protects most types of election disinformation. There is no real space under the contemporary understanding of free speech to allow for government restrictions on this more propagandistic form of misinformation, and little reason to think that such restrictions, even if allowed, would dramatically improve the information environment (and in fact they would almost certainly do more harm than good; a government bureau to monitor and adjudicate this type of speech is a dubious prospect).

All of this points to the difficulties facing those who would hope to improve and secure the information environment surrounding US elections. But understanding the way deception works in the conservative information system is a vital step in addressing the United States' vulnerabilities to election disinformation campaigns. Most deception about elections comes from within the United States, not from foreign actors. There is an information environment that incubates and metastasizes disinformation campaigns, as well as a sizable portion of the electorate that welcomes such deception. Any project that seeks to enhance election security, broadly conceived, in the United States and address disinformation must start there.

NOTES

1 Deen Freelon and Chris Wells, "Disinformation as Political Communication," *Political Communication* 26, no. 2 (Spring 2021): 145–56.

2 Dan Tynan, "How Facebook Powers Money Machines for Obscure Political 'News' Sites," *The Guardian*, August 24, 2016, www.theguardian.com; Heather C. Hughes and Israel Waismel-Manor, "The Macedonian Fake News Industry and the 2016 US Election," *PS: Political Science and Politics* 54, no. 1 (January 2021): 19–23; Rachel Kuo and Alice Marwick, "Critical Disinformation Studies: History, Power, and Politics," *Harvard Kennedy School Misinformation Review*, August 12, 2021, https://doi.org; Election Infrastructure Government Coordinating Council and Subsector Coordinating Council's Joint Mis/Disinformation Working Group, *Mis-, Dis-, and Malinformation: Planning and Incident Response Guide for Election Officials*, accessed January 22, 2024, www.cisa.gov.

3 Paul Starr, *The Creation of the Media: Political Origins of Modern Communications* (New York: Basic Books, 2004); Richard R. John, *Spreading the News: The American Postal System from Franklin to Morse* (Cambridge, MA: Harvard University Press, 1995); Michael Schudson, *The Rise of the Right to Know: Politics and the Culture of Transparency, 1945–1975* (Cambridge, MA: Harvard University Press, 2015); Stéphane Goldstein, ed., *Informed Societies: Why Information Literacy Matters for Citizenship, Participation and Democracy* (London: Facet, 2020).

4 Richard L. Kaplan, *Politics and the American Press: The Rise of Objectivity, 1865–1920* (New York: Cambridge University Press, 2002); Michael Schudson, *Discovering the News: A Social History of American Newspapers* (New York: Basic Books, 1978); David T. Z. Mindich, *Just the Facts: How Objectivity Came to Define American Journalism* (New York: New York University Press, 1998).

5 Matthew Mosk and Avis Thomas-Lester, "GOP Fliers Apparently Were Part of Strategy," *Washington Post*, November 13, 2006.
6 Gilda R. Daniels, "Voter Deception," *Indiana Law Review* 43 (2010): 343–87.
7 Deceptive Practices and Voter Intimidation Prevention Act of 2006, S. 4069, 109th Congress, 2006.
8 Deceptive Practices and Voter Intimidation Prevention Act of 2019, S. 1834, 116th Congress, 2019.
9 Gilda R. Daniels, *Uncounted: The Crisis of Voting Suppression in America* (New York: New York University Press, 2020), 102–5.
10 Richard J. Meislin, "Jersey Controversy Widens over G.O.P. Patrols at Polls," *New York Times*, November 7, 1981, 25.
11 Jane Perlez, "Coalition in Jersey Seeks Evidence of Voters' Fears," *New York Times*, November 16, 1981, B1; Jon Margolis, "Democrats Charge GOP 'Force' in Suit over New Jersey Voting," *Chicago Tribune*, December 15, 1981, A2.
12 Carol Anderson, *One Person, No Vote: How Voter Suppression Is Destroying Our Democracy* (New York: Bloomsbury, 2018); Ari Berman, *Give Us the Ballot! The Modern Struggle for Voting Rights in America* (New York: Farrar, Straus and Giroux, 2015).
13 Daniel Martinez HoSang, *Racial Propositions: Ballot Initiatives and the Making of Postwar California* (Berkeley: University of California Press, 2010), chap. 6; Andrew Wroe, *The Republican Party and Immigration Politics: From Proposition 187 to George W. Bush* (New York: Palgrave Macmillan, 2008); Robin Dale Jacobson, *The New Nativism: Proposition 187 and the Debate over Immigration* (Minneapolis: University of Minnesota Press, 2008).
14 Dave Lesher, "Huffington, Alleging Fraud, May Take Case to Senate," *Los Angeles Times*, November 29, 1994, A1.
15 Kaplan, *Politics and the American Press*; Mindich, *Just the Facts*.
16 Nicole Hemmer, *Messengers of the Right: Conservative Media and the Transformation of American Politics* (Philadelphia: University of Pennsylvania Press, 2016).
17 Mark Major, "Objective but Not Impartial: *Human Events*, Barry Goldwater, and the Development of the 'Liberal Media' in the Conservative Counter-sphere," *New Political Science* 34, no. 4 (2012): 455–68.
18 Hemmer, *Messengers of the Right*, chap. 8.
19 Elizabeth Mendes, "In U.S., Trust in Media Recovers Slightly from All-Time Low," Gallup, September 19, 2013, https://news.gallup.com.
20 Jim Rutenberg and Kate Zernike, "CBS Apologizes for Report on Bush Guard Service," *New York Times*, September 21, 2004.
21 Siva Vaidhyanathan, *Anti-social Media: How Facebook Disconnects Us and Undermines Democracy* (New York: Oxford University Press, 2018).
22 Sam Lebovic, "Fake News, Lies, and Other Familiar Problems," Knight First Amendment Institute, Columbia University, November 18, 2022, https://knightcolumbia.org.

23 Katie Glueck, Michael S. Schmidt, and Mike Isaac, "Dubious Ukraine Report Rejected by Biden Campaign and Social Media Sites," *New York Times*, October 15, 2020.

24 David Gilbert, "Facebook Failed Miserably in Its Attempt to Stop the Hunter Biden Story," *Vice News*, October 23, 2020, www.vice.com; Kari Paul, "'Fundamentally Dangerous': Reversal of Social Media Guardrails Could Prove Disastrous for 2024 Elections," *The Guardian*, June 10, 2023, www.theguardian.com.

5

AFTER THE CIVIL RIGHTS REVOLUTION

THOMAS B. EDSALL

If we were to try to put a date on the origin of contemporary political polarization, a strong candidate would be July 2, 1964, the day that President Lyndon Johnson signed the Civil Rights Act. Johnson's support of the law as the Democratic nominee for president, and the opposition to the law by the Republican nominee, Barry Goldwater, forever changed the politics of race in America. As Edward G. Carmines and James A. Stimson documented in their 1989 book *Issue Evolution: Race and the Transformation of American Politics*,[1] voters first began to distinguish between the two parties on race during the 1964 presidential campaign. Democrats became the party of racial liberalism and Republicans the party of racial conservatism.

I documented this shift in my 1992 book *Chain Reaction*, as issues of race exerted ever-greater pressure on American politics:

> In the immediate aftermath of the 1964 election, a majority of American voters appeared ready to repudiate the ideology of the Goldwater wing of the Republican party, and proceed to the second stage of a liberal revolution: to move government beyond what had been achieved by the New Deal, toward genuine equal opportunity for blacks, Hispanics and other minorities by conducting a major assault on poverty on behalf of a more equitable, color-blind system of economic distribution. . . .

> An ascendant liberalism reached its postwar zenith on August 5, 1965, when Johnson signed into law the Voting Rights Act. . . . Within a year exclusive white control of elections was broken. . . . Johnson declared at the signing ceremony . . . [that] "Today we strike away the last major shackle of those fierce and ancient bonds."
>
> Six days later, on August 11, rioting broke out in the Watts section of . . . Los Angeles. Five days of violent, televised disorder opened the first major fissure in the consensus behind Democratic racial liberalism. Watts provided unmistakable evidence that the drive to achieve black equality would have tremendous costs as well as tremendous rewards. Watts forced acknowledgement of a new reality: that passage of civil rights legislation was not adequate to either assuage black anger, nor to produce the relatively trouble-free integration of the races that had been anticipated by many liberals.[2]

The Watts riots were the first of a chain of events that would push a substantial segment of the American electorate to the right. This chain of events included the following:

- ghetto riots
- the emergence of a separatist Black Power movement
- an abrupt rise in rates of Black crime and children born out of wedlock
- the shift of civil rights protests to the North, where traditionally Democratic voters became polarized on issues of busing and open housing
- an uprising among the nation's college-educated youth that challenged the Vietnam War, conventions of academic discipline, and traditional restrictions surrounding sex and drugs
- the emergence of the women's rights movement and the broader rights revolution
- the surfacing of white backlash as a powerful political force
- the emergence of conflict between white elected officials and Black protest leaders, fostered by the War on Poverty
- an unprecedented surge in the number of applicants for welfare
- intensified demands from Black people for jobs in two beseiged institutions under the control of white Democrats—the labor unions and city hall

The partisan restructuring driven by the post–civil rights racial realignment was soon reinforced by the women's rights and sexual revolutions. Elites, primarily elected officials, began to take stands consistently in favor of or opposed to these three movements. Leaders were soon followed by voters in a sorting process that incrementally but consistently steered Democrats and Republicans into two warring camps.

Over time, this sorting process took on a momentum of its own, propelled by demographics, strategic innovation in election design, and the transforming ideological commitments of the media. As I wrote in 1992, "liberalism had unleashed forces that its leaders could neither control nor keep within the confines of traditional political negotiation, and the once-dominant left-center coalition began to crack."[3] This manifested as voters geographically repositioned themselves by partisanship. The well educated became Democrats and the less well educated became Republicans. Political operatives capitalized on hostility with negative campaigning and microtargeting. Religiosity and morality became sources of political conflict. The media began to divide left or right. Changes in campaign finance law empowered donors with extreme views. Once the party of Wall Street and Main Street, the GOP increasingly became the party of the "left behind," while Democrats, once the party of the working class, became an upstairs-downstairs coalition of relatively affluent white people and predominantly downstairs minorities.

Why would the issues raised by the civil rights movement, the women's rights movement, and the sexual revolution polarize the electorate? These issues brought to the forefront of politics seemingly irreconcilable conflicts that steadily displaced traditional partisan struggles over taxation, spending, and the size of government—issues more amenable to negotiation and compromise.

The older disputes of the New Deal era could be resolved through compromise. The benefits of a tax cut could be shared between the working and upper classes, business and labor; spending could be cut in some places, raised in others. That proved not to be the case in the debates over race, gender, and sex. The relentless nature of such disputes—abortion is a prime example—resists compromise.

There are exceptions. In 2004, George W. Bush successfully used opposition to gay marriage to build his margins against John Kerry. Eight years later, Barack Obama successfully campaigned as a proponent of gay marriage to defeat Mitt Romney. Gay marriage now has the support of a majority of Americans, but the same cannot be said about gender fluidity.[4] If anything, opposition to gender transition has been growing.

In fact, the overall arc of change from 1964 to this writing in early 2024 is from a period of relative consensus, with both parties having a right and a left wing, to the situation now: a Democratic Party split between an upstairs wing and a downstairs wing, and a Republican Party increasingly under the control of election deniers and Christian extremists.

Crucial early developments in the sexual and women's rights revolutions proved to be controversial. These included the introduction of oral contraception in 1961[5] and the promotion of women's rights as evidenced by the 1963 publication of *The Feminine Mystique* by Betty Friedan.[6] Interestingly, Republicans in the early days provided feminists with substantial support—reflected in the 1971 House and 1972 Senate votes for the Equal Rights Amendment (ERA). The House approved the ERA 354–24, with Democrats voting 217–12 in support and Republicans also voting 137–12 in favor. The Senate followed suit, approving the ERA 84–8, with Democrats voting 46–2 and Republicans 37–5.[7]

Polarization on cultural and gender issues was not abrupt. It took over a decade for the Republican Party to stake out an explicitly conservative stance on women's rights. A key development came in 1972, when Phyllis Schlafly, a conservative firebrand and author of the 1964 pro-Goldwater book *A Choice Not an Echo*, founded the powerful Eagle Forum.[8] *Roe v. Wade* in 1973 gave Schlafly a powerful mobilizing tool, and she demonstrated her influence at the 1976 Republican Convention when the party adopted an abortion plank that declared, "The Republican Party favors a continuance of the public dialogue on abortion and supports the efforts of those who seek enactment of a constitutional amendment to restore protection of the right to life for unborn children."[9]

By 1978, Republican support for the ERA had begun to implode. When Congress voted to approve a thirty-nine-month extension of the deadline to win approval in two-thirds of the states, Democrats in the Senate voted 41–15 in favor of the legislation, but a majority of Republicans, 21–16, were opposed.[10] In the House, the collapse of Republican support was more striking, as Republicans voted 103–41 against extension while Democrats backed it 192–86.[11] Women's rights had, in effect, become a partisan issue.

There was also a backlash to the sexual revolution, a counterrevolution that enabled not only Schlafly but other entrepreneurs of the Right, such as Jerry Falwell, who founded the Moral Majority in 1979; Paul Weyrich, who created the Free Congress Foundation in 1977; and Marion G. "Pat" Robertson, who set up the Christian Broadcasting Network in 1960, to become powerful agents of cultural conservatism within the Republican Party.

Issues including crime and punishment, spending on welfare, safety net programs for the poor, and abortion—which soon became a litmus test for presidential candidates in both parties—all became divisive.

Partisan elites, particularly members of Congress, began to polarize on such issues in the early and mid-1970s. DW-Nominate scores,[12] measuring the degree of difference in the voting patterns of Republican and Democratic members of the House and Senate, show the divide starting in roughly the 1972–75 period and steadily widening thereafter.[13]

* * *

A more recent phenomenon, ideological polarization, is closely related to but distinct from what scholars call affective polarization:[14] growing animosity toward members of the opposition party and greater warmth toward members of one's own party.

A common measure of affective polarization in the electorate is based on a thermometer scale in which voters rate their own party and the opposition from 0 (cold) to 100 (warm). American National Election Studies data show ratings of opposition parties holding steady in the mid-40s from 1976 to 1990, then show a modest but steady decline from 46.7 in 1990 to 41.6 in 2000.[15] At that point, affective polarization begins to ramp up as the opposition party thermometer rating steadily falls, reaching 19.3 in 2020.

Republicans have been widely portrayed as prime drivers of conservatism, based in large part on the sharper movement to the right among Republican members of the House and Senate, compared with the more modest shift to the left among their Democratic counterparts.

As Thomas Mann and Norman Ornstein wrote in their 2013 book *It's Even Worse Than It Looks: How the American Constitutional System Collided with the New Politics of Extremism*, "The Republican Party has become an insurgent outlier—ideologically extreme; contemptuous of the inherited social and economic policy regime; scornful of compromise;

unpersuaded by conventional understanding of facts, evidence and science; and dismissive of the legitimacy of its political opposition."[16]

Mann and Ornstein were on target at the time of their writing, but what their analysis failed to consider is that the larger social trends on race, women's rights, and sex were all moving in a decidedly liberal direction, provoking a reaction from those constituencies on the Right that were most threatened by these changes.

In this context, it was the Left, regardless of how morally justified, and not the Right, that initiated the process of pushing these issues to the forefront of political competition. The Right in this context was reacting, no matter how unwarranted the reaction, to an assault, no matter how warranted, from the Left.

The Mann-Ornstein analysis preceded, and thus could not take into account, the very recent sharp shift to the left among Democratic voters, especially white Democrats—in many respects a reaction to the Trump presidency.

In a February 2023 essay, Alan Abramowitz, a professor of political science at Emory, wrote, "The divide between supporters of the two parties has increased considerably since 2012 and most of this increase was due to a sharp leftward shift among Democratic voters. Between 2012 and 2020, the mean score for Democratic voters on a 7-point scale [1 denoting a voter's complete ideological identification as "liberal" and 7 as "conservative"] went from 3.3 to 2.9 while the mean score for Republican voters went from 5.4 to 5.5. . . . The most significant trend in attitudes on these issues has been a dramatic shift to the left among white Democrats."[17]

Two closely linked developments proved crucial in the recent history of polarization. The first is the growth of what's called "issue consistency"—the adoption of consistently liberal or consistently conservative stands on issues, first by political elites, then filtering down into the larger electorate. This marked a substantial divergence from the 1960s and early 1970s when there were, for example, significant numbers of pro-life Democrats and pro–civil rights Republicans.

The second development is the conversion of partisanship from one of many facets of a voter's sense of self to a core or central aspect of a voter's experienced identity, rising from the middle to the top of the list of how one would self-identify.[18]

As growing shares of the electorate have adopted either consistently Democratic or consistently Republican stands on a whole gamut of issues,[19] it has become increasingly clear that American politics is a competition between two separate groups or clusters, each with an antithetical agenda. Where once there was a substantial common ground in Congress and in state legislatures, with conservative Democrats further to the right than liberal Republicans, the two parties have drifted apart, with a no-man's-land separating them. The most liberal Republican in the House of Representatives is now well to the right of the most conservative Democrat.[20]

While the United States stands apart in the salience of race as a polarizing force, it shares with many other European countries the rise of political populism, especially a form of conservative populism that stresses race- and ethnicity-inflected opposition to immigration. "The Far Right is winning Europe's immigration debate: mainstream parties are adopting increasingly radical positions—at their own expense," journalist Anchal Vohra reported on November 1, 2023, in *Foreign Policy* magazine.[21]

Lilliana Mason, a political scientist at Johns Hopkins University, describes this process in a 2016 paper, "A Cross-Cutting Calm: How Social Sorting Drives Affective Polarization":

> It is a primal response to the mega-partisan identity that arises when our social identities all join partisan teams, leaving behind the cross-cutting identities that have previously soothed our emotional reactions. The more sorted we become, the more emotionally we react to normal political events. The anger on display in modern politics is powerfully fueled by our increasing social isolation. As Americans continue to sort into socially homogeneous partisan teams, we should expect to see an emptying out of the emotionally unfazed population of cross-pressured partisans. This should lead to wilder emotional reactions, no matter how much we may truly agree on specific policies.[22]

Along similar lines, five political scientists—Shanto Iyengar, Yphtach Lelkes, Matthew Levendusky, Neil Malhotra, and Sean J. Westwood—write in their 2019 article "The Origins and Consequences of Affective Polarization in the United States,"

> Several features of the contemporary environment have exacerbated partisans' proclivity to divide the world into a liked in group (one's own party) and a disliked out group (the opposing party). First, in the last 50 years, the percentage of sorted partisans, i.e., partisans who identify with the party most closely reflecting their ideology, has steadily increased. When most Democrats are liberals and most Republicans are conservatives, copartisans are less likely to encounter conflicting political ideas and identities and are more likely to see non-identifiers as socially distant. Sorting likely leads people to perceive both opposing partisans and copartisans as more extreme than they really are, with misperceptions about opposing partisans being more acute. As partisan and ideological identities became increasingly aligned, other salient social identities, including race and religion, also converged with partisanship. White evangelicals, for instance, are overwhelmingly Republican today, and African Americans overwhelmingly identify as Democrats. This decline of cross-cutting identities is at the root of affective polarization, according to Mason. She has shown that those with consistent partisan and ideological identities became more hostile toward the out party without necessarily changing their ideological positions, and those who have aligned religious, racial, and partisan identities react more emotionally to information that threatens their partisan identities or issue stances. In essence, sorting has made it much easier for partisans to make generalized inferences about the opposing side, even if those inferences are inaccurate.[23]

The changing makeup of the media environment, the rise of social media, the advent of intensely partisan online outlets, and the growing perception of the mainstream media as liberal have all accelerated cultural antagonism.[24]

The intensifying linkage between partisanship and individual identity has added a new dimension to political competition. Losing means that power has shifted to an enemy determined to dismantle, if not destroy, the principles, tenets, beliefs, and values on which the voter forms his or her identity.

Pollsters have measured the growth and strength of affective polarization. In an August 2022 report, "As Partisan Hostility Grows, Signs of Frustration with the Two-Party System,"[25] the Pew Research Center found that in the relatively short period from 2016 to 2022, the percentage of Democrats who described Republicans as "close-minded" grew from 70 to 83 percent, as "dishonest" from 42 to 64 percent, and as "immoral" from 35 to 63 percent. Republicans' negative views of Democrats on these measures grew by similar percentages.

The same Pew study found that the percentage of Republicans holding a "very unfavorable" view of the Democratic Party grew from 21 percent in 1994 to 62 percent in 2022. Democrats holding a "very unfavorable" view of the Republican Party grew over the same period from 17 to 54 percent.

The disputed elections of 2000 (Bush v. Gore) and 2020 (Biden v. Trump) both exacerbated levels of distrust while further distancing the parties from each other—heightening the danger of more aggressive rejection of results in future contests.

Immediately after the Supreme Court decision in *Bush v. Gore*, Matthew Dowd, Bush's director of polling, found that the swing vote—those who could be persuaded to vote for either candidate—had shrunk to 4–6 percent of the electorate.[26] That meant that it had become far more cost effective to turn out every possible partisan than to spend millions on winning a very small percentage—only 1 or 2 points—of undecided voters. That, in turn, shifted the thrust of campaigns to micro targeting, deploying intensely polarizing themes to motivate supporters who might otherwise fail to turn out.

* * *

Three powerful, overlapping trends now reinforce partisan division: educational, geographic, and economic polarization.

The division between those with and without college degrees is most acute among white people. In a September 2023 paper, William Marble, a political scientist at the University of Pennsylvania, writes, "Over the past 40 years, and especially since 2000, there has been a realignment along educational lines among white voters. College-educated whites are now a reliable voting bloc for Democrats in presidential elections, while whites without a college degree are an increasingly solid Republican voting bloc."[27] To back up his argument, Marble writes, "In 1992, George H.W. Bush captured about 45% of the two-party vote among white voters without a college degree—compared to 52% among white college-educated voters. In 2020, Donald Trump captured nearly 65%

of the two-party vote among non-college whites, compared to just 42% among whites with college degrees."[28] How did this reversal come about? "White college-educated voters have become increasingly liberal on economic issues, pushing them toward the Democratic party. Simultaneously, non-college voters have come to base their voting decisions more heavily on their conservative cultural attitudes. Together, these two trends account for the observed realignment."[29]

The geographic realignment echoes and reinforces the educational realignment. Urban America, where a high percentage of voters have college degrees, is decisively Democratic. In rural America, where voters are disproportionately non–college educated, Republicans predominate. The majority of members of both parties live in the suburbs, which have become the nation's political battleground.

Comparing the geographic patterns of Bill Clinton's victory in 1992 and Hillary Clinton's defeat in 2016 provides a demonstration of the emergence in recent years of these geographically anchored schisms. Bill Clinton won 1,519 counties to 1,582 carried by George H. W. Bush. There was only a modest urban-rural partisan division.

In 2016, Hillary Clinton won majorities in 490 counties, almost all dense and urban, while Trump was victorious in 2,622 counties, almost all of them exurban or rural. A map of the 1992 election shows red and blue counties spread across the country. A map of the 2016 contest shows Democratic victories concentrated on the coasts and in metropolitan centers across the middle of the country, which, except for middle American urban blue islands, forms a sea of red.[30]

A growing economic divide, in turn, overlays the educational and geographic polarizations. Mark Muro, a senior fellow at Brookings, and his colleagues have documented the very different economic paths of red and blue America.[31]

In the 2000 election, Al Gore won 659 counties, which in turn produced 54 percent of the gross domestic product. George W. Bush won 2,397 counties (less densely populated than the Gore counties), which accounted for 46 percent of GDP.

In the 2020 election, the 520 counties that cast majorities for Joe Biden produced 71 percent of GDP, while the 2,564 Trump counties produced 29 percent. In other words, economic wealth in Democratic counties vastly exceeds wealth in Republican counties: the spread between red and blue America grew from 8 percentage points of GDP in 2000 to 42 percentage points in 2020.

More importantly, these three trends—educational, geographic, and economic—reveal a fundamental change in the character of the Republican and Democratic electorates.

The traditional reputation of Republicans as the party of the economically successful and the Democrats as the party of the most economically stressed has been reversed as voters in Republican counties are now having the most difficulty coping with America's transition away from manufacturing. Democratic counties, in contrast, have thrived under globalization.

The same reversal has occurred in the case of class. Republicans now have a much stronger claim to be the party of the working class than Democrats.

William Frey, another demographer at Brookings, captured the results of the class, education, and economic realignments of the two parties in a January 2021 paper, "Biden-Won Counties Are Home to 67 Million More Americans Than Trump-Won Counties."[32]

Frey found, for example, that 62 percent of voters without a high school degree lived in Trump counties, while, at the other end of the spectrum, 64 percent of college graduates lived in Biden counties.

In a reflection of the growing upscale profile of the Democratic electorate, Frey's data show that 68 percent of households making $150,000 to $200,000 and 75 percent of those making more than $200,000 are in Biden counties.

* * *

Over the past three decades, political polarization has continued to intensify. American National Election Studies data measuring the thermometer rating of the two parties show a steady and substantial increase in affective polarization. Virtually all of the increase was in negative views of the opposition party, a central aspect of affective polarization. Put another way, affection for one's own party has remained steady while hostility toward one's adversaries has grown by leaps and bounds.

This essay began by arguing that the cumulative energies driving political polarization in this country since the 1960s originated in racial conflict. The divergence of political attitudes away from the center toward ideological extremes subsequently metastasized into every corner of American politics and policy.

Of the 222 current Republicans in the House, 179, or 80.6 percent, either explicitly denied the outcome of the 2020 election or repeatedly expressed serious doubts.[33] A July 2023 CNN poll found that 69 percent of Republican voters and voters who lean toward the Republican Party believe that Donald Trump won that election—despite overwhelming, irrefutable evidence to the contrary—and that the election of Joe Biden was illegitimate.[34]

Adam Przeworski, a political scientist at New York University, argues that "democracy is a system in which parties lose elections. There are parties: divisions of interests, values, and opinions. There is competition, organized by rules. And there are periodic winners and losers."[35] In rejecting the outcome of the 2020 election, and clearly intending to carry the threat of such a denial forward into 2024, Republicans are challenging these fundamental principles of democracy.

The Republican Party has adopted as its central goal the protection of white hegemony. Faced with inexorable demographic forces that push the goal of white hegemony increasingly out of reach, the Republican Party and its leaders have come to realize they cannot achieve that goal other than by laying siege to the foundations of American democracy.

NOTES

1 Edward G. Carmines and James A. Stimson, *Issue Evolution: Race and the Transformation of American Politics* (Princeton, NJ: Princeton University Press, 1989).
2 Thomas Byrne Edsall, *Chain Reaction: The Impact of Race, Rights, and Taxes on American Politics*, with Mary D. Edsall (New York: Norton, 1992), 48–49.
3 Edsall, *Chain Reaction*, 49.
4 Justin McCarthy, "U.S. Same-Sex Marriage Support Holds at 71% High," Gallup, July 7, 2023, https://news.gallup.com.
5 Audiey Kao, "History of Oral Contraception," *AMA Journal of Ethics* 2, no. 6 (2000): 55–56, https://doi.org.
6 Betty Friedan, *The Feminine Mystique* (New York: W. W. Norton, 1963).
7 "Roll Call Votes: House Vote #197 in 1971 (92nd Congress), to Pass H.J. Res. 208," GovTrack, October 12, 1971, www.govtrack.us.
8 Donald T. Critchlow, *Phyllis Schlafly and Grassroots Conservatism: A Woman's Crusade* (Princeton, NJ: Princeton University Press, 2005).

9 "Republican Party Platform of 1976," August 18, 1976, American Presidency Project, University of California–Santa Barbara, www.presidency.ucsb.edu.
10 *CQ Almanac* 1978, 66th ed. (Washington, DC: CQ-Roll Call Group, 1978), 66-S, http://library.cqpress.com.
11 *CQ Almanac*, 176-H.
12 Keith T. Poole, Howard Rosenthal, and Boris Shor, "About the Project," Voteview .com, accessed January 23, 2024, https://voteview.com.
13 Royce Carroll et al., "DW-NOMINATE Scores with Bootstrapped Standard Errors," Voteview.com, updated September 2, 2015, https://legacy.voteview.com.
14 Lilliana Mason, "A Cross-Cutting Calm: How Social Sorting Drives Affective Polarization," *Public Opinion Quarterly* 80, S1 (2016): 351–77, www.jstor.org; Shanto Iyengar et al., "The Origins and Consequences of Affective Polarization in the United States," *Annual Review of Political Science* 22 (May 2019): 129–46, https://doi.org.
15 "The ANES Guide to Public Opinion and Electoral Behavior," American National Election Studies, November 29, 2023, https://electionstudies.org.
16 Thomas E. Mann and Norman J. Ornstein, *It's Even Worse Than It Looks: How the American Constitutional System Collided with the New Politics of Extremism* (New York: Basic Books, 2013).
17 Alan I. Abramowitz, "Both White and Nonwhite Democrats Are Moving Left: Race, Party, and Ideological Congruence in the American Electorate," Sabato's Crystal Ball, Center for Politics, University of Virginia, February 15, 2023, https://centerforpolitics.org.
18 "Political Polarization in the American Public, Section 1: Growing Ideological Consistency," Pew Research Center, June 12, 2014, www.pewresearch.org.
19 Alan I. Abramowitz, "The Polarized American Electorate: The Rise of Partisan-Ideological Consistency and Its Consequences," *Political Science Quarterly* 137, no. 4 (Winter 2022): 645–74, https://academic.oup.com.
20 Drew DeSilver, "The Polarization in Today's Congress Has Roots That Go Back Decades," Pew Research Center, March 10, 2022, www.pewresearch.org.
21 Anchal Vohra, "The Far Right Is Winning Europe's Immigration Debate," *Foreign Policy*, November 1, 2023, https://foreignpolicy.com.
22 Mason, "Cross-Cutting Calm," 370.
23 Iyengar et al., "Origins and Consequences," 134.
24 Robert J. Barro, "The Liberal Media: It's No Myth," *Business Week*, June 14, 2004, https://scholar.harvard.edu.
25 "As Partisan Hostility Grows, Signs of Frustration with the Two-Party System," Pew Research Center, August 9, 2022, www.pewresearch.org.
26 Thomas Byrne Edsall, *Building Red America: The New Conservative Coalition and the Drive for Permanent Power* (New York: Basic Books, 2007).
27 William Marble, "What Explains the Educational Polarization among White Voters?," williammarble.co, September 2023, 40, https://williammarble.co.
28 Marble, 1.

29 Marble, 3.
30 Thomas B. Edsall, "Reaching Out to the Voters the Left Left Behind," *New York Times*, April 13, 2017, www.nytimes.com.
31 Mark Muro and Sifan Liu, "Another Trump-Clinton Divide," Brookings Institution, November 29, 2016, www.brookings.edu; Mark Muro et al., "Biden-Voting Counties Equal 71 Percent of the Economy," Brookings Institution, November 10, 2020, www.brookings.edu.
32 William Frey, "Biden-Won Counties Are Home to 67 Million More Americans Than Trump-Won Counties," Brookings Institution, January 21, 2021, www.brookings.edu.
33 Karen Yourish et al., "Which 2020 Election Deniers and Skeptics Won and Lost in the Midterm Elections," *New York Times*, November 10, 2022, www.nytimes.com.
34 Jennifer Agiesta and Ariel Edwards-Levy, "CNN Poll: Percentage of Republicans Who Think Biden's 2020 Win Was Illegitimate Ticks Back Up Near 70%," CNN, August 3, 2023, www.cnn.com.
35 Adam Przeworski, *Democracy and the Market* (Cambridge: Cambridge University Press, 2012), 10.

PART II

OVERSEEING SECURE ELECTIONS

6

PRESIDENTIAL POWER AND FEDERAL ELECTIONS

TREVOR W. MORRISON

The president of the United States occupies what the Supreme Court has described as "a unique position in the constitutional scheme."[1] As "the chief constitutional officer of the Executive Branch,"[2] he has duties "of unrivaled gravity and breadth," "rang[ing] from faithfully executing the laws to commanding the Armed Forces."[3] Election administration, however, is not among them. Neither the Constitution nor any federal statute grants the president any direct role in the administration of federal elections. Yet as one scholar recently observed, in a variety of more indirect ways that are not always appreciated, "the President . . . routinely exercises control over elections."[4] This chapter discusses some illustrative dimensions of that control and considers important limitations on it as well.

Part of the undertaking here will relate to the familiar problem of self-dealing in American election law. Because virtually all of the rules for how elections are conducted are made by elected officials who are often candidates in those very elections, there is a risk that incumbents will manipulate the rules for their own electoral advantage.[5] This phenomenon is perhaps most acute when it comes to state legislators who draw the electoral maps governing their own races. By configuring their districts to include more voters likely to support them, incumbents can entrench themselves in a way that violates "the core principle of republican government, namely, that the voters should choose their representatives, not the other way around."[6]

The president has no direct role in electoral boundary setting or election administration. Perhaps for that reason, until recently little sustained attention has been paid to whether and in what ways the self-dealing problem applies to the presidency.[7] But especially in the aftermath of the 2020 presidential election and attempts by former president Donald Trump and his supporters to overturn its results, those questions call out for attention.

LEGAL AND PRACTICAL FRAMEWORK

Federal election administration is decentralized in the American system. The Constitution grants the states, not the federal government, the default responsibility for setting the rules for federal elections.[8] But Congress also has the authority to pass laws preempting state rules for federal elections, enforcing federal constitutional rights in the electoral context, and defining and punishing various election-related crimes.[9] It has exercised that authority to pass a range of important statutes on matters ranging from election fraud to voting rights to campaign finance. In contrast, the text of the Constitution makes no express provision for the president to play a role in elections, but neither does it expressly prohibit him from acting in that space.

Against this backdrop, how should we think about the role of the president in this area? In his landmark concurring opinion in *Youngstown Sheet & Tube Co. v. Sawyer*,[10] Justice Robert Jackson outlined what has become the dominant framework for evaluating assertions of presidential authority. As Jackson put it, "Presidential powers are not fixed but fluctuate, depending upon their disjunction or conjunction with those of Congress."[11] Thus, the president's authority is at its maximum when he acts "pursuant to the express or implied authorization of Congress"; it is at its "lowest ebb" when he takes actions that are "incompatible with the express or implied will of Congress"; and when he acts "in absence of either a congressional grant or denial of authority, he can only rely upon his own independent powers," which may overlap with the legislative power of Congress, rendering this space a "zone of twilight" not always susceptible to clear legal line-drawing.[12]

In the first instance, therefore, the question whether the president may take or direct a particular action in relation to federal elections depends on whether Congress has empowered him (or any other executive official subject to presidential direction) to act.

With the basic legal question thus framed, it is important also to observe that there is a difference between the formal powers granted to the president by law and the practical necessities for exercising that power. As Richard Neustadt explained, "The President of the United States has an extraordinary range of formal powers, or authority in statute law and in the Constitution," yet he "does not obtain results by giving orders—or not, at any rate, merely by giving orders."[13] Instead, he must also convince others (sometimes those serving in his administration, sometimes the public more broadly) to act as he wants them to act. In that sense, as Neustadt famously put it, "presidential power is the power to persuade."[14] True, if the people the president seeks to persuade can be removed from office by him, he can threaten that consequence if they do not follow his wishes. In the ordinary course of governing, express threats of that sort are rarely needed, in part because presidential appointees to high executive office almost always share the president's core policy aims. Still, the possibility of removal likely does have some persuasive power. And yet it won't always be enough. If presidential appointees to a given position are serially unwilling to take certain actions favored by the president, his failure to persuade them will undermine his ability to pursue his goals. Moreover, repeatedly removing recalcitrant appointees may impose a political cost on the president, which could itself constrain him.

Applied to the election context, the point is that the president's need to persuade others in order to achieve his aims operates as a constraint on his practical ability to engage in election interference. If a president tries to use the power of his office to change electoral outcomes (whether his own or others), he will not succeed unless other actors (including his immediate advisers, key officials across the executive branch, and perhaps state and local officials) are willing to follow his orders and accede to his requests.

DELEGATED AUTHORITY

In the most significant study of the president's powers relating to elections, Lisa Marshall Manheim divides statutory grants of such authority into three categories: laws that directly authorize the president to take certain actions not necessarily related to elections but that he might use to address election-related matters; laws relating to elections that are enforced by executive agencies (like the Department of Justice) whose heads are appointed and removable by the president; and laws granting authority to independent agencies specifically devoted to election-related matters (like the Federal Election Commission) whose heads are not subject to at-will removal by the president but may be subject to more informal modes of presidential influence.[15] Without purporting to be comprehensive, this chapter will offer some observations about the first and second categories just mentioned.[16]

STATUTES GRANTING POWERS DIRECTLY TO THE PRESIDENT

As noted earlier, no federal statute assigns the president a role in election administration. However, a number of statutes grant authorities to the president during times of declared national emergency, and at least some of those authorities can be used in ways that relate to election security. Altogether, there are 123 different statutory powers that the president may exercise pursuant to an emergency declaration.[17] The process for making those declarations is governed by the National Emergencies Act,[18] which was intended to impose some degree of discipline and limits on emergency declarations. For a variety of reasons, it has not had that effect. For example, the act provides that emergency declarations automatically expire after one year unless they are renewed, but renewal has become routine across administrations. Indeed, by the summer of 2020 there were thirty-eight declared national emergencies in effect, with the oldest dating back to the 1979 Iranian hostage crisis.[19]

The most frequently invoked emergency authorities are found in the International Emergency Economic Powers Act (IEEPA).[20] Among other things, IEEPA provides that if the president declares the existence of an "unusual and extraordinary threat . . . to the national security, foreign policy, or economy of the United States" that originates outside the country, he may thereafter wield an array of economic powers to do things like block transactions and freeze assets in order to address the threat.[21] IEEPA says nothing explicit about elections, but Presidents Barack Obama, Trump, and Joe Biden all invoked it to issue executive orders relating to election security. The differences among the three orders reflect the divergent priorities of the three administrations.

Obama issued his order in December 2016, in the aftermath of a presidential election beset by concerns about election interference by foreign actors, especially Russia. The Obama order blocked transactions and froze assets of people linked to "significant malicious cyber-enabled activities" connected with "undermin[ing] democratic processes or institutions."[22] Obama was explicit that he imposed the order in response to Russian interference in the 2016 election,[23] although its timing obviously made it impossible for the order to affect that election. Moreover, because it came at the very end of the Obama administration, the order's main effect was to set the status quo for the beginning of the Trump administration.

Trump, however, did not share Obama's priorities, suggesting that it was "time for our country to move on to bigger and better things."[24] Indeed, as one member of Congress put it, attempts to raise the election interference issue were "met with hostility by a President who views any discussion of election security as a threat to his legitimacy."[25] (A parallel pattern may be found in the contrast between the Department of Homeland Security's designation, at the end of the Obama administration, of election infrastructure as "critical," thus triggering a set of requirements to treat election infrastructure as a priority for cybersecurity protection and assurance, and the relative neglect of that issue in the first part of the Trump administration, at the apparent behest of the White House.)[26] Ultimately, Trump did issue his own executive order on election security in 2018,[27] but it was widely criticized as weak and ineffective and appeared to generate no significant new sanctions.[28]

Biden's executive order, signed in April 2021, adopted a stance similar to Obama's, though it was part of a broader set of sanctions against Russian entities and affiliates, in connection with a broader set of concerns.[29] Relating to elections, the Biden order based its declaration of an emergency in part on a finding that the Russian government had made "efforts to undermine the conduct of free and fair democratic elections and democratic institutions in the United States and its allies and partners."[30] In response, the order froze assets and blocked transactions of any person who, acting on Russia's behalf or for its benefit, is deemed to have "interfere[d] in a United States or other foreign government election," or to be responsible for "actions or policies that undermine democratic processes or institutions in the United States or abroad."[31] In doing so, the order treated Russian attempts at election interference as serious threats to national security, on a par with recent cyberattacks on federal agencies.

The lesson of these contrasting executive orders is that although Congress has granted the president significant emergency powers that could be exercised to respond to certain election security threats, whether and how any given president uses that authority may vary greatly from one administration to the next. This is of course true about differing administrations' policy agendas in general. In that sense, election security is no different from any other issue. Yet at the same time, the way a given administration views a potential threat to election security may be a function not simply of the administration's overall policy views but also of how that threat is likely to affect the incumbent president's (or his copartisans') prospects in the next election. That is the self-dealing risk. Because the president retains extremely broad discretion in deciding whether and how to invoke and exercise the emergency authorities granted to him by statutes like IEEPA, there are few if any formal legal mechanisms for mitigating that risk in this particular context.

That is not to say, however, that any of the president's statutory emergency powers can be invoked to intervene directly in the administration of an election, or to change its outcome. Even construed broadly, the authorities conferred on the president by statutes like IEEPA say no such thing. On this point, one other emergency power statute bears specific mention: the Insurrection Act.

Federal law prohibits using the military "to execute the laws" except where "expressly authorized by the Constitution or Act of Congress."[32] This prohibition reflects the deeply held and longstanding view that the military should not be involved in domestic law enforcement. The Insurrection Act recognizes certain limited exceptions to that rule. Specifically, it provides that the president may deploy the armed forces (1) to suppress an insurrection in a state, if requested to do so by the state's legislature; (2) to enforce federal law if unlawful conduct or "rebellion . . . make it impracticable to enforce" federal law "by the ordinary course of judicial proceedings"; and (3) to enforce the constitutional rights of citizens if an "insurrection [or] domestic violence" in any state infringes on those rights and the state authorities are "unable, fail, or refuse" to protect those rights.[33]

Commentators have lamented the Insurrection Act's "broad and undefined" terms.[34] And in the wake of Trump's threat to use the act to suppress nationwide protests after the 2020 police killing of George Floyd, there have been a number of prominent calls to narrow and clarify the law.[35] More recently, evidence has emerged that Trump may have contemplated invoking the Insurrection Act in late 2020 or early 2021, in order to help him remain in office despite losing the election.[36] Yet whatever ambiguity there may be in some of the Insurrection Act's terms, any attempt to invoke it for those purposes would have been entirely unlawful. As a report of the Brennan Center for Justice explains,

> The purposes for which the Insurrection Act may be used are not infinite. Troops may be deployed to suppress armed insurrections or to execute the laws when local or state authorities are unable or unwilling to do so. Their role is then limited to quelling the violence or removing the obstruction to enforcing the law. The Insurrection Act has significant potential for abuse in the form of federal troops being deployed to suppress political dissent. But invoking it does not put the military "in charge" or suspend the normal functions and authorities of Congress, state legislatures, or the courts. It certainly does not grant the president the power to change the outcome of an election or overstay his term in office.[37]

Trump never did invoke the Insurrection Act, in part because leading members of his own administration were adamant that there was no legal basis for doing so. In Neustadt's terms, Trump did not wield his power to persuade successfully. Instead, the episode provides a profound illustration of the power of senior advisers within the executive branch to stymie presidential attempts to interfere with an election.

In sum, although the Insurrection Act, IEEPA, and a number of other federal statutes empower the president to order a broad range of extraordinary actions during declared emergencies and other crises, and although those authorities may be exercised in certain politically self-serving ways, no statute grants the president any power to control election administration or to change the outcome of an election.

STATUTES ENFORCED OR ADMINISTERED BY EXECUTIVE AGENCIES

Congress has enacted numerous laws relating to elections, especially to voting rights. These include, among others, the Voting Rights Act, the Voting Accessibility for the Elderly and Handicapped Act, the Uniformed and Overseas Citizens Absentee Voting Act, the National Voter Registration Act, and the Help America Vote Act. All of these statutes are enforced by the Civil Rights Division of the Department of Justice.[38] Because the attorney general and the rest of the political leadership of the department are nominated and removable by the president, the president is generally able to exercise a degree of influence over them, including in how they establish enforcement priorities.

Those priorities often have obvious partisan valences. As an illustration, Lisa Manheim offers the example of the department's enforcement of the National Voter Registration Act: "Administrations led by Republican presidents have tended to prioritize enforcement of one set of mandates: those requiring states to remove names from the voting rolls. Administrations led by Democratic presidents have tended to prioritize enforcement of the opposite set of mandates: those requiring states to retain names on the voting rolls. Despite perfunctory claims of neutrality, political appointees in both administrations understand this shift in enforcement prioritization to favor the electoral prospects of one political party over the other."[39]

There is nothing new or surprising about the idea that the arrival of a new presidential administration might affect the enforcement priorities of an executive agency whose head is nominated and removable by the president. Indeed, in broad strokes there is nothing undesirable about it either. As a practical matter, no government agency is in a position to enforce the laws for which it has responsibility in 100 percent of the cases that might implicate them. Some amount of priority setting is inevitable. And when the resulting priorities accord with the policy preferences of the presidential administration then in office, the fact that the president is elected gives those policies democratic legitimacy.[40]

It is one thing for a given presidential administration to favor enforcement priorities that align with its policy commitments. That is surely what a rational voter would expect, just as much for laws relating to elections as for any others. But the picture becomes more complicated when we entertain the possibility that shifts in enforcement priorities, or in the interpretation and implementation of law in nonenforcement contexts, could affect electoral outcomes themselves. As Manheim puts it, "Presidential control over executive agencies affects election rules in ways that, particularly in the aggregate, very well may affect who ultimately wins an election."[41] Admittedly, proving—or disproving—any such causal connection is extremely difficult, perhaps impossible. But shifting patterns in enforcement priorities seem consistent with a *desire* to achieve such results.

The census provides an arguable example.[42] The Constitution requires that the federal government conduct a decennial census to count the number of people residing in the country (and their location in it),[43] and the Census Bureau of the Department of Commerce is responsible for that task. The census has huge electoral implications, as it is used to apportion state representation in the House of Representatives and the presidential Electoral College. Electoral lines within states also must be redrawn after each census.

During the Trump administration, Secretary of Commerce Wilbur Ross announced that the "short form" questionnaire for the 2020 census would ask about each respondent's citizenship status. A citizenship question had been included in the census for many years (in every census but one from 1820 to 1950), but it was removed when the "short form" questionnaire was first implemented in 1960.[44] In the ensuing decades, the Census Bureau took the position that "reintroducing such a question was inadvisable because it would depress the count for already 'hard-to-count' groups—particularly noncitizens and Hispanics—whose members would be less likely to participate in the census for fear that the data could be used against them or their loved ones."[45] That, in turn, would cause the jurisdictions with the greatest "undercount" to be underrepresented in the House of Representatives, the Electoral College, and other institutions whose membership is apportioned according to the census results.

However, if a given administration wanted those jurisdictions to be underrepresented (because, for example, voters in those jurisdictions tended to favor the opposing political party), then what had been seen as a drawback of the citizenship question could become a virtue.[46] Moreover, a census that distinguished between citizens and noncitizens "could help to facilitate a technical change to state redistricting practices in future elections that would, in the words of one Republican strategist, be 'advantageous to Republicans and Non-Hispanic Whites.'"[47] In the litigation challenging Ross's decision to reinstate the citizenship question, there was evidence suggesting that he was acting at the behest of the White House.[48] That only exacerbated the concern that the question was being added to pursue partisan advantage.

In the ensuing litigation, however, the argument that the citizenship question was being reinstated for unlawful purposes faced an uphill climb, both at the level of legal doctrine and as an evidentiary matter. Ultimately, the Supreme Court did not hold that the question was being reinstated for unlawful purposes. Instead, it held only that there was "a significant mismatch between the decision the Secretary made [to reinstate the citizenship question] and the rationale he provided" for doing so—namely, to aid the Department of Justice in its enforcement of the Voting Rights Act.[49] Finding that reason "contrived," the Court held that the matter should be remanded to the secretary to provide a better (i.e., more honest) account of why he proposed to reinstate the question, before it could in fact be reinstated.[50]

In reaching that narrow conclusion, the Court emphasized that there was nothing substantively invalid about the citizenship question, and that there would have been nothing wrong if the secretary had decided to reinstate the question after simply "com[ing] into office with policy preferences and ideas, discuss[ing] them with affected parties, sound[ing] out other agencies for support, and work[ing] with staff attorneys to substantiate the legal basis for [the] preferred policy."[51] This left the government with very broad leeway, as long as the reasons it cited for its actions did not appear wholly "contrived."

At a minimum, then, presidential administrations are permitted to change how the census is conducted in order to pursue a range of "policy" justifications—including, presumably, the sort of justification invoked by the secretary in the census case—as long as the record sufficiently connects the justification to the government's actions. And because many purported policy preferences may well track partisan voting patterns, presidents may retain a significant ability to "manipulate the Census for partisan purposes—with an eye toward future electoral prospects."[52] Judicial review of an administration's pursuit of policy preferences through the actions of its executive departments, in other words, may not do much to address the self-dealing problem.

In sum, presidents and their administrations are possessed with a broad range of statutory authorities that can potentially be exercised in relation to elections. How a given presidential administration views issues of election security and integrity, and what they think should be done about risks to that security and integrity, is often itself understood as a matter of legitimate policy disagreement and political contestation. In those circumstances, at least some instances of self-dealing may be nearly impossible to identify, let alone police.

Still, it is important to recall that the federal government does not administer federal elections. Nor does it directly supervise the administration of elections. In a real sense, the closer one gets in time and space to the actual conduct of an election and the counting of the votes, the less of a role there is for the federal executive branch—and thus, the less of an opportunity there is for the president to direct his administration to execute the laws in a way that will interfere with elections.

INHERENT AUTHORITY

Just as no federal statute assigns the president any role in the administration of elections, no provision of the Constitution grants him any inherent authority in that area either. But as in the statutory domain, the president may nevertheless assert some inherent constitutional power to act on—or speak to—election-related matters. Any such assertion must be scrutinized carefully.

First, and critically, the Constitution does not grant the president any roving power to take otherwise unlawful action in periods of emergency or crisis. As Justice Jackson put it in *Youngstown*, the framers of the Constitution "knew what emergencies were, knew the pressures they engender for authoritative action, knew, too, how they afford a ready pretext for usurpation. We may also suspect that they suspected that emergency powers would tend to kindle emergencies."[53] That suspicion animates Jackson's further point that "emergency powers are consistent with free government only when their control is lodged elsewhere than in the Executive who exercises them."[54] And that is why Congress, not the president, has the power to determine the circumstances in which the few emergency powers contained in the Constitution may be exercised. Specifically, the Constitution permits Congress to authorize the domestic deployment of the military in certain emergency situations (the Insurrection Act is an exercise of that power),[55] and it permits Congress to provide for the suspension of habeas corpus in similar circumstances.[56] Beyond that, as Jackson emphasized, the Constitution contains "no express provision for exercise of extraordinary authority because of a crisis."[57]

Having said that, it is of course true that the president's inherent constitutional powers and responsibilities are uniquely far reaching. Those powers and responsibilities are also not all reducible to self-defining grants of power in the Constitution. For example, although Article II of the Constitution vests the president with "the executive Power,"[58] it does not specify the precise metes and bounds of that power. Similarly, Article II provides that the president "shall take Care that the Laws be faithfully executed,"[59] without describing exactly what that entails. The Supreme Court, however, has long understood the "take care" power in broad terms, to include not just "the enforcement of acts of congress . . . according to their express terms" but also "the rights, duties, and obligations growing out of the constitution itself . . . and all the protection implied by the nature of the government under the constitution."[60]

Disagreement over the extent to which the Take Care Clause (or any other constitutional provision) empowers the president to intervene in elections lies at the core of the unprecedented criminal cases now pending against Trump in Washington, DC, and Fulton County, Georgia. To take just one part of the charges in those cases, Trump is alleged to have made knowingly false claims of election fraud to officials in multiple states, in an effort to induce them to change the 2020 election results in his favor. In a January 2, 2021, telephone call, for example, Trump allegedly "lied to the Georgia Secretary of State to induce him to alter Georgia's popular vote count and call into question the validity of the Biden . . . votes," stated that he needed to "find" the precise number of votes required to turn the outcome of the Georgia election in his favor, and "insinuated that the . . . Secretary of State and his Counsel could be subject to criminal prosecution if they failed to find election fraud as [Trump] demanded."[61] If proven, these allegations easily make out prima facie criminal violations.

Trump, however, has responded by arguing that he is immune from such charges because the communications in question were within his constitutional authority. "Ensuring the integrity of federal elections falls within the President's official duty," he asserts, and thus he cannot face legal liability for communicating his supposed concerns about election fraud to state officials.[62] Although a lower court in a separate case recently observed that "a sitting President has no expressly identified duty to faithfully execute the laws surrounding the Certification of the Electoral College,"[63] Trump insists that this formulation describes the president's constitutional responsibilities too narrowly. Congress has passed laws prohibiting election fraud, and the Department of Justice has the conceded power to enforce them. Those laws reflect what Trump, quoting the Supreme Court, describes as a "uniquely important national interest" in the integrity of federal elections, especially for president.[64] Therefore, Trump maintains, the president has the authority under the Take Care Clause to "tak[e] steps to prevent the certification of a federal election tainted by fraud—even if those steps are limited to encouraging other state and federal officials to exercise their responsibilities a certain way where the President allegedly has no direct role."[65] Put another way, "If the President or [the Department of Justice] concludes that significant fraud occurred in the administration of a federal election, the Take Care Clause does not require them to keep that information to themselves. Rather, it authorizes them to report that conclusion to state (and other federal) officials and to urge them to act accordingly."[66]

Trump's alleged actions relating to Georgia and other battleground states were brazenly self-serving and violative of well-established norms of presidential noninvolvement in election administration. But he is not entirely wrong in his account of the presidency. In fact, Trump is surely right that the president possesses inherent authority to communicate with government officials over whom he has no direct control, to express his views on matters of public concern, and to urge them to act in the public interest. Whether understood as an aspect of his Take Care responsibility or as some other dimension of his constitutional office, it is clear that, as the Supreme Court has recognized, "the President of the United States possesses an extraordinary power to speak to his fellow citizens and on their behalf."[67] That power, which Theodore Roosevelt famously called the "bully pulpit," is, as one court recently observed, "an everyday tool of the presidency."[68] Indeed, as Jeffrey Tulis has described, the president's ability to speak to the public to address matters of broad concern, promote policy initiatives, and inspire the nation is, to many, "the heart of the presidency—its essential task."[69]

It is therefore certainly within the president's authority to raise concerns with the American public about voter fraud (or foreign election interference, or ballot access), and to direct his administration to pursue solutions—whether by working with Congress to seek new legislation, or issuing executive orders directing his administration to take certain actions within existing legal authorities, or working with international leaders to address threats of foreign interference, or otherwise. If election security and integrity is a significant national issue, and surely it is, then naturally the president will have an important—indeed, a unique—role to play in directing the nation's attention to the problem and taking care that the government succeeds in addressing the problem. As a matter of effective policy implementation, it may well be imperative for the president to play that role.

Moreover, Trump is likely right that the Constitution provides presidents with some degree of immunity from criminal prosecution for acts taken while in office. Whether that immunity stretches to cover the particular crimes with which he has been charged is still being litigated as of this writing. Trump's arguments on that score are weak. But demonstrating that weakness requires some work, because it is implausible that the president possesses no immunity from prosecution for any of his official acts. Recall Justice Jackson's formulation in *Youngstown*: When the president acts in ways that Congress has forbidden, his authority is at its "lowest ebb."[70] Even at that ebb, some (limited) elements of the president's authority are exclusively his and thus not regulable by Congress. For example, in 2015 the Supreme Court held that "the power to recognize or decline to recognize a foreign state and its territorial bounds resides in the President alone," and therefore that Congress cannot "command" the president "to issue a formal statement that contradicts" his own exercise of this recognition power.[71] The issue in that case was whether Congress could require the executive to issue US passports indicating that a person born in Jerusalem was born in Israel, despite the decades-long determination of multiple presidential administrations not to take a formal position on whether Jerusalem was part of Israel. The Court held that Congress could not compel the executive to take that position. It surely follows, then, that Congress could not make it a crime for a president to refuse to recognize Jerusalem as part of Israel. To be sure, the recognition of foreign states has nothing to do with domestic elections. But this example suffices to demonstrate that Trump's assertion of immunity in the criminal cases against him cannot be defeated by simply rejecting the idea of presidential immunity altogether.

The core problem thus comes into focus. The president must have some authority to address nationwide concerns about election integrity, and the Constitution must confer on him some degree of immunity from criminal prosecution for some of his official acts. Yet if the president is able to wield the power of his office to pressure election officials to overturn legitimate electoral outcomes *for his own benefit* (or even just the benefit of his copartisans), and if he can invoke his office to shield himself from having to face the legal consequences of those actions, the nation's commitment to democratic self-rule will be undermined. The self-dealing problem will have reached its quintessence. To state the obvious, that result should be avoided at all costs.

It may not always be straightforward to differentiate legitimate expressions of concern about voter fraud or electoral malfunctioning from bad-faith attempts to interfere with election outcomes. But finding a way to observe that distinction is critical. On one side of the line, the president can be an important leader in the effort to ensure the security and integrity of our elections. On the other, he could pose an unparalleled threat to the basic functioning of our democracy.

As difficult as line drawing in these matters can be, some distinctions must be made. For one thing, unlike the president's exclusive power to recognize foreign states, there is simply no plausible claim that he possesses any exclusive authority when it comes to matters of election administration or oversight. Thus, whatever inherent power he might have to act in this area is subject to congressional regulation. For another, there is a difference between actions taken by an incumbent president as a *candidate* for reelection and actions taken in his *official* capacity as president. The US Court of Appeals for the DC Circuit made this point recently in the context of a civil suit against Trump for his actions on January 6, 2021: "When a first-term President opts to seek a second term, his campaign to win re-election is not an official presidential act. The Office of the Presidency as an institution is agnostic about who will occupy it next. And campaigning to *gain* that office is not an official act *of* the office."[72]

There are undoubtedly times when drawing even this distinction will be challenging. But sometimes the task is straightforward, as the criminal cases against Trump illustrate. When Trump pressed the Georgia secretary of state to "find 11,780 votes"—the exact number necessary for him to overtake Joe Biden in that state—he was not discharging any presidential duties, no matter how broadly we construe them. He was not merely recommending, in the name of electoral integrity, that Georgia officials investigate claims of voting irregularity and make whatever adjustments to the tally might be factually warranted and legally permitted. Instead, he was pressuring those officials to change the vote count to the extent—and only to the extent—necessary to alter the outcome. Those were the acts of a failed candidate pressuring state officials to take extralegal actions to help him win, not a president discharging his constitutional duties in the national interest. Thus, the fact that Trump was president at the time does not shield him from criminal liability for those acts.

CONCLUSION

To the extent the president has some legal powers relating to elections, the connection is relatively indirect and typically not proximate in time or place to the actual conduct of elections. In exercising those powers, a given president will inevitably reflect and pursue the substantive policy preferences of his administration. And although we may be concerned that policy preferences may operate as proxies for pure electoral self-interest, it is difficult to translate those concerns into robust, judicially enforceable limits. Some amount of self-dealing is likely inevitable.

The main limits on presidential self-dealing lie in the fact that the law does not assign the president *any* role in the actual operation of elections, or in their oversight. In that domain, the president possesses no lawful authority and thus has none to abuse. As the Bipartisan Policy Center puts it, "Presidents don't have much of a role in how elections are run—and that's a good thing."[73]

But of course, as Trump's actions after the 2020 election confirm, the absence of lawful authority alone does not guarantee that a president will not attempt to use his office to interfere with an election. In addition to calling state officials and pressuring them to come up with the requisite votes to flip the election in his favor, and in addition to at least contemplating invoking the Insurrection Act, Trump reportedly pressured officials within his administration to seize voting machines in key swing states in order to undo the reported results in those states.[74] Someone either in his administration or among his nongovernment supporters even drafted an executive order directing that action.[75] But the order was never signed; legal advisers and cabinet-level officials across the government insisted there was no lawful basis for seizing the machines and made clear they would take no part in it.[76]

As with the possibility that Trump might have invoked the Insurrection Act, the reason why the Trump administration did not seize the voting machines lies not simply in the lack of any legitimate legal basis for doing so but also in the willingness of senior executive branch officials to tell the president "no." As extraordinary as the final weeks of the Trump administration were, the lesson here is generalizable: the viability of the legal limits on the president's involvement in elections depends greatly on the willingness of those within his administration to observe and enforce them.

NOTES

1 Nixon v. Fitzgerald, 457 U.S. 731, 750 (1982).

2 *Id.*

3 Trump v. Vance, 140 S. Ct. 2412, 2425 (2020).

4 Lisa Marshall Manheim, *Presidential Control of Elections*, 74 Vand. L. Rev. 385, 405 (2021).

5 *See, e.g.*, Rucho v. Common Cause, 139 S. Ct. 2484, 2509 (2019) (Kagan, J., dissenting) (describing partisan gerrymandering as "enabl[ing] politicians to entrench themselves in office as against voters' preferences"). *See generally* Daryl Levinson & Benjamin I. Sachs, *Political Entrenchment and Public Law*, 125 Yale L.J. 400, 408 (2015) (defining entrenchment as the process by which elected officials "manipulat[e] the ground rules of the democratic process in order to retain their hold on power").

6 Arizona State Legislature v. Arizona Independent Redistricting Comm'n, 576 U.S. 787, 824 (2015) (cleaned up).

7 Manheim at 391.

8 *See* U.S. Const. art. I, § 4, cl. 1 ("The Times, Places and Manner of holding Elections for Senators and Representatives, shall be prescribed in each State by the Legislature thereof"); *id.* art. II, § 1, cl. 2 (providing that, with respect to the selection of members of the Electoral College in connection with presidential

elections, "each State shall appoint, in such Manner as the Legislature thereof may direct," the electors for their state).

9 *See* U.S. Const. art. I, § 4, cl. 1; *id.* amend. XIV, § 5; *id.* amend. XV, § 2; *id.* amend. XIX, § 2 (same). *See generally* Franita Tolson, *The Spectrum of Congressional Authority over Elections*, 99 B.U. L. Rev. 317 (2019).

10 Youngstown Sheet & Tube Co. v. Sawyer, 343 U.S. 579 (1952).

11 *Id.* at 635 (Jackson, J., concurring).

12 *Id.* at 636–37.

13 Richard E. Neustadt, *Presidential Power and the Modern Presidents* 10–11 (3d ed. 1990).

14 *Id.* at 11.

15 *See* Manheim at 388–89, 405–41 (surveying legal arrangements across these three categories).

16 Some of the statutory examples discussed here draw on and extend examples first presented by Manheim.

17 *See A Guide to Emergency Powers and Their Use*, Brennan Ctr. for Justice, www.brennancenter.org (last updated Feb. 8, 2023).

18 50 U.S.C. §§ 1601–51.

19 Bob Bauer & Jack Goldsmith, *After Trump: Reconstructing the Presidency* 341 (2020).

20 50 U.S.C. §§ 1701–09.

21 *Id.* §§ 1701–02.

22 Exec. Order No. 13,757, 82 Fed. Reg. 1 (Dec. 28, 2016).

23 *See Statement by the President on Actions in Response to Russian Malicious Cyber Activity and Harassment*, White House (Dec. 29, 2016), https://obamawhitehouse.archives.gov.

24 Quoted in Manheim at 438.

25 *See* Eric Schmitt, David E. Sanger & Maggie Haberman, *In Push for 2020 Election Security, Top Official Was Warned: Don't Tell Trump*, N.Y. Times, Apr. 24, 2019 (quoting Rep. Adam Schiff).

26 *See* Manheim at 409–10.

27 Exec. Order No. 13,848, 83 Fed. Reg. 46,843 (Sept. 12, 2018).

28 *See* Manheim at 438–39.

29 Exec. Order No. 14024, 86 Fed. Reg. 20,249 (Apr. 15, 2021).

30 *Id.*

31 *Id.* § 1(a)(ii)(B)–(C).

32 18 U.S.C. § 1385.

33 10 U.S.C. §§ 251–53.

34 Thaddeus Hoffmeister, *An Insurrection Act for the Twenty-First Century*, 39 Stetson L. Rev. 861, 905 (2010).

35 *See, e.g.*, Bauer & Goldsmith at 333–40; Statement of Elizabeth Goiten and Joseph Nunn, Brennan Ctr. for Justice, *The Insurrection Act: Its History, Its Flaws, and a*

Proposal for Reform, Submitted to United States Select Committee to Investigate the January 6th Attack on the Capitol (Sept. 20, 2022).

36 *See, e.g.*, United States House Select Committee to Investigate the January 6th Attack on the Capitol, Final Report, H.R. Rep. 117-663 at 692 (Dec. 22, 2022) ("January 6 Committee Final Report") ("The Committee has been troubled by evidence that President Trump's possible use of the Insurrection Act was discussed by individuals identified in this Report"); Indictment, United States v. Trump, Case l:23-cr-00257-TSC, ECF No. 1 at ¶ 81 (D.D.C. Aug. 1, 2023) (alleging that on January 3, 2021, the deputy White House counsel told coconspirator 4, who has been identified in the media as Justice Department official Jeffrey Clark, that if Trump remained in office after Inauguration Day, there would be "riots in every major city in the United States," and that Clark responded, "Well, . . . that's why there's an Insurrection Act").

37 Joseph Nunn & Andrew Boyle, *There Are No Extraordinary Powers a President Can Use to Reverse an Election*, Brennan Ctr. for Justice (Mar. 3, 2021), www.brennancenter.org.

38 *See Statutes Enforced by the Voting Section*, Civil Rights Division, U.S. Dep't of Justice (Nov. 16, 2023), www.justice.gov.

39 Manheim at 388; *see id.* at 413.

40 *See generally* Kate Andrias, *The President's Enforcement Power*, 88 N.Y.U. L. Rev. 1031 (2013).

41 Manheim at 423.

42 The example is discussed in Manheim at 420–23.

43 U.S. Const. art. I, § 2, cl. 3.

44 Dep't of Comm. v. New York, 139 S. Ct. 2551, 2561 (2019).

45 New York v. U.S. Dep't of Comm., 351 F. Supp. 3d 502, 515 (S.D.N.Y. 2019), aff'd in part, rev'd in part, and remanded, Dep't of Comm. v. New York, 139 S. Ct. 2551 (2019).

46 *See* Mannheim at 420–21.

47 *Id.* at 421 (quoting Hansi Lo Wang, *Trump Wants Citizenship Data Released but States Haven't Asked Census for That*, NPR [Sept. 11, 2019, 2:57 PM ET] [in turn quoting Republican redistricting strategist Thomas Hofeller]).

48 *See* New York v. Dep't of Comm., 351 F. Supp. 3d at 548, 552.

49 Dep't of Comm. v. New York, 139 S. Ct. at 2575.

50 *Id.*

51 *Id.* at 2574.

52 Manheim at 422.

53 *Youngstown*, 343 U.S. at 650 (Jackson, J., concurring).

54 *Id.* at 652.

55 U.S. Const. art. I, § 8, cl. 15.

56 U.S. Const. art. I, § 9, cl. 2.

57 343 U.S. at 650.

58 U.S. Const. art. II, § 1.
59 U.S. Const. art. II, § 3.
60 Cunningham v. Neagle, 135 U.S. 1, 64 (1890). *But see Youngstown*, 343 U.S. at 633 (Douglas, J., concurring) ("The power to execute the laws starts and ends with the laws Congress has enacted").
61 Trump Indictment at ¶ 31.
62 Motion to Dismiss Indictment Based on Presidential Immunity, United States v. Trump, Case l:23-cr-00257-TSC, ECF No. 74 at 36 (D.D.C. Oct. 5, 2023).
63 Thompson v. Trump, 590 F. Supp. 3d 46, 78 (D.D.C. 2022).
64 Anderson v. Celebrezze, 460 U.S. 780, 794–95 (1983).
65 Trump Motion to Dismiss at 38.
66 *Id.* at 38–39.
67 Trump v. Hawaii, 138 S. Ct. 2392, 2417–18 (2018).
68 Blassingame v. Trump, __ F. 3d. __, Case No. 22-5069, slip op. at 24 (D.C. Cir. Dec. 1, 2023), https://storage.courtlistener.com.
69 Jeffrey K. Tulis, *The Rhetorical Presidency* 4 (2017); *see also* George C. Edwards III, *The Public Presidency: The Pursuit of Popular Support* (1983).
70 *Youngstown*, 343 U.S. at 637 (Jackson, J., concurring).
71 Zivotofsky ex rel. Zivotofsky v. Kerry, 576 U.S. 1, 5, 28 (2015).
72 *Blassingame*, slip op. at 4.
73 Collier Fernekes et al., *What Presidents Can and Cannot Do for Voting Policy in Executive Orders*, Bipartisan Policy Center (Mar. 23, 2021), https://bipartisanpolicy.org.
74 *See* January 6 Committee Final Report at 222, 396–97.
75 *See* Betsy Woodruff Swan, *Read the Never-Issued Trump Order That Would Have Seized Voting Machines*, Politico (Jan. 21, 2022), www.politico.com.
76 *See* January 6 Committee Final Report at 222, 396–97.

7

ELECTION SECURITY, ELECTION INTEGRITY, AND THE ROLE OF CONGRESS

MATTHEW N. GREEN

Though states are primarily responsible for running elections, the US Congress plays a key role in supporting the security and validity of the electoral process. The Constitution gives Congress the power to determine when and how lawmakers are selected, as well as where House members may be elected; it allows each chamber to be "the Judge of the Elections, returns and qualifications of its own Members"; and it gives Congress the authority to enforce the voting rights of citizens. The Constitution also mandates a bicameral meeting of Congress to count the votes of the Electoral College.[1] In addition, Congress has plenary authority to determine the means of casting those votes, conducts oversight over the election process, and is an important source of funding for states to improve the security and accuracy of balloting.[2]

In this chapter, I review two important ways that Congress contributes to the sanctity of the voting process in the United States. The first is by setting minimum standards of election security and providing financial assistance to states to meet those standards. The second is by establishing the legitimacy of federal elections via its power to adjudicate election outcomes and vouch for their validity. In both spheres of activity, major elements of congressional politics—in particular, *partisan divisions over policy* and a tendency to *respond to crises rather than anticipate them*—have dictated the timing and nature of Congress's actions with respect to the election process. While these twin facets of Congress have led to some improvements in the voting process, they have also contributed to a lack of funding for election security and, in recent years, eroded public confidence in the reliability of elections.

FIRE-ALARM POLITICS AND PARTISAN DIFFERENCES OVER VOTING SECURITY

Generally speaking, Congress's modus operandi is to react to problems rather than anticipate them. There are both behavioral and instrumental reasons for this. It is human nature to delay doing something difficult with unclear long-term payoffs, and legislating is an inherently challenging process that may go unrewarded if it is done on behalf of a policy problem that has not yet manifested itself with voters.[3] As political scientists Mathew McCubbins and Thomas Schwartz argued, the desire to take credit and avoid blame encourages lawmakers to use their time efficiently by responding to complaints rather than seeking out problems to fix; for this reason, Congress prefers "fire alarm"–style oversight of the bureaucracy, in which it responds to complaints of wrongdoing, rather than "police patrol" oversight, in which it tries "detecting and remedying any violations of legislative goals."[4] Even if lawmakers do want to resolve anticipated crises, they are usually focused on dozens of urgent policy issues at any given moment, making it hard for them to dedicate additional attention to future threats.

In addition to being an institution that tends to wait until crises happen, Congress is also partisan, and the two parties differ on a wide range of policy problems and prescriptions—including the kind and degree of threats facing American elections. Congressional Republicans have long claimed that the greatest problem of the electoral process is fraud, including ballot tampering, ineligible voters casting ballots, and people voting multiple times. Democrats, by contrast, have emphasized the danger of unnecessary restrictions being placed on people's ability to vote. These differences derive partly from historical experience: African Americans, who vote disproportionately for Democrats, lost the right to vote in the post–Civil War South for over half a century, while electoral fraud was a hallmark of Democratic machines in Chicago, New York, and other cities.[5] They also stem somewhat cynically from the belief that making it easier for people to vote benefits Democrats more than Republicans, a belief that has only limited empirical support.[6] For instance, one recent study found that Democrats and Republicans vote at almost equal rates when the overall voting turnout is between 40 percent and 60 percent of the electorate, which is typical of most midterm and presidential elections.[7]

Polls have consistently shown that voters' views of electoral threats differ by party as well. In 2004, for example, 30 percent of Democrats were worried about eligible voters being barred from voting, versus 20 percent of Republicans. Surveys in 2007 and 2008 revealed that Republicans emphasized the danger of fraud and voter impersonation far more than Democrats.[8] A poll in 2012 found that nearly two-thirds of Democrats were concerned that citizens would not be able to exercise their voting rights in the upcoming election, whereas a similar proportion of Republicans expressed greater worry about fraud.[9] Four years later, thanks no doubt to Donald Trump's heavy emphasis on claims of election fraud in his run for president, twice as many Republicans as Democrats who were surveyed believed that voter fraud would be a significant problem in the 2016 election. By contrast, while 40 percent of Democrats thought the denial of suffrage rights would be a major problem in 2016, only 22 percent of Republicans did.[10]

CONGRESS'S SUPPORT FOR ELECTION SECURITY

Since the early 1990s, Congress has periodically enacted legislation that directly or indirectly affects voting security. In 1993, it passed the National Voter Registration Act, which was designed primarily to increase voter turnout, namely by requiring motor vehicle agencies to provide voter registration material (thus the law's nickname, "Motor Voter"). However, it also required that states identify a chief election official and made it harder for states to remove the names of registered voters.[11]

After the controversial 2000 presidential election, Congress passed legislation that dealt more explicitly with election security and the modernization of the voting process. The Help America Vote Act (HAVA), which was signed into law in 2002, required that new voters provide identification at voting locations, permitted those who could not do so to cast provisional ballots, and mandated that states upgrade their voting machinery and create an electronic database of registered voters. The law also authorized a new grant program for states to help them meet these requirements and established a commission with the responsibility of distributing those grants.[12]

HAVA represented a major step in improving election security by setting minimum security standards and creating an infrastructure that could provide support to states for modernizing the balloting process. But since HAVA's enactment, Congress has been inconsistent in how much money it actually provides to states. From 2010 through 2018, for example, Congress allocated no funds for HAVA grant programs at all.[13] That changed after widespread allegations of Russian interference in the 2016 presidential election, which ranged from cyberattacks against election infrastructure to providing Trump with information stolen from the Hillary Clinton campaign. A subsequent investigation by the Senate Select Committee on Intelligence revealed that Russia had tried to interfere in US elections as far back as 2014.[14] The allegations and the committee's multivolume report pushed Congress to again appropriate money for states to enhance ballot security. This funding has gone toward improving voter registration recordkeeping and purchasing new voting equipment, but using the monies to improve long-term election security has been a challenge, in part because the amount given by Congress has fluctuated wildly over time, from over $400 million in 2018 to just $75 million in 2023. As a point of comparison, conducting elections costs state and local governments roughly $4 to $6 *billion* per election year.[15]

This legislative history underscores two important facets of the politics of improving ballot security. First, Congress tends to act in response to major problems with the election process rather than in anticipation of such problems emerging in the future. Before HAVA, Congress mostly ignored the fact that states used a wide range of ballot technologies and designs, some of them unchanged since the early twentieth century. The law came about only after embarrassing and highly consequential problems emerged in Florida following Election Day 2000, when state officials struggled to interpret the intent of voters who cast partially punched ballots and elderly voters in Palm Beach County were confused by a faulty ballot layout. The same political dynamic explains the highly variable level of funding for election security and modernization appropriated by Congress, particularly when it stopped providing money after 2010 and only restored it after the 2016 election exposed serious vulnerabilities of electronic voting machines to foreign manipulation. The result, as a report by elections expert Charles Stewart put it, is government help that "has been infrequent and reactive."[16]

Second, long-standing differences between the two parties over whether voter fraud (the view of Republicans) or barriers to voting (the view of Democrats) is the biggest threat to fair and secure elections have sometimes kept Congress from acting more quickly to improve the voting process or have led it to curb efforts to address security issues. When first introduced in the late 1980s, the Motor Voter bill faced objections from Republican president George H. W. Bush and GOP lawmakers, who expressed greater concern about ballot fraud than about making it easier for people to vote; they claimed (with little evidence) that the bill would help Democratic candidates more than Republicans by encouraging voter fraud.[17] As a result, it took four years, a Democratic president, and Democratic majorities in the House and Senate for the proposal to become law. Though HAVA passed with broader bipartisan support, it came only after bill sponsors revised the measure to add voter ID requirements, addressing the objections of Senate Republicans who believed such requirements would prevent fraud and who threatened to filibuster the measure if they were not added to the bill.[18]

CONGRESS JUDGING THE VALIDITY OF ELECTIONS

As previously noted, the Constitution gives Congress a central role in determining the validity of congressional and presidential elections. For elections to the House and Senate, this authority is exercised primarily when the loser of an election challenges the outcome and asks Congress to adjudicate. Such challenges were considered by the House of Representatives with some frequency in the mid- to late nineteenth century before gradually declining after 1900 (Figure 7.1).[19] This decrease was used as evidence by political scientist Nelson Polsby for his famous thesis that the chamber was becoming more institutionalized: that is, the House was accepting election outcomes on neutral, universalistic grounds rather than trying to overturn them for partisan gain.[20] However, a great many of these contested elections had involved southern white citizens using fraud and violence to suppress the Black vote after ratification of the Fifteenth Amendment to the Constitution, and the

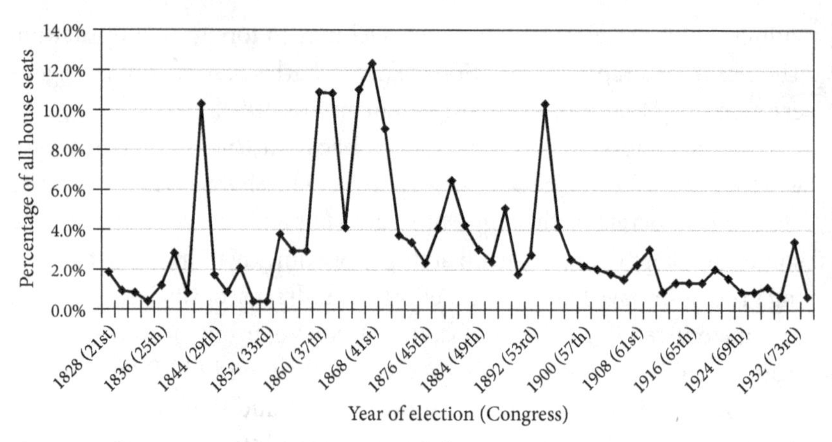

Figure 7.1. Percentage of House Seats Contested, 1828–1934

emergence of state-enforced disfranchisement in the South, which kept Black people from being able to register to vote in the first place, made it harder for losing candidates to challenge the results. That, plus the election of congressional Republicans who shared the South's views on race, and Republicans who viewed the contested election process as using up valuable time when the GOP no longer needed to win southern elections to maintain party majorities, led to the drop in contested House elections.[21] This reflected a durable shift to one-party white rule in the South—and tacit concurrence by the GOP with the end of Black voting rights in the region—as well as a reluctance by the House to review the results of congressional elections that, with a couple of notable exceptions (in 1985 and 1997), lasted even after Black voting rights were restored in the 1960s.[22]

Regardless of the reason for the decline in frequency, contested elections to the House and Senate are extremely rare today. When they do happen, it is usually because the results are extremely close and the election process is marred by obvious irregularities. In 2007, for instance, the House considered the case of *Jennings v. Buchanan*, in which the declared winner, Republican Vern Buchanan, had apparently beaten the Democrat, Christine Jennings, in a high-profile election by fewer than four hundred votes, and a suspiciously large number of voters (nearly twenty thousand) had voted for other offices but not that one. The House eventually voted to dismiss Jennings's appeal of the result.[23]

Indeed, more often than not Congress takes the side of the candidate who is initially declared the winner, which may help explain why candidates who narrowly lose their election choose not to appeal their cases to Congress at all. In 2020, for example, Democrat Rita Hart lost the election to Republican Mariannette Miller-Meeks in the Iowa Second District by just six votes, but after initially asking the House to review the results, Hart opted not to pursue it further, even though Democrats held a slim majority in the chamber and thus had an incentive to reverse Miller-Meeks' victory.[24]

Though Congress almost never acts as an arbiter of congressional elections today, the same has not been true of elections to the White House. Before the twenty-first century, congressional intervention in the count of Electoral College ballots was rare. In 1869 and 1873, objections were raised in Congress over the count of particular states (Georgia and Louisiana in both years, Arkansas and Texas in 1873), but most of the states' votes were upheld.[25] After the tumultuous 1876 presidential election, which was ultimately decided by a special commission made up of members of Congress and Supreme Court justices, Congress enacted the Electoral Count Act (ECA) in 1887. The ECA established that states, not Congress, were principally responsible for determining the winner of presidential elections, though it did allow any state's Electoral College votes to be rejected by majorities in both the House and Senate if one member from each chamber filed a formal objection.

Despite the ECA's incredibly low threshold for objecting to the presidential vote of any state, throughout the twentieth century Congress routinely confirmed Electoral College ballot counts in every presidential election but one: the 1968 election, where lawmakers forced a floor vote over whether to count the vote of a faithless North Carolina elector who had cast his ballot for a third-party candidate, the segregationist former Alabama governor George Wallace. The North Carolina vote was upheld by the House and Senate,[26] but Wallace had made a strong enough showing nationally to threaten to deny any candidate a majority of Electoral College votes, which would have turned the election over to the House. This gave fresh ammunition to reformers in the House and Senate, particularly Senator Birch Bayh (D-IN), who had hoped to elect presidents using the popular vote, thus rendering the ECA obsolete. Southern senators, however, embraced the Electoral College as a source of leverage for their region and a mechanism that ensured (majority) white voters would determine presidential winners in their states, and they successfully filibustered Bayh's constitutional amendment to abolish the Electoral College. Bayh continued pushing for the idea without success until he lost reelection in 1980. The Senate filibuster, increasing congressional partisanship, and the absence of an entrepreneurial advocate for reform in Congress made it exceedingly unlikely that such an amendment would be approved by the necessary two-thirds vote in either chamber.[27]

Lawmakers rediscovered the ability to challenge presidential election results via the ECA after the 2000 election. Vice President Al Gore won more popular votes but lost the Electoral College vote, thanks in part to a Supreme Court decision that put an end to a ballot recount in Florida. Democrats were infuriated, and members of the House Congressional Black Caucus tried to challenge the counting of Florida's votes when the House met to confirm the results, but no senators would join their effort.[28] Four years later, President George W. Bush's Electoral College votes in Ohio were challenged by Senator Barbara Boxer (D-CA) and Representative Stephanie Tubbs Jones (D-OH), who claimed that they were not trying to overturn the results but rather hoping to bring attention to voting practices that had disfranchised voters. Nonetheless, for only the second time in history, Congress had triggered the ECA's provision that required Congress to debate and vote on whether to accept a state's Electoral College count.[29] Though Ohio's results were upheld overwhelmingly by the Senate (74–1) and House (267–31), the objection had opened the door to future challenges by demonstrating that Congress could vote on whether to accept a state's Electoral College ballots for a major party candidate, even if they reflected the popular vote in that state.[30] Some liberal House Democrats tried again to use the ECA to object to Donald Trump's election in 2016, but were not supported by any senators.[31]

Then came the 2020 election, which was marred by false allegations of voter fraud from President Trump and, after the election, from many of his supporters in Congress. This time, far more lawmakers were willing to use the ECA to challenge the election results. When Congress convened on January 6, 2021, to confirm the results of the election, Representative Paul Gosar (R-AZ) and Senator Ted Cruz (R-TX) objected to Biden's win in Arizona, submitting a petition that was cosigned by nearly 60 House members, and Representative Scott Perry (R-PA) and Senator Josh Hawley (R-MO) did the same for Pennsylvania, joined by a whopping 78 House members.[32] The vote results were much closer than in 2004: 7 Senate Republicans and nearly 140 House Republicans—a majority of the House GOP Conference—voted to reject the results in Arizona, Pennsylvania, or both. That so many lawmakers would vote to reverse the results of a presidential election based on an obvious falsehood (that the presidential election was subject to massive, multistate fraud while the lawmakers' own elections were not) showed how loyalty to, and fear of, Trump and his ardent supporters was deep enough for Republicans to abandon Congress's role as a neutral arbiter of elections and treat the ECA as a way to either advertise their loyalty to Trump or carry out a self-coup. Indeed, one study found that lawmakers from more partisan, pro-Trump districts were more likely to object to the ballots in Arizona or Pennsylvania, as were legislators from the House Freedom Caucus, a group that was not only ideologically conservative but also among the most supportive of Trump as president.[33] For some Republicans—including members of the Freedom Caucus and future Speaker of the House Mike Johnson (R-LA)—the attempt to exploit ECA loopholes went well beyond symbolic position-taking via a floor vote. It also included working behind the scenes to try to halt, if not reverse, the counting of Electoral College ballots in favor of Biden, such as by supporting a frivolous Texas lawsuit rejecting the votes in four states and introducing Trump to a midlevel Justice Department official who erroneously claimed that the election in Georgia was tainted by fraud.[34]

In the wake of this unprecedented abuse of the ECA—and the violent siege of the US Capitol Building that same day by Trump supporters hoping to force Congress to stop counting ballots for Biden—Congress passed the Electoral Count Reform Act. The legislation made it far harder for Congress to overturn the presidential election results of any state, in part by raising the minimum number of lawmakers needed to force a vote on objecting to a state's Electoral College results from one member of each chamber to two-fifths of each chamber.[35] It also clarified that the vice president could not play a part in determining the validity of election results, a direct response to a scheme hatched by the Trump White House to have Vice President Mike Pence refuse to count the ballots of certain states.[36]

The 2000, 2004, and 2020 elections also underscored how lawmakers contribute to the validity of national elections through their rhetoric as well as by using their statutory and constitutional authority.[37] Before 2000, when lawmakers took actions in the public sphere on subjects related to presidential elections, it was almost always in the form of endorsing or opposing a candidate, reforming their party's nomination process, or leading a presidential candidate's campaign. But in 2000, for the first time since 1877, such public acts involved challenging the winner of the Electoral College.[38] In that election and the one that followed, some Democrats publicly justified their objections with claims (but no evidence) that the election process had been illegitimate. Such rhetoric reached new heights in 2020. Between November 2020 and the end of January 2021, according to a study led by Representative Zoe Lofgren (D-CA), 120 House Republicans issued over 2,800 posts on social media questioning the validity of the presidential election. Several of Trump's most diehard supporters issued hundreds of such posts, like Paul Gosar (R-AZ) (272 posts), Mo Brooks (R-AL) (158), and Matt Gaetz (R-FL) (155), often with incendiary language insisting the election had been stolen.[39]

As with efforts to improve ballot security, partisan divides have been a major factor in shaping how Congress judges the validity of federal elections. Congressional Democrats raised doubts about both of George W. Bush's election wins and forced the House and Senate to debate the results of Ohio's 2004 presidential election on the grounds that the vote had been suppressed in that state. This opened a Pandora's box in which the ECA's procedures were now a legitimate means of position-taking by lawmakers whose candidate lost the presidential election, if not a way to overturn election results altogether. But while Democrats' use of the ECA reflected their party's concerns about voter suppression, Republicans' historical focus on the dangers of election fraud reached an apotheosis with Trump, who liked to claim his elections were marred by cheating by his opponents regardless of whether he won or lost. In a perverse twist, the GOP alleged the existence of fraud in 2020 not to spur new voting laws and stronger enforcement of existing laws but rather to justify overturning the will of voters and, for Trump and his most ardent allies, committing an extraordinary act of mob violence at the Capitol Building on January 6.

Congress's failure to respond until an actual crisis emerges mattered as well. This was most evident in the long-delayed reform of the ECA. Scholars had pointed to the dangers inherent in the ECA for over a century, and the 2000 election led to renewed calls to revisit the law and fix its most obvious flaws.[40] Yet Congress did nothing. Not until those flaws were exploited by Trump allies—in the wake of the massive assault on the Capitol Building by Trump supporters—did it revise the ECA, albeit only over the opposition of House Republicans who saw it as a rebuke of Trump.

CONCLUSION

Congress plays an important legal and political role in ensuring national elections are secure and confirming the validity of the electoral process. Its budgetary authority allows it to draw from the vast resources of the federal government to help states tighten election security, make it harder to alter or steal votes, and upgrade their voting technology. Both the Constitution and federal law give Congress the responsibility to make sure that federal elections are free and fair and, if need be, decide whether to follow or overturn election results. And Congress's role as a public institution gives its members political megaphones that can be used to create or amplify messages about the legitimacy of election results and the balloting process.

A strong case can be made that Congress—because of its tendency to react to crises rather than anticipate them, and because the two parties have widely different views about the biggest threat facing the electoral process—has done nowhere near enough to increase and maintain election security. Critics have argued that appropriations for ballot security have been inconsistent and woefully insufficient.[41] Years of attempted Russian interference in elections went largely ignored until it became so brazen that it was an issue in the 2016 presidential election and led many Americans to doubt the validity of the results.[42] More disturbingly, the long-documented flaws with the ECA went unheeded—even as congressional Democrats began using the law to challenge the outcome of George W. Bush's election wins in 2000 and 2004—until House Republicans came within seventy-three votes of objecting to Pennsylvania's

Electoral College votes and within ninety-two votes of doing the same for Arizona.[43]

Lawmakers may have thought that their protests against the outcome of a presidential election were harmless position-taking, since in no case did they seriously threaten to overturn the results. But that a handful of congressional Democrats, and later dozens of Republicans, would openly question the results of elections with their rhetoric as well as with their votes—despite scant evidence of fraud or widespread voter suppression—may have helped undermine the electoral process by sowing doubts among citizens about the sanctity and security of the country's elections. Political elites are uniquely positioned to shape the views of citizens, and studies have found that declining faith in elections can affect how elections are run.[44] It is no surprise that, as members of Congress and other political actors increasingly claimed that elections were tainted by irregularities, citizen confidence in election results has declined, and partisans largely followed the cues of same-party elites in identifying the primary culprit. In particular, more Republicans became convinced that election fraud is a regular occurrence after the 2020 election.[45] Given evidence that poorly run elections reduce citizens' faith in the democratic process, should Congress continue to provide insufficient resources to states to run their elections fairly and competently, that may in turn hurt Americans' confidence in elections.[46]

It is extremely unlikely that Congress would shed its chronic habit of waiting until foreseeable crises occur before acting legislatively to improve election security, and there is no evidence that Republicans and Democrats will come to an agreement about the relative dangers of voter fraud versus voter suppression.[47] Nonetheless, it is incumbent upon the legislative branch to ensure that our election process remains secure and respected by the public. HAVA instituted a valuable means of helping states protect the voting process, and the recent reforms to the ECA have taken away a powerful mechanism for lawmakers who might otherwise be tempted toward mischief for political gain. But no law is perfect, and the danger remains that elected officials will consciously ignore the security of the voting process or look for other ways to subvert elections, such as by convincing the necessary two-fifths of senators and representatives to object to a state's Electoral College vote.[48]

If there is hope for the future, it is to be found in one of the two chambers of Congress: the US Senate, which has been better able to avoid putting partisanship above the need to maintain ballot sanctity and election security. It was Republicans in the Senate, not the House, who conducted a thorough investigation into interference in the 2016 election; a far smaller percentage of the Senate than the House challenged the 2020 election results; and it was a bipartisan coalition of senators, not House members, that successfully developed the main elements of the Electoral Count Reform Act and guided it into law. It serves as an example for both chambers that lawmakers must exercise self-restraint—not using their powers to help their party at the risk of undermining American democracy—and remember that the sanctity of the ballot box should concern all members of Congress regardless of party.

NOTES

1 U.S. Const. art. I, §§ 4, 5; art. II, § 1.
2 Garrett 2018.
3 Lieberman 2019.
4 McCubbins and Schwartz 1984, 166.
5 For more on the historical origins of these partisan differences, see the Kohler-Hausmann chapter in this volume.
6 Groarke 2016.
7 Shaw and Petrocik 2020, 108. See also Goidel, MQ Moreira, and Armstrong 2024; Kogan, Lavertu, and Peskowitz 2015.
8 Ansolabehere and Persily 2008; Carroll 2004.
9 Brandon and Cohen 2012.
10 Gass 2016; McCarthy 2016. See also Guskin and Clement 2016.
11 Garrett 2018.
12 "New Voting Standards Enacted" 2003.
13 Orey et al. 2022.
14 US Senate 2020.
15 Boockvar and Sinha 2023; Shanton 2023; Stewart 2022, 3.
16 Stewart 2022, 1.
17 Groarke 2016; Wang 2012, chap. 5.
18 "New Voting Standards Enacted" 2003.
19 Senate contested elections followed a similar historical pattern. See Jenkins 2005.
20 Polsby 1968.
21 Green 2007; Jenkins 2004; Polsby 1968.

22 In 1985, House Democrats voted to declare Democrat Frank McCloskey the winner over Republican Richard McIntyre in Indiana's Eighth Congressional District, which infuriated Republicans and helped expand support for then-backbencher Newt Gingrich (R-GA) (Green and Crouch 2022, 53–56). Republicans had the opportunity to retaliate after incumbent Bob Dornan (R-CA) contested his narrow defeat to Loretta Sanchez in 1996, but a bipartisan majority voted to approve the House Oversight Committee's decision to dismiss the contest (Committee on House Oversight 1998; Wilgoren 1998).
23 Amunson and Hirsch 2008.
24 Pfannenstiel 2021.
25 Three electoral votes from Georgia were rejected after the 1872 election because they were deliberately cast for Horace Greeley even though he had died. Hinds Precedents, vol. 3, ch. 61, §§ 1964–70. For other examples of disputes in Congress over counting Electoral College votes that occurred before 1876, see Edwards 2019, 27–28.
26 North Carolina's Electoral College votes were upheld by a vote of 228–170 in the House and 58–33 in the Senate (Office of the House Historian 2020).
27 Wawro 2000; Wegman 2019.
28 Mitchell 2001.
29 CNN 2005.
30 Associated Press 2005.
31 See the Feingold and Langholz chapter in this volume.
32 Forgey 2021.
33 Strawbridge and Lau 2022.
34 See, e.g., Benner and Edmondson 2021; Broadwater and Eder 2023.
35 Neither the House nor the Senate would have met this threshold had it been in effect in 2020, though the House would have come close to forcing a vote on Arizona's election result, since 18 percent of the chamber signed a petition supporting an objection to the state's Electoral College vote.
36 Parks 2022.
37 Though not examined here, congressional hearings are another way that the House and Senate can seek to telegraph each party's views about the sources of election insecurity to the wider public. In 2021, for example, the House Administration Subcommittee on Elections held a hearing on voter ID laws and the full committee held a hearing on election subversion. With a majority of Democrats on the committee, most of the witnesses at both hearings were Democratic lawmakers or progressive activists. Two years later, the same committee—now with a majority of Republicans—held a series of hearings to promote a bill that imposed a national ID law and cut funds for states that allowed outside groups to help people vote.
38 Mayhew 2002. The original data can be found at https://campuspress.yale.edu.
39 US House of Representatives [2021].
40 See, e.g., Dougherty 1906; Posner 2001, 249–50.
41 Orey 2023.

42 One poll taken over two years after the 2016 election found that 43 percent of Americans agreed with the statement that Russia undermined the legitimacy of that election; 71 percent of Democrats concurred with that statement, while only 13 percent of Republicans did. ABC/Washington Post Poll: Trump/Muller Investigation/2020 Presidential Election, April 22–25, 2019 [Roper #31116359].
43 The vote to object to Arizona's Electoral College ballots was 121–303 in the House, and the vote to object to Pennsylvania's ballots was 138–282.
44 Jacobs and Shapiro 2000; Pastor 1999; Zaller 1992.
45 Bowler and Donovan, forthcoming.
46 Bowler et al. 2015.
47 However, one study found that partisans were equally likely to identify voter fraud or voter suppression as the primary problem with elections. But that same study found that people were more likely to claim an election had irregularities if their preferred candidate lost (Beaulieu 2014).
48 For other weaknesses and potential loopholes in the Electoral Count Reform Act, see the Feingold and Langholz chapter in this volume. For more that Congress could do to prevent voter fraud, see the Hasen chapter in this volume.

REFERENCES

Amunson, Jessica Ring, and Sam Hirsch. 2008. "The Case of the Disappearing Votes: Lessons from the *Jennings v. Buchanan* Congressional Election Contest." *William & Mary Bill of Rights Journal* 17 (2): 397–422.

Ansolabehere, Stephen, and Nathaniel Persily. 2008. "Vote Fraud in the Eye of the Beholder: The Role of Public Opinion in the Challenge to Voter Identification Requirements." *Harvard Law Review* 121 (7): 1737–75.

Associated Press. 2005. "Congress Rejects Election Challenge." NBC News, January 6, 2005. www.nbcnews.com.

Beaulieu, Emily. 2014. "From Voter ID to Party ID: How Political Parties Affect Perceptions of Election Fraud in the U.S." *Electoral Studies* 35:24–32.

Benner, Katie, and Catie Edmondson. 2021. "Pennsylvania Lawmaker Played Key Role in Trump's Plot to Oust Acting Attorney General." *New York Times*, January 23, 2021.

Boockvar, Kathy, and Ashish Sinha. 2023. "Utilization of HAVA Election Funding by States." Institute for Responsive Government, April 1, 2023. https://responsivegoverning.org.

Bowler, Shaun, Thomas Brunell, Todd Donovan, and Paul Gronke. 2015. "Election Administration and Perceptions of Fair Elections." *Electoral Studies* 38:1–9.

Bowler, Shaun, and Todd Donovan. Forthcoming. "Confidence in US Elections after the Big Lie." *Political Research Quarterly*.

Brandon, Michael, and Jon Cohen. 2012. "Poll: Americans Back Voter ID Laws." *Washington Post*, August 12, 2012, A3.

Broadwater, Luke, and Steve Eder. 2023. "Johnson Played Leading Role in Effort to Overturn 2020 Election." *New York Times*, October 25, 2023.

Carroll, Joseph. 2004. "Are Americans Worried about Voter Fraud?" Gallup, October 26, 2004. https://news.gallup.com.

CNN. 2005. "Democrats Challenge Ohio Electoral Votes." January 6, 2005. www.cnn.com.

Committee on House Oversight. 1998. *Dismissing the Election Contest against Loretta Sanchez*. US House of Representatives, Report 105-416.

Dougherty, J. Hampden. 1906. *The Electoral System of the United States*. New York: G. P. Putnam's Sons.

Edwards, George C., III. 2019. *Why the Electoral College Is Bad for America*. 3rd ed. New Haven, CT: Yale University Press.

Forgey, Quint. 2021. "GOP Lawmakers Object to Arizona Electors, Launching Futile Bid to Undo Biden's Victory." *Politico*, January 6, 2021.

Garrett, R. Sam. 2018. *Federal Role in U.S. Campaigns and Elections: An Overview*. Report R45302. Washington, DC: Congressional Research Service, September 4. https://crsreports.congress.gov.

Gass, Nick. 2016. "Poll: 52 Percent of Republicans Call Voter Fraud Major Problem in 2016." *Politico*, August 22, 2016.

Goidel, Spencer, Tiago MQ Moreira, and Brenna Armstrong. 2024. "Party Realignment, Education, and the Turnout Advantage: Revisiting the Partisan Effect of Turnout." *American Politics Research* 52 (1): 23–29.

Green, Matthew N. 2007. "Race, Party, and Contested Elections to the U.S. House of Representatives." *Polity* 39 (2): 155–78.

Green, Matthew N., and Jeffrey Crouch. 2022. *Newt Gingrich: The Rise and Fall of a Party Entrepreneur*. Lawrence: University Press of Kansas.

Groarke, Margaret. 2016. "The Impact of Voter Fraud Claims on Voter Registration Reform Legislation." *Political Science Quarterly* 131 (3): 571–95.

Guskin, Emily, and Scott Clement. 2016. "Poll: Nearly Half of Americans Say Voter Fraud Occurs Often." *Washington Post*, September 15, 2016. www.washingtonpost.com.

Jacobs, Lawrence R., and Robert Y. Shapiro. 2000. *Politicians Don't Pander: Political Manipulation and the Loss of Democratic Responsiveness*. Chicago: University of Chicago Press.

Jenkins, Jeffery A. 2004. "Partisanship and Contested Election Cases in the House of Representatives, 1789–2002." *Studies in American Political Development* 18 (Fall): 112–35.

———. 2005. "Partisanship and Contested Election Cases in the Senate, 1789–2002." *Studies in American Political Development* 19 (Spring): 53–74.

Kogan, Vladimir, Stéphane Lavertu, and Zachary Peskowitz. 2015. "Performance Federalism and Local Democracy: Theory and Evidence from School Tax Referenda." *American Journal of Political Science* 60 (2): 418–35.

Lieberman, Charlotte. 2019. "Why You Procrastinate (It Has Nothing to Do with Self-Control)." *New York Times*, March 25, 2019.

Mayhew, David R. 2002. *America's Congress.* New Haven, CT: Yale University Press.
McCarthy, Justin. 2016. "Four in Five Americans Support Voter ID Laws, Early Voting." Gallup, August 22, 2016. https://news.gallup.com.
McCubbins, Mathew D., and Thomas Schwartz. 1984. "Congressional Oversight Overlooked: Police Patrols versus Fire Alarms." *American Journal of Political Science* 28 (1): 165–79.
Mitchell, Alison. 2001. "Over Some Objections, Congress Certifies Electoral Vote." *New York Times*, January 7, 2001.
"New Voting Standards Enacted." 2003. In *CQ Almanac 2002*. Washington, DC: Congressional Quarterly.
Office of the House Historian. 2020. "Congress and the Case of the Faithless Elector." November 17, 2020. https://history.house.gov.
Orey, Rachel. 2023. "New Election Security Funding Positive but Misses the Mark." Bipartisan Policy Center, February 28, 2023. https://bipartisanpolicy.org.
Orey, Rachel, Grace Gordon, Michael Thorning, and Matthew Weil. 2022. "The Path of Federal Election Funding." Bipartisan Policy Center, June 16, 2022. https://bipartisanpolicy.org.
Parks, Miles. 2022. "Congress Passes Election Reform Designed to Ward Off Another Jan. 6." National Public Radio, December 23, 2022. www.npr.org.
Pastor, Robert A. 1999. "The Role of Electoral Administration in Democratic Transitions: Implications for Policy and Research." *Democratization* 6 (4): 1–27.
Pfannenstiel, Brianne. 2021. "Iowa Democrat Rita Hart, Claiming 'Toxic Campaign of Political Disinformation,' Withdraws Election Challenge in Iowa's 2nd District." *Des Moines Register*, March 31, 2021.
Polsby, Nelson W. 1968. "The Institutionalization of the U.S. House of Representatives." *American Political Science Review* 62 (1): 144–68.
Posner, Richard A. 2001. *Breaking the Deadlock: The 2000 Election, the Constitution, and the Courts.* Princeton, NJ: Princeton University Press.
Shanton, Karen L. 2023. "Election Security: Federal Funding for Securing Election Systems." Congressional Research Service, May 8, 2023. https://crsreports.congress.gov.
Shaw, Daron R., and John R. Petrocik. 2020. *The Turnout Myth: Voting Rates and Partisan Outcomes in American National Elections.* New York: Oxford University Press.
Stewart, Charles, III. 2022. *The Cost of Conducting Elections.* MIT Election Data and Science Lab. https://electionlab.mit.edu.
Strawbridge, Michael G., and Richard R. Lau. 2022. "House Republican Decision Making Following the Capitol Riot." *PS: Political Science and Politics* 55 (3): 484–89.
US House of Representatives. 2021. *Social Media Review: Members of the U.S. House of Representatives Who Voted to Overturn the 2020 Presidential Election.* Washington, DC. US House of Representatives. https://housedocs.house.gov.
US Senate. 2020. *Russian Active Measures Campaigns and Interference in the 2016 U.S. Election.* Report 116-290. Washington, DC: Government Publishing Office, November 10. www.intelligence.senate.gov.

Wang, Tova Andrea. 2012. *The Politics of Voter Suppression.* Ithaca, NY: Cornell University Press.

Wawro, Gregory. 2000. *Legislative Entrepreneurship in the U.S. House of Representatives.* Ann Arbor: University of Michigan Press.

Wegman, Jesse. 2019. "The Man Who Changed the Constitution, Twice." *New York Times*, March 14, 2019. www.nytimes.com.

Wilgoren, Jodi. 1998. "House Dismisses Challenge to Rep. Sanchez's Election." *Los Angeles Times*, February 13, 1998.

Zaller, John R. 1992. *The Nature and Origins of Mass Opinion.* New York: Cambridge University Press.

8

THE SUPREME COURT

MICHAEL WALDMAN

As Thomas Paine wrote at the founding, in America, "the law is king."[1] Of course, we would assume that the US Supreme Court would be at the forefront of upholding democracy. Certainly those trying to undermine free and fair elections have assumed the Court will play a decisive role. In 2020 Donald Trump insisted that Amy Coney Barrett be rushed to confirmation. "I think this [election] will end up in the Supreme Court, and I think it's very important that we have nine Justices," he explained.[2]

Yet history tells a different story. The Supreme Court has rarely played a central role in the struggle to build and define American democracy. Only in the 1960s, when it mandated equal legislative districts, did it act boldly to expand democratic equality. Mostly it has been an absent character in the drama. When the high court did become more aggressively involved over the past two decades, it acted not to bolster democratic rights but to dismantle the legal structures designed to support them. Increasingly it is clear that the Court itself—its structure, its history, and its capture by an ideological faction—is part of the problem.

Many elements of our system, once seen as quirky Americana, now combine to thwart majority rule: the Senate, where California has sixty-eight times the population of Wyoming but each state has two senators; the filibuster, once used sparingly, now deployed against even the most anodyne legislation; the Electoral College, which affirmed the popular vote in every contest from 1888 to 1996—but chose the popular vote loser twice in sixteen years.

Among these constitutional features, the Supreme Court plays an especially anomalous role. It combines vast power with minimal accountability. Its members are unelected. Unlike their counterparts in all but one state supreme court or in the constitutional courts of other countries, they serve for life.[3] The portion of the US Constitution that addresses the judicial branch is one-tenth the length devoted to Congress and the presidency, the democratically elected branches. The Court grew to its current place above the other branches only over time. Once it was seen as a coequal branch of government, but now it is seen as a super-legislature, presiding over and above the others.

In the twentieth century, scholars wrestled with the "countermajoritarian difficulty," the fact that the Supreme Court must at times check the impulses of the political system or wishes of the public.[4] Most of the time that balance was acceptable and at times vitally necessary. Now the Court is actively minoritarian, entrenching the political views of a shrinking segment of the electorate. Its decisions on democracy have increasingly helped one party.

All this has made the Supreme Court uniquely susceptible to domination by an ideological cohort. It has been captured by a faction of a faction. Remedies are few: presidents have limited terms, members of Congress face regular election, but the justices only need fear impeachment, a feeble tool for accountability.

Partisan dimensions are clear, even if they are not mentioned much in law school seminar rooms. Democrats won the popular vote in seven of the past eight presidential elections, the longest such winning streak in American history. Yet Republicans named six of the nine justices. The two parties have roughly split control of the White House for the past half century, but Republican appointees have controlled the Court since 1971. Remarkably, the last time a Democratic president appointed a chief justice of the United States was *1946*.

Republicans know the courts are a redoubt for their political power. They have acted accordingly. When Barack Obama nominated Merrick Garland to fill the open seat created by the death of Antonin Scalia, Mitch McConnell and the Republicans simply refused to consider the nomination, holding the seat open for a full year. This was without modern precedent; the Senate frequently had confirmed nominations close to a presidential election, including when the opposition party controlled the Senate. This may mark a further stage in toxic politicization of the nomination process. As parties polarize, partisan identification matters more. Earl Warren, appointed by Dwight Eisenhower, became the liberal chief justice whose rulings spurred a conservative backlash. Such ideological evolution is unthinkable today.

These factors have shaped the Supreme Court's role in the expansion of American democracy—or more precisely, its minimal role.

SCOTUS ROLE: LESS THAN EXPECTED

John Adams foretold the country's trajectory in 1776 when he resisted expansion of the vote to men who did not own property. "New claims will arise. Women will demand a vote. Lads from 12 to 21 will think their rights not enough attended to, and every man, who has not a farthing, will demand an equal voice with any other in all acts of state. It tends to confound and destroy all distinctions, and prostrate all ranks, to one common level." He warned morosely, "There will be no end of it."[5] That was an astute, if dyspeptic, prediction.

But the Supreme Court rarely had much to do with that expansion of democracy. The doctrine articulated in the 1849 case *Luther v. Borden*, in which the justices opted to stay out of "political questions," grew out of a case where there were two claimants to the governorship of Rhode Island (one of whom supported universal suffrage).[6] The Court refused to decide whether the state had a legitimate government under the Constitution's guarantee of a republican system. After the Civil War, the Fifteenth Amendment and Union army bayonets enabled Black men to be elected to the governorship, to Congress, and to legislatures. No judicial ruling produced that revolution; in fact, the drafters of the Fifteenth Amendment pointedly gave Congress the power to enforce it, just a decade after *Dred Scott*. When "redemption" and Jim Crow laws reversed that progress and ushered in seven decades of suppression, the Supreme Court shrugged. It upheld literacy tests and bans on women voting, and in *Giles v. Harris* in 1903, it said that only military force, not court rulings, could protect the right to vote.[7] A ruling for voting rights would be little more than "declarations in the air."

The clash between Franklin Roosevelt and the Court in the 1930s produced a new constitutional settlement. As articulated in the famous footnote 4 of the otherwise unremarkable *Carolene Products* case, justices would exert "more exacting scrutiny" when considering "legislation which restricts those political processes which can ordinarily be expected to bring about repeal of undesirable legislation."[8] Even so, the Supreme Court stepped gingerly. It would occasionally issue pro-democracy rulings, as when it banned Texas's "white primary" in 1944 in the first case argued by Thurgood Marshall.[9] But it issued few sweeping rulings for voting rights.

The only exception, and it was a big one, came during the liberal heyday of the Warren Court, in cases starting with *Baker v. Carr* in 1962.[10] At the time, inequality in legislative districts gave lopsided power to rural areas, which still dominated even as cities grew. In *Baker*, the Court decided it would hear cases alleging political inequality due to apportionment. Two years later, *Reynolds v. Sims* proclaimed the doctrine of "one person, one vote," decreeing roughly equal-sized legislative districts. "The right to vote freely for the candidate of one's choice is the essence of a democratic society, and any restrictions on that right strike at the heart of representative government," it ruled.[11] By 1968, ninety-three of ninety-nine state legislative chambers had their lines redrawn to comply with the Supreme Court's ruling. That eased the hold of rural districts on state governments and Congress.

But it took legislation, especially the Voting Rights Act, to impose a national floor under elections. For all the focus on the Supreme Court, the job of protecting democracy actually fell far more often to the democratically elected branches. Congress enacted a strong campaign finance system, including voluntary public financing for presidential campaigns, and federal voting bills to require states to expand voter registration activities and to use electronic machines. An end to the poll tax in federal elections and expansion of the franchise to eighteen-year-olds required constitutional amendments. As the country constructed a multiracial democracy after 1965 for the first time, judges policed the edges but largely stayed out.

THE TWENTY-FIRST CENTURY

That all changed in the new century. The Court shed its diffidence, becoming aggressively activist. Especially under the leadership of Chief Justice John Roberts, the justices overturned long-standing and basic democratic rules, striking down federal laws to expand the franchise and promote political equality. (The Warren Court, by contrast, had rarely overturned laws passed by Congress.)[12]

This era began with *Bush v. Gore*, in which the Supreme Court, in a five-to-four vote, cut off the 2000 presidential recount in Florida and awarded the presidency to George W. Bush, who was deemed to have won the state by 538 votes out of 6 million cast. That was a bizarre case—it was, after all, basically a tied presidential election, someone had to decide who won, and lots of people would be unhappy with the result. The ruling would not be cited again for nearly a quarter century in a majority opinion. But the Florida recount exposed the ramshackle electoral system, as well as the stakes for those who could block or expand the vote. And the Court that Bush's presidency left behind, after Roberts and Samuel Alito joined it, immediately began to issue increasingly active rulings on the laws of democracy striking down longstanding protections and statutes.

The Court was transformed, too, by the way justices were appointed. The Federalist Society started as a student club for conservatives who felt marooned at liberal law schools, but eventually became a well-oiled judicial political machine aiming to shift the judiciary.[13] It vetted potential judges for ideological consistency, and candidate Donald Trump announced he would choose only from a list the group provided. Its affiliates spent lavishly on advertising campaigns to support nominees. It backed groups that brought impact suits or filed briefs before those very judges. Cases such as the challenge to the Affordable Care Act were hatched in the hallways of its conferences.[14] This was not just a well-oiled machine but very well funded: in 2021 one donor quietly gave the leader of the Federalist Society, Leonard Leo, $1.6 billion to support the network of conservative legal groups.[15] The transformation of the judicial branch was felt directly in the Supreme Court's rulings on democracy.

Start with voting. The Constitution refers to "the right to vote" five times.[16] But the Court made clear that it would give that right little effective protection starting in 2008, when it allowed states to pass restrictive voting laws with little interference from federal courts. *Crawford v. Marion County*, authored by liberal John Paul Stevens, gave states wide leeway to enact voting rules that might restrict access to the franchise.[17] *Crawford* addressed a "facial" challenge to a voter identification law passed but not yet implemented, and the Court said that new facts might produce a different result. That subtlety was lost on the political world. Already Republicans were insisting there was widespread fraud. Months before, a scandal had erupted when the White House orchestrated the firing of US attorneys who refused to prosecute nonexistent misconduct.[18] The controversy grew hot enough that Attorney General Alberto Gonzales resigned. The Court had blessed the idea that a vague fear of fraud could justify harsh rules. In one case, the justices had written that "voter fraud drives honest citizens out of the democratic process and breeds distrust of our government. Voters who fear their legitimate votes will be outweighed by fraudulent ones will feel disenfranchised."[19] The historian Alex Keyssar reacted with scorn: "*Feel* disenfranchised? Is that the same as 'being disenfranchised'? So if I might 'feel' disenfranchised, I have a right to make it harder for you to vote?"[20]

In 2013, in *Shelby County v. Holder*, the Court gutted the Voting Rights Act, the nation's most effective civil rights law.[21] The act had transformed politics in the South, and it had bipartisan support (when reauthorized in 2006, it passed the Senate with ninety-eight votes). The act's Section 5 had required states with a history of racial discrimination in voting to get clearance in advance from the Justice Department or a federal court before changing voting rules. At the argument, Antonin Scalia groused that the law was nothing more than a "racial entitlement."[22] Spectators gasped. Scalia did not write the opinion, however. John Roberts did, and he was more decorous. Racism was a thing of the past; the South had changed, and the law's strong provisions were no longer needed. Ruth Bader Ginsburg published a memorable dissent. "Throwing out preclearance when it has worked and is continuing to work to stop discriminatory changes is like throwing away your umbrella in a rainstorm because you are not getting wet," she wrote sternly.[23] Political equality in the South had advanced precisely because it had been shielded by federal protection.

Ginsburg proved prescient. Within hours, Texas implemented its harsh voter identification law. A federal judge found that 608,000 registered voters lacked the necessary paperwork and blocked much of the law.[24] The Texas case relied on the Voting Rights Act's Section 2, which still had surprisingly potent force authorizing lawsuits against discriminatory practices. In 2016, for example, a federal appeals court struck down North Carolina's restrictive voting law. The state's plans, the judges ruled, "target African Americans with almost surgical precision."[25] In all, over one hundred restrictive state laws were passed nationwide in the decade after *Shelby County*, and most would have been blocked or slowed by the Voting Rights Act were it at full strength. Racial gerrymanders would have been as well.[26] Many state laws were softened by lower court rulings. But over the decade the gap between Black and white political participation grew across the states once covered by the law.[27] And it has been two decades since the US Supreme Court has struck down a restrictive state voting law.

John Roberts had a long animus toward Section 2 dating from his days as a young Justice Department lawyer. And in 2021, in the first months of the conservative six-justice supermajority's control of the Court, the justices largely neutered Section 2 as a tool against voter suppression laws. At a moment when states were pressing for new restrictive rules, egged on by Trump and his supporters, *Brnovich v. DNC* effectively substituted its approach for the one taken by Congress, even instructing courts to compare a challenged voting rule to the status quo in 1982 as though that was what was being enshrined when lawmakers revised Section 2.[28]

When it came to money in politics, the Court was even more activist. *New Yorker* journalist Jeffrey Toobin noted astutely, "Every Chief Justice takes on a project. Earl Warren wanted to desegregate the South. Warren Burger wanted to limit the rights of criminal suspects. William Rehnquist wanted to revive the powers of the states. It increasingly appears likely that, for John Roberts, the project will be removing the limits that burden wealthy campaign contributors—the 'whole point' of the First Amendment, as he sees it."[29]

Citizens United in 2010 struck down a century of federal campaign finance law enacted by Congress in an effort to counterbalance the power of big money.[30] The ruling built on *Buckley v. Valeo* in 1976, which held in effect that "money is speech" (as one justice said at the oral argument).[31] Campaign finance laws, rather than viewed as a way to advance democratic equality, could survive only if they addressed an increasingly narrow view of corruption.

Citizens United took that logic to its next step. Corporations and unions now could spend unlimited amounts so long as the spending was deemed "independent." Follow-on lower court rulings effectively deregulated all of campaign finance.[32] Small donations increased, but large gifts and spending increased even more. In 2022, nearly four million small donors of $200 or less gave federal candidates over $747 million. Meanwhile, one hundred top individual donors accounted for $1.2 billion in contributions, roughly 60 percent more than all small donors combined.[33] Those who worry most about the polarizing role of campaign cash should look first at the ideologically intense billionaires who now dominate so much of it. Politics was transformed in ways so widespread as to seem invisible. Incumbents now feared having massive sums of "dark money" from undisclosed donors dumped into their primary elections. Before *Citizens United*, Republicans had a climate change bill. After, fearful of funds from the Koch network and other fossil fuel interests, the GOP became the world's only major party that denied the problem.[34] Wealthy individuals gained even more power than corporations. One person, investor Peter Thiel, personally sponsored and largely paid for the campaigns of two US Senate candidates in 2022.[35] One of them, J. D. Vance, is now the junior senator from Ohio. Major presidential candidates came to run their campaigns almost entirely through supposedly independent committees funded by the wealthy. (Ron DeSantis stumbled when his "independent" committee posted his secret debate prep plans on its website.)

On redistricting, the Court's action came through inaction—a refusal to police partisan manipulation of redistricting.

Gerrymandering is as old as the republic. In the very first congressional election, Patrick Henry drew Virginia's congressional map to try to keep archrival James Madison from winning a seat. Both parties gerrymander when they can. But in recent years, the potency of gerrymandering has been enhanced by digital tools and ever more robust data about voters. The Court long understood that redistricting abuses could dampen accountability and worsen polarization. But it despaired of finding a "judicially manageable standard." Finally, in *Rucho v. Common Cause* in 2019, Roberts and his colleagues barred federal courts from even considering cases challenging partisan gerrymandering.[36]

There were still some ways to curb the worst excesses. In some instances, for example, courts could strike down politically gerrymandered maps on the grounds that they were also racially discriminatory. But racial and partisan motives can be hard to disentangle, making partisanship a potential "get out of jail free" card for discriminatory line drawers. Federal courts continued to police highly technical disputes about the Voting Rights Act and what levels of representation it required. But when it came to curbing partisan gerrymandering, that job was now left to states or, in theory, to Congress.

In 2023 there was one surprising exception to the headlong judicial rush to gut voting laws. Alabama Republicans had drawn a congressional map with only one out of seven districts likely to produce a Black victor, even though Black voters now make up almost 30 percent of the state's population. Most expected the Court to use *Allen v. Milligan* to further weaken, or perhaps even completely gut, what remained of the Voting Rights Act in service of its vision of a "color-blind" Constitution. So it was all the more startling when John Roberts and Brett Kavanaugh joined the liberals to ordered Alabama to draw a second district where Black voters were a large enough share of the population to be politically successful. In a modern echo of "massive resistance" from the 1950s, the legislature resisted and refused to comply, and it required another trip to the Supreme Court to make clear that a new district for Black voters needed to be drawn.

NO BAILOUT FOR TRUMP?

Yet despite its plunge into political issues, the Court largely for years declined to do one big thing: help Trump in his assaults on democratic institutions.

Before the 2020 election, the justices assiduously stayed out of the election. That year, the COVID-19 pandemic upended traditional methods of voting, and amid the chaos lawsuits from both parties piled up at the clerk's desk. The Court relied on the *Purcell* principle that judges should refrain from sudden moves too close to an election, an approach that has sometimes meant violations of voting rights could go unaddressed if they were close enough to the election to especially matter. Neither Democrats nor Republicans won major rulings from the Court before Election Day. Most of the time, the high court decides by not deciding: a choice not to grant certiorari to hear an appeal means that lower court rulings stand. Repeatedly the justices resisted the temptation to rule.

Trump's noisy efforts to enlist the courts grew markedly more clamorous after he was defeated for reelection. Sixty-three courts ruled on Trump's cases, and they rejected them using words such as "flimsy," "incorrect and not credible," and "strained legal arguments without merit and speculative accusations . . . unsupported by evidence."[37] The Supreme Court likewise refused to rule. The most audacious suit was filed at the Supreme Court itself, where one state is empowered to sue another. Texas sued Pennsylvania charging that it had allegedly not followed its own election rules. The Court brusquely rejected the move.

In the cauldron of conspiracy theories and legal arguments stirred by Trump and his backers, one bubbled repeatedly: state legislatures had the final word and could reverse the results. This had a faint glimmer of plausibility, since the Constitution's Electors Clause instructs that "Each State shall appoint, in such Manner as the Legislature thereof may direct, a Number of Electors,"[38] a provision eyed by Republicans during the *Bush v. Gore* recount (though it never proved necessary to invoke). Still, the Supreme Court had rejected the idea in a June 2020 ruling that now reads as prophylactic. Elena Kagan and colleagues held that states could pass laws requiring electors to follow the popular vote. They also pointedly noted that legislatures could not interfere after the ballots were cast. "Early in our history, States decided to tie electors to the presidential choices of others, whether legislatures or citizens. Except that legislatures no longer play a role, that practice has continued for more than 200 years," Kagan concluded.[39]

The Court came closest to involvement in *Republican Party of Pennsylvania v. Boockvar*, which involved only a few thousand votes, not enough to have switched the Keystone State's comfortable electoral victory for Biden.[40] Trump relied on an argument that had never been embraced by the Court—what became known as the "independent state legislature theory." Amid the chaos, three justices indicated some sympathy for the idea of legislatures unbound by state courts.[41]

Thus it was ominous when the Court took *Moore v. Harper*. North Carolina is politically divided, with a Democratic governor, Republican senators, and tight presidential margins. But the heavily gerrymandered legislature drew a congressional map likely to produce eleven Republican members and only four Democrats. After the state high court struck down the plan under the North Carolina Constitution, the legislature appealed to the US Supreme Court. It argued that the Constitution's Elections Clause gives legislatures unfettered power to set the "times, places, and manner" of federal elections without checks and balances from state constitutions or state courts. By implication, governors also had no role, nor did voters through ballot measures. Former federal judge Michael Luttig, a prominent conservative, warned the notion was part of "the Republican blueprint to steal the 2024 election."[42] Luttig called *Moore* "the most important case for American democracy in the almost two and a half centuries since America's founding."[43] An avalanche of friend-of-the-court briefs made the same point.

In truth, calling it a "theory" was generous. The Elections Clause was written precisely to curb the power of state legislatures. It used "words of great latitude," James Madison explained at the Constitutional Convention, because "it was impossible to foresee all the abuses" that might come. "Whenever the State Legislatures had a favorite measure to carry, they would take care so to mould their regulations as to favor the candidates they wished to succeed," he added.[44]

In the end, by six to three, an opinion written by Chief Justice Roberts rejected North Carolina's argument. "The Elections Clause does not insulate state legislatures from the ordinary exercise of state judicial review," he wrote.[45] The Court had earlier affirmed that voting laws passed by state ballot measures were constitutional.[46] (Roberts had dissented in that case but switched his views.)

In the winter of 2024, the Court was asked to engage in a way that at last thrust it in the debate over Trump's conduct. For the first time, its actions seemed tailored to help Trump evade accountability, in a way that most helped his political prospects. In one case, the Colorado Supreme Court had ruled that Trump had violated Section 3 of the Fourteenth Amendment and had "engaged in insurrection" leading up to January 6.[47] There was much drama, largely illusory. But there was always a vanishingly small chance that the justices would toss Trump from the ballot, and they quickly and unanimously ruled that an individual state could not reject the eligibility of a national candidate. That was no surprise, and the only question is why the advocates who brought the case thought it might come out otherwise.

Far more consequential was the Court's handling of the former president's claim he was legally immune from prosecution for alleged crimes committed in office.[48] The charges brought over Trump's effort to obstruct the peaceful transfer seemed likely to produce one of the most significant trials in American history. Trump sought broad immunity. At one point his lawyers argued in court he could have ordered Seal Team 6 to assassinate a rival politician, but could not be prosecuted unless he had first been impeached and removed by Congress. It was a legally dubious claim. Special counsel Jack Smith first asked the Supreme Court to rule in December 2023. The justices refused to act. Then after a federal court of appeals unanimously ruled that Trump could face charges, the high court had numerous options: it could have upheld the appeals court's legally strong ruling, for example, or could have unfrozen the trial so it could proceed in spring of 2024. Instead, the justices stalled, scheduling arguments for late April, making it far less likely that Trump would face a jury before the election. In deciding to hear arguments about whether the ex-president was immune from prosecution, the justices appear to have effectively immunized him from a trial.

All this suggests that the supermajority of six highly conservative justices now may be more willing to entertain Trump's challenges to democratic rules should he win another term.

What to make of the Court's rebuff of Make America Great Again legal theories, after so energetically embracing partisan positions on democracy law for the previous two decades? The Court's supermajority, it seems, is conservative—deeply, seriously committed to the project of moving the Court, its interpretation of the Constitution, and the country to the right. It is a conservative Court, not a Make America Great Again Court. Bailing out Trump may not be part of its mission.

THE FUTURE

Where does this all leave the Supreme Court—as a check on democracy, as an enabler of democracy, or as a bulwark against extremism?

In earlier eras, judicial overreach was met with a fierce response, leading to electoral victories and even party realignment. This Supreme Court already has begun to reap the whirlwind of backlash. In the 2022 midterm, Democrats had the best midterm for a party controlling the White House in decades, a result of popular anger at the *Dobbs* decision on abortion rights, along with concerns about the health of democracy. (Many swing voters conflated opposition to *Dobbs* with election denialism as evidence of extremism.)[49] Ballot initiatives supporting abortion rights passed in a half dozen states. In Wisconsin, an electorate that typically divided evenly elected a liberal candidate for state supreme court by an 11-point margin.

Public approval of the US Supreme Court has collapsed to the lowest level ever recorded.[50] It is too early to know whether the supermajority, scalded by the heat, will pull back. In June 2023, the rulings on the Voting Rights Act and the power of state legislatures pleased liberals. That may suggest some of the justices, at least, are acutely attuned to the Court's dwindling support.

Yet there is ample reason for skepticism about a sudden, early course correction. Even *Moore v. Harper* opened the way for more federal judicial involvement in elections. "In interpreting state law in this area," Roberts explained, "state courts may not so exceed the bounds of ordinary judicial review as to unconstitutionally intrude upon the role specifically reserved to state legislatures by Article I, Section 4, of the Federal Constitution."[51] Federal courts can police state courts if they go awry. That could be nothing more than common sense, but it will require vigilance to ensure that partisans do not use it as an excuse to rush to federal court. The central fact—that the Court repudiated the independent state legislature theory while celebrating the role of state courts—should be hammered at every moment.

Another reason for concern: the Court lately has been silent on campaign finance law, but that is because it has not had the chance to whack at that pinata. Before *Buckley*, such laws were seen as vital efforts to curb the overwhelming power of concentrated capital over the political process. Now, decision after decision later, those election rules are seen only through the lens of First Amendment doctrine. Efforts to combat the disinformation spread through hugely profitable social media companies also may fall to the free speech concerns.

Even recent pro-voter rulings should give pause. After *Citizens United* and *Shelby County*, in 2022 the justices merely left well enough alone when they declined to further gut the Voting Rights Act or embrace the fringe state legislature theory. Both cases ratified the status quo. Indeed, the justices should never have heard them in the first place.

All of this forces us to rethink if we are to save American democracy at its moment of peril. We must disenthrall ourselves and stop looking to a noble and largely imaginary Supreme Court to save us. American democracy has advanced, after all, in one of the most glorious struggles in human history. It did so through statutes passed by Congress, through protest movements, through hard-fought political combat, and through energetic enforcement by presidents of both parties. Democracy generally has not advanced through Supreme Court rulings, and it likely never will. Indeed, the Court's doctrines and rulings can be seen as a constraint on future efforts to protect democratic self-government.

When the Court oversteps, citizens can respond. Congress could restore the full strength of the Voting Rights Act, for example. The John Lewis Voting Rights Advancement Act passed the House and had a majority Senate support in 2022 but fell to a filibuster. Matching funds for small campaign contributions, passed by the House as part of the bill eventually known as the Freedom to Vote Act, would negate much damage from *Citizens United* but was similarly stymied in the Senate. Going forward, Democrats are committed to changing Senate rules so these measures can pass. Citizens could enact constitutional amendments as in previous eras to ensure Congress's power to regulate campaign finance, or to protect the right to vote. (Amendments seem impossible; they always do, until things get bad enough, then they come in a burst every half century.) The Court itself could be restructured to ensure greater alignment with the public. The most achievable such reform would be an eighteen-year term for justices, which is broadly popular across the ideological and political spectrum. It could be imposed by amendment, and by statute as well.[52] That could be accompanied by a guarantee that each president can nominate a justice every two years, which could drain partisan toxicity from the nominations process.

Other changes could bolster the Court's accountability. In 2023 ethics scandals rocked the Court when ProPublica revealed that one right-wing billionaire for years had secretly subsidized the lifestyle of Justice

Clarence Thomas. Harlan Crow had, for example, bought Thomas's mother's house and paid for its renovations, and financed the education of the justice's surrogate son. Crow had been introduced to Thomas by the Federalist Society's Leonard Leo, who apparently made a practice of connecting newly confirmed justices with wealthy benefactors. The Court was the only such body without a binding ethics code. All other federal judges, and state judges as well, were governed by such codes. In November 2023, the justices unveiled a "code of conduct" that they explained was necessary to clear up the "misunderstanding" that citizens had about judicial ethics. Unfortunately, that code was toothless—among other things, the justices were still the judges in their own case, with no outside body even to advise on ethics. Congress still has the power to enforce a strong, binding ethics code. The state courts, too, can play a stronger role as an independent bulwark for freedom and democratic equality. Forty-nine of fifty constitutions, for example, have a stronger protection for voting rights than the federal constitution does.[53] State courts, though, have largely interpreted their charters in line with how the federal courts read the US Constitution. That must change. Scholars and advocates have begun a generational effort to invest in these institutions, to encourage them to step up and play their proper constitutional role in our federal system.

Above all we will need to rediscover a virtue that was obvious to democracy advocates in earlier eras and their allies on the bench. If the Supreme Court will not rescue American democracy, and in its activism may undermine it, it should once again practice the virtue of judicial restraint. It may be counterintuitive, but a Supreme Court that found its proper place would strengthen American democracy.

NOTES

1 Thomas Paine, *Common Sense, Rights of Man, and Other Essential Writings* (New York: Signet Classics, 2003), 38.

2 Peter Baker, "Trump Says He Wants a Conservative Majority on the Supreme Court in Case of an Election Day Dispute," *New York Times*, September 23, 2020.

3 Presidential Commission on the Supreme Court of the United States, *Final Report* (December 2021), 112, www.whitehouse.gov.

4 Alexander M. Bickel, *The Least Dangerous Branch: The Supreme Court at the Bar of Politics* (Indianapolis: Bobbs-Merrill, 1962).

5 John Adams to James Sullivan, May 26, 1776, in *The Founders' Constitution*, vol. 1, chap. 13, document 10, https://press-pubs.uchicago.edu.
6 Luther v. Borden, 48 U.S. 1, 12 L. Ed., 581 (1849); Erik J. Chaput, *The People's Martyr: Thomas Wilson Dorr and His 1842 Rhode Island Rebellion* (Lawrence: University Press of Kansas, 2013).
7 Literacy tests: Williams v. Mississippi, 170 U.S. 213 (1898); ban on women voting: Minor v. Happersett, 88 U.S. 162 (1874); Giles v. Harris, 189 U.S. 475 (1903). On *Giles v. Harris*, see Richard H. Pildes, "Democracy, Anti-democracy, and the Canon," *Constitutional Commentary* 893 (2000): 295–319, https://scholarship.law.umn.edu.
8 United States v. Carolene Products Company, 304 U.S. 144 (1938).
9 Smith v. Allwright, 321 U.S. 649 (1944).
10 Baker v. Carr, 369 U.S. 186 (1962).
11 Reynolds v. Sims, 377 U.S. 533 (1964).
12 Rebecca E. Zietlow, "The Judicial Restraint of the Warren Court (and Why It Matters)," *Ohio State Law Journal* 69 (2008): 255–301.
13 See Noah Feldman, *Takeover: How a Conservative Student Club Captured the Supreme Court*, with Lidia Jean Kott (Audible Audio Book, 2021).
14 Josh Blackman, *Unprecedented: The Constitutional Challenge to Obamacare* (New York: PublicAffairs, 2013), 41–43.
15 Andrew Perez, Andy Kroll, and Justin Elliott, "How a Secretive Billionaire Handed His Fortune to the Architect of the Right-Wing Takeover of the Courts," ProPublica, August 22, 2022, www.propublica.org; Kenneth Vogel and Shane Goldmacher, "An Unusual $1.6 Billion Donation Bolsters Conservatives," *New York Times*, August 22, 2022.
16 All references came in the amendments: Fourteenth Amendment (states lose congressional representation when right to vote is abridged), Fifteenth Amendment (banning discrimination in voting due to race), Nineteenth Amendment (guaranteeing the right to vote to women), Twenty-Fourth Amendment (barring poll taxes), and Twenty-Sixth Amendment (guaranteeing the vote to eighteen-year-olds).
17 Crawford v. Marion County Election Board, 553 U.S. 181 (2008).
18 See Michael Waldman and Justin Levitt, "The Myth of Voter Fraud," *Washington Post*, March 29, 2007.
19 Purcell v. Gonzalez, 549 U.S. 1 (2006).
20 Alex Keyssar, "'Disenfranchised?' When Words Lose Their Meaning," *Huffington Post*, October 22, 2006.
21 Shelby County v. Holder, 570 U.S. 529 (2013). For the case and its background, see Michael Waldman, *The Fight to Vote*, rev. ed. (New York: Simon and Schuster, 2022), 229–33.
22 Waldman, *Fight to Vote*, 232.
23 *Shelby County*, 570 U.S. 529 (Ginsburg, J., dissenting).
24 Veasey v. Perry, 71 F. Supp. 3d 627, 633 (S.D. Tex. 2014).
25 North Carolina State Conference of NAACP v. McCrory, 831 F.3d 204, 226 (2016).

26 Jasleen Singh and Sara Carter, "States Have Added Nearly 100 Restrictive Laws since SCOTUS Gutted the Voting Rights Act 10 Years Ago," Brennan Center for Justice, June 23, 2023, www.brennancenter.org.
27 Kevin Morris and Cornyn Grange, "Growing Racial Disparities in Voter Turnout, 2008–2022," March 4, 2024, www.brennancenter.org.
28 Brnovich v. Democratic National Committee, 594 U.S. ___, 141 S. Ct. 2321 (2022).
29 Jeffrey Toobin, "The John Roberts Project," *New Yorker*, April 2, 2014, www.newyorker.com.
30 Citizens United v. Federal Election Commission, 558 U.S. 310, 354 (2010).
31 Buckley v. Valeo, 424 U.S. 1 (1976).
32 Super PACs, which raise money for candidates in unlimited amounts, were authorized by a lower court ruling, *SpeechNow.org v. Federal Election Commission*, 599 F.3d 686, 689 (D.C. Cir. 2010) (en banc).
33 Ian Vandewalker and Mariana Paez, "4 Takeaways about Money in the Midterms," Brennan Center for Justice, November 16, 2022, www.brennancenter.org.
34 Sonere Båtstrand, "More Than Markets: A Comparative Study of Nine Conservative Parties on Climate Change," *Politics and Policy*, August 12, 2015, https://onlinelibrary.wiley.com.
35 Andrew Gumbel, "Peter Thiel's Midterm Bet: The Billionaire Seeking to Disrupt America's Democracy," *The Guardian*, October 15, 2022, www.theguardian.com.
36 Rucho v. Common Cause, 588 U.S. (2019).
37 The quotes come from these cases: Wisconsin VotersAlliance v. Wisconsin Elections Commission, No. 2020AP1920-OA (Wis. December 4, 2020) (Hagedorn, J., concurring) ("flimsy"); Costantino v. City of Detroit, No. 20-014780-AW (Mich. Cir. Ct. November 13, 2020) ("incorrect and not credible"); Donald J. Trump for President Inc. v. Boockvar, 502 F. Supp. 3d 899, 906 (M.D. Pa. November 21, 2020) ("strained legal arguments").
38 U.S. Const. art. II, § 1.
39 Chiafalo v. Washington, 140 S. Ct. 2316 (2020).
40 Republican Party of Pa. v. Boockvar, No. 20A54, 2020 WL 6128193 (U.S. October 19, 2020).
41 When the Supreme Court declined to hear the Pennsylvania GOP's challenge to a state court ruling on ballot counting, Alito, Neil Gorsuch, and Clarence Thomas wrote, "There is a strong likelihood that the State Supreme Court decision violates the Federal Constitution." Republican Party of Pennsylvania v. Boockvar, 592 U.S. ___ (2020). In another case, Justice Kavanaugh veered off the topic (whether a Wisconsin court's ruling on late-arriving absentee ballots would confuse voters) to quote William Rehnquist's assertion, in *Bush v. Gore*, that "'the clearly expressed intent of the legislature must prevail' and that a state court may not depart from the state election code enacted by the legislature." D.N.C. v. Wisconsin State Legislature, 592 U.S. No. 20A66 (Oct. 26, 2020), slip op. at 9 n.1 (Kavanaugh, J., concurring in denial of application to vacate stay).

42 J. Michael Luttig, "Opinion: The Republican Blueprint to Steal the 2024 Election," CNN, April 27, 2022, www.cnn.com.

43 J. Michael Luttig, "There Is Absolutely Nothing to Support the 'Independent State Legislature Theory,'" *The Atlantic*, October 3, 2022, www.theatlantic.com.

44 *Notes of Debates in the Federal Convention of 1787*, reported by James Madison (Athens: Ohio University Press, 1985), August 9, 1787, 423–24. The notes were first published in vols. 2–3 of *The Papers of James Madison* (Washington, DC, 1840).

45 Moore v. Harper, 600 U.S. 1, 143 S. Ct. 2065 (2023).

46 Arizona State Legislature v. Arizona Independent Redistricting Commission, 576 U.S. 787 (2015).

47 Trump v. Anderson, No. 23-719, 2024 WL 899207 (U.S. Mar. 4, 2024).

48 United States v. Trump, 91 F.4th 1173 (D.C. Cir. 2024).

49 Jonathan Weisman and Katie Glueck, "Extreme Candidates and Positions Came Back to Bite in Midterms," *New York Times*, November 14, 2022.

50 Jeffrey M. Jones, "Supreme Court Approval Holds at Record Low," Gallup, August 2, 2023, https://news.gallup.com.

51 Moore v. Harper, 600 U.S. 1, 143 S. Ct. 2065 (2023).

52 Alicia Bannon and Michael Milov-Cordoba, "Supreme Court Term Limits," Brennan Center for Justice, June 20, 2023, www.brennancenter.org.

53 Joshua A. Douglas, "The Right to Vote under State Constitutions," *Vanderbilt Law Review* 67 (2014): 89–149, https://scholarship.law.vanderbilt.edu.

9

POLITICAL REFORMS TO COMBAT EXTREMISM

RICHARD H. PILDES

Understanding the rise of political extremism in the United States—and measures to combat it—raises questions about the causal relationships between political culture, political elites, the information economy, and the institutional design of politics. The question, in essence, is the extent to which extremism is driven from the bottom up versus the top down. The answer helps determine which points of leverage are most likely to be effective in the effort to protect American democracy against political extremism.

Partisan polarization is not necessarily the same as extremism. The political parties might be polarized in the sense that they are clearly ideologically distinct from each other and ideologically coherent internally. But that need not entail extremism, which has more to do with the substantive positions elected officials might take (such as denying the legitimacy of free and fair elections), or the treatment of political opponents as enemies rather than as legitimate opposition, or the refusal ever to compromise with the other side.

That political elites, such as members of Congress, have become highly polarized ideologically is unquestionable. That process of polarization began in the 1980s and has increased relentlessly ever since. Since the Tea Party caucus entered Congress after the 2010 elections, there has been little overlap in congressional voting patterns between Democrats and Republicans. The most conservative Democrat is more liberal than the most liberal Republican and vice versa. In our system of bicameralism and separation of powers, the hyperpolarization of the parties, as I have called it, paralyzes the national political process.[1]

This is obvious during divided government, a situation we have faced 75 percent of the time since 1968. But even during unified government, the filibuster rule in the Senate continues to make the legislative process difficult. Major congressional action even during unified government now sometimes takes place via spending measures, rather than regulation, because the former can be enacted through the reconciliation process, which bypasses the filibuster.[2] Moreover, it is not just elected officials who have become so polarized. The citizens most active in politics, such as those who donate money or work on campaigns, are also highly ideological and polarized.

In the larger political culture, however, the story is more complicated. One of the most striking developments in recent years is the rise of affective polarization: intense enmity toward members of the opposite party, who are regarded more as enemies than as political opponents. Much voting behavior in recent years appears explained more by dislike of the other party than by positive feelings toward one's own party and candidates. Affective polarization is similar across Democrats and Republicans.[3] Scholars note that differing views on policies do not necessarily explain affective polarization: policy preferences are not a good measure of the emotional feelings reflected in affective polarization. Emotional polarization, that is, is not the same as ideological or policy polarization. Instead, affective polarization appears to be more identity based, more tribalistic. For democracy, it is also particularly dangerous. Affective polarization makes it more likely people will tolerate antidemocratic behavior from "their" political figures in order to prevent the other side from gaining power.[4] Affective polarization is part of what has turned politics existential: the belief that if the other side wins, the country will never be the same.

A good deal of scholarship suggests the mass public is not as ideologically polarized on policy issues as are members of Congress or partisan activists, though this issue continues to be debated.[5] To be sure, voters have sorted themselves into the political parties in ways that are more ideologically consistent than in the past. But a number of empirical studies conclude that a majority of Americans who are not political activists still share many policy beliefs, including on issues such as gun rights, immigration, abortion, or how to teach American history.[6] Most partisans, however, *believe* there is far less shared belief, primarily because they themselves have major misperceptions about the policy preferences of other party members.[7] That perception gap is highest among progressive activists and next highest among extreme conservatives.[8]

All this suggests that elite-driven or top-down polarization and extremism play a major role in creating the broader current political culture of tribalistic enmity.[9] And indeed, as studies of the relatively recent phenomenon of affective polarization mount, they are finding that political elites play a major role in driving affective polarization. As a recent synthesis of these studies concludes, "Politicians and political incentives are probably playing a larger role in driving affective polarization than structural issues such as inequality or geographic sorting."[10] This is consistent with long-standing findings in political science about the extent to which citizens take their cues from political elites, as well as the fact that countries such as Hungary, Brazil, and Poland had not been previously polarized but became so under the campaigns and governments of populist leaders who pursued strategies of mobilizing affective polarization.[11]

To the extent affective polarization is driven from the top down, this makes all the more important the institutional framework within which political competition takes place and within which certain types of candidates rather than others are likely to be more successful. A system that permits candidates to win office with only a plurality of the vote gives factional candidates, for example, more of a chance than a system that requires a majority of the vote to be elected. This institutional framework also creates an incentive structure that affects which potential candidates decide to run for office, which approaches to campaigning are most likely to be successful, which candidates get elected, and the governing choices elected officials make with reelection calculations in mind. Given the top-down effects of political elites on mass political culture, and the responsiveness of candidates and elected officials to electoral incentives, a focus on institutional-design reforms to combat elite extremism therefore offers an important point of leverage in seeking to combat the current tribalistic nature of American political culture. At the same time, even if institutional reform can modify the incentives of political elites, we should remain humble about the extent to which those changes can dramatically alter a political culture saturated with cable television, talk radio, and social media.

At the outset, political extremism can be defined in at least two different ways. The first is substantive, based on particular actions or rhetoric (this is sometimes called normative extremism). Those who deny the legitimacy of the 2020 election, for example, might be characterized as substantive extremists. The second is more relative: those who lie at the ideological poles of the political parties, regardless of the specific substance of the positions they take (this is sometimes called empirical extremism).[12] Institutional-design reforms necessarily focus on that second conception of extremism. It is difficult to imagine acceptable institutional reforms that would be viewpoint based and capable of targeting the first type of extremism (one such example is the disqualification provision of Section 3 of the Fourteenth Amendment, though it applies only to the limited number of those who formerly took the oath of office and raises the question of what constitutes engaging in insurrection or rebellion).

Even though institutional-reform measures necessarily focus on the second conception of extremism, they will indirectly affect the first type as well. Those who are substantively extreme tend to come from the ideological wings of the parties. But institutional reforms of the type discussed here will necessarily be overly inclusive; they will make it more difficult for ideologically more extreme candidates in either party, even if they are not extreme in the substantive sense. We have to decide whether the current threats to American democracy are worth that trade-off.

Shortly after January 6, 2021, I wrote a *New York Times* essay arguing that the most urgent task for political reform had become institutional-design changes that would help marginalize the extremist forces in American politics.[13] In this chapter, I'll highlight and discuss briefly five areas of potential evidence-based reform to do just that.

DESIGNING COMPETITIVE ELECTION DISTRICTS

Over the last decade, a great deal of reform effort concerning redistricting has focused on constraining partisan gerrymandering and ensuring outcomes that are fair in partisan terms. I share in those efforts, both in my academic work and as part of the legal team representing Common Cause in the notorious Supreme Court decision *Common Cause v. Rucho*, in which the five-to-four Court held that federal courts could not entertain claims of partisan gerrymandering.[14]

Yet when partisan gerrymandering becomes the exclusive focus of reform, it can eclipse the importance of creating competitive districts. Constructing election districts to be competitive, where possible, is another element of institutional design that can help reduce polarization and extremism. Competitive districts have generally been defined as those in which the winning candidate receives 55 percent of the vote or less. (Given increasing partisan loyalty among voters, which means fewer voters shift back and forth between the parties, swing districts today might have to include no more than 53 percent of likely voters for one party to be competitive.)

Limiting partisan gerrymandering is important, but a map can produce fair partisan outcomes with every seat being completely safe for one party or the other. The dynamics and incentives for candidates running in competitive districts are dramatically different from those candidates face in safe districts. For competitive seats, candidates know they must win over enough voters in the center, who might swing to either party, while also holding on to their base. If they move too far toward the wings of their party, they risk losing the centrist voters needed to win. These dynamics not only weaken the power of the wings of each party but also create incentives for more centrist candidates to run in the first place. Competitive districts also make legislators more responsive to changes in voter preferences; if public opinion on important policies shifts by 5 points, legislators who want to keep or gain office will need to respond to that change.

In safe seats, by contrast, incumbents' main threat is being "primaried." Given the makeup of primary voters, that threat mostly comes from the ideological poles of their party. As the authors of a recent book titled *Rejecting Compromise: Legislators' Fear of Primary Voters* find, "Legislators believe that primary voters are much more likely to punish them for compromising than general election voters or donors."[15] Donald Trump made this point in characteristically bald form in his January 6 speech on the Ellipse, when he mainly attacked Republicans who would not vote to object to the counting of electoral votes: "If they don't fight, we have to primary the hell out of the ones that don't fight. You primary them."[16]

When the major competitive threat that safe-seat incumbents face is from the ideological wings of their party, little incentive exists to appeal to the center of the political spectrum. Primary voters in safe-seat districts also have less incentive to compromise and back moderate candidates because the party's candidate will win the general election regardless of where they fall along the party's ideological spectrum. In turn, moderates are less likely to run in the first place, because they know they can't survive the primary electorate.

The overwhelming dominance of safe seats in Congress contributes to a Congress more polarized than are citizens themselves.[17] From the early 1970s to the early 1990s, around 35 percent of congressional districts were extremely competitive.[18] But by 2022, 84 percent of candidates to the US House were elected from safe seats, with an average victory margin of 28 points. Though the 2022 maps produced a House that was roughly fair in terms of partisan outcomes, given voting patterns, only 16 percent of members were elected from seats in which they faced significant competitive pressure from the other party's candidate. This was similar to 2020, when 83 percent of candidates to the US House were elected from safe seats.[19] This decline, with the loss of incentives to compromise, makes governing in Congress far more difficult.

In a comment that brings together the effects of having fewer competitive districts and the threat that primary-election extremists pose, Tom Davis, a former Republican member of Congress from northern Virginia, recently said, "We ran our caucus to basically support members in swing districts. That's how we got power. Today, they run the caucus now to protect members from R+30 districts [districts the most recent Republican presidential candidate won by more than 30 points] to protect them in primaries."[20]

To be sure, it's not possible to make all districts competitive. The Voting Rights Act requires, where voting is racially polarized, the creation of districts likely to elect the preferred candidate of the minority community. Those districts are generally safe seats for Democrats. In addition, given the extent to which voters have sorted themselves geographically along partisan lines, creating competitive districts in some areas might not be possible or would require unusually shaped districts. But if the number of competitive seats were simply doubled, with about 33 percent of Congress, rather than the current 17 percent, elected from competitive districts, the dynamics on Capitol Hill would change considerably.

Some political scientists, however, disagree that competitive districts marginalize ideological extremism and foster moderation in Congress. This disagreement exposes a striking disjuncture between political scientists and journalists who actually cover Congress. Among those who cover Congress directly, stories with headlines such as "House Democrats in Swing Districts Are Torn over Impeachment"[21] are common. Beyond the headlines, stories covering Congress and state legislatures[22] routinely describe the more moderate positions of members from swing districts compared with those in other seats.[23] That there is often a difference between the ideological views of members from swing districts and others is a simple matter of fact among those who cover Congress most closely. Indeed, legislators themselves strongly believe this, as John Boehner's recent memoir describes in detail.[24]

Yet some political scientists conclude it does not matter whether members are elected from competitive seats or safe seats, because nearly all members of each party vote similarly, regardless of the type of district from which they are elected.[25] What explains this disconnect between those who cover Congress up close and certain social scientists who survey Congress from a greater distance?

The answer is that political scientists define the ideology of members of Congress or state legislatures by aggregating all the roll-call votes taken on bills. This is the easiest data point on legislator policy preferences to measure. But as with quantification in general, basing analysis on the dimensions easiest to quantify can distort reality. For many years now, most legislation has been put together not at the committee level but in leadership-led centralized processes. Behind-the-scenes negotiations among party members take place at this level, when party leaders broker a package that best accommodates the distinct interests within the party. This centralized process also enables party leaders to logroll across bills, giving members who are resistant on one bill what they want in another bill, thus bringing them along to support both measures. By the time a bill is put on the floor for a vote, the party has largely united behind that package. If party leaders can't get sufficient party consensus on a bill, they do not put it to a floor vote.

As a result, counting up only roll-call votes obscures the differences in policy preferences between factions within a party. As leading congressional scholars James Curry and Frances Lee put it, "The roll-call record is censored"; the reality is that the parties "contend with much more intraparty conflict than one might expect from roll-call votes."[26]

In addition, much of roll-call voting in the modern Congress is designed as party messaging. These are votes taken to sharpen and highlight major party differences, rather than to support bills that have a realistic prospect of being enacted. As Curry and Lee document, "Very little actual legislation becomes law by narrow or partisan majorities, but the Congress nevertheless takes many roll call votes that pit one party against the other."[27] Not surprisingly, these messaging roll-call votes display a high degree of party unity—that is part of their point, after all.[28] Yet when political scientists combine all roll-call votes into a single number—without distinguishing bills on minor versus major issues or bills that are purely messaging legislation—they inevitably obscure genuine differences within the parties on significant legislation.

Recent work in political science is starting to undermine the view that legislators from safe seats and competitive seats have the same positions.[29] Rather than treat roll-call voting on all issues as the same, Professors Brandice Canes-Wrone and Kenneth Miller focus on only the most significant bills a given Congress votes on; in their study, that ranges from two to six bills a year.[30] On these bills, they find that members in safe seats respond more to their most polarized donors than do members in competitive districts. This is true for a broad set of issues, including capital gains taxes, partial-birth abortion, the Affordable Care Act, and other highly salient issues.

More specifically, Canes-Wrone and Miller find, first, that national donors are much more polarized than donors from within a member's district. They then find that in competitive districts representatives respond more to the preferences of their constituents, while in safe seats representatives are more responsive to the preferences of this highly polarized national donor class. In other words, in safe seats, members can defect more from their constituents' preferences and embrace the more ideologically extreme positions of their national donors. This is not surprising: if you're going to win a safe seat with 70 percent of the vote, you have a lot of slack to satisfy your national donors with positions your constituents don't support, even if your victory margin winds up dropping next time by several points. But if your district is competitive, you can't afford to stray much from the preferences of your constituents.

Another recent study concludes that when primary electorates are more ideologically extreme, members elected in the general election similarly reflect that extremity in safe seats, but not in competitive districts, where their voting patterns are more moderate.[31]

In sum, those who cover Congress most closely, congressional members themselves, and the most recent work in political science all confirm that members from safe seats tend to be more extreme than those elected from competitive districts. One institutional-design way to combat political extremism is therefore to emphasize the creation of competitive districts, alongside concerns for partisan fairness.

USING INSTANT RUNOFF VOTING

One way to avoid having factional candidates win office is through the use of runoff elections. With runoff elections, the top two candidates in the initial round of voting move on to a second round, which pits them head-to-head. The winner thus has to be supported by a majority of voters in this final round of the election process.

After World War II, a majority of countries that directly elect a president shifted to this type of two-round election system, precisely to ensure winning candidates were supported by a majority of the electorate.[32] This was in response to the view that the Nazis had achieved power in Germany as a factional, plurality-winning party without ever receiving a majority of electoral votes. France is perhaps the most prominent example of such a system. The parties' candidates compete in a first round, but if no one wins more than 50 percent of the vote (which has never happened since the runoff system was created in the Fifth Republic), the top two candidates compete in a second round two weeks later.

In the United States, a few states use runoff general elections, with Georgia being the most visible example in recent years, though the factional candidates those states most feared when these systems were adopted originally were Black candidates. Seven states require even primary-election winners to receive a majority of votes and thus require runoff elections in the primaries if no candidate reaches that level.[33] But most states do not, and in open-seat primaries, about 36 percent of primaries are won with only a plurality of the vote.[34] In competitive districts, these candidates perform slightly less well in the general election than majority-primary victors, which is another benefit of competitive elections. But in noncompetitive districts, there is little penalty for being a factional winner in the primary, if your party dominates the district.[35] Matt Gaetz and Marjorie Taylor Greene, for example, won their first general elections after winning primaries with less than a majority of the primary vote.[36]

In the United States, however, the turnout in runoff elections tends to drop off significantly from the general election (recent Senate runoffs in Georgia, in which partisan control of the Senate was at stake, are an exception). This is not the case in countries like France, in which turnout in the second round of their presidential election is frequently higher than in the first. With much lower turnout, runoff elections run the risk of unrepresentative electorates becoming the decision maker. In addition, a second round of elections imposes significant costs on strapped state and local budgets, and also requires election administrators, including poll workers, to run a second election.

Instant runoff voting (IRV, also called ranked-choice voting) can be understood as an alternative to runoff elections. Its justification is much the same: we should prefer a voting system that rewards candidates who have the broadest electoral appeal, rather than more factional candidates. In theory, a system should select that candidate who would win a head-to-head matchup against each of the other candidates (if there is such a candidate). This is technically known as the Condorcet winner, who is the candidate a majority of the voters prefer to all other candidates. This is another way of saying winning candidates should reflect the preferences of the median voter.

IRV essentially constitutes a multiround election on a single ballot. Voters rank candidates in order of preference (as many as they choose to rank), and when poorly performing candidates are eliminated, the voter's vote on that ballot is transferred to the voter's second-ranked preference. The process continues until a candidate (in a single-office election) receives a majority of the votes.

There are several different *forms* of IRV, however, and the differences between them—which have not yet been widely appreciated—affect whether they do identify the candidate a majority of voters prefer.[37] In the current form of IRV used throughout the United States, the candidate who receives the fewest first-place votes is eliminated; the votes on those ballots are then redistributed to those voters' second-choice preferences. The process is repeated until a candidate wins a majority of the votes in the final round of tabulation.

But how different forms of IRV function in practice depends on the distribution of preferences among voters. When voters are aligned in a normal, bell-shaped distribution, with a substantial number of voters in the center and a smaller number at each wing of the distribution, the currently used form of IRV works well to identify and reward the candidate a majority prefers. If the electorate is split 30–40–30, then one of the two candidates at the wings will be eliminated and their voters' second-choice preferences—presumably predominantly for the centrist candidate—will go to that candidate, who will be elected.

But when voters themselves are highly polarized, so that most voters are located toward either ideological pole and the center electorate is small,[38] the currently used system of IRV will not necessarily reward the candidate with the broadest electoral appeal (the Condorcet winner).[39] In the first round, that candidate (call them the moderate candidate) might well receive the fewest first-place votes and will be eliminated—even though the moderate candidate would defeat either the hard-left or hard-right candidate in a head-to-head match. For example, if 40 percent prefer the hard-left candidate, 40 percent the hard-right candidate, and 20 percent the moderate candidate, the centrist would be eliminated in the first round—even though 60 percent prefer the moderate candidate to either candidate from the ideological poles. This is known as the risk of a "center squeeze" with current IRV systems. Thus, the particular *form* of IRV can matter a great deal if the goal is to avoid anointing factional candidates and to reward Condorcet winners.

Rather than the form of IRV currently in use, other forms of IRV do a better job at identifying the Condorcet winner, or the candidate preferred by a majority of the electorate. This is not the place to go through those alternatives and their properties, which have been described in detail elsewhere.[40] One study of existing uses of IRV in the United States and elsewhere concludes that the current form of IRV, in which the candidate with fewest first-place votes is eliminated first, rarely fails in practice to select the Condorcet winner.[41] But in the type of polarized electorate that characterizes many US states today, it is easy to envision the "center squeeze" becoming a significant issue under the current form of IRV.

Thus, given the justifications for adopting IRV in the first place, it's important to note that IRV comes in different forms and that some forms are better than others at ensuring that the candidate preferred by a majority of voters wins. But the technical properties of a voting system alone are not sufficient to recommend it. Voting systems must be widely perceived as legitimate by voters. That dimension of public acceptance and legitimacy, along with the technical properties of the system, must be taken into account as well.

ELIMINATING THE TRADITIONAL PARTY PRIMARY

The traditional party primary has become a significant source fueling the rise and success of more ideologically extreme candidates. Studies show that incumbent moderates on the Republican side, in particular, have increasingly been challenged in primaries. Similarly, studies show that moderates choose not to run in the first place when they perceive primary electorates to be too extreme for them to survive the primary.[42] This has also led incumbent moderates not to seek reelection, as is the case for several Republican senators who decided not to seek reelection in 2022. In addition, to avoid being primaried in the first place, incumbents tack to the political extremes to preempt such challenges. In *Rejecting Compromise*, Sarah Anderson, Daniel Butler, and Laurel Harbridge-Yong found, based on interviews with members of Congress and aides, that what matters to incumbents is the perception that they risk being primaried if they compromise. Incumbents preemptively change their positions because they perceive they will be challenged, whatever the statistics show about the factual likelihood that they will be challenged.[43]

The early twentieth-century reformers who gave us the direct primary viewed it as a way to avoid the corruption of party machines that chose nominees. They believed primary elections would compel citizens to learn more about candidates and become more engaged. But despite these romantic notions, voters are not champing at the bit to engage in primary elections. Turnout in primaries is notoriously low, as low in midterm primaries as 15 percent of eligible voters in 2014, rarely above 20 percent in the last decade, with a high of 22 percent in 2022.[44] Studies of whether primary voters are more ideologically extreme than other supporters of that party are mixed, though it's widely assumed that they are.[45] That assumption exists because those most actively engaged in political participation tend to be more ideological than those less involved, as a general matter. But empirical evidence does strongly document that primary voters are highly unrepresentative of general election voters; they are older, wealthier, and whiter, and they have higher levels of political knowledge. Circumventing the effects of low turnout, unrepresentative primary elections should be a major focus of reform efforts.

Certain previous reform efforts designed to make election of moderate candidates more likely do not seem to have worked in practice. Little evidence supports the frequently made claim, for example, that open primaries (in which independents can vote) generate more ideologically moderate candidates. The evidence from the two states that currently use top-two primary structures, California and Washington, is mixed about whether the system leads to election of more moderate candidates. Some studies of California conclude it does not; others, that it does.[46] The studies of Washington do not suggest top-two voting has led to election of more moderate candidates. The top-two system also can create a general election in which both candidates come from the same political party.

The most promising form for eliminating the tendency of the traditional primary structure to reward extremism is the top-four or top-five primary. In these systems, all candidates run in a single primary; candidates can identify themselves in partisan terms or as nonpartisan. The top four or five in the primary then go on to the general election, in which ranked-choice voting is used to determine the winner. The theory behind this reform is that any candidate with a strong level of statewide support will get through to the general election, and that with ranked-choice voting the candidate whom a majority of voters support will be elected. This should avoid the elimination of candidates prematurely who would have majority support in the general electorate and avoid plurality or factional winners in the general elections.

Voters in Alaska adopted top-four in 2020, which took effect in the 2022 election cycle (voters in Nevada endorsed top-five but have to endorse it again in a second election before it becomes effective). Thus far, the evidence suggests this new primary structure is working as predicted.

In the most high-profile race, incumbent senator Lisa Murkowski was reelected, even though she would likely have been eliminated had the state used its prior, closed party primary. She was one of the two figures, along with Representative Liz Chaney, whom President Trump targeted most aggressively, and the Trump-supported Republican, Kelly Tshibaka, would likely have won a traditional primary. But under the new system, Murkowski was one of four who made it to the general election, and because she has broad appeal to independents and even some Democrats, she won under the ranked-choice voting system. She received 70 percent of the second-place votes of the Democratic candidate, and when that candidate was eliminated in the ranked-choice voting process, that high level of crossover party support transferred to Murkowski and enabled her reelection. To be sure, she might have won had she run as an independent candidate, but the top-four structure provides an easier path for getting on the ballot.

Less well known is how significantly the new system also affected the twenty-person state senate. Republican Cathy Giessel had been a former state senate president and served for three terms from a center-right district in Anchorage. She had been considered a highly effective legislator but was defeated in 2020 in a traditional Republican primary by a far more conservative, Trump-endorsed candidate who attacked her for compromising too much. Once the top-four system was adopted, she announced a comeback with the intent "to campaign as someone who can work across party boundaries" and form broad electoral coalitions. In the new primary under top-four, three candidates came out effectively tied, two Republicans and a Democrat. When the Democrat, who had finished third, was eliminated, about 40 percent of her vote went to Giessel, while only 8 percent went to her more hard-line conservative opponent. Giessel thus won election with 57 percent of the final vote.[47]

Similarly, in another state senate seat in a conservative rural area, three conservatives ran in an open seat. Of the two dominant candidates, one was considered significantly more conservative than the other. When none of the three received a majority of the vote and the third candidate's votes were redistributed, the more moderate conservative—Jesse Bjorkman—won with 53.6 percent of the vote.

These results also directly affected policy. Giessel was respected enough that she became senate majority leader. She and Bjorkman also became key members of a moderate, bipartisan senate coalition of nine Republicans and eight Democrats (seventeen of the twenty senate seats, which excluded three very conservative Republicans). This coalition agreed to avoid contentious cultural issues on the right and left, such as abortion and transgender issues, and to focus on the state's challenging economic issues. The state passed a consensual budget that differed sharply from prior extreme budget reduction proposals. As one study concludes, "Legislative outcomes were noticeably less contentious and more moderate in ideological terms."[48]

As another form of the effort to minimize the role traditionally structured primaries have in filtering out candidates a majority of the electorate might prefer, states might also eliminate sore-loser laws, if they do not adopt a single primary election. Sore-loser laws prohibit a candidate who loses a party primary from running in the general election; currently, forty-seven states have such laws.[49] One justification for such laws was to avoid the fragmenting of a party's vote in the general election between two candidates, which could enable election of a plurality-winner candidate from the other party. Now that ranked-choice voting is well known, however, states could couple permitting defeated primary candidates to run in the general election with ranked-choice voting. That would avoid these spoiler effect concerns and ensure a candidate with the majority of electoral support would win. Eliminating sore-loser laws would thus enable primary candidates defeated in the traditional primary system to establish, nonetheless, that they had the majority of support in the general election.

THE RIGHT REFORMS OF CAMPAIGN FINANCE

One of the most important facts about our privately financed election system is that individual donors are much more ideologically extreme than the population as a whole. This is one of the most robust social-science findings in the empirical campaign-finance literature.[50] Donors are more ideologically extreme even than nondonor partisans of the same party. Money from individual donors is also the most ideologically motivated source of funds. Traditional business political action committees (PACs) are access-seeking donors; they tend to give to powerful incumbents of each party. Political party committees seek to maximize their party's control of political bodies; they give to competitive challengers and incumbents, regardless of their ideological makeup, because partisan control is the motivating goal.

On top of this, individual contributions and spending have become a much larger share of campaign funds in recent decades. This is partly due to the nationalization of elections, the explosion of small-donor-based funding through the internet, and the rise of unlimited funding for super PACs, whose main source is individual donors. Individual contributions from outside a district or state are all the more ideologically motivated, given the lack of motivation to care about district-specific concerns. In my work, I have shown that more ideologically extreme candidates and members of Congress are most dependent on small donors.[51] I noted earlier that affective polarization is largely driven from the top down, and small donors in particular appear to respond to the outrage and extremism from candidates and incumbents that go viral on the internet and social media.

Small donors are more likely than large donors to make "impulse" contributions in response to politically viral moments; the culture of outrage that generates attention on social media provides the same dynamic that turns on the spigot of small donations. But whether or not small donors are more likely than large donors to fuel the ideological extremes of the parties, the fact remains that our privately financed system of funding, which is so dependent on individual donors, contributes to polarization and extremism.

Given this, properly designed campaign-finance reform, whatever its other virtues, could also have systemic effects in mitigating polarization and extremism. But that depends on the form reform takes. Any system of campaign-finance reform that ties itself to the contribution patterns of individual donors would continue to fuel the ideological extremes. This would be true of the most common current reform proposal among many reform groups, a small-donation matching funds program. In such a program, the federal government would provide a six-to-one match for donations below $200 (or $250, depending on the proposal), up to a certain level. The Democrats' major voting rights reform bill, the For the People Act, included such a proposal. This proposal is based on the system New York City has used for a number of years, which was recently expanded in New York to the state level. But the dynamics of local government elections are very different from those of national elections for Congress.

The appeal of a small-donor matching system is that it would enhance political equality and participation by subsidizing the contributions of small donors. But because this system would base public funding on the preferences of individual donors, it would further fuel the polarization and extremism in our politics. Given the threats American democracy currently faces, we should be hesitant about even well-intentioned reforms that would have those consequences.

But that doesn't mean we have to accept the status quo. The alternative is more traditional forms of public financing, currently used in about ten states. In these systems, candidates must first raise a small, threshold amount from a small number of donors; virtually all credible candidates are able to do so. They then become eligible for grants of public funds. Because these funds come from the general treasury, they are ideologically neutral, unlike public funding that would be based on the preferences of individual donors. In accepting these funds, candidates agree not to raise additional money outside the public-financing system.

To be sure, there are difficulties in designing an effective system of public financing, especially given certain constitutional constraints the Roberts Court has imposed.[52] The system must be able to keep up with the ever-rising costs of campaigns and be funded at high enough levels to make candidates want to accept public funding; given current constitutional doctrine, participation must be voluntary. But well-designed systems of public financing that reduce the weight of individual donors can help mitigate polarization and extremism. Most major democracies do not rely on individual contributions to finance their elections. Instead, they primarily rely on public financing, which is typically run through the political parties. The reforms of the 1970s did bring us public financing of presidential campaigns, but the inability of Congress to keep that system updated with the rising costs of campaigns, and the increasing ability to raise private funds, eventually led candidates to reject the system, which began to become irrelevant when Barack Obama dropped out of public financing in the 2008 general election.

Congress is unlikely to enact any major legislation in the campaign-finance area (or in the political reform area more generally). Thus, movement toward public financing will have to continue to come at the state level. If those reforms come to be seen as successful, they might eventually create demand to adopt them at the national level.

THE PRESIDENTIAL NOMINATIONS PROCESS

One of the most radical changes we made to our democratic process was the shift to the presidential nominations process that took place in the 1970s. That was when the parties moved to the current, primaries-dominated process for choosing the party's nominee. For 170 years before that change to a purely populist system of nomination, elected party figures from around the country played the dominant role in deciding who the party's nominee would be. These figures performed a type of "peer review," in which the judgments of those experienced in government at the national, state, and local levels played a major role in vetting and selecting the party's nominees. Even during the era in which the political party conventions were actual decision makers, there were a few primary elections, which allowed candidates to demonstrate their electoral appeal, but delegates chosen through primary elections never constituted a majority of the delegates.[53]

At the time of the shift to primaries, renowned political scientists with expertise in the nominations process expressed concern that eliminating any role for elected party figures in the process "might lead to the appearance of extremist candidates and demagogues, who unrestrained by allegiance to any permanent party organization, would have little to lose by stirring up mass hatreds or making absurd promises."[54] Many other established democracies continue to give elected party figures at least a filtering, if not decisive, role in selecting the party's standard bearers. In the United Kingdom, for example, Conservative Party members in Parliament first decide on two candidates as potential party leaders, and party members then vote on those two candidates. The Labor Party used to require that potential candidates receive the approval of 15 percent of the Labor members in Parliament before party members could then select among such candidates for the final choice; recent changes have created a more complex system in which elected party figures still play a vetting role (in both cases, the "party electorate" is much smaller than in the United States, because party membership requires paying a fee or dues).

Building back in some role for elected party figures can reduce the risk of extremist candidates winning a party's nomination. Yet building in such a role in a political culture that has gotten used to voters having the exclusive power to choose the nominees is difficult. One way of doing so without undermining the role voters have come to assume would be to change the way delegates are allocated in response to the primary vote in various states. These changes would be designed to make the delegate allocation more proportionate to the actual vote. One of the effects of such changes would be to increase the possibility of a brokered convention. If no candidate receives a majority of the delegates before the convention, the convention would then be brokered; the delegates would then have to decide how to choose among the various candidates.[55]

On the Republican side, primaries become winner-take-all affairs after a certain date in the primary cycle. This enables candidates who might win only a plurality of the vote in a state to capture all that state's delegates, given the winner bonus that follows from winner-take-all rules. On the Democratic side, delegates are allocated proportionately throughout the process. But candidates who receive less than 15 percent of the vote receive no delegates, with those delegates then going to the more dominant candidates instead. This allocation rule also gives bonus delegates to the candidates who receive more than 15 percent of the vote.

Awarding delegates in a more directly proportionate way would eliminate giving extra bumps up to the winning or dominant candidates. It would avoid factional candidates being able to capture all of a state's delegates through winner-take-all allocation rules. When primaries are significantly contested, these changes would make it less likely a candidate would enter the convention having already won a majority of the delegates. No power would be taken away from voters; indeed, the system would reflect their votes more accurately. But the votes in primary elections would be somewhat less likely to definitively determine the outcome, particularly when multiple, serious candidates compete.

For these changes to make sense, the process of selecting convention delegates would also have to change. Currently, the conventions do not matter; delegates serve mainly in a ceremonial role merely to reflect formally the popular vote in the state. But if the possibility of brokered conventions returns, delegates would have to be prominent enough party figures—elected state party leaders, such as governors, for example—to have the legitimacy and support to help choose a nominee in the midst of a contested process that had not yielded a clear winner. In the event no candidate came to the convention with a majority of delegates, party leaders would broker interests within the party in an effort to find a widely acceptable nominee. In doing so, these party leaders would likely value candidates who appealed to a range of interests or factions within the party.

These changes would not stop ideologically extreme candidates from being able to win a majority of delegates through the direct primary process. They would be far from amounting to a return to a full peer-review process. But at a minimum, these changes would make it less likely a factional candidate could automatically capture the nomination. And when conventions were contested, the candidate who emerged would also likely reflect a range of interests within the party.

Other potential ways exist of building back in more of a voice for elected party figures from around the country. In theory, Republicans could allot a certain number of spots to superdelegates, as Democrats currently do, and Democrats could expand the role of their own superdelegates. The Democrats added a role for superdelegates starting with the 1984 convention, after the primary system was perceived to have produced two weak nominees in the first elections under that new system. Superdelegates constitute about 15 percent of the Democratic convention, but they have never acted contrary to the vote of the primary voters. Under recent rule changes, the Democrats have constrained the role of superdelegates; they cannot vote on the first round of balloting but only if the convention goes to a second round. Thus, changes that would add to the role of superdelegates would run directly against the political culture that has developed since the 1970s, in which voters now feel entitled to have their votes determine the outcome.

Not all reforms offered in the name of combatting polarization or extremism are ones I would endorse. I already noted earlier that I believe the reform proposal of a national, small-donor-based matching-funds program would actually further fuel polarization and extremism. I am also skeptical about the proposal that Congress permit or require states to use multimember districts to elect members to the House. This proposal, which has received a fair amount of attention in certain reform circles, seeks to have much larger House districts, each of which would elect five to seven members.[56] The hope is that this would produce a House composed of five to six political parties, and that in such a multiparty House, it would be easier to form majority coalitions on an issue-by-issue basis than it is to find any bipartisanship in our current two-party system. In my view, such a system would instead make Congress even more dysfunctional than it is already. I say that based on my study of the proportional-representation systems of western Europe, which in the last decade changed from being in effect two-and-a-half-party systems to five- or six-party systems—and which have become far more dysfunctional as a result.[57] Having to negotiate legislative deals on an issue-by-issue basis, across multiple parties each with its own self-interested electoral calculations, is likely to make getting bills through the House even harder than it currently is, when one party controls the chamber. And the Senate and White House would remain part of the two-party system, so that any bill that survived the House would then need support from a differently constituted Senate and White House.

A political culture characterized by high degrees of affective polarization is a grave danger to American democracy. Yet there is a good deal of evidence that affective polarization, as well as polarization more generally in the political culture, is driven by political elites in a top-down process. Institutional reforms to make it less likely that ideologically extreme candidates who lack majority support can get elected can thus help to mitigate polarization, both in Congress and in the political culture more generally. That's particularly true if we were to adopt a series of measures involving campaign finance, the structure of primaries, the design of election districts, the types of voting systems, and the nature of the presidential nominations process.

Ideologically extreme political representatives also make delivering effective government more difficult. If party leaders cannot bring them along to support the party line, they make forging the compromises necessary to govern effectively, particularly during divided government, all the more unlikely. Yet when democratic governments appear incapable of delivering effective policies on major issues, it can lead to distrust, alienation, anger, and withdrawal. Even worse, that failure can fuel desires for a strongman figure who promises to cut through this dysfunction and do what democratic governments seem unable to accomplish.[58] If ideologically extreme candidates are supported by a true majority of their electorates, there might be nothing in institutional design that can stand in the way of their election.

Institutional design cannot transform political culture entirely, but it can mitigate ideological extremism to an extent not possible to identify in advance. Such institutional-design reforms might be our best means of combatting some of the most dangerous tendencies in American politics and political culture more broadly.

NOTES

1 Richard H. Pildes, "Why the Center Does Not Hold: The Causes of Hyperpolarized Democracy in America," *California Law Review* 99, no. 2 (2011): 273–333.

2 Jonathan Gould, "A Republic of Spending" (unpublished manuscript, 2023).

3 Nathan P. Kalmoe and Lilliana Mason, *Radical American Partisanship: Mapping Violent Hostility, Its Causes, and the Consequences for Democracy* (Chicago: University of Chicago Press, 2022), 88.

4 Eelco Harteveld et al., "The (Alleged) Consequences of Affective Polarization: Individual-Level Evidence & a Survey Experiment in 9 Countries," OSF Preprints, last modified October 1, 2022, https://doi.org; Eli J. Finkel et al., "Political Sectarianism in America," *Science* 370, no. 6516 (October 30, 2020): 533–36, https://doi.org.

5 See, e.g., Austin C. Kozlowski and James P. Murphy, "Issue Alignment and Partisanship in the American Public: Revisiting the 'Partisans without Constraint' Thesis," *Social Science Research* 94 (2021), https://doi.org (suggesting the American public has become increasingly ideological).

6 See, e.g., Morris Fiorina, *Unstable Majorities: Polarization, Party Sorting, and Political Stalemate* (Stanford, CA: Hoover Institute Press, 2017). See also Andrew Hall, *Who Wants to Run? How the Devaluing of Political Office Drives Polarization* (Chicago: University of Chicago Press, 2019) (concluding that moderate candidates tend not to run, given cost-benefit assessment of doing so); Anthony Fowler et al., "Moderates," *American Political Science Review* 117, no. 2 (2023): 643–60 ("Our findings contribute to a growing literature suggesting that to the extent that elected officials are polarized, it is likely not attributable to mass voting behavior"); Barum Park, "How Are We Apart? Continuity and Change in the Structure of Ideological Disagreement in the American Public, 1980–2012," *Social Forces* 96, no. 4 (2017): 1757–84; and Seth J. Hill and Chris Tausanovitch, "A Disconnect in Representation? Comparison of Trends in Congressional and Public Polarization," *Journal of Politics* 77, no. 4 (2015): 1058–75.

7 Samantha L. Moore-Berg et al, "Exaggerated Meta-perceptions Predict Intergroup Hostility between American Political Partisans," *Proceedings of the National Academy of Science* 177, no. 26 (2020): 14864–72.

8 Rachel Kleinfeld, "Polarization, Democracy, and Political Violence in the United States: What the Research Says," Carnegie Endowment for International Peace, September 5, 2023, https://carnegieendowment.org.

9 On the rise of various populist views in Europe being top-driven by political elites, see Larry M. Bartels, *Democracy Erodes from the Top: Leaders, Citizens, and the Challenge of Populism in Europe* (Princeton, NJ: Princeton University Press, 2023).

10 Kleinfeld, "Polarization, Democracy," 44.

11 See Task Force to Combat Political Extremism, "Report of the Sub-group on Proportional Representation" (2023 draft, in author's possession), 38–39. See also Matt Yglesias, "Polarization IS a Choice," *Slow Boring*, September 12, 2023, www.slowboring.com.

12 The terms *normative extremism* and *empirical extremism* are taken from the work of Cynthia Miller-Idriss, who also identifies *behavioral extremism*, which denotes uncivil and confrontational modes of behavior. Cynthia Miller-Idriss, *Hate in the Homeland* (Princeton, NJ: Princeton University Press, 2022).

13 Richard H. Pildes, "How to Keep Extremists out of Power," *New York Times*, February 25, 2021, https://www.nytimes.com.

14 Some of the material in this section comes from Richard H. Pildes, "Create More Competitive Districts to Limit Extremism," RealClearPolitics, April 29, 2021, www.realclearpolitics.com.

15 Sarah E. Anderson, Daniel M. Butler, and Laurel Harbridge-Yong, *Rejecting Compromise: Legislators' Fear of Primary Voters* (New York: Cambridge University Press, 2020).

16 "Transcript of Trump's Speech at Rally before US Capital Riot," Associated Press, January 13, 2021, https://apnews.com/article/election-2020-joe-biden-donald-trump-capitol-siege-media-e79eb5164613d6718e9f4502eb471f27.

17 Richard G. Niemi, Herbert F. Weisberg, and David Kimball, *Controversies in Voting Behavior* (Washington, DC: CQ Press, 2011).

18 Alan I. Abramowitz, "Redistricting and Competition in Congressional Elections," University of Virginia Center for Politics, February 24, 2022, https://centerforpolitics.org. See also David Wasserman and Ally Flinn, "Introducing the 2021 Cook Political Report Partisan Voter Index," *Cook Political Report*, April 15, 2021, https://cookpolitical.com.

19 Brett Maney, "This Is the Primary Problem with Politics Today," Unite America, April 1, 2021, www.uniteamerica.org.

20 Paul Kane, "McCarthy Thought He Could Harness Forces of Disruption. Instead They Devoured Him," *Washington Post*, October 5, 2023, www.washingtonpost.com.

21 Siobhan Hughes, "House Democrats in Swing Districts Are Torn over Impeachment," *Wall Street Journal*, May 22, 2019, www.wsj.com.

22 Rachael Bade, "Centrist House Democrats Lash Out at Liberal Colleagues, Blame Far-Left Views for Costing the Party Seats," *Washington Post*, November 5, 2020, www.washingtonpost.com.

23 Michael Wines, "Half a Year after Trump's Defeat, Arizona Republicans Are Recounting the Vote," *New York Times*, April 25, 2021, www.nytimes.com.

24 John Boehner, *On the House* (New York: St. Martin's, 2021).

25 See Nolan McCarty, "Hate Our Polarized Politics? Why You Can't Blame Gerrymandering," *Washington Post*, October 26, 2012, www.washingtonpost.com. See also Royce Carroll et al., "DW-NOMINATE Scores with Bootstrapped Standard Errors," Voteview, September 2015, https://legacy.voteview.com.

26 James M. Curry and Frances E. Lee, *The Limits of Party: Congress and Lawmaking in a Polarized Era* (Chicago: University of Chicago Press, 2020), 81, 17.

27 James M. Curry and Frances E. Lee, "Congress at Work," in *Can America Govern Itself?*, ed. Frances E. Lee and Nolan McCarty (Cambridge: Cambridge University Press 2019), 181.

28 Frances E. Lee, *Insecure Majorities: Congress and the Perpetual Campaign* (Chicago: University of Chicago Press, 2016).

29 Brandice Canes-Wrone and Kenneth M. Miller, "Out-of-District Contributors and Representation in the US House of Representatives," *Legislative Studies Quarterly* 47, no. 2 (2021): 361–95.

30 Canes-Wrone and Miller.

31 Rachel Porter, "Estimating the Ideological Extremity of Primary Electorates" (unpublished manuscript, Notre Dame University, 2023).

32 Ben Reilly and Adam Przeworski, "Electoral Systems and Conflict in Divided Societies," in *International Conflict Resolution after the Cold War*, ed. Paul C. Stern and Daniel Druckman (Washington, DC: National Academy Press, 2000), 439.

33 "Primary Runoffs," National Conference of State Legislatures, August 8, 2023, www.ncsl.org.

34 Task Force to Combat Political Extremism, "Report of the Sub-group on Proportional Representation," 15.

35 Task Force to Combat Political Extremism, 15.

36 Jeffrey Lazarus, "Unintended Consequences: Anticipation of General Election Outcomes and Primary Election Divisiveness," *Legislative Studies Quarterly* 30 (2005): 435–61; Alan Ware, "'Divisive' Primaries: The Important Questions," *British Journal of Political Science* 9 (1979): 381–84.

37 Canes-Wrone and Miller, "Out-of-District Donors."

38 Technically, this is a bimodal distribution rather than a normal or Gaussian distribution of voter preferences.

39 Nathan Atkinson, Edward B. Foley, and Scott Ganz, "Beyond the Spoiler Effect: Can Ranked Choice Voting Solve the Problem of Political Polarization?," *University of Illinois Law Review* (forthcoming).

40 Edward B. Foley, "Total Vote Runoff: A Majority-Maximizing Form of Ranked Choice Voting," *University of New Hampshire Law Review* 21 (forthcoming).

See also Nathan Atkinson and Scott C. Ganz, "Robust Electoral Competition: Rethinking Electoral Systems to Encourage Representative Outcomes" (forthcoming 2024).

41 Nicholas O. Stephanopoulos, "Finding Condorcet" (draft manuscript, February 10, 2024).

42 Danielle M. Thomsen, "Ideological Moderates Won't Run: How Party Fit Matters for Partisan Polarization in Congress," *Journal of Politics* 76, no. 3 (2014): 786–97.

43 Anderson, Butler, and Harbridge-Yong, *Rejecting Compromise.*

44 John C. Fortier et al., "2018 Primary Election Turnout and Reforms," Bipartisan Policy Center, November 2018, https://bipartisanpolicy.org.

45 See, e.g., Andrew B. Hall and Daniel M. Thompson, "Who Punishes Extremist Nominees? Candidate Ideology and Turning out the Base in US Elections," *American Political Science Review* 112, no. 3 (2018): 509–24; and John Sides et al., "On the Representativeness of Primary Electorates," *British Journal of Political Science* 50, no. 3 (2018): 677–85.

46 Christian R. Grose, "Reducing Legislative Polarization: Top-Two and Open Primaries Are Associated with More Moderate Legislators," *Journal of Political Institutions and Political Economy* 1 (2020): 267–87.

47 Details in this paragraph and the next two are taken from Glenn Wright, Benjamin Reilly, and David Lublin, "Assessing the Impact of Alaska's Top-4-RCV Electoral Reform" (paper prepared for 2023 Annual Meeting of the American Political Science Association).

48 Wright, Reilly, and Lublin.

49 Barry C. Burden, Bradley M. Jones, and Michael S. Kang, "Sore Loser Laws and Congressional Polarization," *Legislative Studies Quarterly* 39, no. 3 (August 2014): 299–305; Michael S. Kang and Barry C. Burden, "Sore Loser Laws in Presidential and Congressional Elections," in *Handbook of Primary Elections*, ed. Robert G. Boatright (New York: Routledge, 2018), 456–66.

50 Richard H. Pildes, "Participation and Polarization," *University of Pennsylvania Journal of Constitutional Law* 22, no. 2 (2020): 341–408.

51 Richard H. Pildes, "Small-Donor-Based Campaign-Finance Reform and Political Polarization," *Yale Law Journal Online Symposium* 129 (2019): 149–70.

52 Ariz. Free Enter. Club's Freedom Club PAC v. Bennett, 564 U.S. 721 (2011).

53 For a fuller exploration of the issues in this section, see Stephen Gardbaum and Richard H. Pildes, "Populism and Institutional Design: Methods of Selecting Candidates for Chief Executive," *New York University Law Review* 93, no. 4 (2018): 647–708.

54 Nelson W. Polsby et al., *Presidential Elections: Strategies of American Electoral Politics* (Lanham, MD: Rowman and Littlefield, 2016), 230.

55 This proposal comes from Hans Noel. See Hans Noel, "Contested Conventions Would Be Much Better Than Pageants," Vox, July 21, 2016, www.vox.com; and Hans Noel, "How to Fix the Rules to Get More Contested Conventions," Vox, July 22, 2016, www.vox.com.

56 Lee Drutman, *Breaking the Two-Party Doom Loop: The Case for Multiparty Democracy in America* (Oxford: Oxford University Press, 2020).

57 Richard H. Pildes, "Democracies in the Age of Fragmentation," *California Law Review* 110, (2022): 2051–68.

58 See Richard H. Pildes, "The Neglected Value of Effective Government" (New York University School of Law Public Law and Legal Theory Research Paper No. 23-51, 2023).

PART III

ADMINISTERING SECURE ELECTIONS

10

ELECTION ADMINISTRATION AND THE RIGHT TO VOTE

NATHANIEL PERSILY

The 2020 election represented a watershed moment in the history of American election administration. Facing unprecedented challenges related to the COVID-19 pandemic, the nation's army of administrators managed an election that featured the highest voter turnout in a century, with two-thirds of the eligible electorate casting nearly 160 million ballots.[1] The electoral system underwent rapid transformation as the number of voters casting votes by mail nearly doubled, and administrators adopted all kinds of novel measures, such as curbside voting and greater use of ballot drop boxes, to provide safe options for voters to cast ballots.

As Charles Stewart III and I have written elsewhere, however, the 2020 election represented both a "miracle" and a "tragedy."[2] Accompanying the heroism of the administrators was severe polarization in trust concerning the election results. The fact that courts entertained and rejected a range of objections to election practices in more than sixty lawsuits did little to quell the widespread belief among Republicans that the election was stolen. That suspicion reached its apotheosis with the insurrection at the Capitol on January 6. President Donald Trump's continued refusal to accept the results or even to attend the inauguration of President Joe Biden fixed in the minds of at least a third of Americans the notion that the election was somehow illegitimate.

In the three years since the insurrection, public opinion has not moved much on these critical questions. If anything, the polarization in belief in election-related conspiracy theories has hardened further. Consequently, as we approach the 2024 election, election administrators are under greater scrutiny than ever, and the margin for error has shrunk considerably. Indeed, many have now resigned in the face of death threats and the heightened stress of administering elections when trust has collapsed.

Although we now live in an age where each political development is described as "unprecedented," it may be useful, at least with respect to election administration and the right to vote, to take stock of how we got here. Given the unique character and challenges of recent elections, it would be folly to say that where we are now represents the inevitable result of where we have been. Nevertheless, to appreciate the uniqueness of our current era requires an understanding of the pace of development of both voting rights law and election administration.

This chapter takes as its ambitious goal describing the parallel evolution of both voting rights jurisprudence and election administration policy. We tend to tell these two histories as separate chronologies, given that the jurisprudence arises out of court decisions, and administration usually emerges from some combination of legislative and bureaucratic action. But given that the current era features a merging of the two, in which the practice of election regulation is seen (rightly or wrongly) as the primary determinant of the substance of voting rights, much can be gained by telling these histories side by side. Our story begins in the 1960s when both the Supreme Court and Congress began to recalibrate the relationship between federal law—both constitutional and statutory law—and the traditional autonomy that states enjoyed in regulating elections.

FROM WARREN TO REHNQUIST AND THE VOTING RIGHTS ACT TO THE NATIONAL VOTER REGISTRATION ACT

The "Rights Revolution" of the 1960s reenvisioned the federal role in elections. This revolution occurred both in the courts and in Congress. It represented a unique moment, spurred on both by the political environment of the civil rights movement and by leadership that took advantage of the opportunity to rearrange the federal and state roles in elections. Of course, earlier efforts at expanding the franchise—as with the Fifteenth and Nineteenth Amendments or aberrant Supreme Court cases, such as the *White Primary Cases*[3]—cabined state sovereignty over elections. But the 1960s represents the formative era for the construction of the modern framework for voting rights protections.

The Warren Court played a transformational role in reconceptualizing the Fourteenth Amendment's guarantee of "Equal Protection of the Law" to include voting rights. Whereas in 1959 the Court upheld literacy tests in *Lassiter v. Northampton County*,[4] just seven years later it "established" the constitutional right to vote in *Harper v. Virginia Board of Elections*,[5] a decision striking down poll taxes under the Equal Protection Clause. In the intervening years, the Court issued its one-person, one-vote cases, which both drew voting rights into the pro-equality mission that began with *Brown v. Board of Education*[6] and made clear that the Court would act to "clear the channels of political change"[7] and adopt a special role in policing the political process. That role extended beyond race cases or even notorious examples of disenfranchisement, to include regulations of the electoral process, such as ballot access, cases that struck down rules biased against challengers to the two major parties.[8]

In parallel, Congress acted to protect voting rights. In 1964, it eliminated poll taxes for federal elections with passage of the Twenty-Fourth Amendment, which the states ratified soon after. A year later it passed the Voting Rights Act (VRA). With expanded Democratic majorities in the 1964 election, Lyndon Johnson could push through Congress an unprecedented reconfiguration of state and federal power over elections. The famed Sections 4 and 5 placed many southern (and other) jurisdictions under federal supervision for all significant aspects of the electoral process. The law also banned literacy tests and included provisions for federal observers of elections.

Most significantly for the purposes of this chapter, the law represented, in part, a federal regulation of election administration. Due to later court decisions, the preclearance regime of Sections 4 and 5 required covered states to receive federal permission (given by either the Department of Justice or a district court in Washington, DC) for all regulations that implicated the right to vote.[9] Not only would it apply to high-profile laws, such as redistricting plans or voting qualifications, but it would even lead to federal supervision of changes to voter registration, relocation of polling places, and new ballot access requirements. To be sure, the law did not prescribe the "right" way to run an election. But it certainly laid down what constituted a "wrong" way, as it policed each aspect of election administration in covered jurisdictions for possible discriminatory purpose or effect.

When the VRA was amended in 1982, its main focus was on vote dilution, not vote denial or election administration. You would not know that from the terms of the statute, which apply to any "voting qualification or prerequisite to voting or standard, practice, or procedure."[10] But Congress passed the new version of the law in response to the Supreme Court's decision in *Mobile v. Bolden*, which upheld a dilutive at-large election scheme under both a constitutional and VRA challenge. (Vote dilution occurs when, for example, minority voters cannot elect their preferred candidates in a multimember city council elected citywide because the majority will systematically outvote them, unlike in districted elections, in which geographically concentrated minorities might have the power to elect their preferred representative from a given district.) The Court held that such vote dilution claims would require discriminatory purpose. Congress then responded with the effects test of Section 2, which banned such "practices" if they caused minorities to "have less opportunity than other members of the electorate to participate in the political process and to elect representatives of their choice." That provision has been used routinely to challenge redistricting plans or to break up at-large systems into single-member districts. Very few "vote denial" cases were ever brought under Section 2. Indeed, the most fulsome discussion at the Supreme Court of vote denial under Section 2 did not happen until 2021.[11]

For the most part, then, for the thirty years after passage of the VRA and the Supreme Court's decision in *Harper*, the Court's "democracy docket" was preoccupied with redistricting and race cases, and the occasional *Harper*-style disenfranchisement case.[12] The ballot access cases are important exceptions, and they would prove consequential in developing the constitutional test later applied to regulations of election administration. In addition to upholding most restrictions on minor parties and independent candidates,[13] the Court over that period upheld bans on sore-loser (i.e., a primary loser who attempts to run as an independent)[14] and fusion candidacies (i.e., candidates who wish to appear on two parties' ballot lines in the general election)[15] and bans on write-in ballots.[16]

When it comes to federal regulation of the "nuts and bolts" of election administration, the National Voter Registration Act (NVRA) of 1993, or "Motor Voter," represents an important bridge from the VRA era to the Help America Vote Act (HAVA) era. The NVRA's most important provisions required states to facilitate voter registration at departments of motor vehicles and state public assistance agencies. It also required states to allow prospective voters to register up until thirty days before an election. In later years, its prescribed procedures (under Section 8) for maintenance of voter registration lists gained greater significance. The NVRA specifies how and when states can remove from registration lists the names of voters who move or die. Those restrictions have proved quite important as "voter purges" have become a partisan flashpoint in the modern integrity-access debate.

THE 2000 ELECTION, *BUSH V. GORE*, AND THE HELP AMERICA VOTE ACT

The 2000 election brought election administration into the limelight. Anyone who lived through that event remembers the indelible image of the exhausted, cockeyed vote counter splashed on twenty-four-hour cable news coverage for a month between mid-November and mid-December. We tend to view the administrative issues in that election through the lens of the eventual resolution in *Bush v. Gore*, which concerned indeterminate standards for recounting punch-card ballots held to violate the Equal Protection Clause. But the 2000 election was a watershed moment because it laid bare the entrails of every aspect of the electoral system—voter registration, voter purges, felon disenfranchisement, ballot design (recall the famous Palm Beach butterfly ballot), military and mail voting, the shortcomings and diversity of different voting technologies, and the poorly drafted standards and capricious practices for election recounts. Because the election was decided by just a few hundred votes, plaintiffs mined every aspect of the electoral system to investigate whether it may have been outcome determinative. In the quadrennial "Voting Wars"[17] that have followed ever since 2000, *Bush v. Gore* casts a long shadow as to how any small (even seemingly insignificant) aspect of the electoral system might prove outcome determinative for a presidential election.

Although the Supreme Court's resolution of *Bush v. Gore* may have focused on recount standards for punch-card ballots, the civil society and legislative response following the 2000 election was not so limited. The CalTech/MIT Voting Technology Project, the first serious academic effort to study election administration issues, emerged from the ashes of the 2000 election. That initiative performed unprecedented analysis of the voting technology landscape to assess the performance of different types of voting machines. It went even further, though, to develop the concept of "lost votes," which extended beyond technological mishaps to capture the many ways that voter intentions might not lead to a cast and counted vote.[18] The team's findings and approach were important for the legislative response that would follow.

Two commissions emerged to offer reforms to address the problems revealed in the 2000 election. The first, the National Commission on Federal Election Reform,[19] chaired by former presidents Gerald Ford and Jimmy Carter with bipartisan membership of elder statesmen and stateswomen, issued its report in August 2001. It made a series of recommendations relevant to the entire election ecosystem. These included statewide voter registration systems, provisional ballots, a national holiday for Election Day, federal funding and a new federal agency for elections, and elimination of felon disenfranchisement for convicts who had served their sentences. It also recommended that the federal government develop voting system standards and that states set benchmark performance standards for voting machines. The commission went so far as to recommend that news organizations not project winners while polls were still open, and that Congress and states consider legislation to that effect.

Many of these recommendations made their way into HAVA.[20] Although far from transformative for the American electoral system, the legislation nevertheless created federal rules and initiatives that had a significant impact across the election ecosystem. First, given the problems with punch-card ballots revealed in 2000, HAVA appropriated $3 billion of federal funding to upgrade voting equipment. Second, although it did not federalize the voter registration process, it did spur the creation of statewide voter registration databases. Before HAVA, in many states, voter registration was handled at the local (usually county) level. As a result, voters could be registered in multiple places at once and no uniform system existed to clean voter lists throughout a state to account for people who changed residence or died. Third, HAVA created a national system of provisional ballots. The law guarantees that no voter can be turned away from a polling place in a federal election, whether because the voter's name did not appear on the registration book, or the voter failed to produce an appropriate form of identification, or otherwise. Voters who experienced such problems would still be able to cast a ballot, but its legality would be determined after the election. This provision addressed, for example, the problem evinced in the 2000 election in Florida in which many Black voters were prevented from voting because their names were absent from the registration lists due to what turned out to be an error-prone purge of supposed felons. With provisional ballots, voters could vote and then address the impropriety of the purge after the fact. Fourth, HAVA also established the Election Assistance Commission, which serves as a clearinghouse for information on election administration, disburses money to election departments, and certifies voting systems.

In the spirit of bipartisan compromise, HAVA also included, for the first time, a voter identification provision. First-time voters who registered by mail would need to provide one of twenty forms of identification when they voted. The provision was not as restrictive as successive state efforts that required all voters to have government-issued photo identification. Rather, this narrow class of voters covered by HAVA could provide everything from a utility bill or bank statement to a sample ballot.

Nevertheless, the voter ID debate became more passionate and polarizing following HAVA. The integrity-access conversation may not have been new; indeed, ever since the 1982 *DNC v. RNC*[21] consent decree following allegations of "voter caging," the Republican Party had agreed to federal court review for any "ballot security" programs, and the issue came up, often, in the context of the NVRA's voter list maintenance provisions. Moreover, integrity arguments were often lodged against expanding the franchise and other election reforms, ever since the Progressive Era if not long before. But the voter ID debate became the prism through which the partisan debate over election administration would be viewed for the first two decades of the twenty-first century, in large part because several Republican-controlled states passed new voter ID laws at the time. Moreover, voter identification became a flashpoint for the second election commission empaneled following the 2000 election—the so-called Carter-Baker Commission, or the 2005 Bipartisan Commission on Federal Election Reform.[22]

That commission put forward eighty-seven recommendations. Some built on those of the Carter-Ford Commission or others that arose in the debates surrounding HAVA. For instance, the commission recommended greater integration of state voter registration systems with a federal database so voters would only need to register once in their lifetime, and measures to restore voting rights to felons and greater voting access for military and overseas voters as well as voters with disabilities. It recommended uniform procedures for counting provisional ballots and a transition to electronic voting machines with auditable paper backups. The report also contained a set of recommendations to media organizations to avoid calling races before all polls closed around the country and to ensure five minutes of candidate discourse each night in the month preceding an election. Most controversially, though, the commission recommended a uniform system of free voter identification based on the REAL ID card. This caused Commissioners Tom Daschle, Spencer Overton, and Raul Yzaguirre to file a dissent expressing concern about the potential voting barriers such an ID requirement would create. They called the commission's ID proposal "nothing short of a modern day poll tax," with expected socioeconomic and race-based implications.[23]

The constitutional debate over voter ID was largely settled, however, just eight years after the 2000 election, with the Supreme Court's decision in *Crawford v. Marion County*.[24] The controlling opinion in that case, written by Justice John Paul Stevens, upheld Indiana's voter ID law. The opinion accepted the interests the state proffered relating to modernizing elections, preventing fraud, and ensuring voter confidence, despite a lack of empirical evidence suggesting either that in-person voter fraud was a problem in Indiana or that the voter ID requirement would solve it. Regarding the plaintiffs, it is unclear whether the Court was faulting them for not presenting sufficient evidence as to the number of people who would have difficulty voting due to the ID law or whether the nature of the burden—getting an ID—was inherently "non-severe." The case, in this respect, pitted an invisible plaintiff against an imaginary state interest, and the state won. (This dynamic is not unique to *Crawford* or the Indiana law—it is often very difficult to find a plaintiff who has the wherewithal to launch a federal lawsuit but is unable to get a voter ID. In any event, the Court carved out the possibility that severely burdened plaintiffs could bring as-applied challenges to ensure they could vote.)

Crawford is significant beyond the arena of voter ID, though, because it clarified the constitutional standard that would apply to administrative burdens on the right to vote. Administrative burdens, in this sense, are distinguishable from categorical disenfranchisement with respect either to categories specifically mentioned in designated amendments (such as the Fourteenth Amendment regarding race or the Nineteenth Amendment regarding sex) or to the types of categorical discrimination that would trigger strict scrutiny under *Harper*'s interpretation of the Fourteenth Amendment. Rather, *Crawford* made clear that a standard borrowed from ballot access law was the proper standard to adjudicate the constitutionality of laws that made it harder to vote.

The *Crawford* Court borrowed the applicable standard from *Burdick v. Takushi*,[25] a decision upholding Hawaii's ban on write-in ballots. The standard clarifies that "severe" burdens receive strict scrutiny and are presumptively unconstitutional. In contrast, for nonsevere burdens a court should "weigh the asserted injury to the right to vote against the 'precise interests put forward by the State as justifications for the burden imposed by its rule.' . . . As a result, most 'reasonable, nondiscriminatory restrictions' would be presumptively upheld."[26]

The *Crawford* decision is important not only for the constitutionality of voter ID but also for all procedural or administrative restrictions related to voting rights. The Court made clear that the permissive standard related to ballot access, which had generally been used to squash inconsequential minor party candidates, would apply to the more serious business of regulating access to the voting booth. Most voting restrictions in the post-*Crawford* world are based on similar election integrity interests and have a similar character to *Crawford*. As constitutional voting rights lawsuits have proved challenging, other claims, particularly based on racial discrimination under the Constitution or VRA, have become more prevalent. (A similar dynamic has happened in redistricting litigation as the Court has closed off potential partisan gerrymandering claims, forcing litigants to bring similar cases alleging racial discrimination.) In the wake of the Supreme Court's decision in *Shelby County v. Holder*,[27] though, one of the principal tools that prevented election rules with discriminatory effects disappeared. By striking down the coverage formula of the VRA, the Court removed a significant deterrent in certain states that had prevented some restrictive changes to state and even local voting rules.

One other election administration development in the post-*Crawford*, pre-pandemic period deserves discussion. Following the 2012 election, President Barack Obama set up the Presidential Commission on Election Administration (PCEA). Led by the general counsels of the Mitt Romney and Obama campaigns, Ben Ginsberg and Bob Bauer, the PCEA was the last bipartisan effort to grapple with a range of election administration challenges.[28] The commissioners included veteran state and local election officials, as well as representatives from industry such as Disney and Deloitte and Touche.

The long lines experienced by voters in Ohio and elsewhere in the 2012 election led to the creation of the PCEA. However, the PCEA executive order included a broad range of topics relating to election administration—everything from voting technology to preparing for natural disasters that could disrupt elections (given the effect that Hurricane Sandy had on the 2012 election).[29] It specifically avoided certain hot-button topics, though, such as voter identification and reauthorization of the VRA. As such, it was oriented toward nonpartisan election management, rather than the most notorious controversies in election administration. In addition, the PCEA sought to make available an array of tools for election administrators, to deal with problems such as line management and online voter registration, and research related to the areas in the executive order.[30]

After a series of hearings held around the country and meetings with various stakeholder groups and election officials, the PCEA issued its report in January 2014. The report articulated a set of recommendations and best practices related to each of the areas in the executive order. Most notably, it set a goal for election administrators to reduce wait times to under half an hour. It also emphasized the need for alternatives to Election Day polling-place voting, whether through vote-by-mail, early voting, or the creation of vote centers. Finally, with respect to voting technology, the PCEA recommended updating and implementing new voting system guidelines that, among other things, would allow for deployment of commercial off-the-shelf products.

Assessing the independent, long-term impact of the PCEA recommendations presents some challenges. Election officials used the report both to benchmark their efforts (e.g., to ensure wait times did not exceed half an hour) and to lobby state and local governments for more resources to implement the recommendations. The Election Assistance Commission adopted new voting system guidelines in 2015 and 2021, although the PCEA, in that respect, may have been pushing a door already opened. Similarly, the recommended deployment of online voter registration, electronic pollbooks, and alternatives to Election Day polling-place voting, such as mail balloting, vote centers, and in-person early voting, continued a trajectory already underway. Efforts to track progress in implementing the recommendations were facilitated by audits and greater data gathering, which themselves were important recommendations of the report.[31]

The PCEA stands in stark contrast to the presidential commission on voting that succeeded it. In May 2017, President Trump established the Presidential Advisory Commission on Election Integrity. Chaired by Vice President Mike Pence and cochaired by Kansas secretary of state Kris Kobach, the commission's membership was putatively bipartisan, in that five Democrats were originally appointed, although some of them sent letters early on in the process complaining that they were not kept abreast of commission activities.[32]

The commission's mandate was to submit a report detailing the practices that "undermine" or "enhance the American people's confidence in the integrity of the voting [process]." It was also tasked with identifying vulnerabilities that could lead to fraudulent registrations or voting.[33] The commission's work was fraught from its inception. It requested that states provide extensive data on voters, including birthdates, partial social security numbers, party affiliation, and felon status. State officials from both parties balked at the request on privacy grounds, and lawsuits followed. The commission only held two meetings, and the White House shut it down on January 3, 2018.

THE 2020 ELECTION AND ITS AFTERMATH

The COVID-19 pandemic presented unique challenges to an election administration system that was already under great stress. Even before the pandemic hit, seeds had already been planted to delegitimize election results. Critics tend to forget that President Trump claimed the 2016 election was marred by fraud as well, in order to explain why Hillary Clinton won the popular vote. In so doing, Trump achieved the strange distinction of being the first winner of a presidential election to claim election fraud.

As the pandemic hit in the winter and spring of 2020, the presidential primaries were already underway. At the time, it seemed as if the nation might have difficulty pulling off the basic functions of the election. Wisconsin was the first state to experience a severe electoral shock due to COVID-19, as the governor and the courts bickered over how to adjust the relevant processes and deadlines to accommodate people's concerns.[34] For its April 7 primary, Milwaukee ended up closing 97 percent of its polling places and 74 percent of voters in the state cast their primary ballots by mail. Every state that held a primary after Wisconsin's saw a similar rise in mail balloting—on average a 60 percentage point increase from 2016.

Throughout the course of the primary season, it was unclear whether states without experience handling large numbers of mail ballots would be able to manage the load. For example, in New York City, roughly 20 percent of mail ballots (over eighty-four thousand votes) went uncounted due to errors.[35] In the end, a record number of absentee primary ballots were rejected (over half a million nationwide according to one estimate), but the share of primary ballots rejected went down in most states as states learned from each other throughout the primary process.[36]

The baptism by fire of the primaries placed all states on notice for the general election. Different states made different preparations to handle the increase in mail voting. Some states, such as California, New Jersey, Vermont, and Nevada, mailed every voter a ballot for the first time. Others mailed absentee-ballot applications to all voters, expanded eligibility for mail balloting, enacted new notice and cure procedures to allow voters to remedy errors, provided prepaid postage, extended ballot receipt deadlines, and permitted preprocessing of ballots before polls closed. As a result, the rate of mail voting doubled to 46 percent, as seventy million voters cast votes by mail (although Democrats were about twice as likely to vote by mail as Republicans). To be clear, though, only about half of absentee ballots were delivered through the mail—others were dropped off at polling places, vote centers, election offices, or drop boxes.[37] Only 0.8 percent of absentee ballots ended up being rejected in the 2024 General Election.[38]

With the dramatic increase in mail voting and substantial increase in early in-person voting (about a 7 percentage point increase over 2016 to 26 percent of votes cast), it should come as no surprise that Election Day voting experienced a dramatic decline. Only about 28 percent of voters cast their vote in person on Election Day in 2020, less than half the rate (60 percent) from 2016. The number of polling places declined, unsurprisingly, as states like California moved to nearly all-mail voting. Wait times at polling places also increased, as polling places maintained social distancing and enforced other COVID-19 protocols.

By most traditional measures estimated by the Survey of the Performance of American Elections, voters expressed high favorability with the voting process in 2020.[39] Beyond mere self-reporting of the voting experience, the 2020 election was an administrative success. Voter turnout broke records. The share of rejected ballots actually decreased.

Nevertheless, virtually every aspect of the adaptation of the voting system to deal with the pandemic became polarizing and the source of claims of fraud or illegality. The use of drop boxes is a case in point. Allegations of fraud from dumping ballots in drop boxes became a frequent trope during and after the 2020 election—so much so that an entire movie was created to bolster this conspiracy theory[40]—and several states voted to ban them shortly thereafter.[41] The same could be said, of course, with respect to mail balloting in general. At the time of the 2020 election, only 36 percent of Republicans were confident that votes cast by mail or absentee ballots would be counted as voters intended. That number was virtually unchanged two years later, whereas 77 percent of Democrats in 2020 and 88 percent in 2022 were confident.[42] Absentee balloting and all the associated election processes surrounding the casting and counting of mail ballots have become a major source of division between Democrats and Republicans.

But the conspiracy theories did not stop there. The false and persistent allegations of vote switching by Dominion Voting Systems became famous, in large part because Fox News ended up settling a defamation suit brought by Dominion for $787 million. Others claimed election official malfeasance in Atlanta, Philadelphia, and elsewhere, sometimes based on chopped-up or decontextualized video. Allegations of voting by out-of-state, noncitizen, felon, or dead voters—familiar claims in each election—were also lodged against the 2020 results. Some even claimed that Italian hackers used satellites to flip votes.[43]

Maricopa County, Arizona, may have been ground zero for conspiracy theories. One of the most prominent was "Sharpiegate"—a false claim that Election Day voters who voted with Sharpie markers did not have their votes counted.[44] As with so much election-related disinformation, the narrative started on fringe social media accounts and then went mainstream once political and media elites saw its potential. Others claimed that forty thousand ballots were shipped to Arizona from China, leading some to later analyze the ballots for the presence of bamboo fibers.[45] (This was one of several China-related conspiracy theories, some of which were propagated by MyPillow founder, Mike Lindell.)[46] These and other theories were examined by a quasi-audit conducted by the so-called Cyber Ninjas, who were given access to the 2020 ballots for Arizona. In the end, they could not find any evidence for these theories, but belief in them remained strong.[47]

Conspiracies surrounding the 2020 election did not just concern one thing, nor did they arise from a single source. Because they were so heterogeneous, they could not be disproven in a given lawsuit or by an out-of-court rebuttal.[48] Together, however, they led to the conclusion among Republicans that the 2020 election was rigged. Although a confidence gap between Republicans and Democrats had existed before the election (in no small measure because the claims of a rigged election preceded the election itself), it grew in the weeks thereafter. As Charles Stewart III has written,

> Before Election Day, an average 63 percent of Democrats expressed a great deal or quite a bit of confidence that their vote would be counted accurately in the election, compared with 52 percent of Republicans,

> for an 11-point gap. Within a day of the election, that gap grew to 45 points (93 percent for Democrats versus 48 percent for Republicans). The same was true when respondents were asked about the 2020 election being fair. What had been an average 8-point gap before Election Day (54 percent Democrats to 46 percent Republicans) grew to 59 points (84 percent Democrats to 25 percent Republicans) as soon as the results were known.[49]

The partisan gap in confidence persists even three years after the election. As of July 2023, CNN found that 69 percent of Republicans agreed with the proposition that "Joe Biden did not legitimately win enough votes to win the presidency," which is roughly the same share (71 percent) as answered similarly in January 2021.[50] These fears are not merely retrospective. An AP-NORC poll found that only 22 percent of Republicans have high confidence that votes in the 2024 presidential election will be counted accurately, as compared with 71 percent of Democrats.[51]

These concerns about fraud have had practical and legal effects. Many states passed laws to respond to real or imagined concerns relating to deficiencies in administration of the 2020 election.[52] These laws run the gamut from limiting drop boxes, ballot collection, voter registration drives, and private funding of election offices to enacting stricter ID requirements for both in-person and mail voting.[53] Several states also enacted criminal penalties for election officials who violate state law. Arkansas, for example, made it a crime for an election official to send an unsolicited mail ballot, and South Dakota enacted a law that imposes criminal penalties on poll workers for both not making the process of canvassing mail ballots "open" to poll watcher observance and not keeping watchers at a reasonable distance from ballots and personally identifying information.[54] Finally, some states, such as Georgia and Texas, have reorganized supervisory authority over election processes either to reallocate power away from local officials or to transfer power to bodies with a greater number of partisan appointees.[55]

An equal number of states, however, liberalized their laws over the same period. Some, such as Minnesota and New Mexico, passed laws ensuring automatic voter registration and altered felon disenfranchisement laws.

Other states have expanded availability of ballot drop boxes or made it easier to cure defects in mail ballots. In many instances, states codified liberalization of practices that occurred during the emergency situation of COVID-19. Massachusetts, for example, codified its no-excuse mail ballot policy and expanded the number of days for early voting.[56] In short, one group of states (usually those controlled by Democrats, but not exclusively so) viewed the changes made to address the pandemic as an opportunity to permanently liberalize voting laws. A separate group of states (mostly red states) viewed the pandemic response as a warning sign of what to avoid and therefore eliminated those emergency measures or went even further to pass restrictions intended to respond to newfound fears of fraud arising from long-held practices.

In some contexts, election-related conspiracy theories have led states to act in ways that seem perversely inconsistent with the fraud-fighting narrative. The case in point is the collapse of the multistate compact to assist in the cleaning of voter rolls. The Electronic Registration Information Center (ERIC) was a voluntary program among participating states that allowed them to exchange information related to registered voters so that they could remove voters who moved or died and reach out to eligible but unregistered voters. It was one of the programs specifically recommended by the PCEA in order to develop clean voter registration rolls. The program included both Republican and Democratic states and was generally seen as a healthy marriage between those who sought to fight fraud by cleaning voter rolls and those who sought to make it easier for unregistered voters to register. The data from ERIC was even used in Florida in 2022 to prosecute voters who allegedly were ineligible and by Ohio to prosecute voters who voted twice.[57]

In the three years following the 2020 election, however, Republican states left the program en masse. Louisiana, Alabama, West Virginia, Iowa, Missouri, Ohio, Florida, and Texas have left the compact since 2020, even though officials in those states had previously praised the program as a tool for fighting fraud.[58] They did so following publication of rumors in a fringe publication that ERIC was a Soros-funded effort to commit fraud and violate the privacy of voters.[59] Activists then successfully lobbied state officials, and in some cases passed legislation that withdrew the state from the compact.

The ERIC story is instructive because it indicates how placating conspiracy theories can undermine election administration. States that have left ERIC will now be in a worse position to clean their voting rolls. They will have less information about which registered voters may have died or moved. They will need to scramble in the year before the 2024 election to try to build from scratch a less effective tool to clean voter rolls—one that is likely to make errors and lead to confusion among election officials, poll workers, and voters. And as scattershot voter purges are notoriously inaccurate, any newly patched-together system will likely lead to litigation.

The response of Maricopa County to the Sharpiegate controversy represents a similar dynamic. Recall that conspiracy theorists in 2020 falsely asserted that ballots marked with Sharpies would be canceled, because the ink would bleed through the ballot so as to make them unreadable. Despite the absence of evidence for such a claim, Maricopa County nevertheless changed the paper it used for ballots from eighty- to one-hundred-pound paper for the 2022 election. Thicker paper would prevent Sharpies from bleeding through, it was thought.

Maricopa County's 2022 election, which included the very competitive governor's race between Kari Lake and Katie Hobbs, was marred by controversy as well. Some Election Day voters found that the in-precinct ballot scanners could not validate their votes. The votes were still valid and were counted outside the precinct, but any such polling place dysfunction breeds conspiracy theories. In this case, one emerged alleging that Maricopa County was canceling Election Day votes (which trend Republican), or that the resulting disorder in the polling places led to violations of the chain of custody of ballots, which in turn led to fraud.[60] Lake argued then and now that the election was illegitimate and rigged.

As a subsequent analysis of the election led by Arizona Supreme Court justice Ruth McGregor explained, the attempt to address Sharpiegate inadvertently led to the dysfunction in 2022. Thicker paper and a longer ballot in 2022 led some of the printers to misprint ballots that could not then be scanned in the polling place. "The combined effect of the heavy paper, longer ballot, and intermittent burst of print demand pushed the printers to perform at the very edge of or past their capability."[61] By bending over backward to address a meritless accusation of fraud related to the administration of the 2020 election, the county spawned a separate conspiracy theory that further eroded confidence in the electoral system.

The courts in this most recent era have largely been a refuge for sanity in the face of a relentless assault by conspiracy theorists and election deniers. Judges nominated by presidents from both parties disposed of around sixty lawsuits related to the 2020 election in its immediate aftermath. When forced to provide evidence that can be tested in an adversarial process, the conspiracy theories fall apart. Most notable in this regard may be the successful defamation cases brought by Dominion Voting Systems against Fox News and others who spread lies about machines flipping votes. In the upside-down world of election denial, it fell to a voting machine company to be at the forefront of holding accountable those who would try to seed falsehoods about the security of the election system. Finally, both courts and the bar have held lawyers accountable for their baseless misrepresentations in litigation challenging election results.

At the same time, it is important to note that the courts in these past few years have largely served the role of promoting stability in the electoral system, not adopting broad expansions of voting rights. Perhaps the most notable (non-redistricting-related) voting rights case at the Supreme Court in this period was *Brnovich v. Democratic National Committee*,[62] which rejected an interpretation of Section 2 of the VRA that would have invalidated two features of Arizona voting law. In a rare "vote denial" lawsuit that reached the Supreme Court, plaintiffs had argued that Arizona's practices of discarding ballots of voters who voted in the wrong precinct and of prohibiting one person from delivering the mail ballot of another had a disparate impact on Latino and Native American voters. The Court disagreed, or rather held that these practices, given their decades-old pedigree or minor disparate impact, did not rise to a Section 2 violation.

Brnovich, like many of the emergency cases decided on the Court's "shadow docket," illustrates the judicial impulse not to disrupt the system as an election approaches. The so-called *Purcell* doctrine leads courts to freeze the status quo ante in such cases.[63] However, the doctrine sometimes leads the Court to disrupt practices that state and local election officials have deployed to deal with emergencies, as happened in Wisconsin just days before its 2020 primary when the Court overturned the state's extension of deadlines for receipt of mail ballots.[64] What the Court considers a last-minute change and whether and how the *Purcell* doctrine applies to judicial versus administrative disruption of the electoral process remain a bit up in the air (or less charitably, have led to incoherence in the case law).[65] However, the concern for stability underpinning these decisions should be welcomed as every uncertainty or tremor in the administration of an election becomes fodder for polarized arguments and conspiracy theories.

ELECTION ADMINISTRATION IN AN ERA OF POLARIZATION, CONSPIRACIES, ANXIETY, AND HYPERCOMPETITION

The 2024 election is perhaps the third in a row to be perceived as an "existential" election, one in which the future of American democracy is considered at stake. It also promises to be a close election, not only for the presidency but also for both houses of Congress, which are governed by very narrow majorities. While the stakes seem incredibly high and the country appears intensely polarized and equally divided, the anxiety surrounding the election is exacerbated by a loss of trust in the process and a receptivity to the most outlandish conspiracy theories. In addition, with the January 6 insurrection breaking historical norms relating to the peaceful transfer of power, the prospect of political violence seems likelier than in recent decades.

This novel, toxic mix of stresses on the system requires that the country reorient the election administration system in the direction of a safe and secure voting experience that produces trustworthy results. Even apart from the larger trends noted earlier, there are formidable challenges to doing so. First, election administrators are operating in an arena of legal uncertainty. Most states have changed their laws—and many in very significant ways in either a more liberal or more restrictive direction—since the last presidential election. With luck, these laws will be interpreted and litigated in time for local officials to operate with clear understanding of these new policies.

Second, many election officials who are applying these uncertain laws have never run a presidential election before. The job of an election worker has become increasingly difficult—and in some instances, frightening and intolerable—since 2020. Election officials face death threats, burdensome dilatory public records requests, online and offline harassment, and multifaceted political pressure and scrutiny.[66] As a result, a large number of election officials, somewhere in the range of a quarter to a third nationwide, will have resigned between the 2020 and 2024 elections.[67] A large cadre of novice election officials, therefore, will be interpreting and enforcing brand-new election laws. They will be doing so in an environment of unprecedented scrutiny wherein even a perfectly run election may end up being mischaracterized, through decontextualized video or garden-variety conspiracy mongering, as utterly dysfunctional.

Third, election officials and other authoritative sources of election-related information are not trusted by large shares of the population, and in any event, they will have a difficult time breaking through the cacophony of disinformation on social media. Several different phenomena are at work here. Because of the relentless attacks on election officials' trustworthiness, large shares of the population are already predisposed not to believe what these officials have to say. In addition, even for audiences receptive to the messages of election officials and their allies, news related to the election process will be dominated by the loudest elites, not to mention professional disinformation campaigns, sometimes with the aid of artificial intelligence. The 2024 election is unique in that one of the central issues in the campaign relates to election administration—namely, whether the 2020 election was legitimate. Election officials cannot compete in the marketplace of information with the messaging of candidate campaigns and click-baiting social media accounts that benefit from exaggeration and lies.

Fourth, the social media information ecosystem has changed dramatically since 2020. For various reasons, the social media companies will do much less in 2024 to address election-related disinformation than they did in 2020. The whole enterprise of social media content moderation is under attack. With the transformation of Twitter to X, teams that were dedicated to combatting election-related disinformation disappeared. (Moreover, collaboration and information sharing on election-related threats between Twitter and the rest of the industry has evaporated.) But X is not alone: for economic and other reasons, other platforms, such as Facebook/Meta, have also let go a large share of the staff dedicated both to combatting election-related disinformation and to providing accurate information. One of those "other reasons" is the complete politicization of the enterprise of content moderation. Because of mistakes made by the platforms in 2020, such as the demotion of stories about Hunter Biden's laptop or the hypothesis that COVID-19 originated from a Chinese lab leak, conservatives are naturally distrustful of platform content moderation. Congressional investigations, lawsuits, and pressure campaigns have increased the costs considerably for platforms and outside disinformation researchers seeking to expose and act on election-related disinformation.

These challenges cannot be solved, but they can be mitigated. First, we need clear rules for administration of the election. Litigation over the rules in the few months before the election will serve no one's interest. All actors in the system must be clear about the rules of the game by the end of the primary season. Second, election officials need resources both to administer and to communicate about the election process. The half billion dollars in private funding injected into the system in 2020 will not be there in 2024, so the federal government and the states need to provide funds to address the unique challenges election officials face. This includes funds for well-resourced communications departments and for cybersecurity and physical security. Third, local civil society actors from the business and faith communities need to be integrated into the system in order to vouch for the security of the process. There are few, if any, national or statewide figures who are trusted by both sides. Trusted local leaders without clear political affiliations should be enlisted to signal their confidence in the local system of election administration. Finally, states and election departments need to do all they can to discover and address problems at the earliest possible moment and to complete the vote counting as expeditiously as possible. Although officials cannot control the pace of wild falsehoods leveled at the process, they can try to shrink the postelection time period in which those falsehoods might catch fire.

Even with all this preparation, though, we need to be humble in our ability to predict the election administration challenge for 2024. One lesson learned from the recent history of election administration is that new, unforeseen challenges seem to emerge with each election. The best we can do now in this environment of great uncertainty is to support and get resources into the hands of the officials who will administer the election and to do what we can to shield them from the threats posed by the most irresponsible actors in the system.

NOTES

1 "2020 General Election Turnout Rates," ElectProject, last updated December 7, 2020, www.electproject.org.
2 Nathaniel Persily and Charles Stewart III, "The Miracle and Tragedy of the 2020 U.S. Election," *Journal of Democracy* 32, no. 2 (April 2021): 159–78, www.journalofdemocracy.org.
3 Nixon v. Herndon, 273 U.S. 536 (1927); Smith v. Allwright, 321 U.S. 649 (1944).
4 Lassiter v. Northampton County, 360 U.S. 45 (1959).
5 Harper v. Virginia Board of Elections, 383 U.S. 663 (1966).
6 Brown v. Board of Education, 347 U.S. 483 (1954).
7 John Hart Ely, *Democracy and Distrust: A Theory of Judicial Review* (Cambridge, MA: Harvard University Press, 1980), 105.
8 See Williams v. Rhodes, 393 U.S. 23 (1968).
9 Allen v. State Board of Elections, 393 U.S. 544 (1969).
10 42 U.S.C. § 1973(a).
11 Brnovich v. Democratic National Committee, 594 U.S. ___ (2021).
12 See, e.g., Kramer v. Union Free School District No. 15, 395 U.S. 621 (1969) (prohibiting certain voting restrictions for school board elections); Richardson v. Ramirez, 418 U.S. 24 (1974) (upholding felon disenfranchisement).
13 Munro v. Socialist Workers Party, 479 U.S. 189 (1986).
14 Storer v. Brown, 415 U.S. 724 (1974).
15 Timmons v. Twin Cities Area New Party, 520 U.S. 351 (1997).
16 Burdick v. Takushi, 504 U.S. 428 (1992).
17 See Richard Hasen, *The Voting Wars: From Florida 2000 to the Next Election Meltdown* (New Haven, CT: Yale University Press, 2012).
18 CalTech/MIT Voting Technology Project, *Voting—What Is, What Could Be* (July 2001).
19 National Commission on Federal Election Reform, *To Assure Pride and Confidence in the Electoral Process* (Charlottesville, VA: Miller Center of Public Affairs and the Century Foundation, August 2001), https://production-tcf.imgix.net.
20 52 U.S.C. §§ 20901–21145 (2002).
21 Democratic National Committee et al. v. Republican National Committee et al., No. 2:81-cv-03876-DRD-SDW, Document 43-5 (Filed Nov. 3, 2008), www.brennancenter.org.
22 Center for Democracy and Election Management, *Building Confidence in U.S. Elections: Report of the Commission on Federal Election Reform* (Washington, DC: American University, September 2005), https://web.archive.org.

23 *Building Confidence in U.S. Elections: Report of the Commission on Federal Election Reform* (Washington, DC: Center for Democracy and Election Management, September 2005), 89, https://www.eac.gov/sites/default/files/eac_assets/1/6/Exhibit%20M.PDF.

24 Crawford v. Marion County Election Board, 553 U.S. 181 (2008).

25 Burdick v. Takushi, 504 U.S. 428 (1992).

26 *Burdick*, 504 U.S. at 434 (quoting *Anderson v. Celebrezze*, 460 U.S. 780, 789 [1983]).

27 Shelby County v. Holder, 570 U.S. 529 (2013).

28 Disclosure: I was the senior research director of the PCEA.

29 See Executive Order No. 13639—Establishment of the Presidential Commission on Election Administration, March 28, 2013, https://obamawhitehouse.archives.gov/the-press-office/2013/03/28/executive-order-establishment-presidential-commission-election-administr. The following is the full list of issues in the executive order:

i. the number, location, management, operation, and design of polling places;
ii. the training, recruitment, and number of poll workers;
iii. voting accessibility for uniformed and overseas voters;
iv. the efficient management of voter rolls and poll books;
v. voting machine capacity and technology;
vi. ballot simplicity and voter education;
vii. voting accessibility for individuals with disabilities, limited English proficiency, and other special needs;
viii. management of issuing and processing provisional ballots in the polling place on Election Day;
ix. the issues presented by the administration of absentee ballot programs;
x. the adequacy of contingency plans for natural disasters and other emergencies that may disrupt elections; and
xi. other issues related to the efficient administration of elections that the Co-Chairs agree are necessary and appropriate to the Commission's work.

30 *The American Voting Experience: Report and Recommendations of the Presidential Commission on Election Administration* (Presidential Commission on Election Administration, January 2014), https://web.mit.edu.

31 John C. Fortier et al., *Improving the Voter Experience: Reducing Polling Place Wait Times by Measuring Lines and Managing Polling Place Resources* (Washington, DC: Bipartisan Policy Center, April 2018).

32 Jessica Taylor, "Trump Dissolves Controversial Election Commission," NPR, January 3, 2018, www.npr.org.

33 Executive Order No. 13799, May 11, 2017, https://web.archive.org.

34 See Persily and Stewart, "Miracle and Tragedy," 159–60.

35 Carl Campanile, Nolan Hicks, and Bernadette Hogan, "Over 80,000 Mail-In Ballots Disqualified in NYC Primary Mess," *New York Post*, August 5, 2020.

36 Persily and Stewart, "Miracle and Tragedy," 160.

37 Charles Stewart III, *How We Voted in 2020: A Topical Look at the Survey of the Performance of American Elections* (MIT Election Data + Science Lab, 2021), https://electionlab.mit.edu.

38 Stewart.

39 Stewart.

40 See Debbie D'Souza, Dinesh D'Souza, and Bruce Schooley, dirs., *2000 Mules* (D'Souza Media, 2022).

41 Aaron Mendelson and Pratheek Rebala, "'Chaos and Confusion': The Campaign to Stamp Out Ballot Drop Boxes," Center for Public Integrity, October 30, 2022, http://publicintegrity.org.

42 "Midterm Voting Intentions Are Divided, Economic Gloom Persists," Pew Research Center, October 20, 2022, www.pewresearch.org.

43 "Fact Check: Evidence Disproves Claims of Italian Conspiracy to Meddle in U.S. Election (Known as #ItalyGate)," Reuters, January 15, 2021, www.reuters.com.

44 Jessica Huseman, "How Election Lies Led to Real Problems in Maricopa County," Votebeat, April 17, 2023, www.votebeat.org.

45 Sam Levine, "Arizona Republicans Hunt for Bamboo-Laced China Ballots in 2020 'Audit' Effort," *The Guardian*, May 6, 2021, www.theguardian.com.

46 "He 'Proved Mike Wrong.' Now He's Claiming His $5 Million," NPR, April 27, 2023, www.npr.org.

47 Bob Christie and Christina A. Cassidy, "GOP Review Finds No Proof Arizona Election Stolen from Trump," Associated Press, September 24, 2021, https://apnews.com.

48 Justin Grimmer, Michael C. Herron, and Matthew Tyler, "Evaluating a New Generation of Expansive Claims about Vote Manipulation" (unpublished manuscript, July 15, 2023), www.dropbox.com.

49 Charles Stewart III, "Trust in Elections," *Daedalus* 151, no. 4 (Fall 2022): 244, https://direct.mit.edu.

50 Jennifer Agiesta and Ariel Edwards-Levy, "CNN Poll: Percentage of Republicans Who Think Biden's 2020 Win Was Illegitimate Ticks Back Up Near 70%," CNN, August 3, 2023, www.cnn.com; SSRS, "CNN Poll on Biden, Economy, and Elections," conducted for CNN, July 1–31, 2023, www.documentcloud.org.

51 Christina A. Cassidy and Linley Sanders, "GOP Confidence in 2024 Vote Count Low after Years of False Election Claims, AP-NORC Poll Shows," AP News, July 11, 2023, https://apnews.com.

52 "Voting Laws Roundup: June 2023," Brennan Center for Justice, June 14, 2023, www.brennancenter.org.

53 "Voting Laws Roundup: June 2023."

54 "Voting Laws Roundup: June 2023."

55 "Voting Laws Roundup: October 2022," Brennan Center for Justice, October 6, 2022, www.brennancenter.org.

56 "Voting Laws Roundup: October 2022."

57 Gary Fineout, "How DeSantis' Election Police Spent Their First Year," Politico, January 30, 2023, www.politico.com.

58 Jessica Huseman, "These State Officials Praised ERIC for Years before Suddenly Pulling Out of the Program," Votebeat, April 11, 2023, www.votebeat.org.

59 Natalia Contreras, "Conspiracy Theory Whirlwind Threatens to Blow Texas Out of National Program That Keeps Voter Rolls Updated," Votebeat, March 9, 2023, www.votebeat.org.

60 "Kari Lake Loses Challenge of Election Loss in Arizona Governor's Race," CBS News, February 16, 2023, www.cbsnews.com.

61 Ruth V. McGregor, "Maricopa County 2022 General Election Ballot-on-Demand Printer Investigation," Maricopa County Document Center, April 10, 2023, 23–24, www.maricopa.gov.

62 Brnovich v. Democratic National Committee, 594 U.S. ___ (2021).

63 Purcell v. Gonzalez, 549 U.S. 1 (2006).

64 Republican National Committee v. Democratic National Committee, 140 S. Ct. 1205 (2020) (per curiam).

65 See also Richard Hasen, "Reining in the *Purcell* Principle," *Florida State University Law Review* 43, no. 2 (Winter 2016): 427–64.

66 Ruby Edlin and Lawrence Norden, "Poll of Election Officials Shows High Turnover amid Safety Threats and Political Interference," Brennan Center for Justice, April 25, 2023, www.brennancenter.org.

67 Michael Waldman, "The Great Resignation . . . of Election Officials," Brennan Center for Justice, April 25, 2023, www.brennancenter.org; Fredreka Schouten, "Alarm Grows as More Election Workers Leave Their Posts ahead of Election Day," CNN, September 1, 2022, www.cnn.com; Michael Beckel et al., *The High Cost of High Turnover* (Washington, DC: Issue One, September 2023), https://issueone.org.

11

THE DEEP ROOTS OF THE "BIG LIE"

JULILLY KOHLER-HAUSMANN

Alarm about voter fraud reached a frenzied pitch during Donald Trump's presidency, triggering a cascade of extraordinary consequences. At its crescendo, thousands of Americans, convinced that rampant fraud robbed Trump of the presidency, stormed the US Capitol on January 6, 2021. Recognizing that fraud rationalized the violence, many mainstream reporters and pundits hastened to illustrate the claims to be wildly inaccurate. Journalists often stopped short of calling the charges outright lies, but they typically qualified them as "unsubstantiated" or "baseless." Or they invoked the glut of research, court cases, and investigations finding no credible evidence of significant voter fraud. These protestations failed to disabuse the huge swaths of the public that remained convinced widescale fraud had corroded US democracy and installed an illegitimate president.

Many position the democratic crises of the Trump years as a stark break from a more harmonious past. Yet this understandable inclination to distance the 2020 election from earlier periods can limit our understanding of the contemporary predicament. It discourages scrutiny of the institutional and legal levers, cultural tropes, and popular cynicism that the Trump campaign leveraged to undermine the election.

Historians, unsurprisingly, are keen to excavate continuities and antecedents around what appear to be historical ruptures. To contextualize the 2021 attack on the Capitol, some have highlighted the decades-long project to erode voting rights, which led, among other things, to the 2013 Supreme Court decision that struck down preclearance requirements of the Voting Rights Act.[1] Others point to increasing partisan polarization or the development of segmented information ecosystems, which leave some groups siloed in impermeable media echo chambers.[2] This chapter positions the democratic crises of the Trump era in the current of a longer history of voter fraud. This perspective reveals that voter fraud has long shaped US political history. Although the attempts to subvert the 2020 election were unprecedented, the impulse to win power by curating the electorate has long coexisted with the more celebrated determination to build an increasingly inclusive, representative democracy. And those intent on limiting the electorate have long done so by mobilizing fears of voter fraud and questioning particular groups' capacity for self-governance.

VOTER FRAUD AND THE DEEP TRADITION OF CONDITIONAL CITIZENSHIP

Elite accusations of rampant voter fraud are often flagrant lies. They are typically connected to cynical partisan strategies to discredit, dissuade, or disqualify rivals' voters. Nonetheless, such claims would not convince huge numbers of people if they did not resonate at some level or if everyone recognized them as purely crass power grabs. If we are to understand this popular resonance—the efficacy of these particular voter suppression techniques—it is critical to investigate which democratic traditions, racial logics, and institutional arrangements these antifraud campaigns mobilize (and, in turn, promulgate).

Those mobilizing through voter fraud start from a strategic high ground since "free and fair elections" are an uncontroversial, unambiguous value in US democracy. Anyone hoping to impede antifraud crusaders starts off in a rhetorical bind since everyone (publicly) agrees that voter fraud is bad and should be avoided. Anyone minimizing or denying the prevalence of fraud risks being discredited by a few anomalous or decontextualized stories. Public credulity about the prevalence and ease of illegal balloting is enabled by widespread ignorance of the elaborate, complicated procedures officials employ to guarantee election security.

This chapter is not concerned with rehearsing the mendacity of fraud claims or proving fraud's infrequency or irrelevance to electoral outcomes. Dozens of court cases and reams of excellent research and investigations have illustrated this admirably.[3] Instead of debunking the lies about voter fraud, I investigate what insights into US political culture the discourse about it reveals. By focusing on the decades after passage of the 1965 Voting Rights Act, I uncover some of the roots of today's "democratic crises" and highlight the ways charges of voter fraud have long rationalized limiting the electorate and depressing participation.

The late twentieth century is often imagined as a period of democratic consensus and completion, when the nation had finally actualized its founding ideals and embraced an egalitarian citizenship. Despite these popular assertions of consensus, the debates over election administration reflect ongoing controversy regarding a universal, unencumbered franchise and majoritarian democracy. Then, as now, voter fraud was central to these struggles. Lawmakers consistently used this specter to impede efforts to expand the electorate. And then, as now, consternation about voter fraud revealed not only anxiety about illegal balloting but also cleavages in popular understanding of who could legitimately claim the rights, voice, and benefits in the polity. The politics of voter fraud, therefore, can be a window into the ongoing struggles over democratic governance.

Elites' longstanding wariness of mass politics is reflected in the many brakes on the majority's will established by the US Constitution, such as the Senate, the Supreme Court, and the Electoral College.[4] More recent developments—particularly the increasing power of the filibuster in the Senate—also impede the majority's capacity to act, which, for example, enabled minorities to thwart civil rights legislation for years.[5] But ambivalence (even at times outright disdain) for mass democracy is also reflected in the long historical commitment to limiting citizenship and the franchise to those somehow deemed worthy or qualified.

The continuing salience of voter fraud in US politics is best understood as embedded in this deep strain in US political culture that takes full citizenship to be *conditional*, where full standing in the polity is not guaranteed but established through actions or status. Indeed, the very definition of a free, full citizen was produced through contrast with those deemed dependent, subordinate, or otherwise incapable of self-governance.[6] In the early republic, the franchise was typically limited to propertied white men, on the logic that only those with "good character," education, and a vested interest in the community could responsibly elect their representatives. As property-holding qualifications fell, lawmakers still used variations on this logic to restrict the electorate. For much of US history, courts and lawmakers decreed that race, nation of origin, and gender dictated suitability for the franchise. They also barred voters on the basis of character, literacy, felony conviction, pauperism, language, tax paying, mental competency, length of residency, and failure to properly register to vote.

After the explicit racial and gender bars to voting were outlawed by the Fifteenth and Nineteenth Amendments, states preserved the ability to screen out unworthy, uninvested, or uninformed voters. And it was this prerogative that southern lawmakers leveraged to help reassert white supremacy after Reconstruction. With explicit race-based disenfranchisement prohibited, people were instead deemed unqualified for the vote because they were illiterate, uneducated, or nontaxpaying—uncoincidentally all conditions imposed on Black citizens by the Jim Crow South.[7] Claiming that these traits led to incompetent voting and rampant fraud, white southerners fused racial terror with policy, such as poll taxes and literacy tests, to strip the majority of Black citizens of the vote.

Concerns about voter fraud often blurred violations of election law—vote buying, ballot box stuffing—with participation by suspect groups or people. There was also a tendency to conflate corruption with politicians' delivery of resources, benefits, or employment to their constituents. Reformers in the nineteenth and early twentieth centuries denigrated "machine politics" as corrupt not just because of widescale voting irregularities but also because party bosses provided state services and patronage to poor and working-class voters.[8]

Inflected, no doubt, by racial, class, and ethnic suspicions, reformers set out to clean up politics in the late nineteenth century. One of the most important tools designed to curtail fraud was voter registration. The registration regimes that proliferated between the Civil War and World War I aimed to regularize voting rolls and affirmatively establish voters' identities. Yet the imperative to quell technical malfeasance intertwined with efforts to screen out undesirable voters. Often the same device served both functions. In the late nineteenth century, reformers championed the "Australian ballot"—the now-familiar standardized paper ballot printed by the state. It minimized opportunities for fraud and allowed people to cast their votes in more privacy. But many supporters of the reforms also celebrated how the new secret ballots operated as a de facto literacy test that disqualified many poor and foreign-born voters.[9]

Therefore, registration rationalized election administration (and thus mitigated fraud) while also offering elites a tool—however crude and imprecise—for sculpting the electorate. The partisan implications were quickly obvious. Democratic Party leaders often opposed new registration policies for the same reasons that many Republican and middle-class reformers typically supported them: added bureaucratic hurdles disproportionately depressed poor and immigrant votes. While the exact effect of electoral reforms is difficult to establish and varied by location, there is little doubt that these antifraud devices contributed to the dramatic decline in voter participation around the turn of the twentieth century. Between 1888 and 1912, turnout declined from 80.5 percent of the eligible population to 59 percent.[10] Some scholars estimate that registration regimes account for one-third or more of this decline.[11]

Registration took on increased importance as other tools to limit the electorate fell away. By the late-twentieth century, the franchise was no longer contingent upon, for example, good character, race, gender, literacy, tax paying, or property ownership.[12] The 1965 Voting Rights Act (along with amendments, legislation, and court rulings in the same period) banned the most powerful tools for excising undesirable voters, particularly literacy tests and poll taxes. This did not, however, squash the inclination (or partisan incentives) to curate the electorate. The dedication to cultivating a virtuous or competent electorate survived, most explicitly in felon disenfranchisement and mental competency bars.[13] The hyperincarceration of young people of color during the late twentieth century exploded the numbers of people disenfranchised due to criminal convictions and incarceration. Felon disenfranchisement arguably became the most explicit, high-profile articulation of conditional citizenship, where the vote (and standing in the polity) could be forfeited and revoked. But the assumptions structuring felon disenfranchisement—that the vote could be restricted to worthy, invested, and dedicated citizens who fulfill their civic obligations—also structured debates over registration.

REGISTRATION AFTER THE VOTING RIGHTS ACT

The Voting Rights Act did not only renegotiate the legal qualifications for registration; it also inspired efforts to reimagine the practice more fundamentally. Over the following years, groups struggled to redistribute the bureaucratic hassles of registration, particularly in the South, where tens of thousands of African Americans remained unregistered. Battles raged over dispersing this responsibility among individuals, foundation-funded or volunteer registration drives, the federal government, and local election officials.[14] Furthermore, a diverse array of activists and politicians tried to ease or eliminate the hassle of registration. Others endeavored to transfer the responsibility of registration from individuals to the government, pointing out that the state maintained voter rolls in many other democratic nations. Many saw minimizing the barriers to registration as an obvious next step in completing the civil rights revolution or fulfilling the nation's democratic ideals.

Political scientists have extensively debated the precise effect of registration requirements on turnout and election outcomes, often finding minimal effects of various reforms.[15] On the ground, however, party leaders were less sanguine about the risks of altering election administration. Registration reform could seem mundane and technocratic, but elites worried it might have profound, if not entirely predictable, electoral consequences. Therefore, it often encountered fierce resistance. Most assumed that easing registration would disproportionately enlist less affluent voters and voters of color and therefore benefit the Democratic Party. Unsurprisingly, therefore, Republican opposition was much more dedicated and consistent. However, both parties have blocked (or declined to enthusiastically pursue) the injection of new, unpredictable voters into their partisan equations.[16] There were places and times—especially during periods of social upheaval or strident activism—in which Democrats also saw new voters as a risk to existing elites and worked to blunt or derail efforts to expand registration.[17]

Regardless of the actual effect of specific reforms, the debates over election policy revealed (and produced) political culture and democratic norms. Opponents of reform defended cumbersome registration procedures as both a tool to prevent voter fraud and a screen for meritorious voters. They drew on the traditions that positioned the franchise not as an inalienable right but as a privilege reserved for deserving, productive, or engaged citizens. Instead of lamenting the ways registration depressed turnout, some politicians celebrated that voter registration operated as a de facto morals tests for political rights. They welcomed that registration not only impeded fraud but also weeded out voters who were not sufficiently motivated to clear the administrative hurdles of registration. While commentators clearly understood that—in practice—the burdens of registration (just like literacy tests and poll taxes) most dramatically diminished the representation of the poor and people of color, the discourse about civic virtue and voter fraud obscured these underlying political dynamics.

Opponents of easing registration often asserted that lowering the barriers to voting and expanding the electorate clashed with other, more important imperatives, specifically preventing fraud and preserving the sanctity of the ballot. Over and over, discourse positioned these two imperatives as dueling or mutually exclusive. And over and over, elites privileged the "purity of the ballot box" over fuller participation, reasoning that the risk of immoral, fraudulent, or uninformed votes posed a more profound risk to democracy than a limited and unrepresentative electorate.

The campaigns during the 1970s to ease registration happened in the shadow of distressing reports about falling voter turnout. In fact, one of the most perplexing political puzzles of the late twentieth century was why political participation plummeted just as the nation jettisoned many of the legal barriers to the ballot. Elites were already alarmed by the turnout rates in the 1960 elections, when approximately 65 percent of the voting-age population participated. These statistics were especially embarrassing in global comparison, with US participation rates considerably below those of other democratic nations. (President John F. Kennedy appointed a presidential commission to identify the causes and remedies of the low participation in 1963.)[18] In retrospect, the 1960 election would turn out to be a high-water mark. Voter participation would not exceed 1960 levels until the 2020 election. Alarming reports of yet another decline in voter participation became a hallmark of postelection analysis for decades. Almost every election was followed by jeremiads lamenting American civic decline, democratic atrophy, and voter apathy.[19]

While many pundits, academics, and politicians assumed that declining turnout sprang from civic apathy, others argued that it was arcane bureaucratic hurdles that systematically (and unevenly) depressed participation.[20] It was in this context that Wyoming senator Gale McGee first introduced his postcard registration legislation in 1971. He proposed the establishment of a national voter registration administration within the Census Bureau that would oversee the mailing of postcard-sized forms to every household before federal elections. Any eligible citizens interested in registering could simply fill out the postcard and drop it back in the mail. The law also proposed to standardize residency requirements, which varied wildly between different localities. It introduced a federal mandate that any qualified citizen who moved to a jurisdiction thirty days or more before an election was qualified to vote.[21]

The proposal immediately met with staunch opposition from Republicans and southern Democrats. While they surely feared the reforms' electoral implications, their publicly articulated objections focused on the risk of fraud.[22] A version of postcard registration passed the Senate in 1973 after breaking a filibuster by Republicans and southern Democrats. It stalled in the House.

In 1976, the House passed a version of the policy after public encouragement from then–presidential candidate Jimmy Carter. While this iteration was considerably diluted—it allowed registration by mail but did not require sending forms to all homes—it encountered threats of President Gerald Ford's veto and another Senate filibuster. The bill died again in the Ninety-Fourth Congress.[23] Throughout the debates, opponents claimed that there was no way to verify the identity of a person who simply mailed in a card, and warned that unscrupulous people would register the tombstones and empty lots.[24] (Senator Dawson Mathis [D-GA] even offered an amendment on the bill—received with amusement in the chamber—that would have required placing postcard registration forms at the entries and exits of all cemeteries.)[25]

Upon assuming the presidency, Carter championed even more far-ranging election reforms. His package proposed eliminating the Electoral College, expanding federal matching funds to finance congressional elections, and revising Hatch Act limitations on political activity by federal employees. The cornerstone of the reforms, however, was universal voter registration, which would allow citizens to both register and vote on Election Day. It was hoped that the law would sidestep the concerns about fraud raised in the postcard debates because voters were required to present in person with identification. The reforms also included increased criminal penalties for fraud. Unmoved, a coalition of Republicans and southern Democrats again opposed the reforms, again because of fraud risks. This time, opponents claimed officials would not have the time to ascertain the individual's identity and prevent voting in multiple precincts.

Next, advocates proposed requiring that state agencies, such as the offices that administer driver's licenses and social welfare benefits, offer their clients the opportunity to register. Advocates hoped that the agency registration plans—popularly called "Motor Voter"—would neutralize fraud concerns because state officials would be registering people whose identities they had already positively established. Despite some successful state-level experiments with agency registration in the 1980s, the federal motor voter legislation proposed in 1988 encountered staunch resistance from Republican lawmakers. Again, opponents centered concerns about fraud. Senator Mitch McConnell (R-KY) dubbed the measure the "Auto-Fraudo" bill and helped organize the Republican congressional members in almost complete opposition to the reform.[26] After it passed both houses of Congress in 1992, President George H. W. Bush vetoed the bill, explaining that it was "an open invitation to fraud and corruption."[27] After Bill Clinton signed the National Voter Registration Act in May 1993, voting rights advocates spent the ensuing years fending off constitutional challenges to the law and suing the many states that failed, even refused, to implement the law, particularly the provisions that required offering welfare recipients the opportunity to register.[28]

While the alleged dangers of fraud were a key justification for defeating and delaying all these registration reforms, partisan considerations obviously factored into politicians' calculus. The remainder of this chapter examines the normative claims that cloaked these electoral calculations and explained opposition to reforms. These debates illustrate the persistence of conditional understandings of citizenship and the ways voter fraud discourse consistently conflated illegal votes with unworthy voters and illegitimate claims on the state.

MAJORITIES AS CHEATING

The 1965 Voting Rights Act, many claimed, ushered in an era when election administration was a technocratic, apolitical enterprise. Gone was the era in US politics when powerful interests used disenfranchisement or other bureaucratic mechanisms to purge or suppress the votes of would-be opponents. Elites in both parties had reasons to sustain this vision of a fully realized democracy administered through impartial electoral regulations. However, when confronted with possible election reforms, politicians and pundits alike openly acknowledged the political implications of election administration. In these contexts, they would discuss the widely recognized (but rarely openly admitted) fact that the existing distribution of power depended as much on the composition of nonvoters as on the preferences of voters.[29] And many would insinuate that disrupting this status quo was itself a form of cheating.

Newspaper coverage explicitly acknowledged the electoral incentives lurking behind the diverse positions on expanding registration. A 1971 *New York Times* article began, "While publicly proclaiming voter registration to be a non-partisan cause, Congressional Democrats privately see a potential windfall for their party in the estimated 50 million persons who might be converted from Election Day dropouts to voters."[30] Another columnist outlined the issue plainly, explaining that "most of those eligible but not registered were poor, black, young, and undereducated. Statistically, they are thus likely to vote Democratic. That makes it a partisan measure, according to the [Nixon] administration. Therefore most Republicans in Congress will vote against it, and so will conservative southern Democrats." The author explained that those obstructing such reforms risk being portrayed as betraying the nation's democratic ideals: "It is hard enough to justify arguing against full voter registration in a free country on any grounds at all. To fight it because most of the voters thus added will oppose you hardly shines up to the image of a party publicly aspiring to forge a new national majority."[31] Even while insisting prodemocracy norms should act as a check on politicians' desires to prune the electorate, the journalist implicitly acknowledged that election outcomes in the United States depended on candidates' ability to recruit supportive voters *and* exclude opposing ones.

Some Republic insiders publicly acknowledged that their political power depended in part on the existing, constricted registration system. When Carter proposed same-day voter registration in 1977, GOP strategist Kevin Phillips described the reform as "a satchel charge of pure political dynamite," warning readers that it "could blow the Republican party sky-high."[32] Paul Weyrich, the influential conservative activist who helped establish the American Legislative Exchange Council, Moral Majority, and the Heritage Foundation, frankly stated in 1980 that conservatives have a disincentive to increase participation. Before an audience including Pat Robinson, Phyllis Schlafly, and Ronald Reagan, he bemoaned that "many of our Christians have what I call the goo goo syndrome—good government. They want everyone to vote. I don't want everybody to vote. Elections are not won by a majority of people. They never have been from the beginning of our country, and they are not now. As a matter of fact our leverage in the elections quite candidly goes up as the voting populace goes down."[33]

Elites who were threatened by reconstituting the electorate would often characterize registration reforms as a genre of fraud or cheating. Some even implied that Democrats benefited from a natural, numerical majority and that it was unfair when the party attempted to translate that advantage into electoral power. The conservative magazine *Human Events* published a piece explicitly lamenting that liberal Democrats "not content with bringing 18-year-old youths onto the voting rolls" were now "pushing legislation that would result in another serious blow to the Republicans—voter registration by mail." They listed the exact groups that easing registration risked recruiting into the electorate: "Under this scheme, many blacks, chicanos and low-income whites who ordinarily do not bother to register to vote would only have to fill out a card sent to them, put it in the mail and then consider themselves eligible to vote—Democratic, in all likelihood." In this sense, registration reform was trickery, a "gimmick," and "another attempt to legislate their way into national office."[34] In 1977, conservative intellectual and *National Review* founder, William F. Buckley Jr., complained that Democrats, in pushing same-day registration, wanted to "increase a majority that is already vulgar in disproportion."[35]

EARNING THE VOTE: REGISTRATION'S BUREAUCRATIC HASSLE AS A MORALS TEST

The strain in democratic culture that presents the vote as a precious—even sacred—honor reserved for those who fulfill their civic duties has not been hegemonic. It has faced fierce challenges and clashed with alternative visions. However, at almost every effort to expand the franchise, opponents of reforms mobilized both fears of voter fraud and this understanding of the vote as a conditional and earned privilege. Their arguments typically assumed that fraudulently or frivolously cast ballots posed a greater threat to the integrity of US democracy than constricted access.

Critics of registration reform consistently argued that apathy was the true cause of low turnout. They typically positioned the two explanations for declining participation—procedural barriers and public apathy—as mutually exclusive or inherently contradictory. A *Chicago Tribune* editorial opposing postcard registration explained that "the primary cause of low turnouts is voter apathy—a disinterest in the outcome of elections prompted by laziness on the part of some but by a genuine disgust on the part of many with the scandals, bossism, and fraud that have corrupted American Politics to an unfortunate degree." The editorial reasoned that easing registration would not only fail to address the root cause but actually exacerbate the problem: "An effective way to eliminate the corruption—and the consequent apathy—is to make elections more honest. Postcard voter registration would have an opposite effect. . . . The way to get people to vote is not just to make it easier for them (and easier for vote fraud as well). It is to make them want to vote, and that will require more than a piece of legislation."[36] In this logic, apathy and alienation increased as access to the vote expanded and procedural hurdles to participation diminished.

Other lawmakers cautioned that easing registration would not only encourage apathy and fraud but also diminish the value of the franchise altogether. Senator Norris Cotton (R-NH) warned that postcard registration would "cheapen the voting process in the eyes of the American people." In his estimation, the burden and exclusivity of voting produced its allure. Cotton explained that "if you want people to exercise the right of franchise, you should not make it so casual and so cheap and so easy so as to make them, especially young people, feel it is not an important function."[37] Ronald Reagan embraced a similar logic when inveighing against postcard registration in 1977. "Why don't we try reverse psychology & make it harder to vote," he asked. "That might also make it more desirable & attractive."[38]

In the efforts to derail registration reforms, people relied upon (both explicitly and implicitly) the understanding of the vote as a conditional privilege that could be forfeited. They often insinuated that voters who failed to register were demonstrably apathetic and uninterested and therefore risked degrading the electorate. An article in *Human Events* explained that opponents of registration reform doubted the value of incorporating such citizens, questioning "whether democracy should be 'broadened' to include those who have little concern for the important issues involved."[39] A *Los Angeles Times* article acknowledged that curtailing fraud joined with a commitment to cultivating a virtuous electorate, explaining that "opponents contended that the bill would open the floodgates to massive fraud and reward those too apathetic to take the trouble to register according to normal procedures."[40]

During the floor debates on postcard registration, senators acknowledged that citizens possessed a right to vote, but they often articulated this right as one that must be earned or secured through some test or hurdle. Echoing the antiwelfare politics of the time, lawmakers presented postcard registration as akin to an undeserved handout to the ungrateful. Senator James Allen (D-AL) asked, "Why should we spend millions of dollars to hand the franchise, this priceless gift, this right that a person ought to be willing to fight for, and just present it to a disinterested person on a silver platter?"[41] Senator John Stennis (D-MS) positioned the right to vote as one contingent upon fulfilling civic responsibilities. He explained to his colleagues, "To vote is a right. Any right is accompanied by a responsibility. Those who seriously exercise the right also accept the responsibility seriously. . . . Those who do not take the right to vote seriously do not take the trouble to register, and having avoided that responsibility, forfeit the right to cast a ballot." Allowing people to simply mail in their registration, without enduring the hassle and the cost of a stamp, risked polluting the electorate. The senator warned, "What is intended by this bill is that the responsibility to register be so lightened that it can be done by postcard, presumably postage free. Those that take their responsibility so lightly will surely cast their ballots lightly also. Impulse registration will obtain impulse voters."[42]

In a 1977 *National Review* article opposing Carter's election reform package, Buckley argued that fears of fraud were secondary to the more profound concerns about democratic norms:

> Now many Republicans are opposed to the universal registration law proposed by Carter, and they give as the principal reason for their opposition the possibilities of fraud. These possibilities exist, to be sure, but technical fraud is not really the problem. It is a different kind of fraud. When a voter signifies his preference without having given any significant thought to the alternatives, he is guilty of a fraud on the ideals of democracy. . . . And the Republicans, in opposing the contemplated measure, are afraid to say what is surely on their mind. Not that there is such a great possibility of technical fraud, but that the approach—universal registration—belies the gravity of the democratic process.[43]

Registration, in these formulations, served a function akin to the purported purpose of poll taxes and literacy tests: screening out voters deemed frivolous, unengaged, uninformed, or unreasoned.

And just as everyone knew that poll taxes and literacy tests disproportionately disenfranchised voters with low incomes and in communities of color, it was universally recognized, if often unstated, that the burdens of registration weighed most heavily on the least affluent, especially Black and brown citizens. Politicians, academics, and pundits assumed that bureaucratic burdens of registration contributed to the racial and class skew of the electorate, which overrepresented white and middle-class voters. Yet even though commentators would often note (or lament) that registration reforms would increase African American turnout, opponents deployed race- and class-neutral arguments grounded in contractarian logics to block reforms. Their emphasis on civic responsibility and the risks of fraud recast the issue as a technocratic question of election security. It endeavored to distance these debates from explicitly racialized struggles for voting rights that had raged only years earlier.

RACE AND ILLEGITIMATE CLAIMS ON THE STATE

Despite the colorblind discourse, the specter of race and anxiety about mobilized Black, brown, and poor voters saturated debates about fraud. "Good government" Progressive Era reformers found reports of rampant corruption all the more sinister because they assumed that it was committed by suspect ethnic and racial groups.[44] Similarly, the perceived dangers of voter fraud in the 1970s were exacerbated through association with racialized threats. Opponents of registration reform linked voter fraud to other racialized panics of the period, such as welfare cheating, illegal immigration, and street crime.

Victor Riesel wrote an article in *Human Events* that buoyed the danger of voter fraud by invoking tropes about welfare fraud. He recycled the sensationalistic stories circulating about Chicago's "welfare queen," explaining how she stole government benefits by using 250 aliases, thirty-one addresses, three social security numbers, and eight "deceased husbands." Echoing a familiar rationalization for felon disenfranchisement, Riesel reasoned that people who committed one category of crime (such as illegal entry into the country or welfare fraud) would inevitably be inclined to vote illegally. Given all the deception the "welfare queen" was capable of, he asked, "Why wouldn't she vote 10 or 20 times?" He also infused voter fraud with the general panic about immigration. He warned that there were enough "legal" and "illegal aliens" in New York City to "swing an election for the president of the U.S." Riesel explained that a "big alien turnout could swing the big town [New York City], and in turn, the state."[45] Rhetoric like this suggests that the legitimacy of claims about voter fraud depended in part on its linkages to existing racial stereotypes about Black and Latinx criminality and suspect civic status.

The threat of voter fraud also intertwined with a more general anxiety about "democratic overload" that intensified with the economic downturns and high inflation of the 1970s. Theorists such as political scientist Samuel Huntington warned that escalating demands and rising expectations of "special interests" (such as women or African Americans) would invariably outstrip state capacity, triggering spiraling social program costs and inflation.[46] As social movements demanded new rights and resources, many characterized the collective pursuit of subordinated groups' interests as unearned, undeserved, and therefore suspect, even fraudulent.

For example, California state senator Jack Schrade proposed in 1970 to deny "habitual" welfare recipients the right to vote. He complained that they "look out for their own interests at the voting booth."[47] Although courts and legislatures had steadily eliminated pauper exclusions throughout the 1960s, the idea that people "dependent" on state aid or charity were unviable or unworthy actors persisted, and arguably intensified with the escalating racialized antiwelfare politics of the 1970s.[48] Grounded through contractarian conceptions of citizenship, many reasoned that in receiving state aid, people forfeit their right to have a voice or make collective claims on the state. Schrade opposed enabling those "who are not paying their fair share of government" to tell the "taxpayers and property owners of California how to run their state." He continued, "I'd have no objection to the people who are taking advantage of welfare or subsidy programs being relieved of the vote. When they are back gainfully employed again I'd have no objection to giving them their vote back."[49]

Elites worried that easing registration would allow organized blocs, such as women, African Americans, or unions, to make claims on the state. They distinguished these demands from those of legitimate claimants by casting the groups as "special interests." Their demands were illegitimate—even corrupt—because the groups had failed to fulfill the obligations of citizenship or contribute to the polity. Reagan warned that Carter's reforms aimed to increase votes from "the bloc comprised of those who get a whole lot more from the federal government in various kinds of income distribution than they contribute to it." Same-day registration was suspect because it facilitated the distribution of rights and benefits to unproductive and ultimately less worthy members of the polity. Reagan warned, "Don't be surprised if an army of election workers—much of it supplied by labor organizations which have managed to exempt themselves from election law restrictions—sweep through metropolitan areas scooping up otherwise apathetic voters and rushing them to the polls to keep the benefit-dispensers in power."[50] This, Reagan and others implied, was a perversion of liberal democratic norms and a genre of fraud.

* * *

Consternation about voter fraud has morphed in the decades since these 1970s efforts to expand registration. In the wake of the 2020 election, the accusations reached an unprecedented and bizarre intensity. After the debates over hanging chads and butterfly ballots following the 2000 election and over drop boxes and voting machines in 2020, it is difficult to maintain the distinction between technocratic, apolitical voting regulations and partisan combat. After George W. Bush's razor-thin victory in 2000 and Trump's lawsuits over intricate election details of 2020, few would question that the rules of the game—polling station locations, absentee ballot regulations, and identification requirements—have bearing on who wins.

Analysts have had a harder time identifying how this illiberal and antidemocratic temper materialized so quickly or how norms and safeguards seemed to crumble so easily. The earlier debates over election regulations in the 1970s can offer part of the explanation. They suggest that despite the profound legal, political, and cultural transformations ushered in by the civil rights movement and the Voting Rights Act, no democratic consensus solidified in their wake. The country did not, contrary to much rhetoric, dedicate itself uniformly to maximizing political participation or eradicating civic stratification.

Politicians hoping to impede popular will or impose the minority's dictates could rely on the countermajoritarian institutions of the Senate, Supreme Court, and Electoral College. And those hoping to disqualify their opponents' votes were able to draw on the deep current in US democratic culture that is skeptical of political mobilization, especially by collectives of marginalized groups, such as the poor or people of color. And they could mobilize a tradition that sees the vote (and civic standing more broadly) as a conditional, precarious privilege instead of a guaranteed right.

Those who explicitly question the value of increased participation often deploy this vision of a conditional citizenship. Conservative analyst Jonah Goldberg wrote in a 2007 *Los Angeles Times* column, "Maybe the emphasis on getting more people to vote has dumbed-down our democracy by pushing participation onto people uninterested in such things. . . . Maybe the opinions of people who don't know the first thing about how our system works aren't the folks who should be driving our politics, just as people who don't know how to drive shouldn't have a driver's license." Echoing Reagan's musings from decades earlier, Goldberg pondered, "Instead of making it easier to vote, maybe we should be making it harder."[51] Another conservative commentator published similar sentiments in a 2021 *National Review* article titled "Why Not Fewer Voters?" Kevin Williamson wrote, "There would be more voters if we made it easier to vote, and there would be more doctors if we didn't require a license to practice medicine. The fact that we believe unqualified doctors to be a public menace but act as though unqualified voters were just stars in the splendid constellation of democracy indicates how little real esteem we actually have for the vote, in spite of our public pieties."[52]

These arguments recruit from the long tradition in US political culture that champions making political voice contingent upon some criteria, such as education, willingness to endure bureaucratic hassle, or fulfillment of civic obligations. The claims of voter fraud that have been deployed throughout US history are deeply intertwined with this commitment to conditional citizenship. They do not only reveal anxiety about cheating and illegal votes. They are also part of a long struggle to define who can claim voice and standing in the polity and on what terms. In short, controversies about voter fraud are battles over who counts in American democracy.

NOTES

1 Julian E. Zelizer, "'An Instrument of Justice and Fulfillment': The Lost Promise of the Voting Rights Act" (chap. 2 in the present volume); Carol Anderson, *One Person, No Vote: How Voter Suppression Is Destroying Our Democracy* (New York: Bloomsbury, 2018); Ari Berman, *Give Us the Ballot: The Modern Struggle for Voting Rights in America*, repr. ed. (New York: Picador, 2016).

2 Thomas B. Edsall, "After the Civil Rights Revolution" (chap. 5 in the present volume); Nicole Hemmer, "Election Deception: Disinformation, Election Security, and the History of Voter Suppression" (chap. 4 in the present volume).

3 For an example of the meticulous research debunking claims of voter fraud, see Lorraine Carol Minnite, *The Myth of Voter Fraud* (Ithaca, NY: Cornell University Press, 2010). See also the reporting by journalist Ari Berman and the reports by the Brennan Center for Justice. For example, see Justin Levitt, "The Truth about Voter Fraud," Brennan Center for Justice, November 9, 2007, www.brennancenter.org.

4 For just a couple of examples of a huge literature, see Aziz Rana, *The Constitutional Bind: How Americans Came to Idolize the Document That Fails Them* (Chicago: University of Chicago Press, forthcoming); and Robert A. Dahl, *How Democratic Is the American Constitution?*, 2nd ed. (New Haven, CT: Yale University Press, 2003).

5 Adam Jentleson, *Kill Switch: The Rise of the Modern Senate and the Crippling of American Democracy* (New York: Liveright, 2021).

6 Aziz Rana, *The Two Faces of American Freedom* (Cambridge, MA: Harvard University Press, 2010).

7 Eric Foner, *Reconstruction: America's Unfinished Revolution, 1863–1877*, updated ed. (New York: Harper Perennial Modern Classics, 2014); Anderson, *One Person, No Vote*.

8 On the particularities of mid-nineteenth-century democratic culture and different understandings of fraud, see Richard Franklin Bensel, *The American Ballot Box in the Mid-Nineteenth Century* (Cambridge: Cambridge University Press, 2004); Alexander Keyssar, *The Right to Vote: The Contested History of Democracy in the United States*, rev. ed. (New York: Basic Books, 2009).

9 Jamelle Bouie, "Vivek Ramaswamy Has a Gimmick That Republicans Are Sure to Love," *New York Times*, August 11, 2023, www.nytimes.com.

10 "National Turnout Rates, 1789–Present," US Elections Project, accessed January 25, 2024, www.electproject.org.

11 Keyssar, *The Right to Vote*, 128.

12 Keyssar.

13 Jeff Manza and Christopher Uggen, *Locked Out: Felon Disenfranchisement and American Democracy* (New York: Oxford University Press, 2008); Rabia Belt, "Contemporary Voting Rights Controversies through the Lens of Disability," *Stanford Law Review* 68, no. 6 (2016): 1491–550; Rabia Belt, *Disabling Democracy in America: Mental Incompetence, Citizenship, Voting and the Law, 1819–1920* (Cambridge University Press, forthcoming).

14 Steven F. Lawson, *Black Ballots: Voting Rights in the South, 1944–1969* (New York: Columbia University Press, 1976).

15 For a recent investigation of this debate, see Justin Grimmer and Eitan Hersh, "How Election Rules Affect Who Wins," Hoover Institution, June 29, 2023, www.hoover.org.

16 Shifting electoral terrains motivated certain interests within parties (and not others) to expand the electorate. This chapter draws on a larger book project tracking these dynamics and the politics of nonvoting and nonvoters in the decades after the Voting Rights Act. Other scholars have examined the struggles to preserve the racial and class skew of the electorate. See, for example, Frances Fox Piven, Lorraine C. Minnite, and Margaret Groarke, *Keeping Down the Black Vote: Race and the Demobilization of American Voters* (New York: New Press, 2009); Frances Fox Piven and Richard Cloward, *Why Americans Still Don't Vote: And Why Politicians Want It That Way*, rev. ed. (Boston: Beacon, 2000); Spencer Overton, *Stealing Democracy: The New Politics of Voter Suppression* (New York: W. W. Norton, 2007); and Anderson, *One Person, No Vote*.

17 Piven and Cloward, *Americans Still Don't Vote*. On the ambivalent position of liberals, Democrats, and liberalism, see Julilly Kohler-Hausmann, "The Preservation of Conditional Citizenship after the 1965 Voting Rights Act," in

Mastery and Drift: Professional-Class Liberals since the 1960s (University of Chicago Press, forthcoming).

18 John F. Kennedy, "Executive Order 11100—Establishing the President's Commission on Registration and Voting Participation," March 30, 1963, American Presidency Project, www.presidency.ucsb.edu.

19 Kevin Schaul, Kate Rabinowitz, and Ted Mellnik, "2020 Turnout Is the Highest in over a Century," *Washington Post*, last updated December 28, 2020, www.washingtonpost.com. Although the popular press embraced the narrative about declining civic engagement, there have been extensive scholarly debates about the causes and extent of the turnout declines after 1960. See, for example, Thomas E. Patterson, *The Vanishing Voter: Public Involvement in an Age of Uncertainty* (New York: Alfred A. Knopf, 2002); Lyn Ragsdale and Jerrold G. Rusk, *The American Nonvoter* (New York: Oxford University Press, 2017); Robert D. Putnam, *Bowling Alone: The Collapse and Revival of American Community* (New York: Simon and Schuster, 2000); and Jan E. Leighley and Jonathan Nagler, *Who Votes Now? Demographics, Issues, Inequality, and Turnout in the United States* (Princeton, NJ: Princeton University Press, 2013). One of the most widely cited challenges to turnout statistics and the idea of the "vanishing voter" is Michael McDonald and Samuel Popkin, "The Myth of the Vanishing Voter," *American Political Science Review* 95 (December 2001): 963–74.

20 Political scientists also debated the role of registration in declining turnout rates. See, for example, Frances Fox Piven and Richard A. Cloward, "Government Statistics and Conflicting Explanations of Nonvoting," *PS: Political Science and Politics* 22, no. 3 (1989): 580–88; and G. Bingham Powell, "American Voter Turnout in Comparative Perspective," *American Political Science Review* 80, no. 1 (1986): 17–43. On the relationship of academic debates to the struggles over political strategy, see Piven and Cloward, *Americans Still Don't Vote*, esp. chaps. 2 and 9.

21 "Voter Registration," in *CQ Almanac 1971*, 27th ed. (Washington, DC: Congressional Quarterly, 1972), 05-806–05-808; Bruce Winters, "Voter Registration by Mail Approved by Senate Panel," *Baltimore Sun*, November 3, 1971, AAAA8.

22 For a detailed discussion of the ways fraud charges impeded registration reform, see Margaret Groarke, "The Impact of Voter Fraud Claims on Voter Registration Reform Legislation," *Political Science Quarterly* 131, no. 3 (September 1, 2016): 571–95.

23 "Postcard Voter Registration," in *CQ Almanac 1976*, 32nd ed. (Washington, DC: Congressional Quarterly, 1977), 517–19.

24 This was a frequent refrain throughout the postcard registration debates. See, for example, "Demos Plot to Swell Democratic Voting Lists," *Human Events*, February 12, 1972, 4.

25 "Postcard Voter Registration."

26 Mitch McConnell, "Should US Simplify Voter Registration?," *Christian Science Monitor*, October 1, 1991, www.csmonitor.com.

27 "Bush Rejects 'Motor Voter' Legislation," *Congressional Quarterly*, 1992, http://library.cqpress.com.

28 For a discussion of the ways that concerns about fraud narrowed the ambitions of the National Voter Registration Act, see Groarke, "Impact of Voter Fraud." On the history of organizing for the National Voter Registration Act and its implementation, see Piven, Minnite, and Groarke, *Keeping Down*; and Piven and Cloward, *Americans Still Don't Vote.*

29 An example of a particularly cogent analysis of political change that incorporates nonvoters is Thomas Byrne Edsall, *The New Politics of Inequality* (New York: W. W. Norton, 1985).

30 Warren Weaver, "Democrats, Urging Easier Voter Registration, See Party Gain," *New York Times*, October 11, 1971.

31 Ernest Furgurson, "Making Voting Easy," *Baltimore Sun*, November 9, 1971, A14.

32 Kevin P. Phillips, "Election Reform Is Political Dynamite," *Human Events*, April 9, 1977, 11.

33 Samuel L. Perry, Andrew L. Whitehead, and Joshua B. Grubbs, "'I Don't Want Everybody to Vote': Christian Nationalism and Restricting Voter Access in the United States," *Sociological Forum* 37, no. 1 (2022): 4–26, quote on 9.

34 For *Human Events* quotes, including on Democrats' efforts to "legislate their way into public office," see "Demos Plot to Swell." For an example of calling registration reform a "gimmick" to register poor and Black voters, see Spencer Rich, "Senate Vote Set on Mail Registration," *Washington Post*, March 15, 1972, A30.

35 William F. Buckley Jr., "Everybody Vote," *National Review*, April 15, 1977, 456.

36 "Vote Fraud by Mail?," *Chicago Tribune*, July 24, 1973, 12.

37 "Big Labor Key Factor in Postcard Registration Victory," *Human Events*, May 19, 1973, 3.

38 Ronald Reagan, "Postcard Registration," in *Reagan, in His Own Hand: The Writings of Ronald Reagan That Reveal His Revolutionary Vision for America*, ed. Kiron K. Skinner, Annelise Anderson, and Martin Anderson (New York: Free Press, 2001), 245.

39 "Demos Plot to Swell."

40 "Bill to Allow Voters to Register by Mail Killed," *Los Angeles Times*, March 16, 1972, A6.

41 "Voter Registration: Senate Rejects Nationwide Plan," in *CQ Almanac 1972*, 28th ed. (Washington, DC: Congressional Quarterly, 1973), http://library.cqpress.com.

42 John C. Stennis, "The Voter Registration Bill," Congressional Record—Senate, March 15, 1972, 8439.

43 Buckley, "Everybody Vote."

44 Keyssar, *Right to Vote*, 130.

45 Victor Riesel, "How Aliens Could Use Instant Registration," *Human Events*, April 30, 1977, 16, 19.

46 Michel Crozier, Samuel Huntington, and Joji Watanuki, *The Crisis of Democracy: Report on the Governability of Democracies to the Trilateral Commission* (New York: New York University Press, 1975).

47 "Welfare Clients May Lose Votes," *Courier-Post*, September 14, 1970, 6.

48 On ending the disenfranchisement of paupers, see Keyssar, *Right to Vote*, 219–20.

49 "Welfare Clients May Lose Votes." On the broader project of restricting welfare recipients' rights and standing through contractual logics, see Julilly Kohler-Hausmann, *Getting Tough: Welfare and Imprisonment in 1970s America* (Princeton, NJ: Princeton University Press, 2017), chaps. 3 and 4.

50 Rick Perlstein, "Jimmy Carter Tried to Make It Easier to Vote in 1977. The Right Stopped Him with the Same Arguments It's Using Today," *Time*, August 20, 2020, https://time.com.

51 Jonah Goldberg, "Way Too Dumb to Vote," *Los Angeles Times*, July 31, 2007, www.latimes.com.

52 Kevin Williamson, "Why Not Fewer Voters?," *National Review*, April 6, 2021, www.nationalreview.com.

12

HBCUS AND ELECTION INTEGRITY

KAREEM CRAYTON

In the policy dialogue about election integrity and its role in the future of American democracy, it is worth considering carefully what actors who invoke this concept actually mean when they deploy it in practice. The definition of election integrity often lives in the eye of the beholder; at times, one person's election integrity is another's voter suppression, and the perception likely depends on one's beliefs about the burdens and benefits of the policy proposal in question. It is therefore important to be mindful of the likely effects of a policy proposal in this area.

Most would accept the idea that integrity (i.e., having a transparent, reliable system) is necessary for any democracy to maintain free and fair elections; however, identifying how to achieve that objective through specific policies and rules is a more contested proposition. And the devil always lives in the details of the policy consequences for real people. The most commonly invoked justifications for election integrity policies involve ensuring public confidence in the process and safeguarding elections against widescale voter fraud. As integrity agenda proponent and former Alabama secretary of state John Merrill (often a defendant in voter suppression cases) frequently put it, he sought a system where it is "easy to vote but hard to cheat."[1]

Whether these are tropes or truisms, arguments about this approach to integrity are met with observations from research showing that proposed "fixes" to the election system outpace the scope of the observed harms. For example, studies (including those by the Brennan Center) have concluded that election fraud in America is a less frequent occurrence than getting struck by lightning.[2] Not only is it infrequent, but it is also typically detected and therefore not able to affect elections. At best, then, the purported need for many integrity measures is overblown. At worst, however, these efforts tend to justify policies that burden some communities more than others. They also stoke public misinformation about the function of the election system, the good faith of the officials who manage it, and the reliability of outcomes.

Embedded in at least some of the fervent advocacy for election integrity is the expectation that a properly run election may be more challenged with high participation. For one thing, the stance frames the franchise as a privilege (to be exercised by people who deserve the opportunity) rather than a civil right (one that all citizens are entitled to enjoy). Staunch integrity advocates gauge success of the system based on improving voter registration numbers instead of boosting actual voter turnout. For instance, former secretary Merrill and others focus on the number of registered voters and people issued voter ID rather than the number of people who show up to vote. That is, attending to the eligibility to vote is a higher priority to these officials than ensuring that more people visit the polls to select their leaders. In essence, those concerned with safeguarding the effectiveness and integrity of the system appear to view full participation as being inconsistent with a secure election system. Ironically, then, the goal of securing a democratic system involves official efforts and policies that keep people outside the process instead of bringing more people into it.

This distinction raises a critical question that ought to be answered when examining the subject of election integrity: Whose participation is burdened in order to achieve what some view as an appropriately secure election system? This chapter explores why it is the case that, too often, those excluded from this system (whether intentionally or not) are both young and Black. The consequences of this pattern of exclusion are significant, in both moral and practical terms. The point of this chapter is to encourage decision makers to evaluate the impact of election integrity proposals on communities in a more balanced way.

Examining the role that historically Black colleges and universities (HBCUs) have played in the debate over election integrity, this analysis illustrates how election integrity policies have sometimes created distinct barriers that disadvantage Black political participation in these communities. In fact, integrity policies can sometimes pose dangers for HBCU students and faculties by punishing their political engagement on campus. Notwithstanding their central position in the landscape of Black political participation, these educational sites (and their surrounding communities) have become the more frequent targets for disruption, confusion, and intimidation due partly to integrity-related policies whose impact is not always considered fully.

* * *

HBCUs are higher education institutions in the country with a special emphasis on serving the needs of Black communities. These schools are open to all students (today, about a quarter of enrolled students are not Black),[3] but their historical lineage is connected to America's history of supporting racially segregated public facilities during most of the twentieth century. The era of separate but equal in the law produced a distinct social and cultural legacy on these campuses, much of which endures. While the HBCU designation was officially incorporated into federal law in the 1960s, the roots of this network trace back to the nineteenth century. Through Congress's university land-grant program in 1890, these schools became conduits for the economic and labor advancement of Black people, primarily in the South, in the wake of enslavement.[4]

Today, approximately one hundred schools (both public and private) still exist around the country and include graduate and undergraduate programs covering a variety of disciplines. As Table 12.1 shows, these schools are concentrated heavily in the Deep South and its border states. Their distinct impact as sites for Black educational advancement remains a noteworthy accomplishment despite underfunding and significant challenges from often hostile political environments in the segregated South.[5]

While they form only 3 percent of all colleges and universities in the country, HBCUs produce almost a fifth of the nation's Black college graduates. These schools are therefore a major supplier in the pipeline of Black graduates in STEM and other professional disciplines, including law and medicine.[6] Further, the financial impact of these schools as job creators in the broader community is quite immense. According to the United

Table 12.1 Distribution of HBCUs by State

State	Number of HBCUs	Former VRA preclearance coverage?
Alabama	14	Yes
Georgia	10	Yes
North Carolina	10	Partial
Texas	9	Yes
South Carolina	8	Yes
Mississippi	7	Yes
Louisiana	6	Yes
Tennessee	6	No
Virginia	5	Partial
Arkansas	4	No
Florida	4	Partial
Maryland	4	No
District of Columbia	2	No
Kentucky	2	No
Missouri	2	No
Ohio	2	No
Pennsylvania	2	No
Delaware	1	No
Oklahoma	1	No

Negro College Fund (a financial supporter of almost a third of the country's HBCUs), these schools generate annually a total of $14.8 billion in national economic impact and they supply more than 134,000 jobs in the immediate local and regional economies where they are located.[7]

Aside from their being a crucial part of the American higher education ecosystem, there are additional aspects of the HBCU experience that make them especially valued and valuable places to promote the country's continued political development as well.

A primary aspect that distinguishes HBCUs from other institutions of higher learning (called predominantly white institutions) is how the former serves as a platform for cultural and social expression within Black communities. Campus life is shaped by distinctive traditions and celebrations that lift up the contributions of African American culture, which is not commonly observed in other public spaces.

Further, these institutions invite enrolled students to explore their own conceptions of race and social identity in light of the multiple dimensions of culture present on campus. For example, HBCUs are the locus of an active and diverse community that includes a Black sorority and fraternity network (called the "Divine Nine"), faculty and visiting speakers enhance the intellectual experience both in and out of class, and more informal social engagement in rallies, parades, and halftime shows is common. For students who grew up distant from Black communities, the HBCU provides an opportunity to become both familiar with and supportive of the concept of Black excellence in all its forms.

Related to incubating the social development of their students, HBCUs are also a primary site for awakening students to their important role as responsible and engaged citizens. The HBCU not only mobilizes the social thinking and action of students who are on campus but also plays an important part in the broader community as a neighbor. Students' work to become aware of and conversant with important issues of the day, as well as their engagement in mass political behavior that includes activities like petition signing, voter registration, and organizing, has been essential to major change, particularly in the South. These institutions brought together much of the talent and energy to prepare voters to contend with barriers like the literacy test. Given the increasing concerns about the role of citizens in democracy, this function attains even more potential for tremendous good in the current era.

It is no exaggeration to credit HBCUs for enhancing the social mobility of African Americans since Reconstruction. The educational spaces at their founding were among the few places where freedmen in the South could thrive in the Jim Crow era, a significant period of economic transformation within the African American community. The entire purpose of the federal government's investment in land grants in the late nineteenth century (when many HBCUs were established) was to create opportunities for freedpersons to build skills and to enjoy the fruits of equal citizenship. At Tuskegee University (then called Tuskegee Institute), located in the heart of Alabama's Black Belt, that institutional charge meant training students in agricultural science and the business of farming. Other schools focused on preparing students to be educators in segregated K–12 schools or medical professionals. For many African American families during this period, these schools produced the first generation of professionals who could enter the workforce and improve their family's economic standing.

Finally, it is quite difficult to overestimate how much HBCUs contribute to developing America's Black public leadership, which includes corporate officers, social innovators, and political officials at every level of government. As a vital proving ground for organization and skill building in social groups, student government, and political clubs, HBCU campuses have a long history of promoting opportunities for young leaders to find their voices and establish relationships that direct their paths toward significant contributions later in life. Again, much of the South's first wave of Black political leadership in the twentieth century originated with organizing and protest activity on the campuses of the region's HBCUs. For example, the original members of the Student Nonviolent Coordinating Committee (SNCC), including Representative John Lewis, assembled at North Carolina's Shaw University from HBCUs around the region.[8] The trend of training America's Black leadership continues today. The political careers of mayors, cabinet secretaries, members of Congress, and now a sitting vice president are all traceable to HBCUs, which helps underscore the level of success these schools have had in training and promoting strong and visionary figures who help to shape the issues on the public agenda.

THE HISTORICAL ANTECEDENTS OF HBCUS AND VOTER DISRUPTION

Concerns about government interference with the full enjoyment of civil rights, and specifically the right to vote, in HBCU communities is sadly not new. In fact, one of the cases central to the canon of voting rights involved the state's manipulation of jurisdiction borders to limit the political influence of a Black community in the Alabama Black Belt. In *Gomillion v. Lightfoot*, the Supreme Court held that the Alabama legislature had violated the Fourteenth Amendment by redrawing the borders of the city of Tuskegee to create a twenty-eight-sided gerrymandered figure that intentionally excluded all but a few Black residents.[9] The affected community of Black voters who were denied representation in the city included both faculty and students of Tuskegee Institute. Indeed, the named plaintiff in that case, Charles G. Gomillion, was a professor of sociology at Tuskegee and dean of the College of Arts and Sciences on campus. He was a politically active member of the community whose early work promoting voter registration efforts among Black residents in Tuskegee spurred the redistricting tactic by the local white citizens' council.

Only a few miles to the west of Tuskegee, Alabama State University was central to the first recognized act of mass resistance to the Jim Crow system, the Montgomery Bus Boycott. While church-based organizing groups were an important (and also male-dominated) institutional foundation for the yearlong campaign to end segregated busing policy in Montgomery, the formative work of Black women who were professional teachers in the city's Black school (most of whom were educated at Alabama State Teachers College, which later became Alabama State University) developed the networks to establish and manage mass rallies but also the private ride-sharing program used by most of the Black community for transportation needs during the bus boycott. The prolonged effort could not have succeeded without the communications and administrative prowess of people like Jo Ann Robinson and her professional colleagues who were both politically organized and connected to the local HBCU.[10]

Other well-known historical cases of HBCU communities working to entrench fair and equal treatment in the political system come from the Carolinas. In addition to the efforts led by North Carolina A&T students at the Greensboro Woolworths, recognized as the genesis of the national sit-in campaigns, Shaw University in Raleigh was the location of the 1960 founding of SNCC. In its early incarnation, SNCC sought to extend the nonviolent campaign of protest alongside the Southern Christian Leadership Conference to promote strategies that included the Freedom Rides. As it later evolved thanks to the work of Ella Baker, the organization branched out to host training and strategy sessions based at Fisk University in Nashville, Tennessee.[11]

Of course, there were times that these organizational efforts posed grave physical risk to participating students. According to coverage of the time, students at South Carolina State University faced some of most overt and deadly acts of state-sanctioned violence. In 1968, a critical turning point in the civil rights movement, three students were killed and dozens more were injured by state police amid mass protests of segregated public facilities in Orangeburg, South Carolina.[12] The incident marked the first time during the movement that state officials formally authorized explicit violent police action against marchers. The heavily publicized injuries and deaths of the students and other protesters led to commitments by local authorities to desegregate local facilities as well as the pursuit of multiple federal civil rights lawsuits against certain of the officers, whose shooting into a fleeing crowd was inconsistent with what was reasonable under the circumstances.

CONTRIBUTING ELEMENTS IN THE PRESENT ERA

What accounts for the current trend of using voting policy to constrain or suppress voting on HBCU campuses? I identify three major considerations that have made the efforts more frequent and frankly more pernicious: the racial and demographic shift in America's population, the increasing competitiveness and polarization in America's politics, and the elimination of significant safeguards to prevent suppressive policies from being enacted.

The most significant change in the country over the last three decades is the accelerated shift in the racial profile of America's political landscape. The much-anticipated shift toward a more racially diverse country has taken greater shape in the past decade in many states partly due to immigration. The locations where this has become evident range from large metropolitan areas to more rural and suburban settings. Just as important, the patterns of movement of those already in the country have also affected the evolving narrative on racial diversity. A key element of this second factor is the relocation of African Americans to southern states like Texas and Georgia from parts of the country like California or Michigan—areas that had previously boomed during the Great Migration. Consequently, the current pattern of explosive growth in the Sun Belt states has been almost entirely attributable to people of color. For example, nearly 80 percent of the growth in the state of Georgia during the last census was due to people of color, so that these communities represent close to half that state's population.[13] As Table 12.2 illustrates, the locations of the nation's largest HBCUs include states with the highest growth areas in the country. Notably, these schools also represent a significant portion of the black population of their respective counties, making their potential influence on local politics even more salient.

At the same time, the renewed attention to election integrity has also been shaped by the increased competitiveness (and polarization) of the

Table 12.2 Ten Largest HBCUs by Enrollment

University	Enrollment (2021)	Location	2020 local population	2020 local Black population (%)
North Carolina A&T	12,556	Guilford County, NC	541,309	36.3
Florida A&M	9,626	Leon County, FL	297,369	32.5
Howard	9,399	Washington, DC	671,803	45.0
Texas Southern	9,034	Harris County, TX	4,780,913	20.6
Prairie View A&M	8,940	Waller County, TX	61,894	25.5
Tennessee State	8,081	Davidson County, TN	708,144	26.9
North Carolina Central	8,011	Durham County, NC	332,680	35.3
Morgan State	7,763	Baltimore City, MD	569,931	61.2
Southern	7,140	E. Baton Rouge Parish, LA	450,544	47.2
Jackson State	7,020	Hinds County, MS	217,730	73.5

American electorate. Having experienced a worldwide pandemic, a second contested presidential election, and ethical stresses on almost every national institution, the American public has become sharply divided about most matters on the national agenda. Few national leaders or ideas enjoy widespread support in this environment, and people view almost every public concern through a deeply polarized lens. This trend of polarization is enhanced further by recent achingly close outcomes in the last two national elections (resulting in razor-thin majorities in the House and Senate), along with a host of statewide races with stunningly close margins. As a result, even seemingly marginal policy changes that can shift the shape of the electorate can carry profound consequences in electoral outcomes and resulting policy decisions.

A third element contributing to the dynamic between HBCUs and voting rights constraints is the US Supreme Court's role in promoting renewed attention to election integrity. The Court in 2013 invalidated a key part of the Voting Rights Act (VRA) responsible for adding care and prior review to legislation that affected voting in several states. These were many of the same states where preclearance enforcement had led to the improvement of Black political representation and also where most of the country's HBCUs are located. Since the Court rendered the VRA's preclearance provision inoperable over the last decade, the result has been a spike in the number of new (and often suppressive) laws in the previously covered states. While some have been rolled back due to traditional VRA litigation (even with the Court's later requiring more evidence to succeed in these claims), the volume of new rules aimed at reshaping the system has left many of these changes in place.

CURRENT EXAMPLES OF INTERFERENCE ON HBCU CAMPUSES

There are three forms of interference that provide useful illustrations of the ways election integrity policy, when unmoored from an appraisal of effects, can have grave and possibly ruinous consequences for communities in and around HBCUs: unbridled gerrymandering, the disruption of polling place allocation, and harassment and intimidation at the ballot box. These practices follow from election integrity policies not tailored to account for their distinct effects on communities of color. Whether or not they are intentionally designed to do so, they nonetheless can work to undermine the political mobilization and activity of communities of color in a way that is eerily reminiscent of times thought to be long forgotten.

Alongside its terribly misguided decision that effectively ended the operation of the VRA's preclearance regime, the Supreme Court declared in a different case in 2019 that the federal constitution had nothing at all to say about the matter of partisan gerrymandering because the issue was nonjusticiable as a matter of law. In *Rucho v. Common Cause*, the Court determined that there were no discernible standards that could help judges identify and regulate partisan-driven line drawing that produced unfair results.[14] In doing so, the Court left states largely free (absent state constitutional limits) to pursue even the most manipulative district drawing strategies. Ostensibly, this decision was offered in the name of maintaining the Court's distance from the political sphere—designed to ensure public confidence that the unelected branch was not diving into the so-called political thicket.

Yet there are moments where a refusal to decide counts as a decision. The loss of the significant federal guidelines of the voting rights and partisan gerrymandering law is evident in a raft of new state and local laws in previously covered jurisdictions that would undo much of what the era of robust enforcement of the VRA had accomplished in providing meaningful conduits for the expression of preferences by African American voters. And nowhere has the shift of this trend been more pronounced than in redistricting. In the current era, line drawers dispense with even the most cursory procedures to solicit public input on maps (including that of Black voters). Additionally, legislative majorities frequently adopt plans that blatantly divide communities in service to partisan margins in Congress and the state legislature.

Perhaps the most egregious case of this no-holds-barred line-drawing approach that the Supreme Court has unleashed involves Guilford County, North Carolina. Located in the politically competitive Piedmont region of the state, Guilford is also home to North Carolina A&T—the nation's largest HBCU, along with neighboring Bennett College.[15] The North Carolina legislature's preferred district map in 2014 for that region included borders that sliced Guilford County multiple ways, so that one district border ran right down the main street of A&T's campus.[16] The proposed map kept portions of the university and its voters in a district separate from their neighbors, and both were represented by officials who did not prioritize issues relevant to the university and did not even reside in Guilford County. The institution had never been so divided in previous maps, and in fact no other university in the legislature's proposal had been divided in the manner proposed.

Political consequences aside, this single change complicated life for an A&T administration that now had to appeal to different legislators to lobby for campus priorities. Additionally, students now needed to determine which district they lived in each year, depending on where they happened to live on campus, which had effects on their ability to meet and confer about the candidates they might choose to endorse or support in future elections. As a community of interest, people at North Carolina A&T no longer had the ability to mobilize its voters as a unit to advocate for issues that affected the campus. Those interests, now divided, had to compete for the attention of officials with two different sets of electorates largely anchored in other North Carolina counties.

Another tactic of the election integrity agenda (which was supercharged by the functional elimination of VRA preclearance review) is the disruptive reallocation of resources for voter access to the polling place. Without significant federal review of the likely effects of moving a polling place, state legislatures and local election officials have taken steps across the nation to adopt dozens of new proposals for polling places and access rules. These changes include limiting early voting (a process often used by churches and HBCUs to organize voter mobilization strategies), changing polling place allocations, and enacting new identification rules that would not count student IDs as acceptable documents.

With little to no prior announcement or publicity, state and local officials have decreased the number of available polling places, eliminating many that voters and associated organizing groups had come to rely on in elections. For some, this has meant that in order to cast a ballot, they must adjust in response to changes in their assigned polling location and relevant candidates for office. The result, when these changes affect multiple people, is a more confused and slow Election Day experience for voters on these campuses. This negative experience with voting tends to dampen participation and turnout in these precincts, which is particularly concerning among young people whose propensity to vote is still being formed.

These hurdles at HBCUs were among the major institutional flashpoints in recent elections that illustrate the problems voters face when they have little or no notice of such policy changes. The students who live and work in these communities rely on the guidance and experience of people who voted during the last election cycle, so the changes (particularly unexpected and unexplained ones) undermine efforts by groups to build a sustained culture of voting participation on these campuses. Unfortunately, these cases of student voters finding that their polling place has been reassigned—sometimes to a location far from campus—are not isolated.

In the 2022 elections, which featured a historic run for governor by Stacey Abrams, student voters at Morehouse and Spelman Colleges (both part of the Atlanta University Center) were met with overwhelmed and confused poll workers who indicated that many of them were not eligible to cast ballots at the campus polling station. According to reports, many were turned away without sufficient guidance about how to identify the correct location.[17] While private groups hurriedly organized transportation options to ferry students to their newly assigned locations, the effects took hold. In a statewide election decided by a few percentage points, these issues were significant enough to shift outcomes.

At Prairie View A&M, local officials in Waller County, Texas, approved removing early voting sites from campus pursuant to the state's new allocation policy. Since there was no need for preclearance review, few were aware of that change until days before the election.[18] Texas media accounts noted that the removal of polling places had a greater impact on HBCUs than on predominantly white institutions in the state (which were more likely to retain a polling place), though this issue did not appear to sway decision makers. Prairie View students on campus who wanted to vote had a choice of either casting a provisional ballot on campus (which might not be counted) or traveling off campus to the nearest polling place. For more than a few students with significant transportation concerns, this effectively meant they did not have the opportunity to cast a ballot in that election.[19]

Intimidation and harassment are the gravest forms of disruption prompted by voting integrity concerns, and they pose serious threats to robust political participation. Voters are entitled to an election that is free from undue influence and threats, particularly from state officials. This principle allows one's vote to be led only by their conscience. When private or official actors like law enforcement bear down on a polling place with weaponry and the attendant tools of criminal enforcement actions, the message they send to voters is not a welcoming one. This is especially true in the context of campuses that have established histories of painful episodes with police action.

Again, the intersection of high-stakes elections and intimidation tactics should not be ignored as one considers the impact of these policies. In the contested presidential election in 2020, for instance, student voters at Florida A&M University arrived to witness armed police stationed at area polling places in Tallahassee that served Black workers. No explanation at the time was offered, other than to indicate the blockade was not authorized.[20] And more recently, Florida's governor has tried to strengthen his hand by establishing a special task force of prosecutors and enforcement officers solely assigned to look for and prosecute instances of so-called voter fraud.

Similarly, in another recent high-stakes statewide election, Mississippi officials assigned police to a checkpoint very near the state's largest polling place, adjacent to Jackson State University. While that police checkpoint was dismantled on Election Day itself, the message sent to voters was that their activities would be monitored. This policy must also be viewed in connection with the legislature's ongoing efforts to build and manage its own specialized court and police force that would govern enforcement matters in Jackson itself, an 83 percent Black jurisdiction that had its own set of elected government officials. Effectively, that proposal would replace the jurisdiction's entire government service and leave students at Jackson State and their administrators subject to the whims and policies of people who neither reflect their preferred political interests nor even live in the jurisdiction that they do.

* * *

Considerations of election integrity are both relevant and necessary for sustaining a well-functioning election system in any democracy. As the foregoing examples show, though, policymakers who pursue this goal need to attend to the ways voters in different communities might be burdened or excluded in their implementation. This point is most salient in cases involving communities with a prolonged history of exclusion and marginalization.

Serious review and consideration of the likely effects of policies like these were core features of the now-defunct preclearance provisions of the VRA. Over the last decade, without the enforcement of this provision, southern legislatures have not demonstrated great sensitivity to these concerns even when they are expressed. HBCUs' experiences described in this chapter help show that even when the opportunity exists to raise concerns, they usually emerge only after voters encounter problems in elections—and even then, usually in the face of prolonged litigation. More than anything, the challenges faced by HBCUs highlight the ongoing need for structures that ensure that policymaking focused on voting integrity does not undermine other key values essential to confidence and participation in the political process. In our increasingly diverse and multiracial democracy, our future depends on it.

NOTES

1 John Merrill, "John H. Merrill to VP Harris: Photo ID Laws Don't Make It 'Almost Impossible' to Vote," *Montgomery Advertiser*, July 2, 2021, www.montgomeryadvertiser.com. See also "Modernizing Election Administration: 'Make It Easy to Vote, Hard to Cheat,'" Bipartisan Policy Center, October 18, 2013, https://bipartisanpolicy.org.

2 See Tomas Lopez and Adam Gitlin "Analysis: In a Voter Fraud Fog," Brennan Center for Justice, April 14, 2017, www.brennancenter.org.

3 "Spotlight on Minority Serving Institutions," American Council on Education, accessed January 26, 2024, www.equityinhighered.org.

4 Christopher Brown, "The Politics of Industrial Education: Booker T. Washington and Tuskegee State Normal School, 1890–1915," *Negro Educational Review* 50, no.3 (1999): 123–28.

5 Marybeth Gasman and Adriel Hilton, "Mixed Motivations, Mixed Results: A History of Law, Legislation, Historically Black Colleges and Universities, and Interest Convergence," *Teachers College Record* 114, no. 7 (2012): 1–34.

6 "Fact Sheet: Biden-Harris Administration Highlights a Record of Championing Historically Black Colleges and Universities (HBCUs)," Department of Education, September 29, 2023, www.ed.gov.

7 See United Negro College Fund, *HBCUs Make America Strong: The Positive Economic Impact of Historically Black Colleges and Universities* (Washington, DC: United Negro College Fund, n.d.), https://cdn.uncf.org.

8 David Halberstam, *The Children* (New York: Random House, 1998).

9 See Gomillion v. Lightfoot, 364 U.S. 339 (1960); and Allen Mendenhall, "*Gomillion v. Lightfoot*," Encyclopedia of Alabama, May 2, 2011, https://encyclopediaofalabama.org.

10 See Jo Ann Robinson, "The Boycott Begins," in "The Making of African American Identity: Vol. III, 1917–1968," National Humanities Center Resource Toolbox, 2009, https://nationalhumanitiescenter.org. Originally published in Jo Ann Robinson, *The Montgomery Bus Boycott and the Women Who Started It: The Memoir of Jo Ann Robinson*, ed. David J. Garrow (Knoxville: University of Tennessee Press, 1987), 53–87.

11 "Student Nonviolent Coordinating Committee," Martin Luther King, Jr. Research and Education Institute, accessed January 26, 2024, https://kinginstitute.stanford.edu.

12 "The Orangeburg Massacre," South Carolina State University, accessed January 26, 2024, https://scsu.edu.

13 Sonali Seth and Sara Loving, "Local Lockout in Georgia," Brennan Center for Justice, November 28, 2023, www.brennancenter.org.

14 Rucho v. Common Cause, 588 U.S. ___ (2019).

15 "About Bennett," Bennett College, accessed January 26, 2024, www.bennett.edu.

16 Lewis Kendall, "How a Republican Plan to Split a Black College Campus Backfired," *The Guardian*, November 1, 2020, www.theguardian.com.

17 Adam Edelman, "HBCU Students in Georgia Face an Extra Obstacle in Voting," NBC News, December 4, 2022.

18 Murjani Rawls, "Texas Election Laws Are Making It Harder for HBCU College Students to Vote," *The Root*, November 2, 2022.

19 "Prairie View A&M Students Sue Texas County, Allege Voter Suppression of Black Citizens," Associated Press, October 24, 2018.

20 Jerry White, "Florida A&M Students Describe Republican Attack on Voting Rights," World Socialist Web Site, December 6, 2000, www.wsws.org.

13

STATES AS BULWARKS AGAINST, OR POTENTIAL FACILITATORS OF, ELECTION SUBVERSION

RICHARD L. HASEN

States stand at the fulcrum of a decentralized, fragmented, and partially partisan system of election administration in the United States.[1] The continued ability to run free and fair US elections in these polarized and tumultuous times depends in no small part on whether states will continue to serve as bulwarks against election subversion or whether state actors will become facilitators of it, as the 2020 election signaled was possible.

Placing the states at the center of election security may seem odd given other actors' significant roles in the US electoral process. On the one hand, states do not have the final word on election rules governing federal, state, and local elections. Federal statutory and constitutional law trumps state rules by virtue of the US Constitution's Supremacy Clause.[2] For example, federal statutes require states to elect members of Congress from single-member districts, protect minority voters under the Voting Rights Act, and offer a provisional ballot to anyone showing up at the polling place in a federal election who asks to vote but who does not appear to be properly registered.[3] On the other hand, states do not organize and run elections; they generally delegate that task to thousands of local election jurisdictions, typically counties, throughout the United States. Local agencies register voters, organize polling stations, process absentee ballots, and tabulate votes.[4]

The list of tasks and ground rules that states are *not* responsible for in US election administration, however, obscures the key role that states play in federal elections. Under the Constitution, states set qualifications for voting in congressional elections, subject to US constitutional constraints.[5] States also establish the rules for choosing presidential electors and conducting congressional elections, the latter subject to congressional override; the Constitution gives little guidance for how states should do so.[6] As the Supreme Court wrote in the 2023 case *Moore v. Harper*: "Elections are complex affairs, demanding rules that dictate everything from the date on which voters will go to the polls to the dimension and font of individual ballots. Legislatures must provide a complete code for congressional elections, including regulations relating to notices, registration, supervision of voting, protection of voters, prevention of fraud and corrupt practices, counting of votes, duties of inspectors and canvassers, and making and publication of election returns."[7] States also help fund elections and establish statewide rules for their conduct, such as voter identification requirements, standards for parties and candidates to appear on the ballot, and the number of days (if any) of early in-person voting and voting by mail.

The states' central role in the US system of election administration came under close scrutiny during and after the contested 2020 presidential election. US president and presidential candidate Donald J. Trump repeatedly called the integrity of the US election system into question despite all evidence that the election was being run remarkably well under the difficult conditions of the COVID-19 pandemic. His complaints about the potential for fraud led some states to pull back from or seek to shut down efforts making it easier for people to vote in the pandemic.[8]

Following that election, when it was clear that Joe Biden had secured enough Electoral College votes in a fair election to win the presidency, Trump pressured state officials to nonetheless declare irregularities. For example, Trump infamously insisted that Georgia's secretary of state Brad Raffensperger "find" the 11,870 votes he would need to flip the state's Electoral College votes to his column. Trump and his allies wanted to use such declarations as a pretext for Republican state legislators in states that Biden had won to send to Congress alternative slates of presidential electors declaring Trump the winner. Trump was unsuccessful in convincing state officials across many states to subvert the election. The efforts came to a head with the January 6, 2021, insurrection at the US Capitol, when Trump supporters violently disrupted Congress's counting of Electoral College votes in an effort that some hoped would buy more time for state legislatures to send in fake elector slates.

The effort to overturn the 2020 elections failed, but the risk was salient enough that Congress in 2022 passed a new set of rules to clarify that state legislatures do not have the power to send in a slate of presidential electors after the state's voters have already chosen that slate in a fair election. The Supreme Court in the 2023 *Moore v. Harper* decision also rejected a radical version of the "independent state legislature" legal theory that could have given license for state legislatures to subvert voters' will in presidential elections.[9] Trump also faced federal and state charges related to attempted election subversion.[10]

Post-insurrection federal change has not fully eliminated the risk of election subversion in the states, however. Millions of Trump's followers continue to believe the false claim of a stolen 2020 election and have pressured their legislators for faux "audits" of 2020 election results, for laws making it harder to register and vote, and for legislation that would shift power from local governments to states to administer elections. Some local election administrators and county canvassing boards have been swept up in voter fraud hysteria, and it has fallen to states to prevent local governments from opening new pathways to stolen elections.

This chapter considers states' essential role in ensuring the security of the US election system. The first section considers how states have served and can continue to serve as bulwarks against election subversion by local actors in a fragmented system. The second section considers the risks of states themselves as potential facilitators of election subversion, focusing in part on conflicts among state actors and the potential for state actors to check each other's power to ensure free and fair elections. The third section concludes by discussing what Congress and federal courts have done and should do to limit the risks of election subversion by states, local election entities, and private actors.

STATES AS BULWARKS AGAINST ELECTION SUBVERSION

By *election subversion*, I mean sabotage by government officials that leads to an election loser being declared the election winner.[11] The decentralized nature of US election administration creates many potential paths toward election subversion, including through private action and through local election and elected officials. States have both an opportunity and a responsibility to close down those paths and ensure that elections reflect the will of their voters.

Consider first the risks that private actors may pose to free and fair elections. During and after the 2020 election period, election officials and poll workers began to face threats of violence and intimidation, including death threats. These threats primarily have come from Trumpist supporters who believe the false claims of a rigged or stolen 2020 election, but future threats may come from right or left.[12]

Election workers already work in high-pressure, mostly low-paying jobs; retaining such workers, often drawn from the ranks of government bureaucracy, and ensuring they have adequate training is difficult enough without threats of violence. In the aftermath of 2020, attrition rates among election workers have skyrocketed. Such attrition lands a double blow against election integrity: first, elections are likely to be administered less well thanks to the loss of institutional memory and experience as veteran workers leave their jobs; second, in the current conspiracy-laden, threatening atmosphere, talented potential replacement workers may be deterred from seeking election jobs, while conspiracy theorists may be especially attracted to such positions to deter purported "fraud."[13]

Voters too have endured election-related threats and intimidation. In the 2022 midterm elections, a group of armed election truthers in tactical gear watched over ballot drop boxes in an Arizona county; they likely were motivated by the demonstrably false claims that drop boxes were used to facilitate voter fraud in the 2020 elections. It took a federal court injunction to remove these election intimidators from the area.[14]

States have a special responsibility to ensure that voters and election workers can participate safely in the electoral process. Free and fair elections require prevention of private mob violence that can deter turnout and impede the process of balloting and vote tabulation. States control police forces, regularly providing security for many political activities, including political conventions, parades, and protests. Police can implement extra security measures at election-related sites too, and it is incumbent on state leaders to provide adequate resources to ensure equal access to the ballot box in order to encourage widespread electoral participation. It is essential that the police do not position themselves in a way that intimidates voters who may be wary of the actions of law enforcement. Governments can also seek to limit firearms carried by private citizens at polling places and election offices.

Aside from the threats from private actors, in the aftermath of the 2020 election, states have faced a new "insider threat" to their elections from those who have responsibility for running elections or confirming election results. In the first category, consider the actions of Tina Peters, a former election clerk in Mesa County, Arizona. Officials have accused Peters of illegally sharing access to the software used to run election machinery with the 2020 election conspiracy theorist Mike Lindell and others. In Coffee County, Georgia, and Antrim County, Michigan, election officials also have been accused of giving Trump-allied forces unauthorized access to election technology.[15]

Engineers and those who plan and implement election systems design them to be secure primarily against outside tampering; think of the oft-voiced concerns about whether voting machinery has been connected to the internet, making it potentially vulnerable to hacking. Security measures must now deter inside tampering as well, given the reality that not every local election administrator will be an honest partner in ensuring a fair election.

The task of dealing with insider threats is especially tricky because of the necessarily close relationship between state election officials and local election administrators. States set standards and mandates for the conduct of elections, and states typically have certain oversight powers over the conduct of local elections. Local election administrators tabulate ballots and report vote totals under rules set out by the state. When the relationship of trust breaks down between state and local election administrators, the integrity of the election system overall comes under stress.

Aside from the local bodies that *administer* elections, other local bodies such as county boards of supervisors sometimes *certify* election results and *oversee* election officials and local election administrators. Here too states must take into account the risk of a local-level insider threat to the certification and oversight processes.

In the post-2020 election period, a few county officials have resisted certifying election results, primarily stating unwarranted skepticism about the fairness of the vote count or election procedures. In 2022, it took court orders against county boards in Otero County, New Mexico, and Cochise County, Arizona, to get those boards to do their jobs and certify the results of fair local elections. A few rogue county boards also have demanded hand counts of ballots rather than relying on more accurate machine counts (coupled with postelection audits). In Nye County, Nevada, for example, the county board in charge of certifying election results demanded that election officials conduct a hand count of all ballots, including a real-time count of mail-in ballots received before Election Day. Hand counting and public announcement of partial results before Election Day violated state law, and it took a lawsuit to get county officials to back down.[16]

Along similar lines, the board of supervisors in Shasta County, California, voted in 2023 to stop using machines sold by Dominion Voting Systems for ballot tabulation. Dominion was the subject of conspiracy theories in 2020—eventually receiving a $787 million settlement from Fox News for defamatory statements on the network falsely claiming Dominion machines were rigged in the 2020 elections against Trump. After dumping Dominion machines, Shasta County battled the State of California for the right to conduct a slower and less accurate hand count of ballots in the two-hundred-thousand-person county.[17]

These examples suggest that states must exert more control over local election administration to ensure that local officials do not subvert election results. Unfortunately, more centralized state control, while potentially diminishing the risks of *local* election subversion, may increase the risk of *state* election subversion. This chapter now turns to this risk of states acting not as bulwarks against subversion but as facilitators of it.

STATES AS POTENTIAL FACILITATORS OF ELECTION SUBVERSION

Just as power over elections is fragmented across federal, state, and local governments, it is fragmented *within* state governments as well. State legislatures pass voting rules, usually subject to gubernatorial veto or override. Governors may have some role in overseeing or facilitating elections through a state agency; in some cases an elected secretary of state or other executive branch official may have independent power over that office. State attorneys general defend state election laws and otherwise handle much of the state's election litigation; some election litigation is handled by state agencies. State courts interpret state and local election laws, and apply state constitutional provisions to other state and local actors involved in administering elections.

It is not uncommon for state actors to be at odds with one another over election administration. For example, in a suit over North Carolina's voter identification law that made it all the way to the US Supreme Court, the state's Republican-majority legislative body, the general assembly, defended the law while the state's Democratic governor and attorney general opposed it. Eventually the Supreme Court simply threw up its hands and declined to resolve the dispute over the election law because it could not determine who really spoke for the state. A few years later, the legislators had to go back to the Supreme Court for their right to defend such laws.[18]

As we have already seen in the local context, diffusion and fragmentation of election power in the state context provide pathways to potential election subversion. In this section, I consider subversion risks in the legislative, executive, and judicial branches of state government, as well as whether some state actors may serve as a check on other state actors to mitigate such risks.

State legislatures probably represent the greatest risk to election subversion among state actors because of the large role that the Constitution assigns to "legislatures" to set the rules for conducting federal elections. As noted in the introduction to this chapter, in the 2020 election, Trump and his allies tried to cajole state legislatures into appointing alternative slates of fake presidential electors, in the hope of turning Trump's losses in key battleground states into victories. States such as Arizona had Republican-majority legislatures but voters who chose Biden over Trump. The spurious and dangerous theory that state legislatures had the power to appoint alternative electors even after voters in the state had cast their ballots for president was based on a misreading of an 1887 law, the Electoral Count Act, and an extreme interpretation of the US Constitution's provisions setting forth the power of state legislatures to control the manner for conducting presidential elections.

These developments have meant that the threat of election subversion has come in more recent years from Republican legislators and other Republican officials rather than Democratic ones; but the paths to subversion, once opened, could be exploited in the future by either party (or a party not yet in existence). We do not know if this asymmetry will persist.

The next section explains how Congress and the Supreme Court mostly closed off that state legislative pathway to election subversion, but other pathways remain. For example, state legislators may appoint themselves as election judges or canvassing boards when it comes to presidential elections. To understand how, consider that in the 2000 case of *Bush v. Gore*, the Supreme Court confirmed that although each state legislature had given voters the power to choose presidential electors in the state, the legislature could take that power back in future elections (through a duly-passed law signed by the governor or through an override of a gubernatorial veto).[19] Although such a law would be tremendously unpopular and a complete political nonstarter—voters in a state would strongly object to being disenfranchised from voting in the most salient of US elections—the logic of *Bush v. Gore*'s recognition of legislative power suggests the constitutionality of other, lesser tweaks that shift power to state legislatures and facilitate election subversion.

For example, a legislature could try to pass and implement a law granting power to the state legislature rather than to state courts to serve as election judges in the event of a recount or contest of a presidential race. Similarly, the legislature could take it upon itself to act as the canvassing board, officially determining the winner of the presidential election upon the tally of all valid votes as determined by the legislature. A state legislature intent on subverting popular election results could abuse these powers to turn an election loser into an election winner. So far, legislative efforts to grab this power have not advanced to a vote in any state, but at least one Arizona legislator has introduced a bill along these lines.[20]

That state legislatures might engage in such subversion unfortunately is a real risk. In recent years, radicalized elements of the Republican Party elected to state legislative office have passed and proposed more extreme antidemocratic legislation. A *New York Times* count found "at least 357 sitting Republican legislators in closely contested battleground states have used the power of their office to discredit or try to overturn the results of the 2020 presidential election," a tally that "accounts for 44 percent of the Republican legislators in the nine states where the presidential race was most narrowly decided." If some state legislatures are turning some states into "laboratories against democracy," as Professor Jacob Grumbach has put it, then election subversion is possible.[21]

Another potential pathway by which state legislatures may subvert election outcomes is through state takeovers of local election administration offices. In Texas, for example, the state legislature in 2023 passed one bill that allowed the takeover of local election offices with a population of at least three million people and another bill that shifted authority for administering elections from a county election administrator to the tax assessor-collector. Legislators wrote the bills so that they applied to only a single county, Harris County, and Harris County has now sued to block the law.[22] It is easy to view this legislation as an attempt by a Republican legislature to mess with local election administration in Harris, Texas's largest Democratic county. A state takeover could seek to minimize voting opportunities for the county's residents in an effort to shape election outcomes.

By one count, in the last few years, thirteen state legislatures in states dominated by Republicans have passed fifteen laws giving greater control to states over certain local county election administration bodies.[23] Proponents of such laws typically defend them as aimed not at suppressing votes or subverting election results in local areas but instead at ensuring that elections are administered fairly and competently.

Ferreting out motives is hard, as an example from Georgia illustrates. After the 2020 election, the state legislature passed legislation providing a set of steps for potential state takeover of election administration in poorly performing counties. Many on the left believed the law was intended to allow, for partisan reasons, a state takeover of the election administration in Democratic-leaning Fulton County, Georgia. However, after an investigation by the board charged with examining the county's election administration, and after the county implemented improvements, the state board recommended against a state takeover of the county.[24]

The State of Michigan during 2020 also engaged in extra oversight of Detroit, an area with historically poor election administration. Unlike the Georgia and Texas cases involving a Republican legislature and Democratic counties, the takeover here was engineered by the Democratic secretary of state over a Democratic city. Few saw it as a takeover because there was no partisan conflict.[25]

States also must be concerned about deterring local election subversion. As noted in the previous section, states need to guard against insider threats to the integrity of election processes by local election bodies and counties. Given potential partisan motivations for interference, sometimes it may be difficult to know whether a state legislature's attempt at oversight over local election bodies is aimed at preventing election subversion or facilitating it.

The executive branch of a state also could potentially engage in election subversion. For example, a secretary of state charged with reporting vote totals in a presidential election could misreport those totals or falsely report irregularities, as Trump unsuccessfully urged Georgia secretary of state Raffensperger to do. Fortunately, we do not have any current examples of state-level attempts at election subversion like this, but with election denialists running for office (and in some cases getting elected), the risk cannot be dismissed out of hand.[26] Governors too potentially could declare states of emergency or engage in actions related to the state police that could interfere with fair balloting during a presidential election.

The closest examples of attempted executive-led election subversion in current times came in the aftermath of the 2020 elections. Texas attorney general Ken Paxton, the state's chief law enforcement officer (not its chief election administrator), organized the filing of an original action directly in the US Supreme Court that sought to throw out the results of the presidential election in states with Republican-majority legislatures that had voted for Biden over Trump. The suit was based on false and outlandish claims of fraud and election irregularities and unsupported legal theories. Not a single justice supported Paxton's claims on the merits.[27]

One other near attempt at election subversion came in 2020 when a bipartisan canvassing board in the state of Michigan engaged in what was supposed to be a mere formality in declaring Biden the winner of the Electoral College votes in that state. Under pressure from Trump and his supporters, one of the two Republican members of the board abstained from voting for Biden. The other Republican member, along with two Democratic members, nonetheless confirmed Biden's victory by majority vote, averting a crisis. The governor had threatened to seek a judicial order if the canvassing board did not certify the winner of the state's Electoral College votes. After the vote, the state Republican Party refused to renominate the Republican member of the board who voted to confirm Biden's victory.[28]

There is fortunately very little to say about state judicial branch subversion. We have few known instances in the modern period of state judges manipulating election results.[29] The Texas legislature recently considered passing a provision in a larger election law that would have made it easier for (elected) state court judges to throw out the results of disputed elections. It would have done so by lowering the standard of proof in election contests from a clear and convincing evidence standard to a preponderance (or more-likely-than-not) standard. After some lobbying by the business community and others, the legislature removed this provision from the election law before final passage.[30]

Far from being typical sources for election subversion, courts are the primary check on election subversion by other branches in state government. State courts provide definitive interpretation of state election laws. They apply state constitutional provisions protecting voting rights and delineating the separation of powers. State courts can issue injunctions, which are orders to parties to do or not do something, and mandamus orders, which direct other government officials to take particular actions, such as an order to a canvassing board to certify an election result or to an election official to cease a practice found to violate state law.[31]

The executive and legislative branches can seek to check each other through lawsuits as well as political actions. Sometimes there may be clashes between executive officials that could be subject to lawsuits or other political actions, particularly in states where some executive offices (such as secretary of state and attorney general) are elected independently of the state's governor. Governors also have some control over state budgets and spending, power that they can wield to deal with potential subversion from other state actors.

HOW CONGRESS AND FEDERAL COURTS COULD HELP

Congress possesses a wide reservoir of power to counter election subversion in states and by states. Article I, Section 4, of the Constitution gives Congress very broad powers to override state election laws governing congressional elections. Congress also may enforce various provisions of the Constitution barring discrimination in voting rights, including the Fourteenth Amendment's Equal Protection Clause, the Fifteenth Amendment's prohibition on race discrimination in voting, and the Nineteenth Amendment's prohibition on gender discrimination in voting.

As to the actions of private individuals, Congress has the power to criminalize—and has already to some extent criminalized—tampering with voting machines in federal elections, engaging in violence in relation to federal elections, and intimidating and threatening voters and election officials. Federal laws should be strengthened and clarified, ensuring that states need not deal with these problems alone.[32]

Congress also can provide federal penalties against local and state election officials who may endanger the security of the United States by sharing confidential software or other voting technology or who seek to manipulate vote totals. Such actions deprive US citizens of their constitutional rights. (The threat of federal criminal action, however, could be used by nefarious federal officials to try to subvert election outcomes on a state or local level.)

Equally important but perhaps less salient is the power of the purse. Congress can provide adequate funding to ensure that state and local officials may implement voting systems competently and securely. Elections are complex and expensive endeavors, requiring both technical expertise and continuing efforts at vigilance against malicious actors. Congress can enhance state capacity to deal with election threats and problems and provide technical expertise that can assist officials and build trust across different levels of government. Congress also can condition its funding to encourage the adoption of certain secure election technologies and other election-related security measures to ensure free and fair elections.

Finally, Congress can counter potential election subversion at the state level, and indeed it has already begun to do so. In 2022, Congress, on a bipartisan basis, passed the Electoral Count Reform Act. The ECRA updated the antiquated and convoluted 1887 Electoral Count Act that Trump allies tried to rely on in their attempt to have state legislatures purport to appoint alternative slates of electors. The ECRA made a number of other changes as well to the rules for congressional counting of

Electoral College votes. These changes were intended to lessen the risk of subversion by state actors, such as limiting the power of the state's governor to submit to Congress a slate of presidential electors that does not reflect the will of the voters in the state.[33]

Congress could go further, fully nationalizing congressional elections under its Article I, Section 4, powers. It also could pass a constitutional amendment on a two-thirds vote of each chamber that would alter the federal-state-local balance in election administration. Such an amendment would require ratification by three-fourths of state legislatures. Assuming these more dramatic steps are unlikely to be enacted, Congress still can do much to assist states in election security and integrity.

Federal courts too have a significant role to play in assisting states in preventing election subversion and deterring subversion by state actors. When it comes to private actors, federal courts can issue injunctions or other orders that protect constitutional rights (as when a federal court enjoined armed vigilantes in tactical gear near Arizona drop boxes in 2022). Federal law broadly protects voters against intimidation and violence in federal elections, and sometimes an action in federal court is an easier path for investigating and prosecuting election crimes than acting through local prosecutors or state officials.

Federal courts also have jurisdiction to hear claims brought against state or local election officials when they deprive voters of their constitutional rights. Federal prosecutors may bring criminal charges to deal with attempts at election subversion, at least when doing so also interferes concretely with voting rights. An action by a local election official to throw out votes or manipulate vote totals in an election can be a federal crime. Charges against those who attempted to subvert the 2020 US presidential election remain pending at the time of this writing.

The Supreme Court's 2023 decision in *Moore v. Harper* also shuts down the route toward the submission of fake presidential electors that Trump and his allies tried to exploit in 2020. In *Moore*, the Supreme Court held that when state legislatures exercise their powers to regulate congressional elections as authorized by the state constitution, they must do so in the way they ordinarily exercise legislative power. That means, among other things, that the legislature is bound by constraints in the state's constitution and its enacted laws are subject to state judicial review. Legislatures are not free-floating bodies that can act independently of their own state's constitution.[34]

Although *Moore* involved state legislative power in regulating congressional elections, its logic applies equally to the parallel provision of power to state legislatures over presidential elections contained in the US Constitution's Article II. The 2020 fake electors theory implausibly posited that state legislatures maintained plenary power to submit a slate of electors even if state law did not authorize it and even if voters had already voted. The theory was almost certainly wrong under federal law even as it existed before the *Moore* case, but *Moore* put a nail in that coffin by rejecting the argument for free-floating authority. It also preserves authority for state courts to block such attempts to submit electors.

Although *Moore* rejected an extreme version of what has come to be called the "independent state legislature" theory, it adopted a weaker version of that theory. The Court held that state courts do not have unbridled power when it comes to interpreting rules related to congressional (and presumably presidential) elections. When a state court "transgresses the ordinary bounds of judicial review" in interpreting state election law, then the state court usurps the legislature's powers recognized in the US Constitution's Article I, Section 4.[35]

This weaker version of the independent state legislature theory creates a great deal of uncertainty, giving litigants a chance to go to federal court when they disagree with a state court interpretation of state law in a federal election. Ordinarily, state courts are the final arbiters of the meaning of state constitutions and state statutes. The *Moore* ruling may inject federal courts into second-guessing these state interpretations in cases that are going to be highly politically sensitive. It could even get the US Supreme Court deciding the outcome of a presidential election in a very close election where this issue arises.

One salutary benefit of the theory is that it may limit the opportunities for rogue state courts to subvert election outcomes through absurd means of judicial interpretation. This federal judicial oversight lessens the risk that a state court could get away with attempting to steal an election. The problem, as we have seen throughout this chapter, is that giving oversight responsibilities to one body to guard against election subversion may also increase the possibility that the body charged with oversight could itself engage in subverting the voters' will. Do we need to worry about election subversion by federal courts in overruling state courts under the weak version of the independent state legislature theory?

* * *

There is no silver bullet when it comes to the prevention of election subversion in the contemporary United States because power over elections is diffuse and fragmented, and that diffusion provides many potential pathways to thwart free and fair elections. States stand at the intersection of this diffuse system, and well-meaning states can do much to stop both private parties and local entities from subverting the will of the people. But states themselves, and particularly state legislatures, may be the source of election subversion rather than its foil. When a state actor subverts, it falls to other state actors, especially state courts when appropriate and possible, to ensure the election results reflect popular will.

States can benefit from federal assistance in preserving free and fair elections from the federal government, and in rare cases the federal government can act to stop state-driven election subversion. Different levels of government, and different branches of government, ideally should be in partnership to block those who would seek to undermine the results of free and fair elections. Both Congress and the federal courts, including the Supreme Court, can help states secure US elections. In the end, given that election subversion may come from so many different sources, public vigilance will remain the first line of defense. Public attention to the actions of state officials is warranted, to ensure both that states remain bulwarks against subversion and that they do not become sources of subversion themselves.

NOTES

1 Richard L. Hasen, "Three Pathologies of American Voting Rights Illuminated by the COVID-19 Pandemic, and How to Treat and Cure Them," *Election Law Journal* 19, no. 3 (September 2020): 263–88, https://doi.org.

2 U.S. Const. art. VI, cl. 2.

3 Uniform Congressional District Act, 2 U.S.C. § 2c (West 2024); Voting Rights Act, 52 U.S.C. § 10301–10508 (West 2024); Help America Vote Act of 2002, 52 U.S.C. § 21082 (2002).

4 On the general contours of fragmented and divided election administration in the United States, see Kathleen Hale and Mitchell Brown, *How We Vote: Innovation in American Elections* (Washington, DC: Georgetown University Press, 2020), 19–44.
5 U.S. Const. art. I, § 2.
6 U.S. Const. art. I, § 4; art. II.
7 Moore v. Harper, 143 S. Ct. 2065, 2085 (2023) (internal quotation marks and brackets omitted, quoting Smiley v. Holm, 285 U.S. 355, 366 [1932]).
8 For a brief description of the events of and following the 2020 election from which the rest of this account is drawn, see Richard L. Hasen, *A Real Right to Vote* (Princeton, NJ: Princeton University Press, 2024), chap. 5. For additional details, see Richard L. Hasen, "Identifying and Minimizing the Risk of Election Subversion and Stolen Elections in the Contemporary United States," *Harvard Law Review Forum* 135, no. 6 (2022): 265–301.
9 *Moore*, 143 S. Ct. at 2085–88.
10 "Keeping Track of the Trump Investigations," *New York Times*, August 14, 2023, www.nytimes.com.
11 On various definitions of *election subversion*, see Derek T. Muller, "Election Subversion and the Writ of Mandamus," *William & Mary Law Review* 65 (forthcoming), https://papers.ssrn.com (draft at 3). See also Lisa Marshall Manheim, "Election Law and Election Subversion," *Yale Law Journal Forum* 132 (2022): 312–51. Unlike Professor Muller, I would not limit subversion attempts to postelection activities; one could commit sabotage before an election that affects an election outcome afterward.
12 Linda So and Jason Szep, "Reuters Unmasks Trump Supporters Who Terrified U.S. Election Officials," Reuters, November 9, 2021, www.reuters.com; Nick Corasaniti, Jim Rutenberg, and Kathleen Gray, "Threats and Tensions Rise as Trump and Allies Attack Elections Process," *New York Times*, February 1, 2021, www.nytimes.com.
13 Michael Wines, "After a Nightmare Year, Election Officials Are Quitting," *New York Times*, July 2, 2021, www.nytimes.com; Fredreka Schouten, "Personal Threats, Election Lies and Punishing New Laws Rattle Election Officials, Raising Fears of a Mass Exodus," CNN, July 21, 2021, www.cnn.com; "One in Three Election Officials Report Feeling Unsafe Because of Their Job," Brennan Center for Justice, June 16, 2021, www.brennancenter.org.
14 See the press release from the League of Women Voters announcing the settlement of a lawsuit over the incident, "Updates on the Case: Announcement of Case Settlement," Protect Democracy, May 21, 2023, https://protectdemocracy.org, following the issuance of this temporary restraining order against voter intimidation: Ariz. All. for Retired Americans v. Clean Elections USA, No. CV-22-01823-PHX-MTL (D. Ariz. Nov. 1, 2022), https://s3.documentcloud.org. For a debunking of the allegations of drop boxes being used to facilitate voter fraud in the 2020 elections, see Philip Bump, "The Team behind '2000 Mules' Is Called Out for Deception. Again," *Washington Post*, October 17, 2022, www.washingtonpost.com.

15 For an overview of these issues, see Sarah D. Wire, "Are the Feds Ignoring Trump Allies' Multi-state Effort to Access Voting Systems? Experts Raise Alarms for 2024," *Los Angeles Times*, March 9, 2023, www.latimes.com.

16 For an overview of these issues, see Doug Bock Clark, "Some Election Officials Refused to Certify Results. Few Were Held Accountable," ProPublica, March 9, 2023, www.propublica.org.

17 On the Shasta dispute, see Jessica Garrison, "Public Tirades, Recall Threats as Shasta County Roils from Decision to Dump Voting Machines," *Los Angeles Times*, April 28, 2023, www.latimes.com.

18 Berger v. N.C. State Conf. of the NAACP, 142 S. Ct. 2191 (2022); North Carolina v. N.C. State Conf. of NAACP, 137 S. Ct. 1399 (2017) (Roberts, C.J., statement respecting denial of cert.).

19 Bush v. Gore, 531 U.S. 98, 104 (2000).

20 Reid Wilson, "Arizona Bill Would Allow Legislature to Overturn Election Results," *The Hill*, January 27, 2022, https://thehill.com.

21 Jacob Grumbach, *Laboratories against Democracy* (Princeton, NJ: Princeton University Press 2022); Nick Corasaniti, Karen Yourish, and Keith Collins, "How Trump's 2020 Election Lies Have Gripped State Legislatures," *New York Times*, May 22, 2022, www.nytimes.com.

22 S.B. 1933, 88th Legis., 2023 Reg. Sess., 2023 Tex. Sess. Law. Serv. (Ch. 957), to be codified in Tex. Elec. Code. Ann. §§ 31.017–31.022, 31.037, 127.351 (West); S.B. 1750, 88th Legis., 2023 Reg. Sess., 2023 Tex. Sess. Law. Serv. (Ch. 952); Natalia Contreras, "Harris-County Must Remove Its Elections Chief under New Legislation Headed to Gov. Greg Abbott," *Texas Tribune*, May 23, 2023, www.texastribune.org; Shania Shelton, "Houston Area County Sues Texas over Law That Eliminates Its Election Administrator Position," CNN, July 6, 2023, www.cnn.com.

23 Christina A. Cassidy, "GOP State Legislatures Seek Greater Control over State and Local Election Offices," Associated Press, June 25, 2023, https://apnews.com.

24 Election Integrity Act of 2021, S.B. 202, 2020–2021 Reg. Sess., 2021 Ga. Laws 14 (Act 9); Stephen Fowler, "No Takeover Recommended in Fulton County Elections Board Probe," GPB News, January 13, 2023, www.gpb.org. Also see the performance review report: Ryan Germany, Stephen Day, and Rickey Kittle, *Performance Review Board Report on Fulton County Elections*, January 13, 2022, https://s3.documentcloud.org.

25 Alex Ebert, "Meet the Technocrat Who Keeps Killing Trump Voter Fraud Claims," Bloomberg Government, August 5, 2021, https://about.bgov.com.

26 Camille Squires and Daniel Nachanian, "In Secretary of State Races, Election Deniers (Mostly) Lose," *Bolts*, November 14, 2022, https://boltsmag.org ("12 Republicans were running for secretary of state after denying the results of the 2020 election or refusing to affirm the outcome. Eight of them lost. But they won in four red states: Alabama, Indiana, South Dakota, and Wyoming.").

27 Texas v. Pennsylvania, 141 S. Ct. 1230, 1230 (2020) (mem.); Emma Platoff, "U.S. Supreme Court Throws Out Texas Lawsuit Contesting 2020 Election Results in Four Battleground States," *Texas Tribune*, December 12, 2020, www.texastribune.org.

28 Alana Wise, "Michigan Certifies Joe Biden's Election Victory," NPR, November 23, 2020, www.npr.org; Hasen, "Identifying and Minimizing," 278.

29 One possible counterexample involved a dispute over the winner of an Alabama state supreme court race. See Roe v. Alabama, 43 F.3d 574 (11th Cir. 1995); and Edward B. Foley, *Ballot Battles: The History of Disputed Elections in the United States* (Oxford: Oxford University Press, 2016), 267–77.

30 See Hasen, "Identifying and Minimizing," 300.

31 See Muller, "Election Subversion."

32 See Hasen, "Identifying and Minimizing," at 298–99.

33 Electoral Count Reform Act, Pub. L. No. 117-328, 136 Stat. 4459, Div. P, §§ 101–11 (2022); Derek T. Muller, "Congress Passes Legislation That Will Close Off Presidential Election Mischief and Help Avoid Another Jan. 6," *The Conversation*, December 23, 2022, https://theconversation.com.

34 Moore v. Harper, 143 S. Ct. 2065, 2085–88 (2023).

35 *Moore*, 143 S. Ct. at 2088–90.

14

VOTING MACHINES: FRIEND OR FOE?

CHARLES STEWART III

Over 99 percent of all ballots cast in the 2020 presidential election were counted by a computer—a voting machine, some would say.[1] It is hard to imagine that underlying such a ubiquitous use of technology lurk serious questions about the safety and security of elections conducted with the assistance of voting machines. And yet questions persist.

The use of computer technology to count ballots, and more generally to conduct elections, became a major issue in the 2000 presidential election, as the performance of punch-card voting machines was brought under the spotlight.[2] We can trace a line of persistent controversy over the use of voting machines from 2000 to the present. A major strand of dispute has been over the use of paperless voting machines, sometimes called "black box" systems.[3] A variant of this dispute continues to this day with the rise of ballot-marking devices.[4] Episodic issues have arisen when computerized systems have malfunctioned.[5] The apotheosis of this controversy has been the campaign of misinformation that arose in 2020 claiming that voting machines manufactured by Dominion Voting Systems and Smartmatic stole the election from Donald Trump.[6] A social movement demanding that ballots be counted by hand is progeny of this misinformation campaign.[7]

All this controversy boils down to two questions: First, do voting machines make it more likely that the choices of voters will be recorded correctly? And second, should we trust the machines to count the votes correctly?

Asking whether computerized voting systems aid or hinder the accurate expression of voters' preferences is puzzling, considering how thoroughly computers have pervaded everyday life. In a country where 93 percent of households have a personal computer at home[8] and 85 percent have a smartphone,[9] 78 percent of adults prefer to bank online,[10] and 16 percent of all commerce is conducted online,[11] why is there such contention over the use of computers to count votes?

The answer requires us to contend with the inherent limitations of technology as it helps record and count votes, in addition to keeping track of all the information necessary to administer elections accurately and securely. Although much of American commercial and social life occurs online, this everyday activity comes with a degree of imprecision, error, and fraud that we are willing to endure as a cost of doing business, but we would be unwilling to endorse it in electing our leaders.[12] Therefore, the administrative challenge with voting machines is to allow them to do what technology does so much better than humans—such as endure the tedium of counting votes accurately—while confirming that it has performed as expected. This, in turn, means that the challenge of ensuring that voting machines and other election technologies are secure rests more on managing how they are used, instead of depending on them to function perfectly.

This chapter argues that while computerized machines are crucial for the American electoral system, independent verification of election results is essential due to the inherent uncertainty in computer programming. The subsequent sections provide an overview of the voting technology ecosystem, explore its widespread adoption, and conclude by emphasizing the need for independent verification to ensure election security within agreed-on margins of error.

BACKGROUND: THE USE OF TECHNOLOGY TO CONDUCT ELECTIONS

Elections, like complex businesses, heavily rely on the extensive deployment of digital technologies. Before delving into voting machines, it is crucial to assess the broader technology ecosystem governing elections, which helps determine the overall security of voting machines.

While much attention among the public and academic research centers on the security of these machines, their security is contingent on the broader system in which they are embedded. This comprehensive security system aims to verify eligible voters, ensure accurate ballot recording and tabulation, and maintain precision in tabulation reports. This system is secured not only by electronic means but also by physical security and various control management systems.

* * *

Most voters encounter technology in the polling place, where ballots are scanned. This machine is only the tip of the iceberg when it comes to the role of technology in ensuring the accuracy and security of an election.

Figure 14.1 illustrates the broader ecosystem of technology used by local election jurisdictions in the United States, emphasizing the interconnected systems and information flow. In the middle of the diagram is the polling place—it can be the one used on Election Day or during in-person early voting—where voters directly encounter technology. The operation of the polling place depends on information that flows from another major system, the voter registration system. Voter registration, in turn, depends on systems that could be considered part of the general "back-office" operation of a local election office.

Although polling places are where voters are most likely to encounter election technology, a significant portion of ballots are processed elsewhere. Voters in the United States have increasingly had their ballots delivered by mail and have returned them to the local election office to be tallied centrally.[13] The process of managing mail ballots, from the point of request to tabulation, embodies a fourth technology-intensive activity, and is a second place where tabulation occurs.

Finally, election results are accumulated to be reported to the public and form the basis for declaring winners. Results of tabulations at both the precincts and centralized locations are first aggregated by the local election office and then reported to the state. Before these reports are made official, preliminary results are made available to the public and form the basis of reports by news organizations.[14]

The lines that connect the boxes in Figure 14.1 represent flows of information between different systems that are regularly, but not always, digital. When the shared data are digital, this sharing may happen in

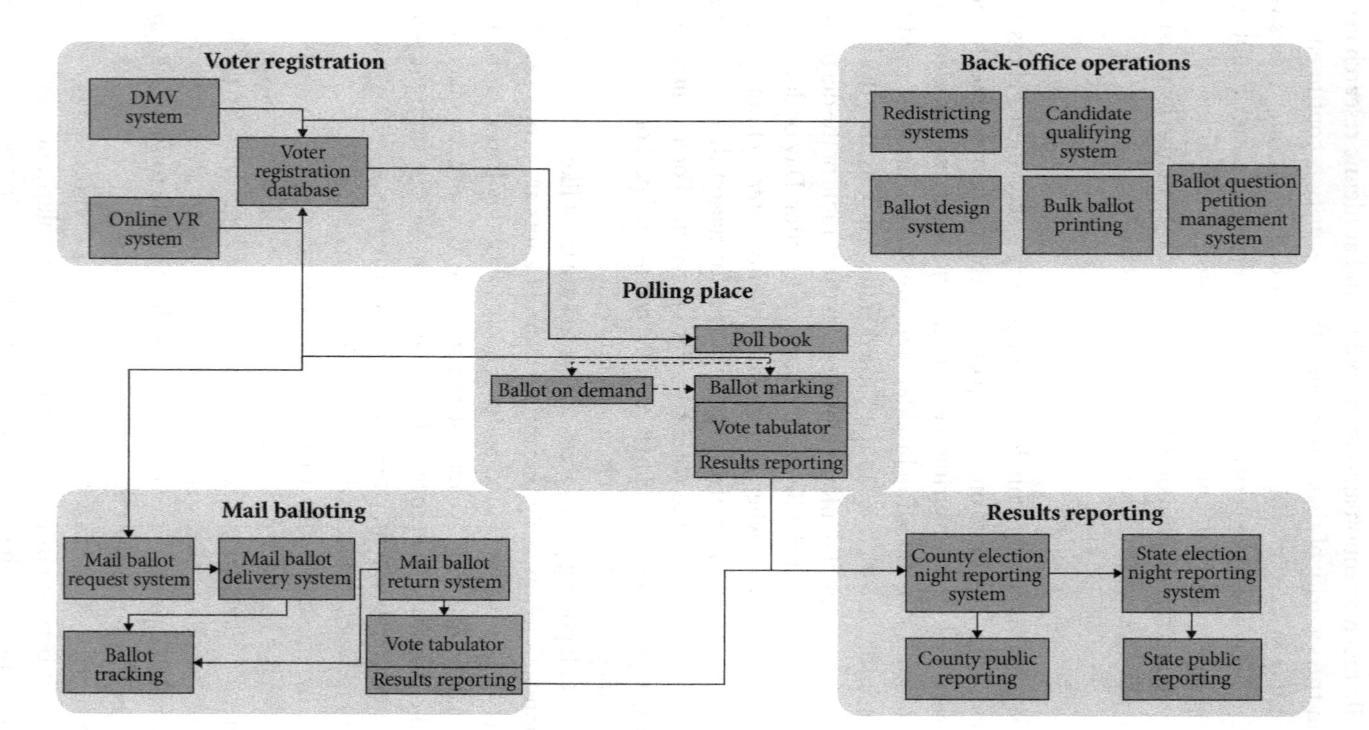

Figure 14.1. Diagram of the Ecosystem of Voting Technology Used by Local Election Jurisdictions

several ways, including through dedicated networks, the internet, and "sneaker net."

This interconnection of electronic devices worries security experts and leads to administrative practices intended to minimize the risk of hacking or other types of intrusions. These practices range from physical security (seals on machines, controlled and monitored entry to server rooms, etc.), to electronic monitoring (e.g., Albert sensors),[15] to the air gapping of critical systems. Election officials generally defend these protections; many computer scientists claim they are not nearly enough.

Returning to the polling place, the check-in station is where the voter's eligibility is checked against a pollbook. Traditionally, this was a paper list, but increasingly local election jurisdictions have come to rely on electronic pollbooks (e-pollbooks).[16] Although e-pollbooks can be configured as essentially standalone devices, they are increasingly connected back to the central office via a computer network using a cellular modem.

The core technology in a polling place is the tabulator, most often a scanner that accepts paper ballots. Paper ballots, in turn, are typically preprinted and organized in stacks at the check-in table. However, for in-person early voting, where a voter is not limited to voting in their geographical precinct, each early voting site must have the capacity to offer any ballot that is used throughout the county.[17] In some cases, this is managed by having a complete selection of hand-printed ballots in each early voting site, a process called "pick and pull." Others manage by printing each ballot as needed using ballot-on-demand printers.

Voters can mark their ballots in two different ways: by hand or using a video screen that presents offices and ballot questions to the voter. With older electronic machines (direct-recording electronic devices, or DREs), when the voter is finished, information about the choice is transferred directly to the tabulator and retained electronically. Nowadays, the video interface is essentially an electronic pencil called a ballot-marking device (BMD). The BMD presents choices to the voter like the older DREs, but when the voter is finished, the BMD prints a ballot reflecting those choices, allowing the voter to verify them before the ballot is scanned. Whether and how thoroughly voters actually scrutinize these paper ballots is another source of controversy.[18] The final step is aggregating the tabulated votes at the polling place and then passing those results off to the central office for further aggregation.

Exploring the voting technology ecosystem underscores the multiple sources of security concern in elections. The general philosophy guiding how the technology ecosystem is designed is to isolate the tabulators completely from other systems, most of which are connected to the internet. It is these other systems, notably the voter registration and election-night reporting systems,[19] that have endured high-profile malicious intrusions and are a major focus of the partnerships established between states and counties and the federal government following the 2016 election.[20] There has never been evidence of malicious cross contamination or "hacking" succeeding in a polling place, probably because of the network isolation of polling places, but prudence dictates guarding against the possibility.[21] Despite the fact that computerized tabulators are designed so that they do not connect to the internet while the polls are open, any potential connection between tabulators and networks is a threat vector that must be protected.

* * *

All the functions of election administration just described have existed in the United States for decades, if not centuries.[22] The function that has regularly attracted the most attention from the public and academics is the technology used to cast and count votes in person. The evolution of this technology has existed in equilibrium with functional and security requirements in the market for election equipment.

The earliest public elections in the United States were conducted viva voce. Voters went to the county courthouse or town hall and announced their votes to a local official, in the presence of anyone who wanted to listen. Some states used paper from the beginning, but even those could not be considered secret. They were often provided by the parties and only had that party's candidates printed on them.[23] Paper ballots were prone to numerous frauds, leading to movements to require that they be cast in secret and that the state print the ballot.

Automation in the casting and counting of ballots began in 1892 with the use of the Myers Automatic Booth lever machine in Lockport, New York, touching off a gradual spread of voting machines across the country.[24] Computerized systems made their appearance in the 1960s with two innovative technologies, at least in the field of election administration: punch cards and optical scanning.[25] Punch cards, as the name implies, were standard computer cards on which voters used a stylus to push out prescored "chads" that corresponded with the candidates they wished to support. At the end of Election Day, all the cards were then gathered up and the votes counted using an electrical-mechanical device.

The full plunge into digital systems began in the 1970s when mechanical lever machines were replaced by fully electronic systems. The next generation of these systems, generically known as DRE systems, borrowed the user interface model of the automatic teller machines used by banks, presenting offices and questions sequentially and allowing the voter to indicate their choice by using a touch screen. When the voter pressed Vote, a memory card would increment a set of counters to indicate how many votes had been received at each ballot position. Electronic memory units also stored electronic representations of the ballots, which could be used as a backup and to "audit" the results of the tabulators, but it is important to emphasize that no paper representation of votes was produced by these early DRE systems for independent verification.

The early deployment of DREs drew some criticism before 2000, but on the whole, they were accepted by election officials and voters as part of the march of progress.[26]

The Help America Vote Act (HAVA) of 2002,[27] passed following the 2000 Florida recount controversy, disrupted the natural upgrade path by outlawing mechanical lever machines and punch-card systems in federal elections. HAVA provided $2 billion to states for upgrading voting technologies. In turn, many counties rushed to adopt the highest-tech voting solutions, DREs. However, this sparked grassroots resistance, particularly in areas accustomed to using paper ballots.

One of the locales where this occurred was Santa Clara County, California, where a Stanford computer science professor, David Dill, led an effort to oppose DREs in that county and, in the process, made the issue one that was taken up nationally by computer professionals.[28] This in turn led to the creation of Verified Voting, a prominent anti-electronic-voting nonprofit that provides thorough coverage of voting equipment on its website and whose board members have been effective advocates for the go-slow path with electronic voting technologies.[29] The opposition to DREs not only slowed the purchase of any new paperless DRE systems, it also led to a dispute over what to do with the systems that had already been bought.

Two responses emerged: one favored by opponents of paperless systems, advocating for hand-marked paper ballots, and one favored by vendors and most DRE-using election officials, which proposed adding a voter-verified paper audit trail (VVPAT) to the existing units. These systems printed the voter's choice on a paper roll, allowing the voter to verify the ballot before hitting the Vote button.[30] Although these VVPATs could be used in recounts and audits, the fact that they were typically on long rolls of paper made them unwieldy to use for these purposes.

In the short period from 2000 to 2004, the share of ballots tabulated on DREs rose from 11 percent to 28 percent while optical scanners' share increased from 28 percent to 37 percent. However, the grassroots rebellion against DREs slowed their growth and prompted election vendors to innovate.

The BMD emerged as a hybrid system combining a touch-screen interface for making one's choices with a print-out that could then be checked by the voter and scanned for tabulation; it could also be used later if an independent recount was needed.

Table 14.1 summarizes the recent evolution of voting technology usage in the United States. In 1980, three-quarters of ballots were counted using either mechanical lever machines (43 percent) or punch cards (32 percent). Optical scanning was rare. Indeed, hand counting was more common (10 percent vs. 6 percent). By the 2008 presidential election, only New York continued to use mechanical lever machines, and punch cards had virtually disappeared, giving rise to the dominance of optical scanning. In 2020, counties representing 77 percent of registered voters relied on optical scanning to tabulate in-person ballots, compared with 20 percent for DREs and 3 percent for all other systems.[31]

The fraction of all ballots tabulated on scanners is even greater than Table 14.1 suggests, because it only reflects in-person voting equipment. In 2020, due to the COVID-19 pandemic, the share of ballots cast by mail more than doubled compared with 2016, from 21 percent to 46 percent.[32] Essentially all these ballots were counted by scanners,

Table 14.1 Voting Technology Usage over Time in the United States (%)

Year	Optical scan	Direct-recording electronic	Mechanical lever	Punch card	A mix of systems	Hand-counted paper
1980	2.1	0.7	42.9	31.8	12.0	10.5
1988	6.5	2.9	31.8	40.8	11.7	6.3
1992	13.2	3.7	28.3	40.2	11.1	3.4
1996	21.0	9.6	20.9	36.8	9.8	2.0
2000	28.3	10.6	16.5	33.9	9.1	1.5
2004	37.2	28.1	12.2	12.2	9.6	0.8
2008	58.2	30.5	5.8	0.1	5.1	0.2
2012	65.2	30.2	*	<0.05	4.3	0.1
2016	66.6	29.4	*	*	3.8	0.1
2020	77.3	19.7	*	*	2.9	0.1

*No reported usage.
Sources: Election Data Services; Verified Voting; state and local election reports. Percentages are the percentage of counties that used the indicated type of voting system.

even in counties that relied on DREs or hybrid systems for in-person voting.

* * *

The evolution of voting machines has been driven by the functional needs of election administration, emphasizing a quick, accurate, secure, and cost-effective counting process. Vulnerabilities that were targeted by late nineteenth-century reforms, such as ballot fraud, tampering, and theft, not only guided early technology choices but continue to influence thinking today.

Awareness of a new class of vulnerabilities inherent in the technology itself emerged with a series of influential studies written by Roy G. Saltman from the late 1970s to the early 1990s.[33] These works stemmed from research done by the National Bureau of Standards (now the National Institute of Standards and Technology) into the security and accuracy of voting systems, in light of a growing number of reports about election-night counting snafus across the country. Saltman identified a variety of vulnerabilities with each type of voting system.[34]

Saltman's analysis categorized vulnerabilities into two main groups: paper-based systems (hand-counted and scanned paper ballots) and paperless systems (DREs and lever machines). Paper-based systems faced issues like ballot-box stuffing, chain voting, and malicious invalidation, while central scanning introduced concerns about transportation, identification, and physical security of the polling place. Hand counting was singled out for being particularly inaccurate.

Paperless systems risked errors made when they were programmed before being deployed to precincts. Both DREs and lever machines were vulnerable to similar perils once they were operational in precincts. They could be "stuffed" with no physical evidence left behind. Most concerning, paperless systems had no independent representation of the ballot. If the tabulators—mechanical or electronic—failed, it might be impossible to detect the error and, if detected, impossible to recover.

Punch-card systems had unique vulnerabilities, including a counterintuitive user interface and fragile punch cards. The problem of chad was identified by Saltman well before it became a national issue. Also, the prescored targets were fragile and could be dislodged while they were handled in the normal course of transporting and tabulating them. This fragility made it unlikely to get the same count twice in a row.

The vulnerabilities that Saltman and others observed in computerized voting systems in the decades before the 2000 election were recognized by officials when they were choosing between systems, although activists and some politicians have questioned the seriousness of the vendors in innovating around security.[35] Saltman was also one of the first to highlight vulnerabilities owing to the difficulty of observing precisely what the computer processors were doing when they tabulated ballots and to highlight the need to ensure against malicious tampering with the machines. These concerns are reflected in best practices suggested by the US Election Assistance Commission for securing voting systems, including designing and securing ballots; programming voting equipment; testing voting equipment; training poll workers; deploying the equipment; managing the equipment on Election Day; reporting results; returning and securing the equipment; and canvassing, certifying, and auditing the results.[36]

DRIVERS OF THE USE OF TECHNOLOGY

I have a buddy in France, and they just had an election there. Polls closed a few hours ago and they already know who the winners are. Must be nice to live in a first world country.
—J. D. Vance, Twitter, April 10, 2022[37]

The question of why automated technologies are used to cast and count ballots is frequently broached by curious Americans, but the question has taken off in frequency since the 2020 election. In the aftermath of that election, and in continuation of baseless claims that the presidential election was stolen from Donald Trump, a social movement has arisen to oppose using voting machines, in favor of hand-counting paper ballots.[38]

This movement has had the effect of changing public opinion on the advisability of hand-counting paper ballots, especially among Republicans, although it still remains a minority opinion. In response to questions posed on the 2022 Cooperative Election Study, 21 percent of Republican respondents stated they would most prefer to vote by a hand-counted paper system, up from 15 percent when the question was asked in 2018.[39]

Amid public agitation about counting ballots by hand, it is valuable to consider why voting machines are used at all, in contrast to most of the rest of the world.[40] There are functional reasons for the prevalent use of voting machines in the United States, but commercial and social factors should not be dismissed. The demand for solutions to logistical and security concerns has created an industry in the United States that sells and services voting machines. This is a small industry, but it is nonetheless one that seeks to turn a profit and lobbies hard to win contracts to expand its business.[41] The presence of technology-selling companies creates a supply-side dynamic that promulgates the diffusion of election technologies throughout the country.

America is also said to be a technological society, with the postwar economic boom tied directly to technological developments that were spawned in large part by the Cold War. Americans' belief that social progress is tied to technological development no doubt has something to do with the embrace of voting machines to tabulate votes. With the explosion of personal computers in the 1980s and the ubiquity of online commerce in the current century, it is easy to regard any governmental process that relies on pencil and paper as outdated.[42]

Still, computerized voting systems are expensive to purchase and operate. In an environment of cost-conscious local governments—voting machines are mostly purchased using local general service revenues—there must be some advantage to using computerized voting machines.

The historical adoption of voting technology, computerized or not, has generally been guided by good-government justifications focusing on economy, efficiency, accuracy, and security. Most of these justifications track back to the speed of counting. Counting speed is a major issue in the United States because of the "long ballot"—that is, the tendency to vote on a large number of offices and policy questions at one time. In contrast to the first round of the French presidential election mentioned in the epigraph of this section, Americans rarely vote on a single question or office when they go to the polls. There are approximately half a million elected officials in the United States at all levels of government, or over 160 for each county.[43]

This large number of elected officials has led to administrative adaptations to handle the volume of votes to be counted. Before mechanical lever machines, the answer was the dispersion of different types of elections across the calendar and the use of precincts with only a few hundred voters assigned to each. These arrangements made it possible to count ballots relatively quickly but created considerable headaches for election officials. A large number of polling places meant that security forces were spread thin in their efforts to protect against physical assaults on the polls.[44]

The earliest justifications for mechanical lever machines were also based on economy, efficiency, accuracy, and security. Although the equipment cost for a lever machine was greater than the plain paper ballots and ballot boxes, a lever machine could last for half a century; over the life of the machine, its cost was more than paid for by savings on ballot printing and personnel. The fact that the tabulation of votes was instantaneous meant that large numbers of votes could be counted as soon as the polls closed, reducing the opportunity to manipulate the ballot count and allowing more voters to go to a single polling place, where a smaller number of staff could oversee voting and single police officers could keep their eyes on a larger number of voters. The risk of chain voting was eliminated, as was the possibility of overvoting. It also became easier to secure the voting equipment: the voting machines weighed hundreds of pounds, which guarded against theft; they could be locked, guarding against tampering.

As technology evolved beyond mechanical lever machines, the alternatives were judged based on these criteria of economy, efficiency, accuracy, and security.[45] The technological evolution of voting machines was scrutinized on many of the same economy and security grounds that were used to assess mechanical lever machines. Both optical scanners and punch cards were cheaper to purchase, store, and transport than mechanical lever machines but required large amounts of expensive, small-batch printing (especially for optical scanners). Both of these paper-based systems required more people to oversee transporting marked ballots to be tabulated; tabulation itself was also personnel intensive.

As the electronic computer age overtook election administration, DREs offered a set of advantages over the incumbent lever-machine systems with what seemed to be few additional risks. Like lever machines, they could be programmed centrally by a small expert staff and checked for accuracy before being deployed. The results could be printed out at the precinct immediately after the polls closed and reported to the county office within minutes. There were no paper ballots to be tampered with; chain voting was impossible. The machines could guard against overvoting, and in a recount, there was no need to subjectively interpret marks on disputed ballots.

To election officials, the main downsides of DREs were the shorter life-span of the technology—years, not decades—and the need to employ technology experts to maintain the equipment.

The growing adoption of voting systems that relied on digital technology occurred despite early rumblings from technologists that these systems contained shortcomings that could potentially be catastrophic. Most notable of these were the papers and reports written by Saltman, but there were many others.[46]

The 2000 election revealed many of the deficiencies of the various computerized election machines then in use, although the deficiencies unearthed pointed more to matters of accuracy than to security. The two major technology problems identified in Florida—hanging and pregnant chad and butterfly ballots—were deficiencies in translating the intentions of voters into representations on a ballot that could be counted. The problems were due to poor ballot design[47] and maintenance,[48] not security.

Over the past decade, as states and counties have retired their DREs, many have adopted the hybrid BMD systems, which offer voters an experience not unlike that of the previous paperless systems, with the added advantage of a paper ballot that is the legal ballot and can form the basis of an independent recount, audit, or both. This transition has sparked controversy, especially in Georgia, where legal challenges are under way.[49] Academic researchers have criticized BMD systems, arguing that the barcodes used for vote recording cannot be directly validated by the voter, that voters do not actually validate the human-readable ballots, that there is no effective remedy if one voter detects an error and corrects it, and that it is impossible to test for all the things that can go wrong with a BMD ahead of an election.[50]

In defense of these systems, other academics have demonstrated that some voters do validate their ballots—probably enough to identify misprogrammed machines—and can be prompted to validate their ballots more often.[51] The hand recount of a BMD system in Georgia following the 2020 general election found no discrepancies among five million ballots cast that were due to the concerns suggested by academics. The identified problems were administrative and not unique to BMDs, such as misplaced ballots.[52]

Election machines are necessary in the United States because of the long ballot that makes rapid, accurate counting of ballots nearly impossible in most of the country. The evolution of voting technologies reflects the adaptation of new technologies to voting, albeit with a notable lag, likely due to the industry's small size, limited capitalization, and stringent performance requirements. This evolution also interacts with the security landscape of voting, where physical attacks remain the most understood and prevalent threats, even in the context of modern cyberattacks, which can most easily be delivered physically, such as through contaminated memory sticks.

DON'T TRUST, VERIFY

So long as Americans have been voting, worries about reliability and integrity have persisted. Since at least the end of the nineteenth century, reformers have assigned great urgency to the need to reduce fraud in elections. This has led to a great deal of worrying about deterring adversaries intent on overriding the expressed intentions of voters, whether by stuffing ballot boxes, stealing ballots, or falsifying election totals. Less public attention has been placed on ensuring that ballots are well designed, that election workers are trained to use the equipment properly, and that equipment performs as intended. Problems related to human error and machine performance are more frequent in the United States than malicious attacks. Old machines break. Poll workers, most of whom are in their sixties or older, are often digital immigrants who find troubleshooting voting machine problems difficult. The most common malicious attacks involve altering paper ballots or falsifying vote reports. In other words, the most commonly observed security shortcomings are low tech and could have easily occurred in the days when hand-counted paper ballots were the norm. But regardless of whether the primary vulnerabilities facing voting machines are due to malicious adversaries, human error, or machine malfunctions, voting systems can fail to record the intentions of voters and, at least sometimes, can produce the wrong outcome in an election.

WHAT SHOULD BE DONE ABOUT THIS?

It is impossible to guarantee that every voter's intention has been properly recorded by a voting machine and that the tally is correct. The best achievable goal is to have each voter's intention properly recorded and to confirm that the tally is correct within a specified level of certainty. Even here, it is infeasible to guarantee 100 percent correctness in election tallies.

The primary challenge of securing the vote in the United States revolves around the secret ballot. Without a secret ballot, it would be possible to independently observe a voter mark a ballot, give that voter a receipt recording their votes, observe the inclusion of each personally identified ballot in the count, and then observe each ballot being tallied. This is essentially the system the nation had at its founding, which ended when the secret ballot became (nearly) universal in the 1890s.[53]

The adoption of the secret ballot fundamentally changed the ability to verify the correctness of the vote count. Constrained by the secret ballot, policymakers, academics, independent researchers, reformers, and others have developed schemes to reduce the likelihood that a voter's intent is disregarded in the vote count. In the reform era of the late nineteenth century, these schemes involved facilitating opportunities to observe all aspects of voting except the marking of individual ballots, which has evolved into the "many eyes" principle that rules thinking about election transparency. The reform era of the late 1800s also saw new requirements about reporting election statistics (registration statistics, turnout statistics, and election results) and enhancing the physical security of polling places and polling equipment. These measures remain the bedrock of security features to this day.

New security practices build on physical security, such as air gapping the transfer of data from one system to the other, which is a physical method to guard against cyberattacks that might flow from one computer system to the other. The consensus that the most secure ballot is a paper ballot is an extension of the long tradition of securing the electoral process by physical means.

However, it has been recognized that physical security and reliance on impartial observers may be insufficient to verify that an election reached the correct outcome. States have developed new approaches to verifying elections. The most common of these approaches is postelection auditing.[54]

* * *

In the 1960s, California kicked off a trend whereby states began mandating postelection tabulation audits by counties. As of the 2022 election, all but eight states allowed some type of postelection tabulation audit, with most requiring it.[55]

The traditional audits that began with California's first foray into the field are conducted using a wide variety of methods and standards.[56] The canonical traditional method involves sampling a fixed percentage of precincts in a county—usually 1 or 2 percent—and recounting the ballots in that precinct. Some of these recounts are by hand, while others are simply retabulations using the equipment that counted the ballots in the first place. Some state laws subject all ballots to being audited, although most states exempt certain ballots.[57] Some states conduct audits before votes are certified, while others conduct postcertification audits. Some states specify whether discrepancies can affect the certification totals, or even the outcome, while others do not. In other words, half a century after postelection audits came into being, the practice of postelection tabulation audits is still the Wild West.

The features of standard postelection tabulation audits most in need of improvement come down to two factors. First, these audits generally do not test whether the chain of custody of ballots has been maintained. Second, the sampling procedures are often unspecified, while the sample sizes are unjustified based on any known model of risk.

Seeking to overcome these deficiencies, statisticians have developed a new form of postelection tabulation audit termed the *risk-limiting audit* (RLA). RLAs rely on three fundamental features: rigorous ballot accounting, adjustment of the sample size based on the closeness of the election, and the ability of the audit to become a full recount automatically if there are enough anomalies or the election is close enough.

Compared with traditional postelection tabulation audits, RLAs are a major conceptual leap and are clearly superior to traditional audits. They are defensible on solid statistical grounds, they are a variant of a quality assurance practice that has been used in industrial production for a century, and in most instances, they are less expensive to conduct than traditional audits.

However, despite their advantages, diffusion of the practice has been slow. RLAs require election officials to explicitly acknowledge that elections can only be verified probabilistically, undermining confidence among a vocal skeptical segment of the public.[58] RLAs require strict chain-of-custody procedures that are difficult to implement and often meet resistance from local election officials. Although RLAs usually require the examination of many fewer ballots than traditional audits, if the initial margin is close, it can require a complete recount. Local governments do not know a priori the size of the sample until after Election Day. Finally, RLAs are based on statistical theories that can be counterintuitive.

* * *

The recent historical record suggests that the primary risk associated with voting machines lies in operational failures or human errors rather than malicious attacks. Postelection audits for the 2020 presidential election revealed that counting errors were vanishingly small.[59] Some will not trust election outcomes regardless of how they are conducted, but it is possible to make elections *trustworthy*, allowing a reasonable person, surveying all the evidence, to independently conclude whether the result was correct.[60]

Critical to ensuring trustworthiness is the ability for the evidence supporting election results to be independently verifiable by the public. Instead of assuming that the equipment has functioned as designed, established techniques, such as using paper ballots as a foundation for robust audits, can enhance the verifiability of elections.

This solution—building a verification system that relies on an ancient technology, paper—may seem odd in a world in which computers control so many parts of our lives, but it is necessary if we are to maintain the secret ballot while demanding that the results are correct with a high degree of certainty.

This is also an attainable solution. The nation is working in the direction of voting entirely by paper, which will likely be achieved by the end of this decade.[61] The bigger hurdle is on the side of auditing. Perhaps because they were distracted by sham reviews of elections in 2020 termed "forensic audits," or just because it is not a sexy topic, state legislators have not taken seriously the need to modernize auditing practices and to support local governments in the transition to more rigorous practices. If there is a federal role in nudging states in the right direction, it is in providing grants specifically targeted at enabling states to carry the administrative burdens associated with bringing auditing into the present.

In the end, as with all aspects of how to use technology to ensure elections are accurate and secure, the biggest challenge is not the equipment itself but the people who manage it and interact with it.

NOTES

1 Data on voting machine usage and turnout were taken from "The Verifier—Election Day Equipment—November 2020," Verified Voting, accessed January 30, 2024, https://verifiedvoting.org; and "Election Administration and Voting Survey (EAVS) Comprehensive Report," US Election Assistance Commission, December 19, 2023, www.eac.gov.

2 Jeffrey Toobin, *Too Close to Call: The Thirty-Six-Day Battle to Decide the 2000 Election* (New York: Random House, 2006); Richard L. Hasen, *The Voting Wars: From Florida 2000 to the Next Election Meltdown* (New Haven, CT: Yale University Press, 2012).

3 Bev Harris, *Black Box Voting: Ballot Tampering in the 21st Century* (Renton, WA: Talion, 2004); Stephen Ansolabehere and Charles Stewart III, "Function Follows Form," in *America Votes! A Guide to Modern Election Law and Voting Rights*, ed.

Benjamin E. Griffith (Chicago: ABA, 2008), 241–60; Charles Stewart III, "Voting Technologies," *Annual Review of Political Science* 14 (2011): 353–78.

4 Andrew W. Appel, Richard A. DeMillo, and Philip B. Stark, "Ballot-Marking Devices Cannot Ensure the Will of the Voters," *Election Law Journal: Rules, Politics, and Policy* 19, no. 3 (2020): 432–50; Philip Kortum, Michael D. Byrne, and Julie Whitmore, "Voter Verification of Ballot Marking Device Ballots Is a Two-Part Question: Can They? Mostly, They Can. Do They? Mostly, They Don't," *Election Law Journal* 29, no. 3 (2021): 243–53; Philip Kortum et al., "Can Voters Detect Errors on Their Printed Ballots? Absolutely," arXiv preprint, April 20, 2022, https://doi.org.

5 Roy G. Saltman, *Effective Use of Computing Technology in Vote-Tallying* (Washington, DC: National Bureau of Standards, 1978); Todd R. Weiss, "Update: Is 'Vote Flipping' an E-Voting Problem or User Error?," *Computerworld*, November 8, 2006, www.computerworld.com; Pam Fessler "Some Machines Are Flipping Votes, but That Doesn't Mean They're Rigged," NPR, October 26, 2016, www.npr.org.

6 David Folkenflik, "Judge Rules Fox Hosts' Claims about Dominion Were False, Says Trial Can Proceed," NPR, March 31, 2023, www.npr.org.

7 Natalia Contreras, "Push to Hand Count Ballots Throws a Texas County's Election Administration into Chaos," Votebeat, October 13, 2023, https://texas.votebeat.org; Jessica Huseman, "Where an Obsession with Election Integrity Can Lead," *New York Times*, October 10, 2023, www.nytimes.com.

8 "QuickFacts," US Census Bureau, accessed November 26, 2023, www.census.gov.

9 "Mobile Fact Sheet," Pew Research Center, April 7, 2021, www.pewresearch.org.

10 Jenn Underwood and Elizabeth Aldrich, "U.S. Consumer Banking Statistics 2023," *Forbes*, March 24, 2023, www.forbes.com.

11 "Quarterly Retail E-Commerce Sales: 3rd Quarter 2023," *U.S. Census Bureau News*, November 17, 2023, www.census.gov.

12 David Jefferson, "If I Can Shop and Bank Online, Why Can't I Vote Online?," Verified Voting, 2014, https://verifiedvoting.org.

13 Voting by mail in 2020 doubled as a share of voting modes compared with 2016, to 43 percent of votes cast. John Fortier and Charles Stewart III, *Lessons Learned from the 2020 Election: Report to the U.S. Election Assistance Commission* (MIT Election Data and Science Lab, September 2021), 10, https://electionlab.mit.edu.

14 Stephen Pettigrew and Charles Stewart III, "Protecting the Perilous Path of Election Returns: From the Precinct to the News," *Ohio State Technology Law Journal* 16, no. 2 (Spring 2020): 587–638.

15 On the issue of Albert monitoring sensors, see "Albert Network Monitoring and Management," Center for Internet Security, accessed January 30, 2024, www.cisecurity.org; and "About the Albert Sensor," Center for Internet Security, accessed January 30, 2024, https://sos.oregon.gov.

16 US Election Assistance Commission, *Election Administration and Voting Survey 2022 Comprehensive Report* (Washington, DC: US Election Assistance Commission, June 2023), www.eac.gov.

17 In most of the United States, elections are conducted by counties, but in New England and much of the upper Midwest, they are conducted by municipalities—cities, towns, and villages. For the sake of simplicity, I refer to all local jurisdictions that conduct elections as "counties" in this chapter.

18 Cf. Appel, DeMillo, and Stark, "Ballot-Marking Devices"; Kortum, Byrne, and Whitmore, "Voter Verification"; and Kortum et al., "Can Voters Detect Errors?"

19 Pettigrew and Stewart, "Protecting the Perilous Path"; US Senate Intelligence Committee, *Illinois Voter Registration System Database Breach Report*, June 21, 2017, www.intelligence.senate.gov.

20 Phil Goldstein, "CISA, Working with Partners, Kept the 2020 Election Secure and Free from Interference," *FedTech*, November 11, 2020, https://fedtechmagazine.com.

21 There has been considerable attention paid to "hacks" of voting machines in controlled environments, most famously in the Voting Village of the annual DEF CON hacker convention held in Las Vegas, but it is important to underscore that these events have been held far removed from the operational environment of the voting machines themselves. See A. J. Vicens, "DEF CON Voting Village Takes on Election Conspiracies, Disinformation," Cyberscoop, August 17, 2022, https://cyberscoop.com; Spenser Mestel, "How an 'Ethical' Hacker Convention Is Fueling Trump's Big Lie," Vice News, January 11, 2022, www.vice.com.

22 This overview of the history of voting technologies is based largely on Douglas W. Jones, "A Brief Illustrated History of Voting," last updated 2003, https://homepage.divms.uiowa.edu; Stewart, "Voting Technologies"; and M. Mesbahuddin Sarker and Tajim Md Niamat Ullah Akhund, "The Roadmap to the Electronic Voting System Development: A Literature Review," *International Journal of Advanced Engineering, Management, and Science* 2, no. 5 (2016): 492–97.

23 Joseph P. Harris, *Election Administration in the United States* (Washington, DC: Brookings Institution, 1934).

24 Jones, "Brief Illustrated History"; Sarker and Akhund, "Electronic Voting System Development."

25 The development of voting technologies followed the development of those technologies for commercial use by decades. For instance, punch cards were first adopted for widespread use in the 1890s. Scanning was developed by IBM in the 1930s.

26 Ansolabehere and Stewart, "Function Follows Form."

27 Help America Vote Act of 2002, Pub. L. No. 107-252, 116 Stat. 1666 (2002).

28 Joanna Glasner, "Silicon Valley to Vote on Tech," *Wired*, February 1, 2003, www.wired.com.

29 Verified Voting, homepage, accessed November 26, 2023, https://verifiedvoting.org.

30 Importantly, the VVPAT was presented behind a barrier, so that the voter could see but not touch it. It was therefore not a "receipt," although many people used that term to describe VVPATs.

31 Hybrid BMD systems are included in the DRE total. In 2020, they were used to cast 22.2 percent of all Election Day votes, compared with only 8.5 percent in 2016. Fortier and Stewart, *Lessons Learned*, 94.

32 Charles Stewart III, *How We Voted in 2020: A Topical Look at the Survey of the Performance of American Elections* (MIT Election Data and Science Lab, March 2021), https://electionlab.mit.edu.

33 Saltman, *Effective Use*; Roy G. Saltman, "Accuracy, Integrity, and Security in Computerized Vote-Tallying," *Communications of the ACM* 31, no. 10 (1988): 1184–218; Roy G. Saltman, "Computerized Voting," *Advances in Computers* 32 (1991): 255–305.

34 Saltman, "Computerized Voting."

35 "Warren, Klobuchar, Wyden, and Pocan Investigate Vulnerabilities and Shortcomings of Election Technology Industry with Ties to Private Equity," Office of Elizabeth Warren, December 10, 2019, www.warren.senate.gov.

36 "Voting System Security Measures," US Election Assistance Commission, accessed January 30, 2024, www.eac.gov. A more detailed discussion of securing voting systems against internet attacks is "Security Recommendations," National Institute of Standards and Technology, updated February 5, 2021, www.nist.gov.

37 J. D. Vance (@JDVance1), Twitter, April 10, 2022, 3:45 p.m., https://twitter.com/JDVance1/status/1513241867726512133.

38 Maggie Astor, "Some Republicans Want to Count Votes by Hand. Bad Idea, Experts Say," *New York Times*, October 18, 2022, www.nytimes.com.

39 These were questions asked in the MIT module of the Cooperative Election Study.

40 "If E-Voting Is Currently Being Used, What Type(s) of Technology Used?," International IDEA, accessed November 25, 2023, www.idea.int. While most democratic countries rely on hand-counted paper ballots, a few have pioneered the usage of electronic equipment, notably Brazil and India. Estonia is the one country that relies heavily on internet voting. See Diego F. Aranha and Jeroen van de Graaf, "The Good, the Bad, and the Ugly: Two Decades of E-Voting in Brazil," *IEEE Security and Privacy* 16, no. 6 (November–December 2018): 22–30; Zuheir Desai and Alexander Lee, "Technology and Protest: The Political Effects of Electronic Voting in India," *Political Science Research and Methods* 9, no. 2 (2021): 398–413; and Piret Ehin et al., "Internet Voting in Estonia 2005–2019: Evidence from Eleven Elections," *Government Information Quarterly* 39, no. 4 (2022): 101718, https://doi.org.

41 Penn Warren Public Policy Initiative, *The Business of Voting: Market Structure and Innovation in the Election Technology Industry* (Philadelphia: Penn Warren Public Policy Initiative, 2017), https://verifiedvoting.org.

42 Charles Stewart III and James Dunham, "Attitudes toward Voting Technology, 2012–2019," *Journal of Political Institutions and Political Economy* 1, no. 2 (June 2020): 159–87.

43 US Census Bureau, *1992 Census of Governments*, vol. 1, *Government Organization*, no. 2, *Popularly Elected Officials* (Washington, DC: US Department of Commerce, 1995), www.census.gov.

44 Richard Franklin Bensel, *The American Ballot Box in the Mid-Nineteenth Century* (New York: Cambridge University Press, 2004).

45 One especially interesting direct comparison of mechanical lever machines with the newer punch-card and optical scanning systems was performed in 1975 by the Kentucky Legislative Research Commission. See Martha Maloney, *Mechanized Vote Recording: A Survey*, Legislative Research Commission Research Report No. 116 (Frankfort, KY: Legislative Research Commission, May 1975), https://apps.legislature.ky.gov.

46 Suleiman K. Kassicieh, Glen H. Kawaguchi, and Len Malczynski, "Security, Integrity, and Public Acceptance of Electronic Voting," *Journal of Systems Management* 39, no. 12 (1988): 6–10; Peter G. Neumann, "Risks in Computerized Elections," *Communications of the ACM* 33, no. 11 (1990): 170–71; Rebecca Mercuri, "Voting-Machine Risks," *Communications of the ACM* 35, no. 11 (1992): 138–39.

47 Jonathan N. Wand et al., "The Butterfly Did It: The Aberrant Vote for Buchanan in Palm Beach County, Florida," *American Political Science Review* 95, no. 4 (2001): 793–810; Walter R. Mebane, "The Wrong Man Is President! Overvotes in the 2000 Presidential Election in Florida," *Perspectives on Politics* 2, no. 3 (2004): 525–35.

48 Douglas W. Jones, "Chad—from Waste Product to Headline," last revised 2002, https://homepage.cs.uiowa.edu.

49 Stanley Dunlap, "Suit Backed by Georgia Lawmaker Challenges State's Ballot Barcode System," *Georgia Recorder*, August 25, 2021, https://georgiarecorder.com; Kate Brumback, "Judge Mulls Whether Voting Machine Case Should Go to Trial," Associated Press, May 2, 2023, https://apnews.com.

50 Appel, DeMillo, and Stark, "Ballot-Marking Devices"; Philip B. Stark and Ran Xie, "They May Look and Look, Yet Not See: BMDs Cannot Be Tested Adequately," in *Electronic Voting: E-Vote-ID 2022*, Lecture Notes in Computer Science, Vol. 13553, ed. Robert Krimmer et al. (Cham: Springer, 2022), 122–38, https://doi.org.

51 Kortum, Byrne, and Whitmore, "Voter Verification"; Kortum et al., "Can Voters Detect Errors?"

52 Georgia Secretary of State, "Risk-Limiting Audit Report: Georgia Presidential Contest, November 2020," November 19, 2020, https://web.archive.org; Kate Brumback, "Georgia Hand Tally of Votes Is Complete, Affirms Biden Lead," Associated Press, November 19, 2020, https://apnews.com.

53 Jonathan N. Katz and Brian R. Sala, "Careerism, Committee Assignments, and the Electoral Connection," *American Political Science Review* 90, no. 1 (1996): 21–33.

54 The other prominent approach, which has barely moved out of the academic journals and a few small pilot projects, is end-to-end verification. On this approach, see National Academies of Sciences, Engineering, and Medicine, *Securing the Vote: Protecting American Democracy* (Washington, DC: National Academies Press, 2018), 96–97, https://doi.org.

55 "The Verifier—Post-election Audits—November 2022," Verified Voting, accessed January 30, 2024, https://verifiedvoting.org.

56 "Post-election Audits," National Conference of State Legislatures, September 22, 2022, www.ncsl.org; MIT Election Data and Science Lab, *Election Auditing: Key Issues and Perspectives* (MIT Election Data and Science Lab, June 2019), http://electionlab.mit.edu.

57 For instance, many states only require ballots cast in person and tallied by scanners in precincts to be audited, leaving absentee ballots or hand-tallied ballots unscrutinized.

58 The *risk limit* that must be set before the RLA begins can be interpreted as measuring the probability the election official is willing to accept that the audit will incorrectly conclude that the result of the vote count is correct. This probability cannot be driven to zero unless there is a complete hand recount of every election.

59 Jacob Jaffe et al., "Efficiency of Risk Limiting Audits" (working paper, MIT Election Data and Science Lab, 2023).

60 Charles Stewart III, "Trust in Elections," *Daedalus* 15, no. 4 (2022): 2334–53.

61 The exception to this prediction concerns certain edge cases, such as for military voters and voters with certain disabilities.

15

THE TRANSITION PERIOD

THE DISRUPTION OF THE ELECTION OF A PRESIDENT DUE TO THE DEATH OF PRESIDENTIAL CANDIDATES AFTER ELECTION DAY

JOHN C. FORTIER

A smooth transition from the November election to the January 20 inauguration of a new president is a sign of a well-functioning democracy. This transition period, however, is fraught with potential obstacles, especially in the instance of a close election and the death of the winning candidate. This chapter lays out several key timeframes within this period, dangers that might arise in these times, and potential reforms to the process.

THE THREE PERIODS OF PRESIDENTIAL TRANSITION

There are three key periods between the November election and the January 20 inauguration day:

1. From Election Day in November (November 3 in 2020) until the day the presidential electors cast their votes (the first Tuesday after the second Wednesday in December; December 8 in 2020)
2. From the December casting of electoral votes until the counting of the electoral votes on January 6
3. From January 6 to January 20, Inauguration Day[1]

There are, of course, other important milestones in the transition period. But a winning presidential candidate passes through each of these distinct periods on the way to assuming the presidency. And disruptions to the transition resulting from the death of the winning candidate or winning ticket look very different in each of these three periods.

First, let us consider each of the three periods and the status of the winning presidential candidate in each period. What are the challenges of the most dire circumstance, when the winning presidential and vice presidential candidates die, and what are those of the still serious but less disruptive scenario in which the winning presidential candidate dies?

Second, what are potential remedies to these dire scenarios to ensure that a legitimate president is inaugurated on January 20?

The presidential election differs from other elections in that voters may believe that they are casting a ballot for a presidential candidate, but in reality they vote for a slate of electors. These electors are preselected people who usually have a strong connection to the party and person of the presidential candidate whose name appears on the ballot. Ultimately, these electors will cast their vote for president and vice president in December.

So a voter who casts a ballot for Joe Biden or Donald Trump would actually be casting a ballot for a group of preselected individuals broadly loyal to the presidential candidate.

There are minor differences in how states and political parties select these electors for the ballot, but broadly speaking they are selected to be loyal to the candidate and candidate's party. Some states actually print the names of the electors on the ballot in small print below the name of the presidential nominee of the party. Most states do not. In addition, forty-eight of fifty states and the District of Columbia award all of the electors from that state to the winner of the popular vote in that state. Two states, Maine and Nebraska, award two electors to the winner of the statewide popular vote, and the remaining electors are awarded one each to the winner of each congressional district.

In December, on the first Tuesday after the second Wednesday, the electors associated with the winning candidate in a particular state meet in the state capitol to cast their votes.

Finally, as the American people are now altogether familiar with, on January 6, the votes of electors cast in December are opened and counted before a joint session of Congress. If a presidential candidate receives a majority of the electors' votes, then he or she is elected president. If no one receives a majority, the election goes to the House of Representatives, under a special contingent election procedure where each state delegation receives one vote and may vote for one of the top three vote getters of electors. A majority of twenty-six states is required to elect a president. If a vice presidential candidate receives a majority of electors' votes for vice president, he or she is elected vice president. If no one receives a majority, then the Senate elects a vice president from the top two vote getters of electoral votes.

At noon on January 20, the terms of the previous president and vice president end. The president-elect and vice president elect become president and vice president.[2]

Typically, this timeline proceeds without incident. The death of the winning presidential and vice presidential candidates, however, poses great difficulties to the successful resolution of the presidential election and inauguration of a new president.

PRESIDENTIAL SUCCESSION PROVISIONS

Before considering the death of winning presidential candidates in each of the three periods before Inauguration Day, it is worthwhile to consider several of our legal and constitutional provisions for presidential succession.

The core constitutional provision is in Article II, Section 1, Clause 6:

> In Case of the Removal of the President from Office, or of his Death, Resignation, or Inability to discharge the Powers and Duties of the said Office, the Same shall devolve on the Vice President, and the Congress may by law provide for the Case of Removal, Death, Resignation or Inability, both of the President and Vice President, declaring what Officer shall then act as President, and such Officer shall act accordingly, until the Disability be removed, or a President shall be elected.

The key point is that when the presidency is vacant, the vice president steps in for the president. (Note that the Twenty-Fifth Amendment makes it clear that the vice president does not just obtain the powers of the president but rather becomes president in the case of death, removal, or resignation.) Beyond that, Congress is empowered to write a law specifying which "Officer" shall assume the powers of the presidency if both the presidency and the vice presidency are vacant.

Over the years, we have had three different versions of a presidential succession act. The current one dates to 1947 and provides for the Speaker of the House, the Senate pro tempore, and the cabinet officers in order of the creation of the departments to be the statutory successors.

But the key point for our purposes is that Congress has written a law that might be activated if there is no president or vice president on January 20.

How the election processes in the transition period play out will determine if we have a president-elect on January 20 ready to take office, or perhaps if we have no president-elect or vice president elect—in which case, we might then go to our presidential succession act and elevate the Speaker of the House to the presidency.

To isolate the issue of the death of the winning candidates, let's assume that the popular vote and Electoral College vote are cast decisively in the November election. While election-night reporting is provisional, and the vote counts will only be certified by states in the following days and weeks, let us assume that on election night, the results are clear and one party's presidential ticket has received sufficient votes in states needed to make a majority of the Electoral College.

In this instance, the death of the winning presidential ticket in the days after Election Day would be a terrible tragedy and jarring to the nation. But what would be the status of the election, and how would a president emerge to be inaugurated on January 20?

The death of the winning presidential candidates before the casting of votes by the presidential electors in December would raise a certain type of confusion, but one that might be resolved by actions of the winning political party. The indirect election of the president by presidential electors poses a challenge, but also potentially provides a solution. While the voters have spoken on Election Day, they will not have completely lost their voice, as their actions on the popular ballot have elected electors, who are still living and able to meet in December to cast their electoral votes.

Take, for example, the 2020 election. Joe Biden and Kamala Harris received enough popular votes in states to select 303 electors, who would then go on to cast their electoral votes on December 14. Then 303 votes were cast for Biden as president and 303 votes were cast for Harris as vice president. If tragedy struck and Biden and Harris were killed in a terrorist attack or cut down by the pandemic or some other terrible event, the 303 electors who were prepared to vote for Biden and Harris might be convinced by the Democratic Party to cast their ballots instead for some other choice of the Democratic Party. If the electors could be persuaded to cast their ballots for a new Democratic ticket, then those electoral votes could be counted on January 6, a president-elect and vice president elect would emerge, and on January 20 the new ticket would take office and serve a four-year term.

Legally, it would be straightforward. And the way that slates of electors are selected to be loyal to the Democratic nominees would make it likely that the electors could be persuaded to vote for a newly chosen Democratic ticket. The main difficulty would not be legal but rather would be to get party consensus on a replacement ticket, then to communicate the choice to the electors and persuade them all to vote for the new ticket. But most difficult of all would be to persuade the American people of the legitimacy of this new ticket. Yes, the new ticket would be of the same party that had won enough electoral votes in the 2020 election to win the presidency. But this new ticket would not have stood before the American people for election.

One could imagine the party committee reconvening to select a new presidential ticket as they might have if the candidates had died before Election Day. Perhaps sober leaders would choose a new presidential ticket that was similar in politics and temperament to the now-deceased winning ticket. And an effort to publicize the choice and seek input from party members or from the broader public could further legitimize the choice. This is likely the best circumstance one could hope for. Even so, there would likely be grumbling, especially from the opposing party, that the new presidential ticket had not stood for popular election. But a less than best-case scenario might see calls for the winning party to choose an ideological ticket that might not have been successful if it stood for popular election.

Assuming that the winning party could select a new ticket, the remainder of the election transition process would be mostly straightforward. The electors would meet in December and cast their votes for the new ticket. On January 6, the ballots would be counted at the joint session of Congress for the new ticket. Then this new ticket would assume presidential office on January 20.

One alternative exists for the winning political party if their ticket dies before the counting of electors in December. If the winning party controls both houses of Congress in the upcoming Congress, then an alternative to selecting new candidates would be for the party to encourage its electors to vote for the deceased candidates. Then, on January 6, the new Congress would not object to the counting of the electors of deceased candidates. The deceased ticket would effectively be elected president-elect and vice president elect. But on January 20, they would not be able to take office, and the vacancy in the presidency would mean that the Speaker of the House would be next in the line of succession and would become president on January 20 to serve a four-year term.[3]

NEW PROBLEMS ARISING FROM RECENT LAWS BINDING PRESIDENTIAL ELECTORS

One other difficulty that has arisen in recent years is related to new state laws strongly binding the presidential electors to vote for the candidate who has won the popular vote.

For many years, states have made efforts to bind their electors to vote only for the choice made by voters on the November ballot. These earlier laws attempted to limit the possibility of so-called faithless electors. In this case, electors exercise their discretion to cast a ballot for president and vice president of their choice at odds with what the voters of their state had selected on the Election Day ballot. Often, in recent years, these faithless electors have been protest votes, and in small numbers they do not change the outcome of the election. But as one could imagine a small group of electors casting faithless votes to deny a candidate an Electoral College majority, states have rightly been interested in trying to limit these faithless electors.

But these early laws sought to bind the electors to voters' choice on the ballot by very weak means. Typically, earlier laws had a provision binding the electors with no penalty to the electors, or they imposed very small monetary penalties of $500 or $1,000.

One state, North Carolina, had a more stringent law of binding. This law bound electors to vote for the candidate who had won on the popular ballot in that state. And if an elector did not vote appropriately, the law provided for the removal of the elector and replacement with an alternative elector who could then vote the appropriate way. In theory, this stringent law would eliminate faithless electors because any such elector would be replaced by a faithful elector who would vote the correct way.[4]

In the past two decades, more states have adopted the strict North Carolina law that replaces faithless electors.[5] And the Supreme Court affirmed the propriety of such a strong binding law in *Chiafolo v. Washington*.[6] While these laws limit the prospect of faithless electors, they make the job of replacing deceased presidential candidates more difficult. If a political party were to attempt to select new candidates for the electors to vote for, in a number of states the electors would not be able to vote for such new candidates. If, for example, the party instructed its electors to vote for a new candidate, then some states' slates of electors would comply, while others would be forced to cast their ballots for the deceased ticket. In the end, this could divide the presidential vote and perhaps prevent any candidate from receiving a majority of the electors counted on January 6.

In this case, the strategy of instructing all slates of electors to vote for the deceased candidates could be employed, but if Congress were not fully controlled by the winning presidential candidates' party, then there would be the possibility of objections to votes cast for deceased presidential candidates. Or if the Speaker of the House in the new Congress was of the party opposite that of the winning presidential candidate, then the presidency would go to the party that lost the November general election.

Finally, in considering the difficulties of getting a new president in the case of candidate death before the casting of votes by electors, we should consider the less dire circumstance in which only the winning presidential candidate dies and the winning vice presidential candidate survives.

The difficulties here are similar to those in the death of the entire ticket. A political party might consider instructing its electors to vote for a wholly new presidential candidate to go along with the still-living winning vice presidential candidate. For example, if Biden passed away shortly after the election, perhaps the Democratic Party would instruct the electors to vote for Hillary Clinton as president and Harris as vice president. This strategy would run into some difficulties with the binding elector laws, as perhaps not enough states for a majority of the Electoral College could be assembled to vote for Clinton (some states' electoral slates would be bound to vote for the deceased Biden).

If instead the party instructed its electors to vote for the deceased Biden for president and the living Harris for vice president, this method would ultimately place Harris in the presidency if the party controlled both houses of Congress and did not object to any votes for the deceased candidates. If the opposing party controlled both houses of Congress in the new Congress, then perhaps the party would object to the Biden votes as invalid because they were for a deceased presidential candidate and then elect the losing presidential candidate to be president. The uncertainty of what would happen with electoral votes for a deceased president could lead to confusion, and the opposite party could take advantage of the confusion for its own benefit.

Let us skip to the third period in the transition before returning to the more difficult second period. If the winning presidential ticket died after the electoral votes had been counted on January 6 (but before January 20), then on January 20 at noon, the presidency would be vacant and, following the Presidential Succession Act, the Speaker of the House would take the oath of office and become president for the four-year term.

This is a clean and straightforward legal situation. The main objection, however, is that the presidency could be assumed by a Speaker from the opposite party of the winning presidential candidates. A winning Reagan-Bush ticket would end in President Tip O'Neil, or a winning Clinton-Gore ticket in 1996 would lead to President Newt Gingrich.

In the case of the death of only the winning presidential candidate in this third period, the situation is perfectly clear. The vice president elect would become president on January 20.

* * *

If the winning ticket died after the electors had met and cast their votes for the winning ticket, but before those electoral votes were counted in the joint session on January 6, there would be great confusion of the outcome of the electoral process. Would Congress count the electoral votes cast for the deceased winning candidates?[7]

The makeup of the Congress that would count the votes and the inclination of the Congress to create mischief would also be unknown. One could imagine a few troubling scenarios. Congress could choose to count the votes of the deceased candidates. This scenario would lead to a vacant presidency on January 20 with the Speaker of the House becoming president. This Speaker could be of the same party as the winning presidential ticket, or they might not be.

Congress might also consider two other courses of action that would result in the election of the losing presidential candidates. If Congress rejected the slates of electors themselves (not just the votes of the electors), then Congress might find itself with only the slates of electors who had voted for the losing candidate. And as the winning slates had been disqualified, then Congress's action would result in the election of the losers of the popular vote. If, on the other hand, Congress chose to reject the votes of the electors but not the slate of electors, then it would find that there is no majority of electors for any candidate. For president, the choice would go to the House of Representatives, and the House could choose among the top three vote getters in electors. In most scenarios, Congress would only be able to vote for the losing presidential candidate, as all of the electoral votes for the deceased winning candidates would be disqualified. The House contingent election requires the House to vote by state delegation, with each delegation counting as one vote and a required twenty-six votes to elect a president. Again this could lead to the election of the losing presidential candidate or perhaps deadlock in the House. The Senate would determine the outcome of the vice presidential election, but again would likely only be able to vote for the losing vice presidential candidate, as all of the votes for the deceased winning candidates would have been dismissed by objections on January 6.

The second period is the most difficult in the transition period. Unless the winning party controls the new House, confusion, the installation of the losing presidential candidates, the installation of a Speaker of the House of the opposite party of the election winners, and outright deadlock are all possibilities.

The remainder of this chapter will consider three sets of reforms: first, a set of recommendations made by the first Continuity of Government Commission that provided solutions tailored to each of the three periods in the transition period;[8] second, recommendations made by a later reconvening of that commission that developed a new set of recommendations depending on a never-used provision of the Twentieth Amendment;[9] third, if the winning presidential ticket were killed, the possibility of a temporary president, who would hold office until a special election for president could be held. The winner of that special election would fill the remainder of the presidential term.

CONTINUITY OF GOVERNMENT COMMISSION

The Continuity of Government Commission was a joint effort of the American Enterprise Institute and the Brookings Institution after 9/11. It consisted of former high-level government officials of all three branches and both political parties. Chaired by former senator Alan Simpson and former White House counsel Lloyd Cutler, it made recommendations on presidential succession during the transition period, along with recommendations on other aspects of continuity of government.

The commission made recommendations tailored to each of the three periods of the transition.

For the first period of the transition, from the November Election Day to the December casting of the votes of electors, the commission stressed the role of the political party in selecting new presidential candidates and instructing electors to vote for these newly selected candidates of the party. This recommendation echoes the discussion earlier in this chapter about the need for the party to legitimize the new presidential candidates, who will go on to become president and vice president without having stood for election before the American people.

At the time of these recommendations, there was only one state law on the books that strongly bound electors by replacing them with alternates if they voted "faithlessly."[10] An update to this recommendation might be to recommend that states adopt exceptions to their binding statutes in the case of the death of the candidate (as a few of these state laws already do).

The commission recognized the great confusion that would result from the death of the winning candidates during the second period of the transition, the period between the December casting of electoral votes and the January 6 counting of the electoral votes. The outcome of the election would be very uncertain with the prospects of political mischief by the opposing party, deadlock over the counting of votes, and likely heated political combat as real possibilities.

The commission had no great reforms to address this period, but it did note that the dates of the casting and counting of the electors' votes were set by statute and that the period of time could be shrunken or nearly eliminated. If the casting of the electoral votes took place a short period of time before the counting of the votes, then the death of the candidates would be very unlikely to occur during this short window.

The third period of the transition, when the deaths of political candidates would occur after the electoral votes have been counted on January 6 but before January 20, should lead to a vacancy in the presidency on January 20, filled by the Presidential Succession Act. The current act has the Speaker of the House as the first statutory successor to the president and vice president.

The first commission, however, had several special considerations regarding this period. First, the commission (and its successor commission) recommended that the general line of succession be changed to cabinet succession, removing the Speaker and president pro tempore from the line of succession. Second, the commission, in the aftermath of 9/11, was particularly concerned about a mass attack, perhaps on Inauguration Day, which would wipe out the whole line of succession. And the commission rightly noted that the cabinet of the incoming president would not be in place until at earliest a few hours after the inauguration ceremony. The commission laid out a scenario in which a mass attack on Inauguration Day would lead to a wiping out of the whole line of succession or reliance on the outgoing president's cabinet as a line of succession.

The key recommendation for the inauguration problem was to have the outgoing president appoint and confirm a few key figures in the line of succession for the incoming president before the incoming president takes office. As most of the incoming cabinet is subject to confirmation hearings before Inauguration Day, the idea would be for the outgoing president to appoint (and the Senate confirm) the incoming president's secretary of state and perhaps other cabinet posts a few days before the inauguration. In this case, the sudden death of the president-elect, the vice president elect, and congressional leaders during an attack on the inauguration ceremony would result in the presidency being assumed by the now-confirmed incoming secretary of state.

The commission was reconvened in 2020–21 with some remaining members of the previous commission and new members. Chaired by former secretary of Health and Human Services Donna Shalala and former White House counsel A. B. Culvahouse, it rethought these earlier recommendations about presidential succession during the transition period.

The second commission took a different approach to the death of candidates during the transition period. First, this commission was particularly concerned with the possibility of the death of the winning candidates leading to a president of the opposing party. Essentially, it would mean that the party that lost the presidential election in November would assume the presidency on January 20. This, of course, could occur in the most straightforward scenarios when the president-elect and vice-president elect were killed a few days before the inauguration if the Speaker of the House were of the opposing party. (Like the first commission, this second commission also broadly favored cabinet succession for presidential succession in all other cases, in part to ensure the continuity of the party in the White House.)

A second worry that the second commission stated was that the polarized political system made it unlikely that there would be cooperation between the two parties to confirm the incoming president's cabinet, or that this polarization might make the problems of counting electoral votes and the possibility of partisan mischief even more prominent.

The key new insight of the commission was to employ the never before used powers of Congress under Section 3 of the Twentieth Amendment. The key language in this section reads, "The Congress may by law provide for the case wherein neither a President elect nor a Vice President elect shall have qualified, declaring who shall then act as President, or the manner in which one who is to act shall be selected." Congress has not exercised this power. And little or no commentary has been made on this section. The use of the authority under this section is helpful because it is broader than the authority granted to Congress to write a presidential succession act in Article II of the Constitution, according to which Congress may only specify a list of people in the line of succession. Also, the word "Officer" has generated debate over whether this refers to executive branch officials only or includes legislative officers. But it also is limiting even in the specific case of congressional officers, as certain officials such as the Speaker and Senate president pro tempore are clearly officers, but the minority leader of each chamber is not.

Section 3 of the Twentieth Amendment is much more flexible in that it does not require Congress to limit itself to "Officers." Also, it does not require that the law specify individuals who might succeed to the presidency. It gives Congress the ability to provide in law for a process to select the president, not just provide a list.

With the possibility of a more flexible succession act for the problem of a dead presidential ticket, the commission fashioned a few options that ensured that the new president would be of the same party as the winning presidential candidate.[11] And it avoided some of the pitfalls of the various periods during the transition.

The commission recommended two options for Congress:

1. Pass a law stating that the death of the winning presidential candidates would result in the House leader of the winning candidates' party as the successor to the presidential candidates. If the Speaker of the House is of the same party as the winning presidential candidates, then the Speaker will assume the presidency on January 20. But if the Speaker is of the opposite party, then the minority leader of the House would assume the presidency.
2. Pass a law stating that the death of the winning presidential candidates would trigger a process by which the party caucus of the winning presidential candidate would convene to pick a successor. (The commission made the specific recommendation that a joint caucus of the House and Senate members of the winning presidential candidate make the choice.)

Finally, one of these two options would be combined with a provision in law that electoral votes for a deceased candidate shall be counted on January 6 (not thrown out by objection). The combination of these provisions would mean that the death of the winning presidential candidate in the time before the casting of electoral votes in December would result in the electors casting their votes for the deceased candidates, but because of the law, they would not fear that those votes would not be counted by Congress. And they could be secure in the knowledge that someone of their political party would assume the presidency in a process laid out in advance by law.

Similarly, if the deaths occurred after the electors had cast their votes but before they had been counted on January 6, all of the ambiguities as to how those votes would be treated by Congress on January 6 would be eliminated by the provision in law to count the votes for deceased electors.

Finally, if the deaths occurred in the period after January 6 but before January 20, a process would be in place for the selection of a president of the same party as that of the winning presidential candidates.

A SPECIAL ELECTION

One last reform should be considered that addresses the problem of the death of the winning presidential candidates: the possibility of a temporary president assuming office on January 20, who would serve only until a special election could be held to fill the remainder of the term.

Both the original language of Article II of the Constitution and the language of Section 3 of the Twentieth Amendment could authorize such an election. Our first presidential succession act had an explicit provision for a special election. Our second presidential succession act included an option for Congress to call for such an election. Our current act does not have such a provision.

This special election was a recommendation of the first Continuity of Government Commission but not the second. It does, however, deserve consideration as an option separate from the specifics of each commission's recommendations for the transition period.

We have been fortunate in our history in that we have never had a statutory successor take office. Presidents and vice presidents have died in office, but we have never had a double vacancy that would trigger a statutory successor. In the case of the death of candidates during a transition period or a mass attack killing many figures in government, there is the possibility that a more obscure or more controversial figure takes office on January 20. Under current law, the successor would serve the whole four-year term. One partial solution to the problem of having a less than perfect successor in office is to limit the term of that successor and to go back to the people to find a more permanent successor.

Our transition period has the potential to become a tangled mess of electoral procedures and difficult succession issues, combined with partisan polarization, which would be exacerbated by the circumstances. All of this calls out for solutions that would ensure clarity of succession and the greatest likelihood that the will of the people in the November election will be respected.

NOTES

1 John C. Fortier and Norman J. Ornstein, "If Terrorists Attacked Our Presidential Elections," *Election Law Journal* 3, no. 4 (December 2004): 597–612.
2 John C. Fortier, ed., *After the People Vote: A Guide to the Electoral College*, 3rd ed. (American Enterprise Institute for Public Policy Research, 2004).
3 Fortier and Ornstein, "If Terrorists Attacked."
4 Fortier, "After the People Vote."
5 See https://fairvote.org (accessed February 16, 2024) for a catalogue of current state faithless elector laws.
6 Chiafalo v. Washington, 140 S. Ct. 2316 (2020).
7 See the case of Horace Greeley, discussed in Akhil Reed Amar, "Presidents, Vice Presidents, and Death: Closing the Constitution's Succession Gap," *Arkansas Law Review* 48 (1994): 215.
8 Continuity of Government Commission, *Preserving Our Institutions: The Second Report of the Continuity of Government Commission; Presidential Succession* (Washington, DC: AEI and Brookings, 2009), https://www.brookings.edu.
9 John C. Fortier and Norman J. Ornstein, "Continuity of Government: Presidential Succession," Continuity of Government Commission, American Enterprise Institute, December 5, 2022, https://www.aei.org.
10 Fortier, "After the People Vote."
11 Fortier and Ornstein, "Continuity of Government."

16

THE POTENTIAL IMPACT AND LIMITATIONS OF THE ELECTORAL COUNT REFORM ACT OF 2022

RUSS FEINGOLD AND LINDSAY LANGHOLZ

The 2020 presidential election and its aftermath exposed flaws in the constitutional and statutory framework that governs the counting of electoral votes and certification of presidential elections. Uncertainty surrounding key provisions of the Electoral Count Act of 1887 left the United States vulnerable to a constitutional crisis and violent rebellion. While stark, this was not the first time a presidential election had exposed cracks in the system. To evaluate the potential impact and importance of recent reforms and the vulnerabilities that remain, we look back to previous elections that placed strains on this framework, the ways in which these flaws were often papered over through the creation of and adherence to norms prioritizing a peaceful transition of power, and the ways in which the Electoral Count Reform Act of 2022 addresses this history while leaving other vulnerabilities unaddressed.

THE CONSTITUTION AND TEMPORARY MEASURES GOVERNING PRESIDENTIAL ELECTIONS (1789–1877)

The process by which members of the Electoral College selected a president and vice president was first governed exclusively by Article II, Section 1, Clause 3, of the US Constitution. Electors were to meet in their respective states and vote by ballot for two people.[1] Once all votes were tabulated, the list was to be sent in the form of a signed and sealed certificate to the vice president in their role as president of the Senate.[2] In the presence of both chambers of Congress, the president of the Senate would then open all certificates and count all votes received. The constitutional text also required a successful candidate to receive a majority of votes from electors; should no candidate receive a majority of electoral votes, the House would choose from the five highest vote recipients, with each state's House delegation having one vote to cast. The candidate with the highest number of votes would be elected president, and the second-highest vote getter would be elected vice president. Should two candidates receive a majority of votes equal in number, the House would choose between the two, again with each state's House delegation casting one ballot.[3]

This selection scheme was born out of indecision and fatigue among attendees of the Constitutional Convention and, according to one delegate, was "the most difficult" issue the framers confronted.[4] According to historian Alexander Keyssar, one of the primary sources of their difficulty was the lack of available models to draw on.[5] Selection by legislature was the most prominent model available, utilized by several nascent states to select their governor, but even after delegates accepted this model multiple times, the convention reopened the issue repeatedly. Key delegates, including James Madison, proposed a national popular vote, but slavery created insurmountable complications. Delegates unsuccessfully proposed numerous other designs until a committee tasked with resolving lingering issues put forward the final design, which was adopted by the convention and ratified with little fanfare.

This system worked until George Washington declined to seek a third term. Under the stress of competition, the flaws in the constitutional text began to show. In the 1796 election, several newspapers reported issues with the certificate of one state whose votes would prove decisive.[6] Thomas Jefferson wrote to John Adams, who served as president of the Senate during the proceedings, to express his desire for the votes to be counted for Adams regardless of technical errors, as the voters had clearly expressed their intent. A crisis was averted due to Jefferson's desire to "prevent the [phenomenon] of a Pseudo-president at so early a day."[7] This was the first instance of one candidate prioritizing such a transition over sustained protest in an effort to prevent constitutional crisis and, in doing so, papering over a procedural defect of the system.

The election of 1800 resulted in a tie between Jefferson and his running mate, Aaron Burr, after their entire set of electors voted a straight ticket, not following an unofficial procedure established twelve years prior to avoid such situations.[8] This problem was caused by the Constitution's original design[9] and exposed when the norm established in the prior three elections was not followed. Additionally, historical sources indicate that Jefferson, in his role as president of the Senate, likely knowingly ignored irregularities on Georgia's certificate, creating a two-way tie among candidates (himself being one) who had received a majority of electoral votes rather than a plurality, setting in motion a very different procedure under Article II.[10] Jefferson was eventually sworn in as the third president, creating with his rival once more a norm that would govern future presidential elections, peacefully transitioning power between political rivals.

Congress quickly took action to refine the constitutional procedure for the Electoral College ahead of the next presidential election, proposing language that would supersede Article II, Section 1, Clause 3, and sending it to the state legislatures on December 9, 1803, under the procedure established in Article V. The amendment was ratified and published as the Twelfth Amendment.[11]

The Twelfth Amendment is the only amendment to have altered the presidential elector selection process.[12] The following are the key provisions of the amendment for the purposes of our analysis:

- Separate ballots are to be voted by electors for president and vice president.
- A list of all votes cast is to be compiled, with the votes received by each candidate enumerated, signed, and certified.
- The certified list is to be sealed and transmitted to the president of the Senate, who shall, in the presence of both chambers of Congress, open all certificates and the votes shall be counted.
- If any candidate receives a majority of the electoral vote for president, that candidate shall be elected president, but if no candidate receives a majority, a procedure is established for the House of Representatives to vote, with each state's contingent casting one vote.
- A parallel procedure is established for the Senate to choose by ballot the vice president should no candidate receive a majority of electoral votes.[13]

In the 1824 presidential election, John Quincy Adams won the presidency as a result of a House vote under the Twelfth Amendment, despite losing the popular vote and a plurality of electoral votes to Andrew Jackson.[14]

In 1861, supporters of President-Elect Abraham Lincoln feared that the man who came in second in the Electoral College, sitting vice president John Breckinridge, would find a way to interfere with the electoral certificates he was charged with receiving and counting before Congress as part of a larger potential threat to Lincoln's ascent to power and the safety of the capital.[15] Breckinridge ultimately conducted the count without incident, and while the country would soon be plunged into a constitutional crisis with the outbreak of the Civil War, the process for counting electoral votes survived.

In 1865, Congress adopted the Twenty-Second Joint Rule, a tool Republicans created "to assure control over the votes of recently rebellious southern states."[16] The rule created a procedure for hearing objections to any state's certificate, requiring each chamber to vote to count any electoral votes in question.[17] Still in the shadow of the Civil War and with Reconstruction front and center, the election of 1872 put the Twenty-Second Joint Rule to the test. Electors from five states were challenged based on irregularities,[18] and Congress rejected the electors from Arkansas and Louisiana.[19] These challenges did not affect the final result of the presidential election, and Congress chose not to readopt the Twenty-Second Joint Rule in 1876.[20]

* * *

The uncertainties and defects in the presidential election system built on constitutional text alone were fully exposed in the aftermath of the election of 1876. During the campaign between Rutherford B. Hayes and Samuel Tilden, "both sides believed that the other was engaging in massive fraud, or would if it could, to guarantee a win."[21] Two weeks before Election Day, Hayes would write in his diary that "danger is imminent: A contested result. And we have no such means for its decision as ought to be provided by law."[22] The prediction came to fruition and was nothing short of a "four-alarm conflagration."[23] All three states that were then occupied by federal troops, Florida, Louisiana, and South

Carolina, submitted multiple electoral vote certificates.[24] Congress created a commission to resolve the dispute consisting of five senators, five representatives, and five Supreme Court justices.[25] After the 1877 Electoral Commission determined by a party-line vote that Hayes had won all states in question, and Congress declined to order otherwise,[26] Hayes was elected president by a single electoral vote. The decision was not well received by Democrats, who created "wild disorder" on the House floor, blocking any possible action on the commission's report.[27] Eventually a deal was allegedly struck.[28] Hayes would be sworn in two days later. And despite all that was sacrificed to allow for one candidate to emerge from the election of 1876 victorious without violence,[29] Hayes's "legal and moral title to the presidency was never accepted as legitimate by at least half the country."[30] He served only one term, and Grover Cleveland would later sign into law the Electoral Count Act of 1887.

THE ELECTORAL COUNT ACT OF 1887 AND UNFORESEEN COMPLICATIONS (1877–2021)

With the expiration of the 1877 Electoral Commission, the law once again reverted to the patchwork provided by Article II of the Constitution, the Twelfth Amendment, and whatever norms remained after the Twenty-Second Joint Rule, with "no permanent mechanisms for resolving" disputes in which the two chambers of Congress could not agree on which state electors were to be counted, and with a risk that the states would face disenfranchisement.[31] To address this risk, the Electoral Count Act of 1887 provided a procedure by which Congress should receive, process, tabulate, and count the electoral votes of each state. Among its key provisions, the 1887 act

- charges the executive of each state with ascertaining their state's electors and transmitting a signed and sealed certificate of ascertainment to designated officials in Washington, DC, for the purpose of being counted as the state's electoral votes;
- sets a date on which a joint session of Congress, presided over by the president of the Senate, will meet to count all electoral votes and announce a winner;

- provides instructions on how the president of the Senate, with assistance from appointed tellers, should open and read aloud all certificates of electoral votes submitted by state officials;
- creates a procedure by which objections to any state's certificate will be considered, including a requirement that every objection be submitted in writing by at least one senator and one congressmember and a requirement that debate be limited to two hours in each chamber, with members limited to five minutes for remarks;
- establishes a date by which a state's certified submission of its slate of electors will be considered by Congress to be conclusive, so long as it has been determined under the laws enacted before the day on which electors are appointed and any and all controversies have been resolved, a provision that has come to be known as the "safe harbor" deadline;
- addresses how multiple certificates submitted for one state should be treated; and
- requires that the joint meeting not be dissolved until all electoral votes have been counted and a winner declared.

The 1887 act's new procedural requirements for counting electoral votes created greater clarity in certain sets of circumstances while leaving others unaddressed. Norms and luck, rather than careful statutory design, largely allowed Congress to successfully navigate election uncertainties under the 1887 act in the 133 years between its enactment and the fallout of the 2020 election.

In 1960, Hawaii submitted dueling slates of electors in the 1887 act's first significant test.[32] While initial results gave Vice President Richard Nixon a narrow victory over Senator John F. Kennedy, Kennedy eventually won the state following a recount ordered after the safe harbor date. The recount had not concluded by the time electors were required by law to meet, and Nixon's Hawaiian electors cast their ballots at an official ceremony, with Kennedy's electors performing the same ceremony, unofficially, the same day. Both slates' certificates were submitted to Congress.[33] Once the recount was complete, but after the safe harbor date, the governor of Hawaii sent a third certificate, certifying the Kennedy slate. Vice President Nixon presided over the joint session of Congress, where he remarked, "In order not to delay the further count of the electoral vote here, the Chair, without the intent of establishing a precedent, suggests that the electors named in the certificate of the Governor of Hawaii dated January 4, 1961, be considered as the lawful electors from the State of Hawaii."[34] Hawaii's votes were counted and Congress took no further action to address the uncertified certificate Kennedy's electors submitted before the recount had been completed.[35]

In an effort to draw attention to a particular weakness of the Electoral College, Representative James O'Hara and Senator Edmund S. Muskie, joined by thirty-seven members of the House and six members of the Senate, objected to the vote cast in 1968 by a "faithless elector" from North Carolina who was pledged to Nixon, once again a candidate, but cast a ballot for third-party candidate George Wallace, former governor of Alabama. Vice President Hubert Humphrey presided over the joint session, and the objection was voted on but defeated.[36]

In the 2000 election, with all other states' electoral counts decided for either Vice President Al Gore or Texas governor George W. Bush and as the safe harbor date neared, Florida's electoral votes were certified by the secretary of state but all controversies had not yet been resolved.[37] The Florida State Supreme Court ordered a recount under state law, which the US Supreme Court first stayed and then ruled unconstitutional and violative of Florida election law mere hours before the safe harbor deadline.[38] In its five-to-four decision, the Court reached the questionable conclusion that Florida had expressed an intent to avail itself of the protections afforded by the 1887 act's safe harbor provision.[39] Gore conceded hours later, mooting the controversy before it reached Congress.[40]

When Congress met to count all electoral votes, members of the Congressional Black Caucus objected to the Florida slate due to the disenfranchisement of Black Florida voters.[41] The objections were quickly gaveled down by Vice President Gore, as House members did not have a senator who joined in the objection. Bush was elected without winning the popular vote.

The election of 2000 brought the 1887 act out of obscurity and onto the front pages of newspapers throughout the country. In her dissent in *Bush v. Gore*, Justice Ruth Bader Ginsburg characterized the safe harbor deadline as "lack[ing] the significance the Court assigns it," asserting that the time crunch was due in part to the Court's own actions and would yield a less equitable result than allowing the recount to continue until the Electoral College was scheduled to meet and cast their votes.[42]

The controversy surrounding the Court's decision also brought renewed attention to, and with it scrutiny of, the Electoral College itself and sparked momentum for reform.

President Bush's reelection also came down to the wire. In Ohio, the secretary of state declared Bush the winner of the state's twenty electoral votes one day before the safe harbor deadline, leaving no time for controversies to be resolved.[43] Senator John Kerry did not challenge the result, avoiding a sequel to the constitutional crisis of four years prior.[44]

As Vice President Dick Cheney presided, Representative Stephanie Tubbs Jones and Senator Barbara Boxer objected to the Ohio slate of electors on the grounds of disenfranchisement of Black Ohio voters.[45] The objection was sent to each chamber, with thirty members of the House joining Tubbs Jones in voting to sustain the objection[46] and Boxer the lone vote to sustain in the Senate.[47]

After a tumultuous election in 2016, Donald Trump defeated Secretary of State Hillary Clinton despite losing the popular vote by nearly three million votes.[48] Members of the Progressive Caucus in the House attempted to object to the results of the election, citing voter suppression, improper elector qualifications, and Russian interference.[49] As in 2001, no senators joined the objections, and Vice President Joe Biden gaveled them down, as they could not be entertained under the 1887 act.[50]

In 2021, the many shortcomings of the patchwork of laws and norms governing electoral vote counts would come home to roost.[51] The problems plaguing the post–Election Day period read like the lowlights of past electoral count controversies. In an effort to push states' certifications past the safe harbor deadline, President Trump's campaign filed frivolous lawsuits.[52] Wisconsin failed to meet the deadline, with rival electoral slates meeting concurrently to send certificates to Washington.[53] Republican officials in Wisconsin and four other states sent signed certificates falsely purporting to represent the "duly elected and qualified" electoral votes of their respective states.[54] As the date of the joint session approached, President Trump personally began a pressure campaign on Vice President Mike Pence to take advantage of allegedly vague language in the 1887 act regarding the vice president's role.[55] Meanwhile, Senator Ted Cruz unsuccessfully led a group of eleven senators and senators-elect in calling for an electoral commission to investigate an emergency audit of electoral returns in key states, citing the 1877 Electoral Commission as precedent.[56] Once the joint session was called to order on January 6, 2021, Representative Paul Gosar raised an objection, joined by eight senators and fifty-seven other representatives, to the electoral votes of Arizona.[57] And as each chamber met separately to consider the objection, a violent mob, fueled in part by "misunderstandings about the process established by the [1887] Act,"[58] breached the Capitol and temporarily disrupted the electoral count.[59] The joint session reconvened later that evening, with Joe Biden receiving 306 electoral votes to Trump's 232.

THE ELECTORAL COUNT REFORM ACT OF 2022

Noting President Trump's "corrupt[] attempt[s] to violate the Electoral Count Act of 1887 in an effort to overturn the 2020 Presidential Election," the first recommendation of the final report issued by the Select Committee to Investigate the January 6th Attack on the United States Capitol (Select Committee) directly called for reform to the 1887 act, "to deter other future attempts to overturn Presidential Elections."[60]

The Select Committee specifically called on the House of Representatives to pass the Presidential Election Reform Act (PERA) and the Senate to "act promptly to send a bill with these principles to the President."[61] Both chambers of Congress took up the charge. Substantially similar bipartisan bills were introduced in the Senate (the Electoral Count Reform Act, or ECRA)[62] and the House (PERA).[63] Only the House passed its standalone legislation,[64] but ultimately a version of the Senate's bill became law through the 2023 appropriations omnibus.[65]

These reforms will replace the outdated sticks-and-straw structure of unclear legal text and political norms with statutory brickwork should wolves appear at the electoral count's door again.

ECRA clarifies that the role of the vice president, serving as president of the Senate and presiding over the joint meeting of Congress to tabulate the electoral votes received from the states, is "solely ministerial."[66] In an effort to leave no doubt, ECRA also "explicitly deni[es]" that the vice president has any power to "solely determine, accept, reject, or otherwise adjudicate or resolve disputes over the proper certificate of ascertainment of appointment of electors, the validity of electors, or the votes of electors."[67]

In an effort to eliminate frivolous objections, ECRA raises the threshold for objections to one-fifth of each chamber's membership.[68] Additionally, the revised language limits the grounds for objections to situations in which either there has been unlawful certification of electors or "the vote of one or more electors has not been regularly given."[69] While the objections raised in 1969, 2005, and 2021 all met the previous threshold of one member joining from each chamber, none would have met the revised criteria established by ECRA.[70]

Each state's governor, unless otherwise specified by state law in effect by Election Day, is now identified as the single state official recognized by Congress as authorized to submit the state's certificate of ascertainment. ECRA further provides a procedure by which presidential candidates, and only presidential candidates, can bring a challenge to a state's certificate in the federal district court where the state capital is located. A three-judge panel, consisting of two circuit court judges and one district court judge, will hear the challenge.[71]

With the ability to challenge a governor's certification in federal court, ECRA also addresses the possibility raised by legal scholars of a "rogue governor" recognizing an illegitimate slate of electors and receiving the support of one chamber of Congress.[72] This situation has thankfully not been successfully achieved, but not for lack of trying by President Trump in 2021.[73] At least one vulnerability remains on this front. If a rogue governor sets about delaying certification rather than submitting illegitimate electors, they could put stress on an untested system. Under the new ECRA procedures for judicial review, an expedited review is expressly contemplated. But if a governor or other designated state official has until six days before the electors meet to issue a certificate of ascertainment, "a legal challenge to the certificate would need to be handled with extraordinary speed."[74]

In 1845, Congress established a national election day for the first time and included a provision that if a state "holds an election on the prescribed day but 'fail[s] to make a choice,' it does not forfeit its electors"[75] but is permitted to appoint electors on a later day "in such a manner as the legislature of such State may direct."[76] ECRA replaces this failed election language to more explicitly provide guidance on how to handle an "extraordinary and catastrophic" situation arising in one or more states on Election Day.

ECRA clarifies that electors shall be appointed "in accordance with the laws of the State enacted prior to election day."[77] In *Bush v. Gore*, the majority asserted that "the State, of course, after granting the franchise in the special context of Article II, can take back the power to appoint electors."[78] This has never been attempted by a state, but the theory that a state legislature could take back that power once votes had been cast and choose their own electors "was the heart of Trump's plan" in the weeks leading up to January 6, 2021.[79] Florida governor Ron DeSantis and other conservative commentators directly called on state legislatures to step in after Election Day to overturn the results in their respective states.[80]

In the aftermath of the 2020 election, conservative advocates advanced the independent state legislature theory, that state legislatures have "plenary" power to set the rules for all federal elections, including presidential elections, and therefore would be within their constitutional powers to select their own set of electors regardless of what voters chose.[81] The updated language in ECRA and the Court's rejection of this maximalist reading of Article II has addressed the specific circumstances that arose in the 2020 election.

VULNERABILITIES LEFT UNRESOLVED

While ECRA addressed a significant number of flaws exposed by previous elections, several vulnerabilities remain.

States are under significant stress to meet the federal timetable for certifying elections and avail themselves of the safe harbor provision.[82] With the growing use of mail ballots that, depending on state law, can require extra time after Election Day to process, this pressure is not likely to ease in the near future.[83] And of course, the process is far from over once these ballots, as well as provisional ballots, are processed. The state must then canvass and certify all votes, and in some cases conduct a recount. This creates an unnecessary rush to certify in order to secure safe harbor protection.[84] This pressure was amplified by the Court's decision in *Bush v. Gore*, which read a state's apparent desire to avail itself of the safe harbor provision as determinative while cutting off further legal redress to disenfranchised voters and Gore's campaign.

The gap in time between the safe harbor date and the meeting of the electors was set at a time when the speed of horses and buggies was accounted for in determining the required amount of time to transport certificates to Washington, DC. The issue "can be easily addressed by having Congress push the date for final certification of electors—the 'safe harbor' date—from mid- to late-December and have the electoral college meet closer to the Jan. 6 date on which the certified votes are formally counted"[85] or abolishing the safe harbor provision altogether.[86]

The Twelfth Amendment procedure for a contested election, with each state's delegation in the House allotted one vote, compounds a political imbalance created by the Electoral College[87] itself in "treat[ing] large states and small states on equal terms and, as a result, generat[ing] a conceptually similar . . . bias against contemporary Democrats."[88] The resolution of the 1824 election, with the House selecting John Quincy Adams to become president despite his loss of the popular vote, cast a shadow of illegitimacy on Adams's single term. Numerous constitutional amendments aimed at changing this procedure have been introduced and failed.

The threat of Wallace's third-party candidacy in 1968 to force a contested election was enough to create bipartisan consensus that Electoral College reform was necessary. Indiana senator Birch Bayh first introduced legislation to replace the Electoral College with a national popular vote in 1966, but this effort would not gain traction until Wallace's presidential run. The proposed amendment, introduced by Bayh and Representative Emanuel Celler, would go on to pass the House with bipartisan support by a vote of 338–70. However, the measure fell six votes short of the number needed for cloture in the Senate. Bayh's amendment was the furthest any proposed amendment on Electoral College reform has advanced in modern times, but it was by no means the only attempt at such reform through constitutional amendment. In fact, no issue has been the subject of more proposed amendments. Between 1800 and 2020, more than eight hundred amendments aimed at reforming the Electoral College were introduced in Congress.[89] While Bayh's proposed amendment and several others in recent history have advanced a replacement of the Electoral College with a national popular vote, earlier popular proposals included a proportional system, wherein a state's electoral votes were allocated according to the popular vote of the state, and a district-based system, with electors chosen by congressional district.

Since modern polling on Electoral College reform began in the 1940s, a majority of Americans have consistently supported change.[90] In 2023, that number is nearly two-thirds of US adults, according to Pew Research Center. Congressional interest and public support remain consistent in support of changing the mechanisms by which we elect a president, but the constraints of Article V have proved too strict for this project thus far.

Amending constitutionally required processes was beyond the remit of those who took on the work of reforming the statutory structures that govern our presidential elections after the 2020 election. After months of negotiations on legislation that would potentially reshape the presidential electoral system, it became clear that only a bill narrow in scope would be politically viable in the Senate. Given these political realities, no one could expect ECRA itself to redress the foundational inequalities rooted in constitutional text, but the fact remains that the antidemocratic nature of the Electoral College and the procedures laid out for a contested election create a sense of illegitimacy among many American voters. With ECRA now in place, attention should be afforded to potential reforms to deal with these inequalities.

Similarly, voter suppression remains a significant problem and threat to our pursuit of a multiracial democracy. The Roberts Court has consistently shut the courthouse door in the faces of voters seeking to vindicate their voting rights, often hiding behind procedural rules it created from whole cloth.[91] The legitimacy of an election is rooted in the opportunity of all qualified voters to meaningfully participate. Focusing on the procedure by which electoral votes are counted without any examination or redress of underlying problems with the election system itself is insufficient.

The joint session held to count electoral votes is not the appropriate time to entertain objections beyond a very limited scope, given Congress's proper role in certifying the results of a presidential election and the need to protect the rule of law and peaceful transition of power. The clarification ECRA makes on the limited, acceptable grounds for a proper challenge to a state's electors is welcome. However, we can also recognize the underlying injustices that have motivated members to raise objections in previous years. In *Bush v. Gore*, "the Court's implicit stance is that voters whose votes are counted but improperly weighted lose something that the Constitution protects, but that disenfranchised voters do not."[92] Should we address the shortcomings of the 1887 act with no further action to provide meaningful redress for voter suppression, we risk making the same mistake.

As with the Electoral Count Act of 1887, there was genuine bipartisan support for reform as a direct result of the chaotic aftermath of the 2020 presidential election.[93] This is no small feat at a time when bipartisan legislation has become increasingly rare. It should be celebrated. However, we note that PERA and ECRA were unable to secure passage as standalone legislation by the 117th Congress, and it was only through the vehicle of an omnibus bill incorporating ECRA that reform to the 1887 act was finally passed.[94]

While the Senate never voted on the ECRA provisions alone, the House successfully passed PERA in 2022. Nine Republican members of Congress voted in favor of the bill. All nine have now left Congress, having lost primary elections to right-wing challengers or retired.[95] While polling conducted in 2021 showed that there was strong bipartisan support for updating the 1887 act, with 52 percent of Republican voters polled expressing support,[96] Republican primary voters in 2022 chose candidates who had either questioned or fully rejected the official results of the 2020 election, espousing what has come to be known as the "Big Lie." In the 2022 midterm elections, the *Washington Post* found that a majority of Republican nominees for House, Senate, and key state offices publicly embraced the Big Lie.[97] While some notable Big Lie proponents lost in swing states, many candidates throughout the country were successful.

The 2020 election was the most secure in US history, despite unprecedented challenges created by the COVID-19 pandemic.[98] A series of postelection recounts and "audits" have confirmed the results time and again, and yet disinformation about the election being stolen continues to spread. Conservative political operatives have been actively recruiting proponents of the Big Lie to run for office and take over election administration offices.

Officials from both parties were crucial in conducting a safe and secure election in 2020 and resisting calls to subvert the results from the highest levels of government. In Georgia, Republican secretary of state Brad Raffensperger resisted pressure from the president of the United States and his staff to "find" enough votes to change the outcome of the presidential election.[99] In Michigan, Democratic secretary of state Jocelyn Benson chose to expand access to the ballot box during a global health crisis by sending absentee ballot applications to all eligible voters in the state and in the wake of the election was targeted at her home by angry protesters.[100]

The pressure to subvert our elections and to penalize those who refused to do so has not stopped, with poll workers and secretaries of state continuing to receive threats to themselves and their families and field a wave of inquiries and accusations rooted in conspiracy theories. As a result, there are a record number of administrators retiring, and this has flung open the doors for proponents of the Big Lie to take over these critical positions. This attempted takeover of key election administration positions, including those of governors in their newly clarified role under ECRA, by Big Lie proponents is a threat to the security of our election system. It also threatens the public's faith in our electoral process.

Some scholars seek to address concerns about such state actors subverting the will of the voters by pointing to the federal judiciary as a backstop, but we find little comfort in such a fail-safe. For example, Professor Edward Foley, a preeminent scholar in this space, has argued, "While all of us concerned for the future of democracy should worry about partisan state officials seeking to manipulate the counting of the state's popular vote, we should calibrate our concern so that it is commensurate with the threat. In doing so, we must recognize that the federal judiciary, if it adheres to long-standing principles and precedents, will not permit any state official to proclaim an electoral outcome contrary to what a true count of the ballots would provide."[101] The word "if" in his final sentence is carrying quite a bit of water. We know, and continue to learn, that we cannot assume the federal judiciary will adhere to "long-standing principles and precedents." From recent decisions in *Dobbs v. Jackson Women's Health Organization*[102] to *Kennedy v. Bremerton School District*[103] to *Students for Fair Admissions v. Harvard and UNC*,[104] the Roberts Court has "cast decades of established precedent to the wind" in pursuit of conservative policy objectives.[105]

The potential threat is not limited to the Supreme Court. One recent study showed that federal judges appointed by Trump "are significantly more conservative than judges appointed by other Republican presidents in recent decades."[106] The near-wholesale rejection of the lawsuits filed by Trump's legal team in 2020 is encouraging,[107] but as we've seen historically, "traditional norms of judicial behavior seem to have constrained neither the justices who sat on the 1877 Electoral Commission, nor the Court that decided *Bush v. Gore*."[108] As one side of the political spectrum plays constitutional hardball[109] in an effort to pack the federal judiciary with idealogues, such a systemic constraint should not be ignored.

CONCLUSION

ECRA revises the system by which states certify presidential electors and Congress counts their votes, with the benefit of over two centuries of historical experience to draw on. The legislation's important clarifications and refinements will undoubtedly make the system more secure. But one piece of legislation cannot fully account for vulnerabilities in the system by which we elect a president, and real questions of legitimacy will remain as systemic inequities in the electoral process go unaddressed.

NOTES

The authors would like to thank Christopher Wright Durocher and Claire Collin Comey for their editorial support.

1 U.S. Const. art. II, § 1, cl. 3.
2 U.S. Const. art. II, § 1, cl. 3; U.S. Const. art. I, § 3, cl. 4.
3 U.S. Const. art. II, § 1, cl. 3.
4 Alexander Keyssar, *Why Do We Still Have the Electoral College?* (Cambridge, MA: Harvard University Press, 2020), 17.
5 Keyssar, 17.
6 Bruce Ackerman and David Fontana, "Thomas Jefferson Counts Himself into the Presidency," *Virginia Law Review* 90 (2004): 570–77.
7 Ackerman and Fontana, 577.
8 Ackerman and Fontana, 585.
9 Russ Feingold and Peter Prindiville, *The Constitution in Jeopardy* (New York: Public Affairs, 2022), 80–81.
10 Ackerman and Fontana, "Jefferson Counts," 587–603 (detailing the defects with the certificate submitted by Georgia that created confusion over the acceptability of a certificate clearly out of format but nonetheless reflecting the expected results given the press's reporting on the electoral results in the state).

11 Sanford Levinson and Ernest A. Young, "Who's Afraid of the Twelfth Amendment?," *Florida State University Law Review* 29, no. 2 (Winter 2001): 971.
12 Feingold and Prindiville, *Constitution in Jeopardy*, 81.
13 U.S. Const. amend. XII. The full process by which the House votes should no candidate receive a majority of electoral votes is as follows: "If no person have such majority, then from the persons having the highest numbers not exceeding three on the list of those voted for as President, the House of Representatives shall choose immediately, by ballot, the President. But in choosing the President, the votes shall be taken by states, the representation from each state having one vote." U.S. Const. amend. XII.
14 Thomas H. Neale, *Contingent Election of the President and Vice President by Congress: Perspectives and Contemporary Analysis*, R40504 (Washington, DC: Congressional Research Service, 2020), 8.
15 Ted Widmer, "How Lincoln Survived the Worst Election Ever," *New York Times*, October 30, 2020, www.nytimes.com. See also "Affairs at Washington," *Holmes County Republican* (Millersburg, OH), February 21, 1861, www.loc.gov ("Since the Presidential votes have been counted, and the election formally declared by Mr. Breckenridge [*sic*], the feeling of apprehension about the safety of the Capital is much relieved").
16 L. Kinvin Wroth, "Election Contests and the Electoral Vote," *Dickinson Law Review* 65, no. 4 (1961): 328.
17 Wroth, 328 (citing House Special Committee on Counting Electoral Votes, 44th Cong., 2d Sess., H.R. Misc. Doc. 13, 87-144 [1877]).
18 Wroth, "Election Contests," 329n37.
19 In the case of Louisiana, two different electoral slates were submitted, one with eight abstentions for president as voting took place after Horace Greeley had passed and eight votes for Benjamin Gratz Brown for vice president, Greeley's running mate. This certificate was signed and sealed by Governor Henry Warmoth. The other slate contained eight votes for President Ulysses S. Grant and eight for his running mate. In the final count, no votes were included for Louisiana. Hans Rasmussen, "Infighting, Fusion, and Fraud in the Election of 1872," *Civil War Book Review* 24, no. 4 (2022): 5. Arkansas's electoral votes were determined to have not been certified according to law and not properly appointed.
20 Wroth, "Election Contests," 330.
21 Lawrence Lessig, "The Mess Congress Could Make," *The Atlantic*, October 19, 2020, www.theatlantic.com.
22 John Copeland Nagle, "How Not to Count Votes," *Columbia Law Review* 104 (2004): 1732.
23 Edward Foley, *Ballot Battles* (New York: Oxford University Press, 2016), 8.
24 Nagle, "Count Votes," 1735. In addition to the three Southern states, a controversy arose over the eligibility of one of Hayes's pledged electors from Oregon. Nagle, 1735.
25 Nagle, 1744–45. The commission itself was not embraced by the two candidates. Nagle, 1744.

26 Act of Jan. 29, 1877, ch. 37, § 2, 19 Stat. 227, 229 (granting Congress the authority to object to the commission's report).

27 Chris Land and David Schultz, "On the Unenforceability of the Electoral Count Act," *Rutgers Journal of Law and Policy* 13 (Fall 2016): 353.

28 Eric Foner, *Reconstruction: America's Unfinished Revolution, 1863–1877*, rev. ed. (1988; New York: HarperCollins, 2014), 581.

29 Franita Tolson, "In the Messiest Contested Election, One Man Saved the System from Itself," *New York Times*, November 3, 2020, www.nytimes.com.

30 Roy Morris Jr., *Fraud of the Century: Rutherford B. Hayes, Samuel Tilden, and the Stolen Election of 1876* (New York: Simon and Schuster, 2004), 2.

31 Eric Schickler, Terri L. Bimes, and Robert W. Mickey, "Safe at Any Speed: Legislative Intent, the Electoral Count Act of 1887, and *Bush v. Gore*," *Journal of Law and Politics* 16 (2002): 735.

32 Wroth, "Election Contests," 321.

33 Associated Press, "Electoral College Votes, Kennedy Gets Illinois," *Evening Star* (Washington, DC), December 19, 1960, A6, www.loc.gov.

34 Vice President Nixon, speaking on the electoral votes of Hawaii, 87th Cong., 1st Sess., 107 Cong. Rec., pt. 1, p. 290 (January 6, 1961).

35 Kyle Cheney, "See the 1960 Electoral College Certificates That the False Trump Electors Say Justify Their Gambit," *Politico*, August 25, 2023, www.politico.com.

36 Objection to counting electoral votes from North Carolina, 91st Cong., 1st Sess., 115 Cong. Rec., pt. 1, pp. 146–71 (January 6, 1969).

37 Todd S. Purdum, "Counting the Vote: The Overview; Bush Is Declared Winner in Florida, but Gore Vows to Contest Results," *New York Times*, November 27, 2000, www.nytimes.com.

38 Bush v. Gore, 531 U.S. 98 (2000).

39 *Bush*, 531 U.S. at 111. The Court's other conclusions, including that the recount as ordered by the Florida Supreme Court violated the Equal Protection Clause and that the Court held the ability to overrule a state supreme court's interpretation of state law, are outside the scope of this chapter.

40 "Text of Gore's Concession Speech," *New York Times*, December 13, 2000, www.nytimes.com.

41 Alison Mitchell, "Over Some Objections, Congress Certifies Electoral Vote," *New York Times*, January 7, 2001, www.nytimes.com.

42 *Bush*, 531 U.S. at 143.

43 Daniel P. Tokaji, "An Unsafe Harbor: Recounts, Contests, and the Electoral College," *Michigan Law Review First Impressions* 106 (2008): 86.

44 Matthew Jaffe and Tim Skoczek, "John Kerry: It Was Right for Me to Concede Quickly in 2004," CNN, October 17, 2016, www.cnn.com.

45 Representative Tubbs Jones, speaking on counting electoral votes, 109th Cong., 1st Sess., 151 Cong. Rec. H85–86 (January 6, 2005): "Unfortunately, objecting to the electoral votes from Ohio is the only immediate avenue to bring these issues

to light. . . . I raise this objection because I am convinced that we as a body must conduct a formal and legitimate debate about election irregularities."

46 151 Cong. Rec. H127.

47 Russ Feingold, co-author of this chapter, was a member of the 109th Congress and voted against the objection.

48 Richard Pérez-Peña, "Donald Trump Completes Final Lap, Electoral College, to White House," *New York Times*, December 19, 2016, www.nytimes.com.

49 Counting electoral votes, 115th Cong., 1st Sess., 163 Cong. Rec. H185–90 (January 6, 2017).

50 163 Cong. Rec. H185–90.

51 Even before a single vote had been cast, President Trump rejected the long-established norm of committing to acceptance of an electoral loss and a peaceful transition of power. Felicia Sonmez, "Trump Declines to Say Whether He Will Accept November Election Results," *Washington Post*, July 19, 2020, www.washingtonpost.com. The myriad conspiracy theories and disinformation peddled by Trump and his camp could and undoubtedly will fill volumes. We limit ourselves in this subsection to a discussion of the 1887 act's interaction with the relevant theories advanced in the aftermath of the 2020 presidential election.

52 Katherine Shaw, "A Mystifying and Distorting Factor: The Electoral College and American Democracy," *Michigan Law Review* 120 (2022): 6.

53 Molly Beck, "With Case Pending in State Court, Wisconsin Is Only State to Miss Election Safe-Harbor Deadline," *Milwaukee Journal Sentinel*, December 9, 2020, www.jsonline.com.

54 Kyle Cheney and Nicholas Wu, "'Dangerous Precedent': Jan. 6 Committee Trains Its Sights on False Pro-Trump Electors," *Politico*, January 21, 2022, www.politico.com. Republican officials in two additional states submitted certificates that contained a qualifier that their votes should only be counted if Trump's legal challenges to their respective states' results ultimately prove successful. Trump's role in organizing these "fraudulent slates of electors" is cited as evidence of his conspiracy to defraud the United States, as charged by the Department of Justice in ongoing litigation. Indictment, United States v. Donald J. Trump, No. 23-257 (D.D.C. filed Aug. 1, 2023).

55 Brian Naylor, "Pence Says Trump Is Wrong to Insist VP Could Have Overturned Election Results," NPR, February 4, 2022, www.npr.org.

56 "Joint Statement from Senators Cruz, Johnson, Lankford, Daines, Kennedy, Blackburn, Braun, Senators-Elect Lummis, Marshall, Hagerty, Tuberville," Office of Ted Cruz, January 2, 2021, www.cruz.senate.gov. See also Elizabeth Thompson, "Cruz Makes 'Historically Misleading' Comparison in Citing 1876 as Precedent for Special Inquiry on Biden's Electoral Win," *Dallas Morning News*, January 4, 2021, www.dallasnews.com.

57 117th Cong., 1st Sess., 167 Cong. Rec. H77 (January 6, 2021).

58 Matthew A. Seligman, "Disputed Presidential Elections and the Collapse of Constitutional Norms," SSRN, November 13, 2018, 64, https://papers.ssrn.com.

59 117th Cong., 1st Sess., 167 Cong. Rec. H77 (January 6, 2021).
60 Select Comm. to Investigate the Jan. 6th Attack on the US Capitol, H.R. Rep. No. 117-000, 689 (2022).
61 Presidential Election Reform Act, H.R. 8873, 117th Cong., 2d Sess. (2022).
62 Electoral Count Reform and Presidential Transition Improvement Act of 2022, S. 4573, 117th Cong., 2d Sess. (2022).
63 For a comparison of the two bills, see Andy Craig, "Lofgren, Cheney Introduce Bill to Reform the Electoral Count Act," Cato Institute, September 20, 2022, www.cato.org.
64 Presidential Election Reform Act Roll Call 449, H.R. 8873, 117th Cong., 2d Sess. (2022), https://clerk.house.gov.
65 Consolidated Appropriations Act of 2023, Pub. L. No. 117-328, § P (2022).
66 3 U.S.C. § 15(b)(1).
67 3 U.S.C. § 15(b)(2). These clarifications address the concerns that arose over Breckenridge's ability to interfere with the electoral count on the eve of the Civil War and Pence's ability to do the same in 2021. Rather than rely on the intuitions and political motivations of Jefferson and Nixon in analogous circumstances as historical precedent, the new language in ECRA creates a formal process by which to resolve potential disputes and defines the vice president's role in doing so.
68 3 U.S.C. § 15(d)(2)(B)(i).
69 3 U.S.C. § 15(d)(2)(B)(ii).
70 Some scholars have argued that this raised bar is still too low given the fact that nearly one-third of House members voted to sustain an objection to Arizona's electoral slate in 2021. See, e.g., Lawrence H. Tribe, Erwin Chemerinsky, and Dennis Aftergut, "The Electoral Count Act Must Be Fixed. A New Proposal Doesn't Go Far Enough," *Washington Post*, August 1, 2022, www.washingtonpost.com.
71 This process mirrors the one established in the Bipartisan Campaign Reform Act of 2002, Pub. L. No. 107-155 (commonly known as the McCain-Feingold Act).
72 Adam Edelman and Peter Nicholas, "'Rogue Governor' Scenario Spooks Senators Working to Prevent Stolen Elections," NBC News, May 5, 2022, www.nbcnews.com.
73 Indictment, Georgia v. Donald John Trump, No. 23SC188947, 2023 WL 6309346 (Ga. Sup. Ct. filed Aug. 14, 2023). Other situations that would have benefited from the clarity and judicial review process provided in this section of ECRA include the uncertainty caused by defective electoral certificates in 1801, and the conflicting state certificates filed in 1872, 1876, and 1960.
74 3 U.S.C. § 5(a)(1); Thomas A. Berry, "Some Potential Improvements to the Electoral Count Reform Act," CATO Institute, July 27, 2022, www.cato.org.
75 Richard D. Friedman, "Trying to Make Peace with *Bush v. Gore*," *Florida State Law Review* 29 (2001): 816.
76 3 U.S.C. § 2 (repealed 2022). The repeal of this provision should eliminate claims that a state has failed to make a choice because votes were not perceived to have been counted and certified fast enough, as was argued in the weeks after Election Day in 2020.

77 3 U.S.C. § 1.
78 *Bush*, 531 U.S. at 104.
79 Barton Gellman, "Trump's Next Coup Has Already Begun," *The Atlantic*, December 6, 2021, www.theatlantic.com.
80 Zac Anderson, "Florida Republicans Rally around Trump as He Claims Voter Fraud," *Sarasota Herald-Tribune*, November 6, 2020, www.heraldtribune.com.
81 J. Michael Luttig, "Opinion: The Republican Blueprint to Steal the 2024 Election," CNN, April 27, 2022, www.cnn.com. The Supreme Court rightfully rejected the legal fiction of the independent state legislature theory in its recent decision in *Moore v. Harper*. Moore v. Harper, 600 U.S. 1 (2023).
82 Tokaji, "Unsafe Harbor," 88.
83 For a comprehensive list of when each state can begin processing mail ballots, see "Voting outside the Polling Place: Absentee, All-Mail and Other Voting at Home Options, Table 16: When Absentee/Mail Ballot Processing and Counting Can Begin," National Conference of State Legislatures, January 18, 2023, www.ncsl.org.
84 Tokaji, "Unsafe Harbor," 86–88.
85 Tribe, Chemerinsky, and Aftergut, "Electoral Count Act." One such proposal was introduced by Senator Marco Rubio in 2020 but gained no traction. Safe Harbor Extension Act, S. 4517, 116th Cong. (2020).
86 Presidential Election Reform Act of 2022, § 6. See also Andy Craig, "How to Pick a President: A Guide to Electoral Count Act Reform," CATO Institute, June 28, 2022, www.cato.org ("[The safe harbor mechanism] is a failed idea whose purposes can be better achieved in other ways").
87 Kate Shaw, "The Other Cause of January 6," *The Atlantic*, June 10, 2022, www.theatlantic.com.
88 Jonathan S. Gould and David E. Pozen, "Structural Biases in Structural Constitutional Law," *New York University Law Review* 97 (2022): 116.
89 Feingold and Prindiville, *Constitution in Jeopardy*, 80.
90 Keyssar, *Why Do We?*, 1.
91 David Gans, "The Roberts Court, the Shadow Docket, and the Unraveling of Voting Rights Remedies," American Constitution Society, October 2020, www.acslaw.org.
92 Peter M. Shane, "Disappearing Democracy: How *Bush v. Gore* Undermined the Federal Right to Vote for Presidential Electors," *Florida State Law Review* 29 (2001): 538.
93 Donna Brazile and Michael Steele, "The Bipartisan Reform of the Electoral Count Act Is No Coincidence," *The Hill*, December 23, 2022, https://thehill.com.
94 The 1887 act similarly experienced multiple false starts before passage. For a thorough examination of the legislative history of the 1887 act, see Schickler, Bimes, and Mickey, "Safe at Any Speed."
95 Andrew Solender, "House Passes Jan. 6 Panel's Bill to Reform Electoral Count Act," Axios, September 21, 2022, www.axios.com.
96 "Bipartisan Poll Finds Strong Support for Updating the Electoral Count Act," Campaign Legal Center, October 27, 2021, https://campaignlegal.org.

97 Amy Gardner, "A Majority of GOP Nominees Deny or Question the 2020 Election Results," *Washington Post*, October 12, 2022, www.washingtonpost.com.

98 "Joint Statement from Elections Infrastructure Government Coordinating Council & the Election Infrastructure Sector Coordinating Executive Committees," press release, Cybersecurity and Infrastructure Security Agency, November 12, 2020, www.cisa.gov.

99 Michael D. Shear and Stephanie Saul, "Trump, in Taped Call, Pressured Georgia Official to 'Find' Votes to Overturn Election," *New York Times*, May 26, 2021, www.nytimes.com.

100 Arit John, "State Election Officials Survived Trump's Attacks. Will They Survive the Ballot Box?," *Los Angeles Times*, February 8, 2022, www.latimes.com.

101 Edward B. Foley, "As Part of Electoral Count Act Reform, Liberals Should Learn to Love *Bush v. Gore*," *Lawfare*, February 4, 2022, www.lawfaremedia.org.

102 Dobbs v. Jackson Women's Health Organization, 142 S. Ct. 2228 (2022).

103 Kennedy v. Bremerton School District, 142 S. Ct. 2407 (2022).

104 Students for Fair Admissions v. Harvard and UNC, 600 U.S. 181 (2023).

105 Aziz Huq, "No, the Roberts Court Is Not Moderating," *Time*, July 6, 2023, https://time.com.

106 Kenneth L. Manning, Robert A. Carp, and Lisa M. Holmes, "The Decision-Making Ideology of Federal Judges Appointed by President Trump," in *Judicial Process in America*, 12th ed. (forthcoming), https://papers.ssrn.com.

107 See Rosalind S. Helderman and Elise Viebeck, "'The Last Wall': How Dozens of Judges across the Political Spectrum Rejected Trump's Efforts to Overturn the Election," *Washington Post*, December 12, 2020, www.washingtonpost.com.

108 Stephen A. Siegel, "The Conscientious Congressman's Guide to the Electoral Count Act of 1887," *Florida Law Review* 56, no. 3 (2004): 566.

109 Mark Tushnet, "Constitutional Hardball," *John Marshall Law Review* 37 (2004): 523.

EPILOGUE

KAREN J. GREENBERG AND JULIAN E. ZELIZER

Nearly four years after the horror of January 6, 2021, when a violent mob exposed just how far certain elements in American politics are willing to go to achieve victory, the risks to our democratic system remain clear. The stability of the voting system and the transfer of power are vulnerable. If enough bad actors are willing to challenge the results of the democratic will, it is possible to undermine the collective decision. Efforts to protect the ability of Americans to fully participate in the decision-making process, moreover, have eroded since the landmark victory of the civil rights movement in 1965 with the Voting Rights Act.

And the insecurity of our democratic system means that our national security is at risk. If the electoral system is not sound, we cannot count on a government that will be able to make decisions about war and peace, both at home and abroad, with confidence. The legitimacy of the elected officials who are responsible for making key decisions will never be strong in vast parts of the electorate. Moreover, the nation's adversaries—from overseas governments intent on threatening our safety to national militia groups seeking to overturn our constitutional system—will continue to perceive weakness and be tempted to try exploiting our fragility to strengthen themselves.

Some of the risks that our democracy faces are products of the moment. They grow out of the intensified political polarization that has diminished the number of elected officials who are able to bridge the red and blue divide. As feelings of political difference have worsened, the cost of electing leaders from the other side of the aisle has seemed more dangerous and intolerable. The willingness to do whatever it takes to prevent that outcome has become greater. As the GOP has radicalized with leaders such as former president Donald Trump, moreover, there has been one major party that understood acceptable tactics to include restricting the franchise, despite constant warnings of the detrimental racial impact of doing so, and embracing election denialism as a defining theme.

But the risks also grow out of much broader and more long-term problems that are intrinsic to our national political culture and the design of our institutions. The authors in this book have attempted to explore the problem of election security through this wide-angle lens. They have probed the original structure of our elections, inscribed in the Constitution, which has perpetually opened the door to great instability on Election Day, starting as early as 1800 when the nation had barely taken form. They remind us of how the localism and federalism that has been so central to the manner in which we determine our leadership has created multiple points where it is possible to create dysfunction. Although we love to boast of the great democratic pulses that have shaped the nation, antidemocratic ideologies have been equally powerful throughout American history, pushing back against efforts to broaden the franchise.

Reform to secure our elections must start at the institutional level. Our authors have endeavored to heed the call of the moment by providing us with a fresh look at the fragility of our electoral process so that reform can begin. The argument of most of the authors in these pages suggests that the best path toward fulfilling the promise of the founding would be to address key institutional weaknesses. Together, the wisdom gathered here suggests that a more secure future is possible. Congress has started some of this work through the Electoral Count Reform Act of 2022, which tightened up processes in which Trump's allies were being pressured, and had the potential, to reverse the vote in states. These were problems that had emerged during several elections over the course of American history. Reforms that curb disinformation, improve election administration, and secure voting rights for all Americans will all be essential to the stability of the system.

The authors also make clear that institutional reform alone cannot save us. Yes, systemic changes can make it more difficult for individuals to subvert our democracy. Derelict actors, however, will always be able to find ways to undermine what has been built. In the end, the decisions that voters make about who should be their leaders at the national and local levels will always be essential to the sanctity of democracy and to ensuring that, next time around, they will still have the ability to vote.

ACKNOWLEDGMENTS

We would like to thank the many people and organizations that made this book possible. First, we want to thank all the contributors who made this book such a pleasure to write. They were smart, reliable, and engaged, always thinking of the collective rather than the individual.

We also want to thank Princeton University's Center for Collaborative History and the School of Public and International Affairs for providing the funding that we needed to hold a weekend conference where authors discussed drafts of the chapters. Bernadette Yeager and Jennifer Loessey were essential to making sure that everything ran smoothly. Thanks as well to Fordham University School of Law's Center on National Security for its generous assistance.

Finally, thanks to NYU Press and Clara Platter, who have been enthusiastic about the book from the start and moved it to completion with diligence, care, and speed.

ABOUT THE CONTRIBUTORS

KAREEM CRAYTON is Senior Director for Voting and Representation at the Brennan Center for Justice at NYU Law School. A seasoned expert on the intersection of law, politics, and race, Crayton has served on law and political science faculties across the country and written more than two dozen publications that explore the connections between race and politics in governmental institutions. During the 2020 redistricting cycle, he advised nearly a dozen local jurisdictions, commissions, and legislative caucuses on legal and policy matters. Additionally, he has influenced key developments in political representation in the south, served as special counsel and chief of staff to the Democratic house leader in the Alabama legislature during its special session on redistricting and later hiring and training a litigation team in a regional public law firm to argue in two key gerrymandering cases before the US Supreme Court. A native of Montgomery, Alabama, Crayton is a magna cum laude graduate of Harvard College and holds a doctorate in political science and a law degree from Stanford University.

THOMAS B. EDSALL is a columnist for the *New York Times*. He has been a weekly contributor to the Opinion section since 2011. He covered politics for the *Washington Post* from 1981 to 2006, and before that for the *Baltimore Sun* and the *Providence Journal*. He has written five books: *The Age of Austerity*; *Building Red America*; *Chain Reaction: The Impact of Race, Rights, and Taxes on American Politics*; *Power and Money: Writing about Politics*; and *The New Politics of Inequality*. From 2006 to 2014 he held the Joseph Pulitzer II and Edith Pulitzer Moore Chair in Public Affairs Journalism at the Columbia University Graduate School of Journalism. He has been a contributing writer for the *New York Review of Books*, *The New Republic*, *The Atlantic*, *National Journal*, the *Washington Monthly*, *Harper's*, *Dissent*, and other magazines. He has won the Carey McWilliams Award of the American Political Science Association and the Noel Markwell Media Award and was a Pulitzer finalist in 1992 in General Nonfiction.

RUSS FEINGOLD is President of the American Constitution Society. He served as a US senator for Wisconsin from 1993 to 2011 and a Wisconsin state senator from 1983 to 1993. From 2013 to 2015, he served as the US special envoy to the Great Lakes Region of Africa and the Democratic Republic of the Congo. During his eighteen years in the US Senate, Feingold was ranked sixth in the Senate for bipartisan voting. He is a recipient of the John F. Kennedy Profile in Courage Award, and he co-sponsored the Bipartisan Campaign Reform Act (McCain-Feingold Act), the only major piece of campaign finance reform legislation passed into law in decades. He was the only senator to vote against the initial enactment of the USA PATRIOT Act during the first vote on the legislation and was well known for his opposition to the Iraq War and as the Senate's leading opponent of the death penalty. He served on the Judiciary, Foreign Relations, Budget, and Intelligence Committees. Feingold was chairman or ranking member of the Constitution Subcommittee. He is the honorary ambassador for the Campaign for Nature, which is a global effort calling on policymakers to commit to address the growing biodiversity crisis. The campaign sought a science-driven, ambitious new deal for nature at the Fifteenth Meeting of the Conference of the Parties to the UN Convention on Biological Diversity in Kunming, China, in 2021. Feingold recently co-authored *The Constitution in Jeopardy: An Unprecedented Effort to Rewrite Our Fundamental Law and What We Can Do about It* with Peter Prindiville. Feingold also is the author of *While America Sleeps: A Wake-Up Call for the Post-9/11 Era* and contributes regularly to various publications such as the *New York*

Times, the *Washington Post*, and *The Guardian*. He appears frequently on MSNBC and CNN.

John C. Fortier is a senior fellow at the American Enterprise Institute, where he focuses on Congress and elections, election administration, election demographics, voting (and absentee voting), the US presidency, and the Electoral College. He is also continuing his work on the continuity of government. He is the author and editor of *After the People Vote: A Guide to the Electoral College*, *Second-Term Blues: How George W. Bush Governed*, and *Absentee and Early Voting: Trends, Promises and Perils*. A prolific writer, Fortier has been published in scholarly journals and the popular press, including *Politico* and *The Hill*. He is a frequent guest on radio and television, and he has appeared on ABC News, Bloomberg, BBC News, C-SPAN, CBS News, CNN, Fox News, NBC News' *Today*, National Public Radio, and *PBS NewsHour*, among others.

Matthew N. Green is Professor of Politics at the Catholic University of America. His recent books include *Newt Gingrich: The Rise and Fall of a Party Entrepreneur*, co-authored with Jeffrey Crouch; *Legislative Hardball: The House Freedom Caucus and the Power of Threat-Making in Congress*; and *Choosing the Leader: Leadership Elections in the U.S. House of Representatives*, co-authored with Doug Harris. He has also published articles in a number of scholarly journals, including *Legislative Studies Quarterly*, *Political Research Quarterly*, and *American Politics Research*.

Karen J. Greenberg is Director of the Center on National Security at Fordham Law. Her most recent book is *Subtle Tools: The Dismantling of American Democracy from the War on Terror to Donald Trump*. Her books include *Rogue Justice: The Making of the Security State* and *The Least Worst Place: Guantanamo's First One Hundred Days*. She has edited many volumes, including *Reimagining the National Security State: Liberalism on the Brink*, *The Enemy Combatant Papers: American Justice, the Courts, and the War on Terror*, *The Torture Papers: The Road to Abu Ghraib*, and *The Torture Debate in America*. She is Editor in Chief of the *CNS Soufan Group Morning Brief* and the *Aon Cyber Brief*. Her work has been featured in the *New York Times*, the *Washington Post*, the *Los*

Angeles Times, the *San Francisco Chronicle*, *The Nation*, the *National Interest*, *Mother Jones*, *The Atlantic*, the *New Republic*, the *American Prospect*, and TomDispatch.com, as well as on major news channels. She is a permanent member of the Council on Foreign Relations, a Future Security Initiative Research Fellow at New America, and a visiting fellow at the Soufan Center.

RICHARD L. HASEN, Professor of Law and Political Science at UCLA School of Law, is an internationally recognized expert in election law, writing as well in the areas of legislation and statutory interpretation, remedies, and torts. He directs UCLA Law's Safeguarding Democracy Project. His newest book is *A Real Right to Vote: How a Constitutional Amendment Can Safeguard American Democracy.*

NICOLE HEMMER is associate professor of history and director of the Carolyn T. and Robert M. Rogers Center for the American Presidency at Vanderbilt University. She is the author of *Messengers of the Right: Conservative Media and the Transformation of American Politics* and *Partisans: The Conservative Revolutionaries Who Remade American Politics in the 1990s*. She cofounded Made by History, the historical analysis section at the *Washington Post*, and has been a columnist at a number of national and international outlets. She cohosts the podcasts *Past Present* and *This Day in Esoteric Political History.*

JULILLY KOHLER-HAUSMANN is Associate Professor of History and American Studies at Cornell University. She studies the United States, with a focus on political, legal, social, and women's history after World War II. Her first book, *Getting Tough: Welfare and Imprisonment in 1970s America*, won Honorable Mention for the 2018 Frederick Jackson Turner Award from the Organization of American Historians and was listed as one of "CHOICE's Outstanding Academic Titles for 2017." Kohler-Hausmann's research has been supported by numerous fellowships, such as those of the Charles Warren Center for Studies in American History at Harvard University, the American Association of University Women, the American Council of Learned Societies, and the Institute for Advanced Study in Princeton. She is currently writing a history of US democracy since the 1965 Voting Rights Act that centers those people assumed to be outside politics: those who did not or could not vote.

LINDSAY LANGHOLZ is Senior Director of Policy and Program at the American Constitution Society. In this capacity, she works with legal scholars and advocates to protect and expand the right to vote, ensure that our elections are fair and accessible, and promote laws and policies that protect individual liberty and address inequality resulting from discrimination. Before joining ACS, Langholz directed voter protection programs on behalf of two presidential campaigns, a national party, and two state party organizations. She has also advised nonprofit voting rights organizations, managed several political campaigns, and worked as a campaign coordinator for the AFL-CIO.

TREVOR W. MORRISON is the Eric M. and Laurie B. Roth Professor of Law and Dean Emeritus at New York University School of Law. He teaches and writes in the areas of constitutional law and the federal court system, with a particular focus on the constitutional separation of powers, presidential power, and legal interpretation within the executive branch. His scholarly publications cover a wide range of topics, including the role that the historical practice of the political branches plays in structuring the constitutional separation of powers, the extent to which (and mechanisms through which) law constrains the president, and the norms of legal advice-giving within the executive branch. He served as Dean of NYU Law from 2013 to 2022. Before that, he was on the faculties of Cornell Law School and then Columbia Law School. Outside academia, he has served in the White House Counsel's Office and the Justice Department's Office of Legal Counsel and Office of the Solicitor General, and as a law clerk to Judge Betty Binns Fletcher of the US Court of Appeals for the Ninth Circuit and to Justice Ruth Bader Ginsburg of the US Supreme Court. He is also Of Counsel at the law firm Kaplan Hecker & Fink LLP.

NATHANIEL PERSILY is the James B. McClatchy Professor of Law at Stanford Law School, with appointments in the departments of Political Science, Communication, and FSI. Persily's scholarship and legal practice focus on the "law of democracy," which addresses issues such as voting rights, political parties, campaign finance, redistricting, and election administration. He has served as a special master or court-appointed expert to craft congressional or legislative districting plans for Georgia, Maryland, Connecticut, New Hampshire, New York, North Carolina, and Pennsylvania. He also served as Senior Research Director for the Presidential Commission on Election Administration. In addition to dozens of articles on the legal regulation of political parties, issues surrounding the census and redistricting process, voting rights, and campaign finance reform, Persily is co-author of the leading election law casebook, *The Law of Democracy: Legal Structure of the Political Process* (with Samuel Issacharoff, Pamela Karlan, Richard Pildes and Franita Tolson). His current work, for which he has been honored as a Guggenheim Fellow, an Andrew Carnegie Fellow, and a Fellow at the Center for Advanced Study in the Behavioral Sciences, examines the impact of emerging technologies, such as artificial intelligence, on political communication, campaigns, and election administration.

RICHARD H. PILDES is one of the nation's leading scholars of constitutional law and a specialist in legal issues affecting democracy. He is a member of the American Academy of Arts and Sciences and the American Law Institute, and he has received recognition as a Guggenheim Fellow and a Carnegie Scholar. His acclaimed casebook, *The Law of Democracy: Legal Structure of the Political Process* (now in its sixth edition), helped create an entirely new field of study in the law schools. *The Law of Democracy* systematically explores legal and policy issues concerning the structure of democratic elections and institutions, such as the role of money in politics, the design of election districts, the regulation of political parties, the design of voting systems, the representation of minority interests in democratic institutions, and similar issues. He has written extensively on the rise of political polarization in the United States, the Voting Rights Act, the dysfunction of America's political processes, the role of the Supreme Court in overseeing American democracy, and the powers of the American president and Congress, and he has criticized excessively "romantic" understandings of democracy. In addition to his scholarship on these issues, he has written on national security law, the design of the regulatory state, and American constitutional history and theory. Respect for his expertise in these areas is reflected in frequent citations of his work in US Supreme Court opinions, the translation of his work into many languages, and his frequent public lectures and appearances around the world, including his nomination with the NBC News team for an Emmy Award for coverage of the 2000 presidential election litigation. His work has been translated into Chinese, French, Spanish, and Portuguese. In addition to his scholarship, Pildes plays an active role litigating in his areas of expertise. He has won two cases before the US Supreme Court, including a 2015 victory in *Alabama Democratic Conference v. Alabama*, a case involving race and redistricting. He served as counsel to a group of former chairpeople of the Securities and Exchange Commission in litigation defending the constitutionality of the Sarbanes-Oxley Act; as counsel in election litigation to the Puerto Rico Electoral Commission; as counsel to the government of Puerto Rico; as a federal court-appointed independent expert on voting rights litigation; and as counsel in successful Supreme Court litigation that challenged the way the United States Tax Court operated. He was also a senior legal adviser to the 2008 and 2012 campaigns of President Barack Obama. Pildes received his AB in physical chemistry summa cum laude from Princeton and his JD magna cum laude from Harvard, where he served as Supreme Court Note Editor on the *Harvard Law Review*. He clerked for Judge Abner J. Mikva of the US Court of Appeals for the District of Columbia Circuit and for Justice Thurgood Marshall of the US Supreme Court. After practicing law in Boston, he began his academic career at the University of Michigan Law School, before joining the NYU School of Law in 2001.

Charles Stewart III is the Kenan Sahin Distinguished Professor of Political Science at MIT and a fellow of the American Academy of Arts and Sciences. His research and teaching interests include American politics, elections, legislative politics, and American political development. For over a decade, he has been a member and codirector of the Caltech/MIT Voting Technology Project; in 2017, he founded the MIT Election Data and Science Lab, which is dedicated to the scientific analysis of election administration and closer collaborations between academic researchers and election practitioners to improve the practice of elections in the United States.

JEREMI SURI holds the Mack Brown Distinguished Chair for Leadership in Global Affairs at the University of Texas at Austin. He is the author and editor of eleven books on politics and foreign policy, most recently *Civil War by Other Means: America's Long and Unfinished Fight for Democracy*. His other books include *The Impossible Presidency: The Rise and Fall of America's Highest Office*; *Liberty's Surest Guardian: American Nation-Building from the Founders to Obama*; *Henry Kissinger and the American Century*; and *Power and Protest: Global Revolution and the Rise of Détente*. His writings have appeared on CNN.com and in the *New York Times*, the *Washington Post*, the *Wall Street Journal*, *The Atlantic*, and *Foreign Affairs*, as well as other media. Suri hosts a weekly podcast, *This Is Democracy*.

MICHAEL WALDMAN is President and CEO of the Brennan Center for Justice at NYU School of Law, a nonpartisan law and policy institute that works to strengthen the systems of democracy and justice. His books include *The Supermajority: How the Supreme Court Divided America*, *The Fight to Vote* (a *Washington Post* notable nonfiction book for 2016), and *The Second Amendment: A Biography*. Waldman served as Assistant to the President and Director of Speechwriting for President Bill Clinton from 1995 to 1999, and previously he was Special Assistant to the President for Policy Coordination from 1993 to 1995. He served as a member of the Presidential Commission on the Supreme Court of the United States. Waldman is a graduate of Columbia College and NYU School of Law.

JULIAN E. ZELIZER is the Malcolm Stevenson Forbes, Class of 1941, Professor of History and Public Affairs at Princeton University. He is also a CNN political analyst and a contributor on NPR's *Here and Now*. He is the award-winning author or editor of twenty-five books, including *The Fierce Urgency of Now: Lyndon Johnson, Congress, and the Battle for the Great Society*, the winner of the D. B. Hardeman Prize for the Best Book on Congress; *Fault Lines: A History of the United States since 1974* (co-authored); and *Burning Down the House: Newt Gingrich, the Fall of a Speaker, and the Rise of the New Republican Party*. The *New York Times* named the last book an Editor's Choice and one of the 100 Notable Books in 2020. His most recent books are *Abraham*

Joshua Heschel: A Life of Radical Amazement; *The Presidency of Donald J. Trump: A First Historical Assessment*, which he edited; and the *New York Times* best seller *Myth America: Historians Take on the Biggest Lies and Legends about Our Past*, which he co-edited with Kevin Kruse. His newest book, *In Defense of Partisanship*, is forthcoming. Zelizer, who has published over 1,300 op-eds, has received fellowships from the Brookings Institution, the Guggenheim Foundation, the Russell Sage Foundation, the New-York Historical Society, and New America.

INDEX

Abramowitz, Alan, 95
Abrams, Stacey, 249
absentee ballots, during 2020 US presidential election, 202–3
activism, judicial, in Supreme Court, 149–53
Adams, John, 14, 147, 310
Adams, John Quincy, 15, 312, 320
affective polarization: Democratic Party and, 164; nominations process and, 183; political partisanship and, 164–66; Republican Party and, 164
Affordable Care Act, US (2010), 149
Afghanistan, US foreign policy interference in, 61–63
Alabama: civil rights movement in, 38–39; gerrymandered districts in, 153, 243–44; Republican Party in, 153
Alaska, party primary system in, 175–77
Alito, Samuel (Justice), 44, 149, 161n41
Allen, James, 228
Allen v. Milligan, 50, 153
Allen v. State Board of Elections, 41
American Enterprise Institute, 303
American Legislative Exchange Council, 226
American National Election Studies, 94, 100
Anderson, Sarah, 174
Arizona: ballot issues in, 207–8; Cyber Ninjas in, 204; objections to Electoral College votes in, 140n35; restrictive voting laws in, 51; "Sharpiegate" in, 204, 207; state role in election subversion, 258–59; 2020 election conspiracies in, 204–5
Arkansas, election laws in, 205
"Australian ballot," 220
authoritarian governments, as US national security risk, 3–4
authority. *See* presidential authority

Baker, Ella, 244
Baker v. Carr, 20, 40, 148
ballot-marking device (BMD), 275, 278, 284
ballots, balloting and: absentee ballots, 202–3; in Arizona, 207–8; "Australian ballot," 220; mail-in voting of, 48–49; paper, 275–76; purity of, 222; secret, 285–86; write-in, 199
Barrett, Amy Coney (Justice), 145

Bauer, Bob, 27, 200
Bayh, Birch, 133–34, 320
behavioral extremism, 185n12
Benson, Jocelyn, 322–23
Biden, Hunter, 85–86, 211
Biden, Joe, 24–28, 85, 316; election denialism and, 51; International Emergency Economic Powers Act and, 110–12; on US democracy, 11. *See also* 2020 US presidential election; 2024 US presidential election
"Big Lie," 216–17, 322
Bipartisan Policy Center, 122
Bjorkman, Jesse, 176–77
Black Americans: elected to public office, 41, 147; Great Migration for, 35, 245; migration movement to Georgia, 245; migration movement to Texas, 245; violence against during civil rights movement, 37–39, 56, 244–45; voter discrimination against, 47; voter registration numbers after VRA, 41; World War II veterans, 35. *See also* Black voters; civil rights movement; historically Black colleges and universities; slavery, slave trade and
"black box" systems, 271
Black communities, in US: Jim Crow laws in, 2, 33–34; literacy tests for voting access, 20, 34, 147–48; poll taxes and, 20, 34; voter suppression in, 43; voting restrictions on, 3, 5, 33–34. *See also* historically Black colleges and universities
Black Power movement, 91
Black voters, political partisanship responses to, 35
"Bloody Sunday," 39
BMD. *See* ballot-marking device
Boies, David, 11–12
Boxer, Barbara, 134, 316
Branch, Taylor, 36
Brazil, US foreign policy interference in, 61
Brnovich v. DNC, 151, 208
Brooks, Mo, 136
Brown, Benjamin Gratz, 325n19
Brown v. Board of Education, 193
Buchanan, Vern, 132–33
Buckley, William F., Jr., 226–27, 229
Buckley v. Valeo, 151–52, 157
Burdick v. Takushi, 199
Burger, Warren, 151
Burgess, John, 18
Burr, Aaron, 14, 311
Bush, George H. W., 44, 134, 224; resistance to National Voter Registration Act, 131; white voter support for, 98
Bush, George W., 21–27, 84, 99, 137–38, 149, 232, 315; foreign policy of, 62; opposition to gay marriage rights, 92–93. *See also* 2000 US presidential election; 2004 US presidential election
Bush v. Gore, 21–25, 45, 98, 154, 161n41, 324; Electoral Count Reform Act and, 26–27, 319, 321–22; Help America Vote Act and, 195–201; Supreme Court's activist role in, 149, 196
Butler, Daniel, 174

California: mail voting in, 48–49, 203; misinformation campaigns in, 80–81; Proposition 187, 80–81; state role in election subversion, 258
campaign finance laws, 5–6; *Buckley v. Valeo*, 151–52, 157; *Citizens United* case, 151–52, 158; donor ideology and, 177–78; For the People Act and, 178–79; for political action committees, 178; political extremism and, 177–80; public funding of elections, 178–79
Canes-Wrone, Brandice, 170
Capitol attacks, on January 6th, 2021, 49, 216–17; congressional hearings on, 1
Cardin, Ben, 77–79
Carmines, Edward G., 90

U.S. v. Carolene Products Company, 148
Carter, Jimmy, 45, 196; voter registration reform and, 223–24, 229
CBC. *See* Congressional Black Caucus
Celler, Emanuel, 320
Census Bureau, federal administration of elections and, 115–16
Central Intelligence Agency (CIA): foreign operations by, 58–59; involvement in French elections, 59–60; involvement in Italian elections, 58–59
Chain Reaction (Edsall), 90–91
Cheney, Dick, 316
Cheney, Liz, 176
Chiafolo v. Washington, 300
Child, Julia, 58
Chile, US foreign policy interference in, 61
China: US foreign policy and, 62; US interference in leadership selection, 63
Choice Not an Echo, A (Schlafly), 93
CIA. *See* Central Intelligence Agency
citizenship: conditional, 217–21; contractarian conceptions of, 233; egalitarian ideals for, 218; historically Black colleges and universities as influence on, 242; voting restrictions through, 116
Citizens United v. Federal Elections Commission, 151–52, 158
Civil Rights Act, US (1957), 36
Civil Rights Act, US (1964), 37–38, 90
civil rights movement: in Alabama, 38–39; Black Power movement as element of, 91; "Bloody Sunday," 39; Congress of Racial Equality, 35; Edmund Pettis Bridge confrontation, 38–39; Freedom Rides, 244; March on Washington, 37; National Association for the Advancement of Colored Peoples, 35; political influence of, 36; sit-in movement, 244; Southern Christian Leadership Conference, 35, 244; Student Nonviolent Coordinating Committee, 35, 39, 56, 243–44; on television, 39; violence against Black people during, 37–39, 56, 244–45
civil rights policies: under Civil Rights Act (1957), 36; congressional response to, 39–40; Dixiecrats and, 36–37; under Johnson, L., 36–41; under Voting Rights Act, 2–3, 5, 20, 40–46; white backlash to, 36–37
Civil War, in US, 2, 56
Clark, James, 38–39
Clark, Jeffrey, 125n36
Clay, Henry, 15
Clegg, Roger, 43
Cleveland, Grover, 19, 75, 313
Clinton, Bill, 83; impeachment of, 21; National Voter Registration Act, 114, 129, 131, 195, 224. *See also* 1992 US presidential election; 1996 US presidential election
Clinton, Hillary, 48, 99, 316; misinformation campaigns about, 84; Putin and, 65; Russian hacking of, 66, 130. *See also* 2016 US presidential election
code of conduct, for US Supreme Court, 159
Cold War: Communism fears during, 60; misinformation/disinformation campaigns during, 73; US national security during, 57, 60
Communism, expansion during Cold War, 60
competitive election districts: definitions of, 167; design of, 166–71; national donors and, 170–71; political extremism countered by, 166–71; political scientists and, 169; safe seats and, 167–68, 170–71; under Voting Rights Act, 168–69
conditional citizenship, 217, 220–21; requirements for, 218–19
Condorcet winner, in runoff voting systems, 172–74

Congress, US: certification of election results, 25; Congressional Black Caucus, 41, 134; contested seats in, *132*; election security and, 127–31; Electoral Count Act and, 18–19; For the People Act in, 77–78, 178–79; Freedom to Vote Act in, 158; ideological polarization in, 163; intervention in Electoral College, 133; John Lewis Voting Rights Advancement Act in, 51, 158; presidential authority by, 108; presidential authority over elections by, 108; Presidential election Reform Act, 317, 322; role in election security, 127–39; roll-call voting in, 170; safe seats in, 167–68, 170–71; state role in election subversion and, 263–67; Twenty-Second Joint Rule, 15–16, 312–14; 2022 midterm elections, 49–50; validity of elections assessed by, 131–37. *See also* competitive election districts; gerrymandering; redistricting; *specific legislation*

Congressional Black Caucus (CBC), 41, 134

Congress of Racial Equality, 35

Connor, Bull, 37

conspiracy theories. *See* election conspiracies

Constitution, US: elections and electoral systems under, 13–14; Elections Clause in, 27, 155; Electoral College and, 4; Electors Clause, 154; federal administration of elections under, 108, 112; First Amendment, 86; Fourteenth Amendment, 19–20, 22, 160n16, 166, 193; measures for presidential elections, 309–13; Nineteenth Amendment, 5, 34, 160n16, 219; presidential authority under, 107, 117–22; presidential immunity in, 120; presidential transition of power and, 296; state role in election subversion and, 264; Take Care Clause in, 118–19; Twelfth Amendment, 14–15, 17, 22, 24–25, 311; Twentieth Amendment, 305–7; Twenty-Fourth Amendment, 40, 160n16; Twenty-Sixth Amendment, 5, 160n16; voter identification laws and, 198. *See also* Fifteenth Amendment

constitutional system, in US: vulnerabilities of, 2. *See also* Constitution, US

Continuity of Government Commission, 303–7

Cooperative Election Study, 281

Cotton, Norris, 227–28

COVID-19 pandemic: mail-in voting during, 48–49; 2020 US presidential election and, 153, 202–3; voting machines during, 278–79

Crawford v. Marion County, 150, 198–99

Crow, Harlan, 158–59

Cruz, Ted, 134–35, 316

Culvahouse, A. B., 305

Cutler, Lloyd, 303

Cyber Ninjas, in Arizona, 204

Cybersecurity and Infrastructure Security Agency, US, 73

Daschle, Tom, 198

Davis, David (Justice), 17

Davis, Tom, 168

death threats, to election officials, 210

Deceptive Practices and Voter Intimidation Prevention Act, US (2016), 77

democracy, in US: Biden on, 11; in crisis, 218; during nineteenth century, 2, 75; role of federal government in, 32; Tocqueville on, 55. *See also specific topics*

Democracy in America (Tocqueville), 56, 70

Democratic Party: affective polarization and, 164; Black voters and, 35; Dixiecrats in, 36–37; expansion of voting rights and, 114; Freedom Democratic

Party, 38; nominations process for presidential candidates, 181–82; as party of racial liberalism, 90; Southern voters and, 37; superdelegates and, 182; voter confidence in integrity of 2020 election, 203. *See also* partisanship
Department of Homeland Security, US, 73
Department of Justice, US: Civil Rights Division of, 114; enforcement of Voting Rights Act, 116; federal administration of elections and, 110; role in federal administration of elections, 110
DeSantis, Ron, 152
Dill, David, 27
Dionne, E. J., Jr., 21
direct presidential authority, over elections, 110–13
direct-recording electronic devices (DREs), 275, 277–78, 280, 283–84
Dirksen, Everett, 40
disinformation campaigns. *See* misinformation/disinformation campaigns
Dixiecrats, 36–37
DNC v. RNC, 197
Doar, John, 36
Dobbs v. Jackson Women's Health Organization, 323
Dole, Robert, 41–43
Dominion Voting Systems, 204; state role in election subversion and, 258
donors, political: in competitive election districts, 170–71; extremism of, 177–78; impulse donations by, 178–79; matching systems for, 179; small, 178. *See also* campaign finance laws; *Citizens United* case
Dornan, Bob, 140n22
Dowd, Matthew, 98
Dred Scott decision, 147
DREs. *See* direct-recording electronic devices
drop boxes, during 2020 US presidential election, 203
Eagle Forum, 93
Eastman, John, 24–25, 30n34
ECA. *See* Electoral Count Act
ECRA. *See* Electoral Count Reform Act
Edmund Pettis Bridge, racial confrontation on, 38–39
Edsall, Thomas, 90–91
Ehrlich, Robert L., 77
1800 US presidential election, 12
1824 US presidential election, 12, 15, 312, 320
1860 US presidential election, 312
1872 US presidential election, 15, 312
1876 US presidential election, 12, 17–19; Electoral College in, 16; Fifteenth Amendment and, 16
1888 US presidential election, 18–19
Eisenhower, Dwight, 36, 83, 147; foreign policy under, 60–61; "New Look" strategy under, 60–61
election commissions: Election Assistance Commission, 23; under Electoral Commissions Act, 17; Federal Election Commission, 56, 86, 110; Presidential Advisory Commission on Election Integrity, 201; Presidential Commission on Election Administration, 200–201, 213n29
election conspiracies: in Arizona, 204–5; election administration and, 209–12; after 2020 US presidential election, 204–5
election denialism: "Big Lie" and, 216–17, 322; growth of, 1–2; over 2020 US presidential election, 101, 191–92; within Republican Party, 101, 205; seizure of voting machines and, 123; by Trump, 101, 191; during 2022 midterm elections, 49–50; in 2024 US presidential election, 51
election integrity: advocates for, 239; historically Black colleges and universities and, 238–51; "many eyes"

election integrity (cont.)
principle and, 286; Supreme Court role in, 246; theoretical approach to, 238–40; Trump's claims about, 24–25, 254. *See also* "Big Lie"; voter fraud
election interference, at historically Black colleges and universities, 247–51
election law, in US: in Arkansas, 205; Electronic Registration Information Center program, 206–7; in Georgia, 205; in Massachusetts, 206; in Minnesota, 205–6; in New Mexico, 205–6; self-dealing in, 107, 122; in South Dakota, 205; in Texas, 205; validity of elections and, 131–37; voter fraud and, 219. *See also* Congress; election security; Supreme Court; *specific legislation*
elections, electoral systems and, in US: congressional certification of, 25; Constitutional requirements and structure for, 13–14; corrupt, 75; early structural issues in, 12–16; Election Assistance Commission, 23; election conspiracies and, 209–12; under Electoral Commissions Act, 17; under Electoral Count Act, 4, 18–19, 22; under Electoral Count Reform Act, 4; existential elections, 209; foreign influences on, 6; foreign interference in, 57–63; historical technology used for, 272–76; hypercompetition in, 209–12; legitimacy of, 127; limited federal scrutiny of, 57; methodological approach to, 6–7; political polarization and, 209–12; prohibition of military intervention in, 112; Putin interference in, 65, 67; reform movements for, 16; social media as influence on, 210; under Twenty-Second Joint Rule, 15–16, 312–14; two-vote system, 14. *See also* Electoral College; federal administration of elections; incumbent candidates; *specific elections; specific topics*
Elections Clause, in US Constitution, 27, 155
Elections Clause, US Constitution, 155
election security, election interference and: conceptual approach to, 74, 76; congressional authority over, 127–31; congressional role in, 127–39; Cybersecurity and Infrastructure Security Agency, 73; under Deceptive Practices and Voter Intimidation Prevention Act, 77; Democratic priorities for, 128–29; minimum standards of, 127; in Pennsylvania, 76–77; political partisanship and, 128–29; public opinion polls on, 129; reform approaches to, 331–33; Republican priorities for, 128–29; by Russia, 65, 67, 111–12; state funding for, 130; by US in foreign elections, 58–60, 63. *See also* Electoral Count Act; Electoral Count Reform Act; misinformation/disinformation campaigns; voter fraud
election subversion: definition of, 255, 268n11; state role in, 253–58. *See also* state authority
Electoral College, Electors and: apportioning of Electors, 13; in Arizona, 140n35; Certification of, 119; congressional intervention in, 133; 1876 US presidential election and, 16; under Electoral Commissions Act, 17; establishment of, 4, 123n8; faithless electors, 24, 300; fake electors and, 154, 266; for Hawaii, 314–15; independent state legislature theory for, 154; legal binding of, 299–303; for Louisiana, 325n19; in North Carolina, 299–300; proposed elimination of, 223–24; reform of, 320–21; rules of, 123n8; Trump attacks against, 167–68; under Twelfth Amendment, 14–15; 2000 US presidential election and, 2–3; 2020 US presidential election, 26; winner-take-all systems,

295. *See also* Electoral Count Act; Electoral Count Reform Act
Electoral Commissions Act, US (1977), 17
Electoral Count Act (ECA), US (1887), 4, 18–19; complications of, 313–17; dangers of, 137; goals and purpose of, 133; key provisions of, 313–17; manipulation of, 134–35; reforms of, 138; safe harbor provision in, 315–16; state role in election subversion under, 259; under Twelfth Amendment, 25; 2000 US presidential election and, 22; after 2020 US presidential election, 134–35
Electoral Count Reform Act (ECRA), US (2022), 4, 50, 135, 141n48, 317–18; *Bush v. Gore*, 26–27, 319, 321–22; clarification of, 321; state role in election subversion under, 264–65; as untested, 28; vulnerabilities in, 319–24
Electors Clause, US Constitution, 154
Electronic Registration Information Center program (ERIC program), 206–7
emergency powers, presidential authority and, 117–18
empirical extremism, 185n12
e-pollbooks, 275
Equal Opportunity Commission, 37–38
Equal Rights Amendment (ERA), 92–94
ERIC program. *See* Electronic Registration Information Center program
extremism, political: behavioral, 185n12; campaign finance reform and, 177–80; competitive election districts as response to, 166–71; definition of, 166; of donors, 177–78; empirical, 185n12; institutional-design reforms for, 166, 184; normative, 185n12; political partisanship as distinct from, 163; in presidential nominations process, 180–84; runoff voting systems, 171–74; theoretical approach to, 163–66; traditional party primaries and, 174–77
Facebook, 66, 85–86, 210
faithless electors, 24, 300
"fake news," 73
Falwell, Jerry, 94
FBI. *See* Federal Bureau of Investigation
federal administration of elections: Census Bureau and, 115–16; decentralization of, 108–9; Department of Justice role in, 110; Federal Election Commission, 56, 86, 110; under Johnson, L., administration, 193; legal framework for, 108–9; practical framework for, 108–9; presidential authority and, 108; prohibition of military intervention, 112; under US Constitution, 108, 112
Federal Bureau of Investigation (FBI), 56
Federal Election Commission, 56, 86, 110
Federalist Party, 14
Federalist Society, 149–50, 159
Fein, Bruce, 43
Feinstein, Dianne, 81
felon disenfranchisement, voting restrictions through, 220–21
The Feminine Mystique (Friedan), 93
Fifteenth Amendment, US Constitution, 75, 160n16; 1876 US presidential election and, 16; election of Black politicians as result of, 147; Republican Party and, 33; voting rights under, 3, 5, 33, 131–32, 219
First Amendment, US Constitution, 86
Florida: election issues in, 130; restrictive voting laws in, 51. *See also* *Bush v. Gore;* 2000 US presidential election
Florio, James, 45
Floyd, George, 113
Flynn, Michael, 65
Foley, Edward, 323
Foner, Eric, 33
Ford, Gerald, 196, 223

foreign elections: Geneva Conventions and, 68; interference in, 69; international agreements, 68; noninterference in, 67–70
foreign policy, US: under Bush, G. W., 62; China and, 62; double standards of, 62–64; under Eisenhower, 60–61; election interference in foreign countries, 59–62; under Obama, 62; political warfare as element of, 60; propaganda, 60; Putin response to, 64–67; Russia and, 62, 64–67
For the People Act, 77–78, 178–79
Fourteenth Amendment, US Constitution, 19–20, 160n16; disqualification provision, 166; one-person, one-vote mandate, 22; voting rights under, 193
France, elections in: CIA involvement in, 59–60; runoff voting systems in, 171–72
Franklin, Benjamin, 4
Free Congress Foundation, 94
Freedom Democratic Party, 38
Freedom Rides, 244
Freedom to Vote Act, US, 158
free speech: under First Amendment, 86; misinformation/disinformation campaigns and, 74–75
Frey, William, 100
Friedan, Betty, 93

Gaetz, Matt, 136, 172
Garfield, James, 33
Garland, Merrick, 146–47
Gasperi, Alcide De, 59
gay marriage rights, 92–93
Gellman, Barton, 25–26
gender, voting restrictions by, 5
Georgia: election laws in, 205; migration of Black Americans to, 245; rejected electoral votes in, 140n25; restrictive voting laws in, 51; runoff voting system in, 171; Secretary of State for, 118–19, 122, 254–55, 262; state role in election subversion, 261–62
Georgia v. Ashcroft, 46
gerrymandering, partisan: in Alabama, 153, 243–44; history of, 152–53; limitations on, 151, 166–71; near historically Black colleges and universities, 247; in North Carolina, 248; Roberts' response to, 153; in *Rucho v. Common Cause*, 123n5, 153, 167, 247; of safe seats, 167–68; under Voting Rights Act, 151
Giessel, Cathy, 176–77
Gingrich, Newt, 140n22, 301
Ginsberg, Ben, 200
Ginsburg, Ruth Bader (Justice), 3, 22, 46, 150, 315
Goldberg, Jonah, 232
Goldsmith, Jack, 27
Goldwater, Barry, 37–39, 83, 90. *See also* 1964 US presidential election
Gomillion, Charles G., 243–44
Gomillion v. Lightfoot, 243–44
Gonzales, Alberto, 150
Goodwin, Richard, 39–40
Gore, Al, 45, 99, 134, 315; concession after 2000 presidential election, 23; Klain and, 11–12. *See also Bush v. Gore;* 2000 US presidential election
Gorsuch, Neil (Justice), 161n41
Gosar, Paul, 134–36, 317
Grant, Ulysses S., 15, 33, 56, 325n19
Great Migration, of Black Americans, 35, 245
Great Society, 43
Greeley, Horace, 15, 140n25, 325n19
Greene, Marjorie Taylor, 172
Grumbach, Jacob, 261
Guatemala, 60

Haley, J. Evetts, 83
Hamer, Fannie Lou, 38
Harbridge-Young, Laurel, 174

Harper v. Virginia Board of Elections, 193–94
Harrison, Henry, 19
Hart, Rita, 133
Hasen, Richard, 50–51
HAVA. *See* Help America Vote Act
Hawaii: slates of electors for, 314–15; write-in ballots in, 199
Hawley, Josh, 135
Hayes, Rutherford B., 16–19, 312. *See also* 1876 US presidential election
HBCUs. *See* historically Black colleges and universities
Helms, Jesse, 41–42
Help America Vote Act (HAVA), US (2002), 23, 114, 129–31; *Bush v. Gore* and, 195–201; Election Assistance Commission as result of, 197–98; provisional ballot system under, 197; 2000 US presidential election and, 195–201; voter fraud and, 224; voter identification guidelines, 198–99; voting equipment upgrades under, 196; voting machines under, 277
Henry, Patrick, 152
Herbert, Gerry, 44
Heritage Foundation, 43–44, 226
historically Black colleges and universities (HBCUs): Black public leadership influenced by, 243; cultural and social expression at, 241–42; distribution by state, *241*; election integrity and, 238–51; election interference at, 247–51; engaged citizenship and, 242; enrollment statistics, *246*; establishment of, 240; gerrymandered districts around, 247; historical antecedents of, 243–45; during Jim Crow era, 242; as job creators, 240–41; limitations of voter mobilization strategies, 248–50; polling places near, 250; sit-in movement at, 244; social identification at, 242; Student Nonviolent Coordinating Committee, 243–44; United Negro College Fund and, 240–41; voter disruption and, 243–45; voter suppression at, 245
Hobbs, Katie, 207
Hoover, Herbert, 57
House Freedom Caucus, 135
Huffington, Michael, 81
Human Events (conservative journal), 82, 226, 228, 230, 236n34
Humphrey, Hubert, 315
Huntington, Samuel, 230

IEEPA. *See* International Emergency Economic Powers Act
immigration policy: Huffington and, 81; Proposition 187 and, 80–81; race/ethnicity-based opposition to, 96
immunity, for presidents: Trump's claims of, 118–20, 156; in US Constitution, 120
incumbent candidates, political entrenchment of, 107
independent state legislature theory, 154, 266–67
Indiana: congressional elections in, 20–21, 140n22; voter identification laws in, 198–98
Indonesia, US foreign policy interference in, 61
inequality in voting districts, *Baker v. Carr*, 20, 40, 148
instant runoff voting (IRV): Condorcet winner in, 173–74; forms of, 172–73
Insurrection Act, US, 112–13, 123; Trump and, 155–56
International Emergency Economic Powers Act (IEEPA), US, 110–12
Iran, US foreign policy interference in, 60
Iranian hostage crisis, 110
IRV. *See* instant runoff voting
Israel, 120–21
"issue consistency," 95

Issue Evolution (Carmines and Stimson, J. A.), 90
Italy, elections in: CIA involvement in, 58–59; Soviet involvement in, 59
It's Even Worse Than It Looks (Mann and Ornstein), 94–95
Iyengar, Shanto, 96

Jackson, Andrew, 15
Jackson, Ketanji Brown (Justice), 50
Jackson, Robert (Justice), 108, 117, 120
Jefferson, Thomas, 14, 310–11
Jennings, Christine, 132–33
Jennings v. Buchanan, 132–33
Jim Crow laws, 33–34; historically Black colleges and universities and, 242; racism through, 2; during Reconstruction Era, 2; Supreme Court response to, 147
John Lewis Voting Rights Advancement Act, US, 51, 158
Johnson, Lyndon, 56, 83; Civil Rights Act (1964), 37–38, 90; civil rights legislative agenda for, 36–41; civil rights movement and, 36; federal administration of elections under, 193; federal power over elections under, 193; Great Society, 43; Medicare program, 37–38; War on Poverty and, 91. *See also* 1964 US presidential election; Voting Rights Act
Johnson, Mike, 135
Jones, Stephanie Tubb, 134
judicial activism. *See* activism
Justice Department, US, 56

Kagan, Elena (Justice), 14–15, 24, 50, 154
Kamarck, Elaine, 51
Karzai, Hamid, 61–63
Kavanaugh, Brett (Justice), 50, 153, 161n41
Kean, Thomas, 79
Kennan, George, 58–59
Kennedy, John F., 36–37, 63, 222, 314–15
Kennedy, Ted, 42
Kennedy v. Bremerton School District, 323
Kentucky, election disputes in, 19
Kerry, John, 84, 92, 316. *See also* 2004 US presidential election
Keyssar, Alexander, 32, 150
King, Martin Luther, Jr., 35, 39–40; March on Washington and, 37
King, Rufus, 12–13, 28
Klain, Ron, 11–12
Klobuchar, Amy, 77–79, 86
Kobach, Kris, 48, 201
Kosar, Kevin, 27
Krebs, Christopher, 71n28
Ku Klux Klan, 34

Lake, Kari, 207
Lassiter v. Northampton County, 193
Latino communities, in US: voter discrimination in, 47; voter suppression in, 43; voting restrictions on, 3
Lelkes, Yphtach, 96
Leo, Leonard, 149, 159
LePage, Paul, 78
Levendusky, Matthew, 96
Lewis, John, 39, 243
Lincoln, Abraham, 312
Lindell, Mike, 204, 257
literacy rates, misinformation campaigns and, 75
literacy tests, for voting: under Jim Crow laws, 20, 34, 147–48; voter discrimination through, 20, 34; voter suppression through, 147–48; voting restrictions through, 20, 34
Lofgren, Zoe, 136
Louisiana, electoral slates from, 325n19
Luther v. Borden, 147

Macedonia, 73
Madison, James, 13, 152, 155, 310
mail-in voting: in California, 48–49, 203; during COVID-19 pandemic, 48–49;

expansion of, 48–49; by state, 48–49; Trump's fear of, 49; during 2020 US presidential election, 202–3
Malhotra, Neil, 96
Manafort, Paul, 65
Manhattan Project, Soviet Union infiltration of, 58
Manheim, Lisa Marshall, 109–10, 114–15
Mann, Thomas, 94–95
Marble, William, 98
March on Washington, 37
Marshall, Thurgood (Justice), 148
Mason, Lilliana, 96
Massachusetts, election law in, 206
Mathis, Dawson, 223
McCloskey, Frank, 21, 140n22
McConnell, Mitch, 146–47, 224
McCoy, Alfred W., 71n27
McCubbins, Mathew, 128
McGee, Gale, 223
McGregor, Ruth, 207
McIntyre, Rick, 20–21, 140n22
McLeod, Daniel, 40–41
Meese, Edwin, 43
Merkel, Angela, 62
Merrill, John, 238–39
Michigan, state role in election subversion, 261–62
military, intervention in elections, prohibition of, 112
Miller, Kenneth, 170
Miller-Idris, Cynthia, 170
Miller-Meeks, Marianette, 133
Minnesota, election law in, 205–6
misinformation/disinformation campaigns: in California, 80–81; about Clinton, H., 84; during Cold War, 73; conceptual approaches to, 73–74; "fake news," 73, 85; free speech protections, 74–75; through journalism, 74–75; literacy rates and, 75; about Obama, 84; political partisanship and, 81–87; Proposition 187, 80–81; through robocalls, 78; security frameworks for, 74–76; through social media, 78, 86; sources of, 2; voter fraud and, 76; as voter suppression, 75–76
Misinformation Review, 73
Mississippi, voter discrimination in, 38
Mobile v. Bolden, 194
Moore v. Harper, 27–28, 155, 157, 254–55, 265–66
Moral Majority, 94, 226
Motor Voter Act. *See* National Voter Registration Act
Mueller, Robert, 65–66
Murkowski, Lisa, 176
Musk, Elon, 86
Muskie, Edmund, 315
Myers Automatic Booth lever machine, 276–77

National Association for the Advancement of Colored Peoples (NAACP), 35
national emergencies, presidential authority during, 110
National Emergencies Act, US, 110
National Review, 82–83, 226, 229, 233
national security, in US: Central Intelligence Agency, 58; during Cold War, 57, 60; definition of, 3; external risks to, 3; non-state terrorist networks and, 3–4; Office of Strategic Services, 58; political warfare and, 60
National Security Act of 1947, US, 58
National Voter Registration Act, US (1993), 114, 129, 195, 224; political resistance to, 131
nativism, voter fraud and, 81
Neustadt, Richard, 109
Nevada: party primary system in, 175–76; state role in election subversion, 258
New Deal, 35, 92
New Jersey, voter intimidation in, 78–79
New Mexico: election law in, 205–6; state role in election subversion, 258

1940 US presidential election, 82
1952 US presidential election, 82–83
1964 US presidential election, 83; Black American vote in, 38
1968 US presidential election, 315, 320
1992 US presidential election, 83, 99
1996 US presidential election, 301
Nineteenth Amendment, US Constitution, 5, 34, 160n16, 219
nineteenth century, US democracy during, 2, 75
Nixon, Richard, 37, 42, 314–15; Republican Right and, 83–84
nominations process, for presidential candidates: affective polarization as result of, 183; for Democratic Party, 181–82; historical development of, 180; ideological extremism as result of, 183–84; for Republican Party, 181; superdelegates in, 182
non-state terrorist networks, 3–4
normative extremism, 185n12
North Carolina: binding of Electors in, 299–300; gerrymandering in, 248; *Moore v. Harper*, 27–28, 155, 157, 254–55, 265–66; restrictive voting laws in, 151; state role in election subversion, 259; voter identification law in, 259
Nuclear Non-proliferation Treaty, 68

Obama, Barack, 45–46, 79, 86; Deceptive Practices and Voter Intimidation Prevention Act, 77; foreign policy under, 62; gay marriage policy and, 92–93; International Emergency Economic Powers Act and, 110–11; misinformation about, 84; Presidential Commission on Election Administration and, 200–201, 213n29; rejection of Garland nomination, 146–47. *See also* 2008 US presidential election
Office of Strategic Services (OSS), 58
O'Hara, James, 315
Ohio: voter suppression claims in, 136; voter turnout in, 200
O'Neil, Tip, 301
one person, one vote mandate, 22; *Reynolds v. Sims*, 20, 40, 148
Operation Red-Map, 46
Ornstein, Norman, 94–95
OSS. *See* Office of Strategic Services
Overton, Spencer, 198

PACs. *See* political action committees
Paine, Thomas, 145
paper ballots, 275–76
partisan gerrymandering. *See* gerrymandering
partisanship, political: affective polarization and, 164–66; in Congress, 163; identity and, 97; "issue consistency" in, 95; journalistic objectivity and, 82; misinformation campaigns and, 81–87; Nixon and, 83–84; political extremism as distinct from, 163; Republican Right ecosystem for, 83–84; social media as influence on, 97; in US Supreme Court, 146
party primary systems, traditional: in Alaska, 175–77; ideological extremism and, 175; in Nevada, 175–76; reform strategies for, 175; sore-loser laws and, 177; top-five voting system, 175; top-four voting system, 175–76; voter demographics, 175; voter turnout for, 174–75. *See also* nominations process
Paxton, Ken, 262
PCEA. *See* Presidential Commission on Election Administration
Pence, Mike, 2, 25, 48, 50, 135, 201, 316
PERA. *See* presidential election Reform Act
Perino, Dana, 49
Perry, Scott, 135
Peters, Tina, 257
Phillips, Kevin, 226
Pildes, Richard, 23

Podesta, John, 66
polarization: affective, 164–66; presidential transition of power and, 308; top-down, 165
political action committees (PACs), 178
"political questions" doctrine, 20
political warfare, 67; conceptual development of, 60
polling places, near historically Black colleges and universities, 250
poll taxes, 20, 34; under Twenty-Fourth Amendment, 40, 160n16; under Voting Rights Act, 148
Polsby, Nelson, 131
populism, as political movement, rise of, 96
postcard registration legislation, 223–24
Powel, Elizabeth Willing, 4
Powell, Adam Clayton, Jr., 35
preclearance requirements, in Voting Rights Act, 40, 217
Presidential Advisory Commission on Election Integrity, 201
presidential authority, elections and: by Congress, 108; constitutional foundations of, 107; as delegated authority, 109–10; direct powers, 110–13; emergency powers, 117–18; by executive agencies, 114–17; federal administration of elections and, 108; as inherent to office, 117–22; under Insurrection Act, 112–13, 123; under International Emergency Economic Powers Act, 110–12; during national emergencies, 110; under National Emergencies Act, 110; self-interest as factor in, 122; statutory grants of, 109–17; Take Care Clause and, 118–19; under US Constitution, 107, 117–22
Presidential Commission on Election Administration (PCEA), 200–201, 213n29
Presidential Election Reform Act (PERA), 317, 322
presidential elections, in US: constitutional measures for, 309–13; foreign government interest in, 56; Supreme Court involvement in, 2–3; Tocqueville on, 55. *See also* nominations process; *specific presidential elections*
Presidential Succession Act, US, 304
presidential succession provisions, after death of winning candidate, 296–301, 304–5
presidential transition of power: constitutional provisions for, 296; Continuity of Government Commission and, 303–7; partisan polarization and, 308; periods of, 294–96; presidential succession provisions after death of winning candidate, 296–301, 304–5; special elections after death of winning candidate, 307–8; Trump's rejection of, 327n51; under Twentieth Amendment, 305–7
Prigozhin, Yevgeny, 65
propaganda: through social media, 66; during 2016 US presidential election, 66; US foreign policy and, 60
Proposition 187, in California, 80–81
Przeworski, Adam, 101
public funding, for elections: campaign finance laws and, 178–79; Obama rejection of, 179
punch-card systems, 280
Purcell doctrine, 153–54, 208–9
Putin, Vladimir, 62; Clinton, H., and, 65; response to US foreign policy, 64–67; US election interference by, 65, 67

race: as polarizing political force, 96; voting restrictions by, 5. *See also* racial discrimination; racism
race relations, in US: public shift to Republican right influenced by, 91. *See also* racism
racial discrimination: under Jim Crow laws, 2; under Voting Rights Act, 5

racism: under Jim Crow laws, 2; opposition to immigration policy influenced by, 96; voter fraud and, 81, 230–31
Radical Republicans, 33
Raffensperger, Brad, 118–19, 122, 254–55, 262, 322
Ramos, Nelva Gonzalez, 47
ranked-choice voting, 172. *See also* instant runoff voting
Rather, Dan, 84
Reagan, Ronald, 41–42; opposition to expanded voter registration, 226, 228, 232–33
Reconstruction Era: democracy during, 2; expansion of voting rights during, 32–36; Jim Crow laws, 2, 33–34; Ku Klux Klan during, 34; Mississippi voting restrictions during, 34–35; poll taxes during, 20, 34; restriction of voting rights during, 33–36
redistricting: under Operation Red-Map, 46; political extremism and, 166–71; "political questions" doctrine and, 20; Supreme Court rulings on, 20; voter suppression through, 20. *See also* gerrymandering
Rehnquist, William (Chief Justice), 22, 43, 151, 161n41
Rejecting Compromise (Anderson, Butler, and Harbridge-Young), 167, 174
Republican Party: affective polarization and, 164; in Alabama, 153; Black voters and, 35; election denialism within, 101, 205; enforcement of voting requirements, 114; Federalist Society and, 149–50, 159; Fifteenth Amendment passed by, 33; Heritage Foundation and, 43–44; House Freedom Caucus, 135; nominations process for presidential candidates, 181; Operation Red-Map, 46; opposition to expansion of voter registration, 226; as party of racial conservatism, 90–91; Radical Republicans, 33; *Roe v. Wade* and, 93; Tea Party caucus, 163; voter caging allegations against, 197; voter confidence in integrity of 2020 election, 203; voter intimidation strategies by, 78–79; voter suppression by, 43–44; voting restrictions by, 47–48. *See also* partisanship
Republican Right, as political movement: Eagle Forum and, 93; ecosystem for, 83–84; Free Congress Foundation, 94; Moral Majority, 94; Nixon and, 83–84; race relations as influence on public shift to, 91; *Roe v. Wade* and, 93; Schlafly and, 93–94
Reynolds v. Sims, 20, 40, 148
Richards, Richard, 79
Riesel, Victor, 230
Rights Revolution, 192
risk-limiting audits (RLAs), 287
Roberts, John (Chief Justice), 27, 43–44, 46, 50; criticism of Voting Rights Act, 149–51; judicial activism under, 149; judicial response to gerrymandering, 153
Robertson, Marion G. "Pat," 94, 226
Robinson, Jo Ann, 244
robocalls, 78
Roe v. Wade, 93
Rollins, Ed, 44
Romney, Mitt, 93, 200
Roosevelt, Franklin D.: conflicts with Supreme Court, 148; foreign European military operations under, 57–58; New Deal, 35, 92. *See also* 1940 US presidential election
Ross, Wilbur, 115
Rove, Karl, 46
Rucho v. Common Cause, 123n5, 153, 167, 247
runoff voting systems: Condorcet winner, 172–74; expansion after World War II, 171; in France, 171–72; instant runoff voting, 172–74; political extremism

and, 171–74; in US states, 171–72; voter turnout for, 172
Russia: Clinton, H., and, 66; interference in US presidential elections, 65, 67, 111–12, 141n42; Internet Research Agency, 65; response to US foreign policy, 62, 64–67; US foreign policy and, 62; US interference in leadership selection, 63

safe harbor provision, in Electoral Count Act, 315–16
Saltman, Roy G., 279–80
Sanchez, Loretta, 140n22
Scalia, Antonin (Justice), 146, 150
Schlafly, Phyllis, 93–94, 226
Schrade, Jack, 231
Schwartz, Thomas, 128
secret ballots, 285–86
September 11th terrorist attacks, 64
1796 US presidential election, 13–14
Shalala, Donna, 305
"Sharpiegate," in Arizona, 204, 207
Shaw v. Reno, 46
Shelby County v. Holder, 46, 56, 150, 158, 200
Silkworth, Ron, 77
Simpson, Alan, 303
Sinatra, Frank, 59
sit-in movement, 244
slavery, slave trade and: Civil War and, 56; *Dred Scott* decision, 147; expansion of, 56
Smartmatic voting system, 271
Smith, Jack, 156
social media: elections influenced by, 210; misinformation campaigns on, 78; political partisanship influenced by, 97; in 2016 US presidential election, 66. *See also* Facebook; X
sore-loser laws: for traditional party primaries, 177; under Voting Rights Act, 194
Sotomayor, Sonia (Justice), 50
South Carolina v. Katzenbach, 40–41
South Dakota, election laws in, 205
Southern Christian Leadership Conference, 35, 244
South Korea, US foreign policy interference in, 61
South Vietnam, US foreign policy interference in, 61
Soviet Union: infiltration of Manhattan Project, 58; involvement in Italian elections, 59. *See also* Russia
special elections, after death of winning presidential candidate, 307–8
Starr, Kenneth, 43
state authority, election subversion and, 256–57; in Arizona, 258–59; in *Bush v. Gore*, 260; in California, 258; congressional involvement in, 263–67; constitutional provisions for, 264; Dominion Voting Machines and, 258; Electoral Count Act and, 259; Electoral Count Reform Act and, 264–65; facilitation of, 258–63; federal courts' role in, 263–67; in Georgia, 261–62; governors and, 258, 260; independent state legislature theory and, 154, 266–67; in Michigan, 261–62; in Nevada, 258; in New Mexico, 258; in North Carolina, 259; Republican, 260–61; in Texas, 263; theoretical approach to, 253–55
Steele, Michael S., 77
Stennis, John, 228
Stevens, John Paul (Justice), 3, 150
Stevens, Thaddeus, 32–33
Stewart, Charles, III, 131, 191, 204–5
Stimson, Henry, 57
Stimson, James A., 90
Stone, Roger, 65
Student Nonviolent Coordinating Committee, 35, 39, 56, 243–44
Students for Fair Admission v. Harvard and UNC, 323

superdelegates, in Democratic Party nomination process, 182
Supreme Court, US: activist era of, 149–53, 196; code of conduct for, 159; election integrity influenced by, 246; Elections Clause ruling, 155; establishment in US Constitution, 146; Federalist Society and, 149–50, 159; future legal responses of, 156–59; gutting of Voting Rights Act, 150–51; involvement in presidential elections, 2–3; Jim Crow laws and, 147; judicial overreach of, 157; political partisanship as influence on, 146; presidential election rulings, 2–3; public approval of, 157; *Purcell* doctrine and, 153–54, 208–9; redistricting cases, 20; rejection of Obama nomination to, 146–47; Roosevelt administration in conflict with, 148; state election rulings, 19; Trump appointees to, 145; 2000 US presidential election and, 2–3, 22–23; Voting Rights Act rulings, 3, 150–51; voting rights legislation and, 147–48. *See also Bush v. Gore; specific cases; specific justices*
Swift Boat Vets for Truth, 84

tabloid journalism, misinformation campaigns through, 74–75. *See also* free speech
Taft, Robert, 82–83
Take Care Clause, in US Constitution, 118–19
Taylor v. Beckham, 19, 20
Tea Party caucus, 163
Tennessee, mail-in voting in, 48–49
terrorist networks, non-state, 3–4
A Texan Looks at Johnson (Haley), 83
Texas: election laws in, 205; migration of Black Americans to, 245; state role in election subversion, 259; voting restrictions in, 3, 46–47; Voting Rights Act application in, 151; "white primary" in, 148
Thiel, Peter, 152
Thomas, Clarence (Justice), 44, 161n41; Crow and, 158–59
Tilden, Samuel, 16–19, 312. *See also* 1876 US presidential election
Tocqueville, Alexis de, 55–56; on election interference, 69–70
Toobin, Jeffrey, 151
top-down polarization, 165
top-five voting system, in party primary system, 175
top-four voting system, in party primary system, 175–76
transgender rights, 93
transition of power. *See* presidential transition of power
Tribe, Lawrence, 43
Truman, Harry, 58
Trump, Donald, 2, 26–28, 316; attempts to overturn 2020 presidential election, 12, 153–56; Biden, H. and, 85–86; "Big Lie" and, 216–17, 322; claims about election integrity, 24–25, 254; claims of presidential immunity, 118–19; criticism of mail-in voting, 49; Eastman and, 24–25, 30n34; election denialism and, 101, 191; election fraud claims by, 129; on electoral vote counts, 167–68; Federalist Society and, 149; Georgia Secretary of State and, 118–19, 122; Insurrection Act and, 113; insurrection claims against, 155–56; International Emergency Economic Powers Act and, 110–11; January 6th Capitol attacks, 1, 49; manipulation of Electoral Count Act, 134–35; Presidential Advisory Commission on Election Integrity, 201; Raffensperger and, 254–55; rejection of transition of power norms, 327n51; removal from 2024 Presiden-

tial ballot, 155–56; seizure of voting machines under, 123; Supreme Court justices appointed by, 145; voting fraud claims by, 48; voting restriction strategies by, 48; white voter support for, 98–99. *See also* Capitol attacks; 2016 US presidential election; 2020 US presidential election; 2024 US presidential election
Tshibaka, Kelly, 176
Tubbs-Jones, Stephanie, 316
Tulis, Jeffrey, 119–20
Twelfth Amendment, US Constitution, 17; Electoral Count Act under, 25; establishment of Electoral College under, 14–15, 311; 2000 US presidential election and, 22, 24
Twentieth Amendment, US Constitution, 305–7
Twenty-Fourth Amendment, US Constitution, 40, 160n16
Twenty-Second Joint Rule, 15–16, 312–14
Twenty-Sixth Amendment, US Constitution, 5, 160n16
Twitter (X), 66, 85–86
2000 US presidential election: early call of winner in, 12, 21–22; Electoral College winner, 2–3; Electoral Count Act and, 22; Florida role in, 22; Gore concession after, 23; hand recounts in, 22; Help America Vote Act and, 195–201; political partisanship as influence on, 21; popular vote winner, 2–3, 21, 134; Supreme Court involvement in, 2–3, 22–23; Twelfth Amendment and, 22, 24; validity questions for, 136; voter demographics for, 99; voting machines during, 283–84. *See also Bush v. Gore*
2004 US presidential election, 92–93; validity questions for, 136
2008 US presidential election, 45–46
2016 US presidential election: Internet Research Agency, 65; Mueller Report, 65–66; Russian interference in, 65, 141n42; social media propaganda during, 66; voter demographics for, 99; voter fraud claims after, 48
2020 US presidential election, 27–28; absentee ballot applications during, 202–3; attempts to overturn results of, 11–12, 153–56; constitutional crisis after, 26; COVID-19 pandemic and, 153, 202–3; Democrat confidence in election integrity, 203; Dominion Voting Systems and, 204; drop boxes during, 203; Eastman and, 24–25, 30n34; election conspiracies after, 204–5; election denialism over, 101, 191–92; election integrity claims, 24–25; Electoral College winner, 26; Electoral Count Act and, 134–35; fake electors and, 154, 266; independent state legislature theory and, 154; in-person voting during, 203; mail-in voting during, 202–3; *Purcell* principle and, 153–54; Republican confidence in election integrity, 203; *Republican Party of Pennsylvania v. Boockvar*, 154; undecided vote count in, 11–12; validity questions for, 136; voter turnout in, 235n19. *See also* Capitol attacks
2024 US presidential election: collective anxiety over, 209–12; election denialism as element of, 51; as existential election, 209; removal of Trump from ballot, 155–56; voting restrictions as impact on, 51

UN. *See* United Nations
Uniformed and Overseas Citizens Absentee Voting Act, US, 114
United Kingdom (U.K.), nominations process in Parliament, 180–81
United Nations (UN), 69

United Negro College Fund, 240–41
United States (US): Affordable Care Act, 149; Civil Rights Act (1957), 36; Civil Rights Act (1964), 37–38; Civil War, 2, 56; Cybersecurity and Infrastructure Security Agency, 73; Deceptive Practices and Voter Intimidation Prevention Act, 77; democratic crises in, 218; Electoral Commissions Act, 17; Help America Vote Act, 23, 114, 129–31, 195–201; Insurrection Act, 112–13, 123, 155–56; interference in foreign elections, 58–60, 63; International Emergency Economic Powers Act, 110–12; National Emergencies Act, 110; National Security Act of 1947, 58; National Voter Registration Act, 114, 129, 131, 195, 224; Presidential Succession Act, 304; September 11th terrorist attacks, 64; Uniformed and Overseas Citizens Absentee Voting Act, 114; Voting Accessibility for the Elderly and Handicapped Act, 114. *See also* Congress; Constitution; Electoral Count Act; Electoral Count Reform Act; Supreme Court; Voting Rights Act; *specific agencies; specific states; specific topics*
US Constitution. *See* Constitution

Vance, J. D., 152, 281
Vietnam War, 91
Vohra, Anchal, 96
voter caging, 197
voter discrimination: against Black Americans, 47; Freedom Democratic Party evidence of, 38; against immigrant populations, 35; through intimidation, 34; through literacy tests, 20, 34; in Mississippi, 38; in the North, 35; through poll taxes, 20, 34; in the South, 20, 33–35. *See also* voter suppression; Voting Rights Act
voter fraud: analysis of, 231–33; conditional citizenship and, 217–21; election law violations and, 219; expansion of voting registration as, 225–26; Help America Vote Act, 224; misinformation campaigns and, 76; nativism as foundation of, 81; racism as foundation of, 81, 230–31; Trump's claims of, 48; unsubstantiated claims of, 47; welfare fraud compared to, 230
voter identification laws, 140n37; constitutional debates over, 198; *Crawford v. Marion County*, 150, 198–99; Help America Vote Act, 198–99; in Indiana, 198–98; in North Carolina, 259
voter intimidation: in New Jersey, 78–79; Republican Party strategies, 78–79
voter registration: for Black Americans, 41; under Carter, 223–24, 229; citizen apathy and, 227–28; expansion of, 225–26; institutionalization of, 219–20; morality and, 227–29; under National Voter Registration Act, 114, 129, 131, 195, 224; political science debates over, 221; postcard registration legislation, 223–24; Reagan's opposition to, 226, 228, 232–33; reform movement for, 221–24, 227–29; Republican response to expansion of, 226; special interest voting blocs through, 231; after Voting Rights Act, 221–25. *See also* Voting Rights Act
voter suppression: in Black communities, 43; under Deceptive Practices and Voter Intimidation Prevention Act, 77; at historically Black colleges and universities, 245; through intimidation, 34; Ku Klux Klan and, 34; in Latino communities, 43; through literacy tests, 147–48; misinformation campaigns as, 75–76; in Ohio, 136; through redistricting, 20; by Republican Party, 43–44; in the

South, 56. *See also* redistricting; voter discrimination
voter turnout: historical declines in, 220; in Ohio, 200; with runoff voting systems, 172; for traditional party primary systems, 174–75; in 2020 US presidential election, 235n19
voter-verified paper audit trail (VVPAT), 278, 290n30
Voting Accessibility for the Elderly and Handicapped Act, US, 114
voting machines: ballot-marking device, 275, 278, 284; "black box" systems, 271; during COVID-19 pandemic, 278–79; digital technology for, 277; direct-recording electronic devices, 275, 277–78, 280, 283–84; Dominion Voting Systems, 204, 258; drivers of use of, 281–84; early justifications of, 281–82; ecosystem diagram for, *274*; e-pollbooks, 275; future approaches to, 285–88; hacking of, 276, 290n21; under Help America Vote Act, 277; historical use of, 272–77, *279*, 282; interconnection of electronic devices, 275; limitations of, 272; Myers Automatic Booth lever machine, 276–77; optical scanning, 278; paper ballots and, 275–76; post-election auditing of, 287–88; punch-card systems, 280; risk-limiting audit, 287; Smartmatic, 271; trustworthiness of, 287–88; during 2000 US presidential election, 283–84; verification strategies with, 284–85; voter-verified paper audit trail, 278, 290n30
voting restrictions: on Black communities, 3, 5, 33–34; through citizenship questions, 116; through felon disenfranchisement, 220–21; historical types of, 219; impact on 2024 US presidential election, 51; on Latino communities, 3; through literacy tests, 20, 34; in North Carolina, 151; under Operation Red-Map, 46; poll taxes and, 20, 34; by race, 5; by Republican Party, 47–48; at state level, 3, 46–47; Trump and, 48; against women, 5, 147–48. *See also* gerrymandering; redistricting
voting rights: for Black Americans, 3, 5, 33, 131–32; *Citizens United* case, 151–52; under Civil Rights Act (1957), 36; expansion during Reconstruction Era, 32–33; under Fifteenth Amendment, 3, 5, 33, 131–32; under Fourteenth Amendment, 193; under Freedom to Vote Act, 158; under Help America Vote Act, 23, 114, 129–31; John Lewis Voting Rights Advancement Act and, 51, 158; political pushback against, 42–51; during Reconstruction Era, 32–36; under Twenty-Sixth Amendment, 5, 160n16; Uniformed and Overseas Citizens Absentee Voting Act, 114; under Voting Accessibility for the Elderly and Handicapped Act, 114. *See also* voter discrimination; voter intimidation; voter suppression
Voting Rights Act (VRA), US (1965), 2, 114; *Allen v. Milligan* and, 50, 153; amendments of, 194; Black Americans elected to public office after, 41; Black voter registration after, 41; *Brnovich v. DNC*, 151, 208; competitive districts designed under, 168–69; Department of Justice enforcement of, 116; dilution claims, 194; fusion candidates under, 194–95; gerrymandering limitations under, 151; government enforcement of, 56; invalidation of, 246–47; legal challenges to, 43–46; legislative legacy of, 192–95; national impact of, 148; one-person, one-vote mandate, 22, 40; political legacy of, 41–42; poll taxes prohibited under, 148; preclearance

Voting Rights Act (VRA) (cont.)
requirements in, 40, 217; prohibition of racial discrimination under, 5; reauthorization of, 42–43; Roberts' criticism of, 149–51; *Shelby County v. Holder* and, 46, 56, 150, 158, 200; sore-loser laws under, 194; states' rights under, 40–41; Supreme Court rulings on, 3, 150–51; Supreme Court's gutting of, 150–51; in Texas, 151; violations of, 79; voter registration after, 221–25; voting discrimination prohibitions under, 20
VVPAT. *See* voter-verified paper audit trail

Wallace, George, 133, 315, 320
Warmoth, Henry, 325n19
War on Poverty, 91
Warren, Earl (Chief Justice), 20, 41, 147, 151, 193
Washington, George, 13–14, 310
Wesberry v. Sanders, 20
Westwood, Sean J., 96
Weyrich, Paul, 94, 226
White Primary Cases, 193
white voters: for Bush, G. H. W., 98; for Trump, 98–99
Whitman, Christine, 44
Williamson, Kevin, 233
women: under Nineteenth Amendment, 5, 34, 160n16, 219; voting restrictions against, 5, 147–48. *See also* gender
women's rights movement, 91; Equal Rights Amendment and, 92–94; as partisan issue, 93–94; *Roe v. Wade*, 93
World War II, runoff voting systems after, 171
write-in ballots, in Hawaii, 199

X (Twitter), 66, 85–86

Youngstown Sheet & Tube Co. v. Sawyer, 108, 117, 120
YouTube, 86
Yzaguirre, Raul, 198